The Witches of Abiquiu

The WITCHES of ABIQUIU

THE GOVERNOR, THE PRIEST, THE GENÍZARO INDIANS, AND THE DEVIL

Malcolm Ebright
&
Rick Hendricks

Illustrations by Glen Strock

University of New Mexico Press

Albuquerque

PRINTED IN THE UNITED STATES OF AMERICA

YEAR   PRINTING
12 11 10 09 08 07 06   1 2 3 4 5 6 7

PAPERBOUND ISBN-13: 978-0-8263-2032-2
PAPERBOUND ISBN-10: 0-8263-2032-5

Library of Congress Cataloging-in-Publication Data

Ebright, Malcolm.
  The witches of Abiquiu : the governor, the priest, the Genízaro Indians, and the
Devil / Malcolm Ebright, Rick Hendricks.
      p. cm.
  Includes bibliographical references and index.
  ISBN-13: 978-0-8263-2031-5 (cloth : alk. paper)
  ISBN-10: 0-8263-2031-7 (cloth : alk. paper)
    1. Indians of North America—New Mexico—Abiquiu—History—18th century.
2. Indians of North America—New Mexico—Abiquiu—Religion. 3. Indians,
Treatment of—New Mexico—Abiquiu—History—18th century. 4. Catholic
Church—Missions—New Mexico—History—18th century. 5. Witchcraft—New
Mexico—Abiquiu—History—18th century. 6. Trials (Witchcraft)—New
Mexico—Abiquiu—History—18th century. 7. Abiquiu (N.M.)—History—18th
century. 8. Abiquiu (N.M.)—Social conditions. 9. Abiquiu (N.M.)—Politics and
government. I. Hendricks, Rick, 1956– II. Title.
  E78.N65E26 2006

                              2005032951

Illustrations by Glen Strock

Book design and composition by Damien Shay
Body type is Minion 10/14
Display is Calligraph 421

CONTENTS

LIST OF ILLUSTRATIONS

PARTIES TO WITCHCRAFT PROCEEDINGS

SPANISH CIVIL AUTHORITIES

Fernández, Carlos — Alcalde

García Parejas, Manuel — Alcalde

Marín del Valle, Francisco Antonio — Governor of New Mexico, 1754–1760

Vélez Cachupín, Tomás — Governor of New Mexico, 1749–1754 and 1762–1767

PRIESTS

Ordóñez, fray Félix — First resident priest at Abiquiu, said to have been killed by Vicente Trujillo

Toledo, fray Juan José — Second resident priest at Abiquiu

GENÍZAROS

Agueda, María — Sister of Francisca Varela who was possessed by the devil known as Diablo Cojuelo

Chávez, María — Twelve-year-old girl choked by Atole Caliente and Jacinta to prevent her from talking to Father Toledo

Isabel, La Pastora — La Pastora no. 1/ Abiquiu Genízara

Jacinta	Daughter of Atole Caliente
Janisco, Ambrosio	Abiquiu Genízaro, said to be the chief *hechicero* (sorcerer/witch, medicine man, shaman) in all of New Mexico and to have been taught "the art of divination" by an unnamed Navajo
María Francisca	Abiquiu Genízara, married to Pedro Trujillo and accused him of trying to kill her in the form of a cat.
Menchero, Antonio	Sandia Genízaro who moved to Abiquiu; accused of trying to kill Father Irigoyen of Sandia by putting a poisonous herb in the priest's water jar
Ontiveros, Miguel, El Cojo	Abiquiu Genízaro, singled out by Father Toledo in Phase One as being the primary sorcerer who ran the School of the Devil.
Pacheco, Juana, La Pastora	La Pastora no. 2 / Abiquiu Genízara
Petrona, Come Gallinas	Abiquiu Genízara
Rafael	Abiquiu Genízaro; told Alcalde Fernández that El Cojo, Vicente, and his wife María, and Agustín Tagle and his son Diego were the main sorcerers and that Diego was the chief of all of them
Tagle, Agustín, El Viejo	Sorcerer of Abiquiu, said to have been the most powerful sorcerer
Tagle, Diego, son of Agustín	Abiquiu Genízaro, said to be a chief sorcerer
Tagle, Juan, son of Agustín	Abiquiu Genízaro, said to be a chief sorcerer

Tagle, María, wife of Vicente Trujillo	Abiquiu Genízaro accused of trying to kill Father Toledo; she told Governor Vélez Cachupín under torture how she made the priest ill and how she would cure him
Trujillo, Joaquinillo, El Descubridor	The chief informer who obtained leniency by naming other sorcerers; brother of Vicente Trujillo; he was a Kiowa captured by the Comanches and sold to a Spaniard at Taos
Trujillo, Juan (Largo)	Santa Ana Genízaro; brother of Joaquinillo, El Descubridor; said he was taught divination by an unnamed Navajo
Trujillo, María Salvia	The first person to become possessed during Phase Three, the exorcisms
Trujillo, Paula	Accused María and Vicente Trujillo, her aunt and uncle, of trying to kill Father Toledo "by putting herbs in his food and making a doll in his image" to stick pins into
Trujillo, Pedro, El Paseño	Abiquiu Genízaro accused by El Cojo of bewitching people in the form of a cat
Trujillo, Prudencia	Cured when Juan Largo sucked pieces of shells and hair from her body
Trujillo, Vicente	Governor of the Genízaro pueblo during the administration of fray Félix Ordóñez; was said to have killed Ordóñez and many people at Santa Ana Pueblo through witchcraft
Ulibarrí, Antonio, El Chimayó	Abiquiu Genízaro
Vallejo, María	One of the possessed persons at Abiquiu who named suspected sorcerers and pointed out places of "idolatrous" worship while she was possessed

Varela, Francisca

One of the possessed women exorcised by Father Toledo, who disrespectfully called him a *chivato coletudo mulato* (an insolent, kid goat, mulatto)

ACCUSED SORCERERS FROM OTHER PUEBLOS

Agustín

Son of Cristóbal, interpreter from Santa Ana

Arias, Miguel

Santa Fe Genízaro

Cascabel

Chimayo Genízaro said to have his art in a small black stone and to be extremely powerful

Joaquinillo, the Suma

Indian from Sandia

Martín

Isleta Indian

Mauricio

Ojo Caliente coyote

Temba

San Juan Indian

Vicente

Nambe Indian (comes and goes by his art and spreads the news he brings from the people of Chimayo)

ACKNOWLEDGMENTS

This book began on a distant day sometime around 1996 when Benito Córdova appeared at Malcolm's doorstep in the wilds of northern New Mexico with two important manuscripts: one from the Inquisition records in the Archivo General de la Nación in Mexico City; the other from the Bancroft Library in Berkeley, California. The documents dealt with a little-known witchcraft trial that took place at Abiquiu, New Mexico, between 1756 and 1766, a crucial period in the colony's history. Benito suggested that Malcolm should continue the research he had started, and Malcolm agreed, planning to try to publish a book about this arcane but fascinating glimpse of mid-eighteenth-century New Mexico. Little did Malcolm know what he was getting into.

First to come to his aid was Julián Josué Vigil, a friend in Las Vegas, New Mexico, a professor and longtime collaborator, and an expert paleographer. For many weeks during a period of about two years around 1997 to 1998, Julián and Malcolm transcribed and translated the portion of the witchcraft documents that Benito had not already done. In the basement of the Carnegie Library in Las Vegas, New Mexico, they discovered some of the amazing events described in the following study. The Carnegie Library has an excellent collection and is a great place to work. Our thanks go to Director Joann Martinez and Archivist Roselee Romero.

When most of the basic documents had been transcribed and translated, there were some archival materials that still had not been deciphered, particularly Father Juan José Toledo's long and intricate petitions. At this stage of the work, Malcolm combined forces with Rick Hendricks. They agreed on a long-term plan to finish translating all the witchcraft documents and to begin to try to make sense of them. Rick has an abiding interest in Franciscan history and religious history in general, so he was able to add an important perspective about fray Juan José Toledo, his background, and training. The final manuscript evolved out of the partnership between Rick and Malcolm.

The authors soon realized that there were several stories embedded in these manuscripts. The first story was the blow-by-blow description of the charges and countercharges leveled during the witchcraft trial itself. The first story was complicated by numerous ambiguities and ironies, particularly the question of whether some of what was reported as witchcraft was in fact Native American ceremonialism which the Franciscans did not understand and therefore categorized as evil Devil worship. By reading between the lines and interpreting the documents the Spaniards wrote, it was possible to discern hidden Indian voices.

Another equally important story had to do with the situation of New Mexico at the mid-eighteenth century. Little has been written on eighteenth-century New Mexico, and most of what has been written glorifies the genuine accomplishments of Governor Juan Bautista de Anza, but fails to mention the equally important career of Tomás Vélez Cachupín. Governor Vélez Cachupín is a fascinating figure whose reputation should be equal to that of Anza and Diego de Vargas.

Just as the authors were learning more details about Vélez Cachupín's life, they met an indirect descendant of Vélez Cachupín named Teresa Escudero, a native of Laredo, Spain. Teresa was teaching Spanish in Santa Fe under a program sponsored by the Spanish government and was trying to find information about her famous ancestor. Teresa told us that Vélez Cachupín was buried in Laredo and that she spends her summers in a house known as the Casa Cachupín owned by the Vélez Cachupín family. The authors began doing research together with Teresa, who searched the archives in Spain during her summer vacations while Rick communicated via e-mail his suggestions to Teresa about what to consult in the archives. Soon Teresa found Vélez Cachupín's will, which was the subject of an article the three wrote in the summer 2003 issue of the *New Mexico Historical Review*. Much of the information about Vélez Cachupín's life in Spain came from that collaboration.

The authors wish to thank Julián Josué Vigil and Robert Martinez for assistance in transcribing the witchcraft documents, and John Kessell for answering numerous questions. Richard Salazar, Richard Ford, Charlie Carrillo, Virgil and Isabel Trujillo, and Darlene Torres read parts of the manuscript and made helpful comments. Special thanks goes to Carroll Riley,

Benito Córdova, and Cordelia Snow for reading and commenting on the entire manuscript. Dede Snow was especially generous with her time and provided many helpful insights. Richard Greenleaf, Robert Tórrez, Virgil and Isabel Trujillo, and Estevan Rael-Gálvez contributed ideas and materials and numerous lively discussions. Mark Adams, Al Regensberg, Daphne Arnaiz-DeLeon, Gail Packard, Melissa Salazar, and Sandra Jaramillo of the New Mexico State Records Center and Archives greatly facilitated our research, as did the staff of the Southwest Room of the New Mexico State Library. Steve Hardin assisted with the field work in Abiquiu. Lois Stanford provided guidance to the anthropological literature on resistance. Any errors herein are the authors' responsibility.

The authors are grateful as well to Danté Ruiz and Glen Strock (for the drawings), Robert Wittwer (for the map), Helene Boudreau (for typing drafts of the manuscript), Robin Collier (computer guru), and Kay Matthews (for creation of the index). Malcolm wishes to thank Rae Lunden, Maddie McDougal, and Martín Prechtel for their support. The authors of this book hope that it will provide a rich source for further research into New Mexico's multicultural history and provide an example of the still unsolved mysteries and utter fascination incorporated in the people and the land of the Southwest.

A NOTE ON STYLE

The expository style of fray Juan José Toledo and some of his contemporaries is often convoluted. To aid the reader, we have supplied punctuation and modern orthography and have modernized Spanish names. New Mexico place names appear without accents unless they are part of a longer Spanish phrase. Hence, Abiquiu appears without an accent, but Santo Tomás Apóstol de Abiquiú carries an accent. Explanations of all Spanish words and phrases retained in the English text are given immediately after the first occurrence or in notes. They are also italicized only on the first usage. Frequently used Spanish terms are included in the glossary. According to *Webster's Third New International Dictionary of the English Language Unabridged*, which we have taken as our authority, certain words, accented in Spanish, are now accepted as English words of Spanish origin, without accents. Examples are alferez and cedula. Titles of Spanish nobles we have retained in Spanish. We have left saints' names in English, unless they are mentioned as part of the name of Spanish churches, organizations, or places.

INTRODUCTION

This book is about a witchcraft outbreak at Abiquiu, New Mexico, between 1756 and 1766, and about the main protagonists in those dramatic proceedings: the governor, Tomás Vélez Cachupín; the priest, fray Juan José Toledo; the Genízaro Indians of Abiquiu; and the Devil, who was thought to have possessed many of the Abiquiu Genízaros. The events leading up to the witchcraft trial in the early 1760s began with the establishment of the Abiquiu Genízaro land grant by Governor Vélez Cachupín in 1754. This book uses the Abiquiu witchcraft litigation as an emblematic event shedding light on many heretofore unexplored aspects of New Mexico history in the mid-eighteenth century.

The witchcraft trial unfolded in four phases. In the first phase, Father Juan José Toledo complained to Governor Francisco Antonio Marín del Valle (1754–60) about being bewitched by Genízaros from Abiquiu pueblo, specifically by an Indian known as Miguel, El Cojo. Father Toledo had been assigned to the Genízaro pueblo as its priest soon after Governor Vélez Cachupín made the Genízaro land grant in 1754, and Toledo was at the center of the entire witchcraft litigation. In the second phase of the witchcraft proceedings, an informer known as Joaquinillo, El Descubridor, took Alcalde Carlos Fernández, the governor, and other civil officials, to places of "idolatry," which those Spanish officials proceeded to exorcise and destroy. Most of these sites were indigenous ceremonial ones, such as the Stone Lions and rock art sites that the Franciscan priests viewed as locations of Devil worship. Also important in phase two were the accusations that Alcalde Fernández documented against numerous Genízaros in Abiquiu charged with various aspects of witchcraft, including killing other Genízaros. The third phase of the witchcraft trial consisted of a series of exorcisms performed by Father Toledo on women and girls claiming to be possessed by the Devil. The more women Toledo exorcised, however, the more new ones became possessed. In the fourth and final phase of the witchcraft proceedings, Governor Vélez Cachupín calmed the epidemic of demonic possessions and exorcisms by convening a *junta* (meeting) of religious leaders who deliberated about the strange goings-on in Abiquiu, arguing about it for two days. They then sent the case to the Inquisition in Mexico City where it languished because the Holy Office had lost interest in demonic possession as a form of heresy.

As things calmed down at Abiquiu, Vélez Cachupín meted out fairly light punishments to the accused sorcerers and witches who survived their stay in the Santa Fe prison; public shame, the threat of two hundred lashes, and service in an *obraje* (textile workshop) were the worst. No one was hanged, as had been the case at Salem in 1692, or burned at the stake, as had been the case in Europe.

The Abiquiu witchcraft trial itself is worthy of note as the last big witchcraft outbreak in North America, similar to the Salem, Massachusetts, witchcraft trials of 1692, although not as deadly. Salem has been thought by scholars to be the end of the long string of witchcraft eruptions that started in Europe in the fifteenth century, but the Abiquiu witch craze was the last major witchcraft and demonic possession outbreak in North America.[1]

Some readers may be interested primarily in the witchcraft proceedings themselves, which are found in Chapters 7 through 11. We hope, however, that most will also read Chapters 1 through 6 to learn about the background of the witchcraft proceedings and to assess their importance. Each chapter is designed to prepare the reader for the fantastic events described in Chapters 7 through 11 by describing in detail historic and prehistoric Abiquiu (Chapter 1), the Genízaros (Chapter 2), Father Juan José Toledo (Chapter 3), Governor Tomás Vélez Cachupín (Chapter 4), the Abiquiu Genízaro land grant (Chapter 5), prior witchcraft trials in New Mexico (Chapter 6), and the Devil (Chapter 9).

The social dislocation and anxiety concerning life at Abiquiu in mid-eighteenth-century New Mexico in the middle ground between civilization and the *tierra de la guerra*, or zone of open warfare, made the community ripe for an outbreak of witchcraft. Yet the Abiquiu witchcraft trials were symbolic of several other important developments in the early history of New Mexico. Each of the important players in this drama—the priest, the governor, the Genízaro Indians, and the Devil—represented different aspects of these sweeping changes and were themselves radically changed by these events. To understand the Abiquiu witchcraft outbreak it is necessary to have a sense of the forces shaping New Mexico in the middle of the eighteenth century.

After the Pueblo Revolt of 1680, Spaniards attempted to reestablish a foothold in the austere and unforgiving New Mexico landscape, returning in 1692 only to face unrelenting attacks by Comanches, Utes, and Apaches. Abiquiu bordered the Spanish-settled area to the south, and its fate as a viable and stable community was an important test for other New Mexico settlements. If Abiquiu could not survive nomadic Indian attacks, other New Mexico settlements might not be able to make it either. The fate of New Mexico as a Spanish colony hung in the balance.[2]

Abiquiu had been a middle ground for contending warriors even before the Spanish under Juan de Oñate arrived in New Mexico in 1598. The ruins of prehistoric pueblos, many an enigma to scholars, still dot the landscape around Abiquiu. When and why they were abandoned has not been fully explained, but drought, attack by outside invaders, and the Little Ice Age are likely causes. Chapter 1 sets the stage for the events of the witchcraft litigation by describing how the Abiquiu area has always been a middle ground between contending forces. Before the arrival of the Spaniards, those forces were the prehistoric Pueblos of the region and enemy invaders from the south. The charred ruins of the Riano pueblo provide stark evidence of this warfare.[3]

During the seventeenth century, when slave trading by corrupt governors pitted the Pueblos of New Mexico against Apaches and Navajos, with whom the Pueblos had formerly been at peace, Abiquiu continued to be a middle ground.[4] After the Pueblo Revolt, Spanish settlements in the Abiquiu area found themselves in the middle ground between the communities of Santa Fe and Santa Cruz de la Cañada and raiding Utes, Navajos, and Comanches to the north and northwest. The Abiquiu Genízaro pueblo—the brainchild of Governor Vélez Cachupín—was a means of providing a buffer zone or defensive bulwark between the Spaniards and the nomadic tribes they were attempting to replace. Composed of members of nomadic tribes themselves, the Genízaros were squeezed in several directions. They were able to acquire land and potential *vecino* status by their membership in the Abiquiu Genízaro pueblo, but to achieve this improvement in their social and economic status they had to give up their Indian identity. This led to the existential quandary faced by Genízaros in the 1760s: they were not Spaniards because they were designated as an Indian pueblo, but neither were they typical Pueblo Indians because the wellspring of their Indian identity—their ceremonies, their religious beliefs, and their religious shrines—were from different cultures and were thoroughly repressed and destroyed by Spanish officials and priests.[5]

The common definition and description of a Genízaro has been too narrow and has suffered from an excess of scholarly pedantry and a shortage of real-life examples of people who were called Genízaros. Fray Angélico Chávez's definition in the *Handbook of North American Indians* is "Indians of mixed tribal derivation living among [Hispanos]...having Spanish surnames from their former masters, Christian names through baptism in the Roman Catholic faith, speaking a simple form of Spanish, and living together in special communities or sprinkled among the Hispanic towns and ranchos." We use a broad definition that includes as the primary markers of Genízaro status the elements of servitude or captivity and Indian blood. Such a definition includes nomadic Indians who lost their tribal identity, spent time as captives and or servants, and who were living on the margins of Spanish society. It is more in keeping with the usage the Genízaros themselves employed.[6] By looking at specific individuals who fit the broader Genízaro classification and who called themselves Genízaros, we hope to enlarge the dialogue and discussion about who the Genízaros were.[7]

The Abiquiu Genízaros occupied that middle ground called *nepantla*, known to Indians from Peru to Mexico as a place where they were neither the Indians that they had been, nor the Spaniards they would become. This place of uncertainty and ambiguity was exactly the place where witchcraft would find fertile ground to extend its roots. Painted, incised, and pecked on the boulders and sandstone rocks around Abiquiu are images revealing the two sides of nepantla: the pictographs reflecting the Indian side of the dichotomy, and the crosses reflecting the Spanish Christian side. This paradox of Genízaro identity was never fully resolved in eighteenth-century Abiquiu. Chapter 2 discusses the Genízaros in general and includes short biographies of specific Genízaros.[8]

Chapter 3 deals with Father Juan José Toledo and with Franciscan attempts at Christianization of the Genízaros of Abiquiu. Father Toledo's biography helps one understand why this priest was partially but not entirely prepared for the challenges he faced at the mission of Abiquiu. He arrived at Abiquiu in 1755 to replace Father Ordóñez, who died shortly after he left Abiquiu, allegedly from a witchcraft attack. Undaunted, Father Toledo weathered all four stages of the witchcraft proceedings and remained at Abiquiu for six years afterward. He had his own run-in with the Inquisition for allegedly approving of Genízaro concubinage and seems to have softened his opinions in the period after the conclusion of the witchcraft proceedings. Together with Governor Vélez Cachupín, Father Toledo deserves credit for enduring the Abiquiu witchcraft outbreak, at great peril to his own health. The seeds he planted in the 1750s to the early 1770s flowered and bore fruit during the 1820s when a very different priest forced the Abiquiu Genízaros to take part in fashioning their own form of Catholicism. Often, what the Spaniards called "witchcraft" was actually resistance to priests such as Father Toledo who were attempting to eradicate the native belief systems and convert the Indians to Catholicism.

With the end of the Abiquiu witchcraft trials in 1766, the accommodation among Hispanic settlers, Genízaros, Pueblos, and the marginalized population of mestizos in between, was well under way. The beginnings of a relative peace with raiding Plains Indians and Navajos had been established, and the groundwork had been laid for the expansion of Spanish settlements. Governor Vélez Cachupín had achieved peace with all neighboring nomadic tribes. This important period of New Mexico history should be seen as of at least equal importance with the later administration of Governor Juan Bautista de Anza (1778–88) which has received greater attention. Beyond telling the story of the last major witchcraft trial, this book highlights a turning point in New Mexico history when for the first time new permanent settlements such as the one at Abiquiu were established on the frontier, and peace was achieved with the Utes and Comanches.

Governor Vélez Cachupín was successful in achieving peace with hostile Indians partly because of his policy of establishing community land grants, and partly through his leadership on crucial military campaigns where he learned of the Genízaros' fighting prowess when they served as auxiliaries to Spanish forces.[9] The Abiquiu Genízaro grant was one of these community grants. Vélez Cachupín realized that the old system of making land grants primarily to elite members of society was not conducive to frontier defense. The elites could not always be relied on to defend their land to the death. Genízaros were the best Indian fighters because they knew the enemy. They knew the Comanches and the Utes' strategies and tactics intimately, because among them were members of these Indian tribes.

Vélez Cachupín made seventeen land grants during his two terms as governor, including the Abiquiu Genízaro grant. The Abiquiu grant was entirely made up of Genízaros; the Carnuel, San Gabriel de las Nutrias, Sabinal, and Las Trampas grants were made to groups of Spaniards and Genízaros. These grantees became landowners, capable of supporting themselves and their families on their tracts of private land together with their use rights to the common lands. Vélez Cachupín's grants to the above communities and to Truchas were the first true community grants.[10]

Chapter 5 sets the stage for the witchcraft trial by detailing the establishment of the Abiquiu Genízaro pueblo with a discussion of the land grant and its place in Governor Vélez Cachupín's frontier defense policy. This chapter takes the story of the Abiquiu grant, which Governor Vélez Cachupín made in 1754 to sixty families, through its abandonment in the early 1770s, the increase in population in the area from 1,000 in 1790 to around 3,600 in 1827, the battle in the 1820s between the last Franciscan priests and the community wanting their own form of Catholic religion, the fights over private and common land on the Abiquiu grant, the submission of the Abiquiu grant for confirmation to the surveyor general and the Court of Private Land Claims, and its confirmation to the land grant board at more than 16,500 acres.

Moving into the witchcraft portion of the book, Chapter 6 discusses several representative witchcraft trials in colonial New Mexico, from the 1668 Bernardo Gruber matter that never did come to trial, to the 1707 witchcraft charges by Leonor Domínguez against three San Juan women that turned out to be entirely fabricated, to the case of *Antonia Luján v. Francisca Caza* in which another San Juan woman was accused of witchcraft. In the latter case when the plaintiff Luján refused a potion offered by defendant Caza as a means of bringing an abundance of material objects into her life and attracting important people, Antonia Luján got sick, even when Francisca Caza tried to cure her with powder from a large shell. When questioned about why she used the powdered shell in what may have been an attempted poisoning, Francisca Caza told her interrogators that the Devil had tricked her and put the idea into her head. We do not know the outcome of this case, but Caza's answer was like a confession that told her questioners what they wanted to hear. The concept of the Devil had many connotations in Abiquiu, and Chapter 9 deals with the many faces of the Devil. (We capitalize the Devil [Satan] to distinguish him from the lesser devils who made their appearance at Abiquiu.) Since the exorcism of demonic possession implies the existence of the Devil, Chapter 9 is inserted before Chapter 10, which is devoted to the exorcisms.

Father Toledo was greatly influenced by the concept of the Devil found in the *Malleus Maleficarum* by Kramer and Sprenger and in Bishop De la Peña Montenegro's *Itinerario,* or Guidebook for Priests. The 1486 *Maleficarum* was a witch-hunting handbook that defined the three elements of witchcraft as evil, a witch, and the permission of God. The concept of evil outside of God was embodied in the Devil; not to believe in the Devil was considered heresy. Missionaries in Central Mexico and beyond learned to depict the Devil and his realm of Hell in vivid detail to convince the Indians to repent their sins. The Indians, however, held a different worldview in which creative and destructive forces existed side by side in their gods. They had no deity like the Devil and no word for evil. The Nahuas of Central Mexico and the Incas of the Andes believed in concepts of order and disorder rather than good and evil. In the Andes, for instance, the serpent did not embody evil as it did for Christians, but rather a destructive force attempting to re-create balance when relations of equilibrium had not been maintained.

Father Toledo had to deal with the Devil, both in the abstract and concrete manifestations. Toledo's viewpoint changed gradually as he found that the devils he encountered during the marathon exorcisms he performed differed from the abstract concept of the Devil he had been taught. In many instances the devils Toledo encountered fit Father Toledo's preconception: they spoke Latin; they tried to corrupt those they possessed; and they often retreated in defeat when confronted with Christian symbols such as the cross. By contrast, some devils did not fit the pattern of absolute evil. Some of these devils said they were sent to help rid the pueblo of witchcraft, some made predictions about when the Abiquiu witch craze would end, and some gave personal advice to individuals much like modern therapists. As the outlandish nature of the demonic possessions at Abiquiu became more and more bizarre, neither the governor, the priests making up the junta, nor the Inquisition took them seriously.

After discussing what happened in the Abiquiu witchcraft proceedings, the final chapter attempts to draw some conclusions. We do not try to ascribe physical or medical explanations as was done in studies of Salem witchcraft. Neither ergot-induced hallucinations nor animal-borne disease such as encephalitis have proved to be logical and consistent explanations of the Salem events. Although there may be some physical explanation of the Abiquiu witchcraft outbreak, so far such an explanation is elusive. If an epidemic disease like smallpox swept through Abiquiu, why did it not affect other communities? Rather than being simply a matter of disease, the answers must run deeper. Indian resistance to Christianization is an important factor not found at Salem. A climate of fear induced by warfare with the Plains Indians is a factor similar to that found at Salem, according to the most recent Salem witchcraft scholarship in Mary Beth Norton's, *In the Devils' Snare: The Salem Witchcraft Crisis of 1692.*

In the Epilogue we bring the history of Abiquiu down to the present. We grapple with the question of identity at Abiquiu, using the Genízaros' battle to retain their land as a lens through which to view Genízaro identity. As the Genízaros struggled with land speculators such as José García de la Mora, Father Teodoro Alcina, and later J. M. C. Chávez, the Genízaros found their Indian identity to be a two-edged sword. On the one hand, they could use Spanish laws protecting Indian land; on the other, Hispanos found ways to acquire and encroach on Indian land as they did at Pecos, Galisteo, and other pueblos whose population was dwindling. Indian identity helped Abiquiu under the surveyor general and the Court of Private Land Claims as Surveyor General Julian noted the leniency of Spanish laws toward Indians and Genízaros. Then in the early 1900s Abiquiu shifted toward a Hispanic identity.

From a religious standpoint the Genízaros began by resisting forced Christianization and then in the 1820s embraced the Penitente form of Catholicism as one of the first communities to have a strong Penitente Brotherhood in the 1820s. Today Abiquiu still has a dual identity, which is its strength and uniqueness. Abiquiu celebrates its Indian identity at the feast day of Santo Tomás in November and its Hispano identity at the feast day of Santa Rosa de Lima in August. Abiquiu is still known as the Pueblo of Abiquiu, the land grant still owns most of the land confirmed to it by the Court of Private Land Claims, and Abiquiu's people are retaining and nurturing their traditions as they gird their loins to protect their land, water, and culture in the twenty-first century.

Figure 1
Father Toledo and Alcalde Fernández exorcise stone with a Contract with the Devil on it.
Drawing by Glen Strock.

CHAPTER ONE

Abiquiu, the Middle Ground

The Cross and the Petroglyph

Positioned on the western edge of prehistoric New Mexico, the Abiquiu region served as an outpost for thousands of years, much like Pecos was a frontier sentinel on the eastern frontier of the region. Present-day Abiquiu is situated on the ruins of one of the prehistoric Pueblo villages that dotted the area, in the watersheds of the Ojo Caliente, El Rito, and Chama Rivers. After the villages were abandoned, inhabitants of these early pueblos migrated to San Juan, Santa Clara, and other Tewa-speaking pueblos. Some of these early dwellers of the Chama Valley and Abiquiu area are said to have journeyed to Hopi country and established an independent settlement there, arriving during the latter part of the Pueblo-Spanish War of 1680–96. Less than fifty years later a group

of Hopis were resettled at Abiquiu; they were perhaps the descendants of
the earliest occupants of the Abiquiu area thus completing a cycle and possibly creating a homecoming.[1]

Life was perilous in the Chama River Valley around Abiquiu, even
before the arrival of the Spaniards, for the region was frequently raided
by southern Athapaskans, such as the Apaches. The early Pueblos were con-
stantly on the lookout, watching for the approach of hostile parties of warriors who often traveled along the waterways. Tipi rings evidencing former
lodge sites were usually at some distance from the nearest river because
it was easier to travel a few miles for water than it was to put one's life at
risk in the path of enemy raiding parties moving along these streams.[2]
Grisly evidence of this peril was found at the Riano ruin, which was set
on fire around 1348. Archaeologist Frank Hibben described the horrific
scene revealed by his excavation:

> The presence of a partially charred skeleton in the
> rooms seems to argue for a destruction of the
> pueblo by invaders or armed forces...which would
> cause a sudden exodus of the inhabitants. This con-
> tention is further borne out by the appearance of
> the pottery and the artifacts of the rooms—all the
> pottery being in place on the floors where it had
> been crushed by the falling roof. The metates and
> manos yet leaned against the walls in some cases,
> and bone awls had been placed in the corner. If the
> pueblo had been fired accidentally it seems improb-
> able that the kiva would have burned, yet such was
> the case. Every room, including the kiva, showed the
> marks of fire.[3]

These ancient Pueblos left another record of their stay in the Chama
Valley, leaving behind petroglyphs and pictographs on the sandstone cliffs
surrounding their villages. Near the site of the Riano ruin a petroglyph
panel known as the "Abiquiu Pictures" was photographed as part of
Hibben's excavation of the Riano site. The photos reveal rich images of
animals, birds, human forms, geometrical forms, snakes, corn plants, and
later, examples of Christian crosses. Unfortunately, the reservoir behind

Abiquiu Dam flooded these petroglyphs along with the associated ruins of Riano Pueblo.[4]

An important petroglyph showing a Comanche attack on the Pueblos was destroyed in the 1930s as a result of road construction. All that remains of that site north of Abiquiu and west of Ghost Ranch is a description in *New Mexico Magazine*:

> A panel of apparently Comanche authorship was discovered showing a raid upon Pueblos by a band of Comanches on horseback, and shooting guns. This places the date as sometime after the coming of the Spaniards, for before their advent firearms were unknown among the Indians. There are nearby a dozen Comanches in feathered war bonnets mounted on pudgy ponies, attacking a Pueblo man who is running away as fast as possible, a Pueblo woman with bow and arrow is bravely trying to defend her man.[5]

The information contained in these petroglyphs is invaluable, and an important subtlety has been lost through their destruction. Nothing can substitute for viewing the rock art on site, in part because of the layering of images one over the other. Some of this layering was intentional, as when an animal image was superimposed over the image of a man in the belief that the man pecking or painting the images on the rock would acquire the power and strong attributes of the animal depicted.[6] Another reason has to do with the way in which the rock art artist often utilized creases, holes, slits, protuberances, and other qualities of the rock. Indigenous cultures often saw a hole or slit in the rock as a gateway to the place where power resides: the spirit world. By having the petroglyph or pictograph incorporate a feature of the natural landscape, especially a crack in the rock surface, a rock artist or shaman could journey through that orifice to contact the gods in the spirit world. This relationship between the rock art and the natural features surrounding it can be suggested but cannot be captured in a photograph.[7]

During Phase Two of the Abiquiu witchcraft trial, fray Juan José Toledo, Alcalde Carlos Fernández, Genízaro informer Joaquinillo, and three

Figure 2
Basalt boulder with pre-contact ancestral Puebloan petroglyphs and post-contact crosses located at the base of Mesa Prieta. *Photograph by Richard I. Ford.*

witnesses were taken to a site called El León Fuerte (the strong lion), two thousand varas south of Abiquiu. To date, this site has not been discovered, but it is described in several places by Fernández. The alcalde was sent to the site south of Abiquiu "with the intention of destroying and annihilating as much as possible the heathen temples [*adoratorios*], and places where they might have been worshipping."[8] Alcalde Fernández destroyed the petroglyphs on the stone lion and erected a cross on the spot. Then he ordered Father Toledo to exorcise the spot. When he had completed the rite of exorcism (a rite he repeated many times during the witchcraft proceedings), Toledo and Fernández moved to another site north of Abiquiu where, again guided by the informer Joaquinillo, they found some additional petroglyphs drawn on the side of a cliff.

The petroglyphs found at the second site were similar to drawings on the wall of a nearby cave where one of the most powerful of the sorcerers accused in the witchcraft proceedings, Agustín Tagle, called El Viejo, was said to bring his followers to engage in secret rites. It is unclear whether those rites were witchcraft, or native ceremonialism, although it appears that both were occurring in mid-eighteenth-century Abiquiu. The images drawn in the margin of Fernández's report are all that remain, unless this cave is one day discovered. If it is, one would expect to find some crosses that Father Toledo inscribed there in 1763 as part of the rite of exorcism.

Ethnobotanist Richard Ford recently examined rock art images around Abiquiu and noted numerous examples of crosses associated with petroglyphs and pictographs within a mile radius of Abiquiu, with few crosses outside this zone. These crosses and rock art sites represent some of the few such sites clearly linked to historical documents. It seems likely that Father Toledo and other individuals placed many of these crosses as part of the exorcisms carried out during the witchcraft proceedings.[9]

In addition to the exorcism performed by Father Toledo, Fernández attempted to remove the rock drawings, as he describes in his report:

> On the side of a cliff were drawn the figures which appeared in the margin of my previous *diligencia*. They were erased and destroyed by me, and in the surroundings we drew crosses and the place was exorcised by the Reverend Padre Minister [Toledo].[10]

It seems clear that these drawings had religious significance to the Indians living near Abiquiu. Like the stone lions, they were undoubtedly ceremonial sites that the ancient residents of the Chama Valley pueblos visited, just as members of Cochiti Pueblo still visit and consider the stone lions within Bandelier National Monument sacred. How they became seen as sites of Devil worship in mid-eighteenth-century New Mexico is a major theme of this book.[11]

The rock art images found in Abiquiu and elsewhere in the Chama River Valley tell a multifaceted story of religious observance, trading, and warfare. The Athapaskans who surrounded the pueblos had a well-established trading relationship with the now vacant prehistoric pueblos involving a good deal of interdependence and cooperation.[12] This was reflected in the trade between the Plains Apaches and the Tiwas of Picuris and Taos pueblos on the eastern frontier of New Mexico. This trade was documented in 1598 when these Tiwa pueblos were trading blankets, pottery, maize, and "some small green stones" (probably turquoise), for meat, hides, tallow, and salt from the Plains Apaches."[13] This trade pattern was similar to what occurred at Abiquiu along the western frontier where the primarily agricultural pueblos may have traded their produce for meat and animal by-products of hunter-gatherer tribes.

Rock art images of shields, shield-bearers, and the War Twins tell a parallel story. Contrary to the image of peaceful Pueblos eschewing armed conflict whenever possible, warfare existed among New Mexico Pueblos and between the Pueblos and Plains Indians. Rock art images and evidence from historical documents reveal what Polly Schaafsma has called "a highly developed ceremonial war cult or warrior society among the Southern Tewa."[14] The presence of similar petroglyphs in and around the Abiquiu area showing warriors with weapons and shields are further indications that the Abiquiu region was also a war zone.[15]

Abiquiu was the center of la tierra de guerra, at the same time as it was the focus of trading networks among Pueblos, Apaches, and Navajos. Abiquiu represented a middle ground before Spanish contact and even more so as Spanish settlement began to penetrate the area beginning in the 1720s and 1730s. The mind-set of fear and anxiety that possessed Spanish settlers, repeatedly driven out of their settlements by Utes and Comanches, must have been similar to that of the prehistoric pueblo dwellers at Tsama, Sapawe, Poshuouinge, and Tsiping, who manned their rooftops, straining to catch sight of the next raiding party. These early Pueblos did not want to be surprised by an attack such as the one that destroyed the Riana Pueblo.[16]

Abiquiu and the surrounding area also became the middle ground for the Navajos, who at one time claimed the entire Piedra Lumbre-Abiquiu environs as their hunting ground, as did some Tewas of the Rio Grande Pueblos who also frequented ancestral shrines and sacred springs in the area. The Navajos primarily used this middle ground in the seventeenth and early eighteenth centuries, although there was some penetration and interaction with the Northern Tewa pueblos after the Pueblo Revolt. In 1696, for example, Tewas from Santa Clara took refuge with Navajos at Los Pedernales.[17]

In a similar manner, the Apaches and the southern Rio Grande Pueblos engaged in a trading and raiding relationship before the arrival of Spanish settlers under the leadership of Juan de Oñate. Before the entry of the Spaniards this relationship was primarily one of cooperative trading. Although the Plains Apaches preferred trading to raiding, by the late 1620s the Apaches "were goaded to war against the Spaniards by a slave raid."[18] The Spanish policy of divide and conquer reached its nadir around 1628 when Governor Felipe Sotelo Osorio (1625–29), induced a rival faction of Apaches to attack and take captive a group of peaceful Plains Indians who had come to Santa Fe interested in becoming Christians and in trading. As a result the Apaches declared war, and the Spaniards, who were trying to pacify them and Christianize the Pueblos, confronted an additional challenge.[19]

Another example of the disruptive effect of the Spanish policy of fomenting divisiveness involved the use of Pueblo allies by the Spaniards during slave raids on other Indians.[20] In 1659 Governor Juan Manso (1656–59) and his successor Bernardo López de Mendizabal (1659–61) quarreled over who owned some Apache captives taken in a raid carried out by the Spaniards and their Picuris allies. Manso claimed the eighteen captives as his, but Mendizabal said he had purchased the Apaches from the Picuris. Whether Governor Lopez de Mendizabal had actually bargained with the Picuris for the Apaches, this dispute over Apache captives certainly was not good for Apache-Pueblo relations.[21]

Abiquiu became a middle ground among hostile enemies because of the Spanish pursuit of their divide-and-conquer policy. The Utes also considered the Abiquiu-Piedra Lumbre area their hunting grounds during the seventeenth century before the Pueblo Revolt. The Utes were subjected to the same kind of slave raids that the Apaches suffered, thus aggravating tensions between Utes and Spaniards. An example illustrative of this situation occurred when Governor Luis de Rosas (1637–41) captured about eighty Moache Utes and forced them to labor in his Santa Fe workshops.[22] The Utes also came into conflict with Navajos and Northern Tewa Pueblos over the use of the Abiquiu-Piedra Lumbre area, a conflict exacerbated by the arrival of the Spanish settlers. Many elite Spaniards wanted land grants in the Abiquiu area, but few were willing to put themselves in the path of Ute, Comanche, and Navajo raiders.[23]

Despite the inherent cultural clash between Spaniards and Pueblos in the Abiquiu region, Spanish settlers demonstrated a remarkable willingness to embrace Pueblo knowledge of the healing arts and even the indigenous practice of witchcraft. This permissive posture stood in stark contrast to the priests' attempts to eradicate all vestiges of Pueblo religious beliefs. The Pueblos did not see a contradiction between healing power and witchcraft, what Europeans called white and black magic, respectively.

In the Zuni origin myth, a witch pair came up from the underworld bringing the people two gifts: death, to keep the world from being overcrowded; and corn, to feed the people. The story indicates that at Zuni (and other pueblos), magical power or sorcery was not always differentiated as good or evil. "Pueblo curing societies work against witchcraft, but there are said to be [curing] society practices in black magic as well as in white, particularly among the clown societies....Although black magic is plainly distinguished from white magic and the witch is he or she who is habitually engaged in the practice of black magic, witchcraft may be practiced by any person or by any group."[24] Before the Pueblo Revolt, Indians and Spaniards often came into contact when Indian servants imparted their curing and witchcraft knowledge to their Spanish masters. For example, between 1627–28 Governor Sotelo Osorio, the same individual who was accused of slave-raiding, sent an agent to San Juan Pueblo to bring an Indian woman "versed in magic and black art to Santa Fe to try to save the life of a soldier who was said to be bewitched."[25]

The prelude to Spanish settlement of the Abiquiu-Piedra Lumbre area and of the Genízaro land grant of Abiquiu, which was the setting for the witchcraft trial described in this book, was the decades-long Pueblo-Spanish War, and in particular, the great Pueblo Revolt of 1680. One of the primary causes for this cataclysmic event was the violent suppression of native ceremonials by the clergy.[26] In August 1680, the combined Pueblo forces led from Taos by Popé of San Juan and from Picuris by Luis Tupatú, together with some Apache allies, forced all Spanish settlers to abandon the province and to retreat to El Paso for twelve years. The Pueblo-Spanish War lasted until 1696 when Diego de Vargas consolidated the Reconquest of New Mexico he began in 1692. The aftershocks of this protracted military confrontation endured until the mid-eighteenth century and profoundly affected the Abiquiu witchcraft trials.

The contradictions and ambiguities characteristic of pre-Revolt Spanish-Indian relations began to fade into an uneasy accommodation as the eighteenth century wore on. The inconsistency between the ideal of improving the lot of the Pueblos through Christianization and the reality of appalling abuses inflicted on them by both Church and State began to be resolved somewhat after the Pueblo Revolt. During the eighteenth century, Franciscans, such as Father Toledo, sought support from civil authorities to suppress dances, such as the Turtle Dance. Provincial governors, however, were dependent on Pueblo allies in their campaigns against Apaches, Comanches, Utes, and Navajos. Oppression of the Pueblos occurred only when governors felt relatively secure from raiding, as they did early and late in the eighteenth century. Thus, while Spanish governors ordered the destruction of kivas in 1714 and 1793, for much of the rest of the century the friars ignored the continuance of Pueblo ceremonial dances. At the same time, the Pueblos and the Abiquiu Genízaro pueblo, adopted—at least on the surface—the ritual trappings of Christianity.[27]

Ute/Comanche depredations against the Spaniards were examples of the kind of all-out warfare that had been one of the reasons the prehistoric Chama Valley pueblos were abandoned, with warfare again being waged as Abiquiu and other frontier areas became the middle ground between contending forces.[28] The extent of the Ute and Comanche threat, as well as the psychological impact of the raids in the Abiquiu area, was immense. Before 1747 the Comanches, allied with the Utes, engaged in joint raids against Pueblo and Spanish settlements south of Abiquiu. Then, in August 1747, a large body of Utes and some Comanche warriors attacked Abiquiu, taking twenty-three women and children captive and killing "a girl and an old woman for having defended themselves."[29] Initially the Spanish thought the Utes and, to a lesser extent, the Comanches were responsible for the raid. The Spanish attacked a peaceful rancheria of about a hundred Ute tipis, provoking the Utes to respond by attacking Santa Cruz de la Cañada. The Abiquiu region again became the center of la tierra de guerra. The alliance between Utes and Comanches made possible this devastating raid, leaving Spanish settlers on edge, not knowing when the next attack would come or which Indian group was responsible.

Even though the Spanish mounted a retaliatory expedition in October 1747 against both Utes and Comanches held responsible for the August raid, attacks on Spanish settlements continued with such severity that the settlers in Abiquiu, Ojo Caliente, and other frontier settlements asked Governor Joaquín Codallos y Rabal (1743–46) for permission to withdraw from their communities.[30] Through their alcalde, the settlers told the governor that Indian raids were certain to occur as "the settlers are almost within view of the pagan Indian enemies, the Utes, [and] Comanches." They wanted to withdraw "to other places more secure and convenient because of the imminent danger of losing [their] lives." Governor Codallos y Rabal granted the request "for the time being," although it was three years before Abiquiu was resettled. In the meantime, Utes, Comanches, and Navajos again had unfettered access to their traditional hunting grounds in the Abiquiu region.[31]

It seemed possible at midcentury that the Spanish presence in the entire Abiquiu-Rio Chama watershed was over. Unless settlements could be reestablished that were fortified and protected by Spanish troops, Abiquiu and its vicinity would remain an abandoned middle ground between Spanish settlements around Santa Cruz de la Cañada and the Utes, Navajos, and Comanches to the north.

The problem of expanding Spanish settlements in the face of resistance by indigenous tribes had preoccupied the viceregal government in Mexico City since the Pueblo Revolt. Yet there was a good deal of confusion within the Spanish government regarding how much accommodation between Christianity and native belief systems was acceptable. On the one hand, the viceroy ordered the destruction of all "idols, temples of idols, and altars of false gods," as well as the prohibition of all native dances and ceremonies.[32] Governor Vélez Cachupín, on the other hand, made it a point to try to understand and to permit native religious customs whenever possible. In 1754 Vélez Cachupín left a set of recommendations for his successor, Marín del Valle, which included the following suggestion regarding the Comanches: "Permit their familiarities and take part in their fun at suitable times. Sit down with them and command tobacco for them so they may smoke, as is their custom."[33] As Comanche and Ute raids intensified it was important to be on good terms with the Pueblo Indian allies, so Vélez Cachupín and a few other governors were fairly tolerant of the Pueblos' performance of their dances and other ceremonials. Vélez Cachupín also told Marín del Valle that he had "extended to [the Pueblos] executive protection and rendered justice" so that during his first five-year term the Pueblos had been loyal "and very prompt to serve the king in war."[34]

A few decades after the Abiquiu witchcraft trials, a military reorganization throughout northern New Spain and a few decisive battles, such as Governor Juan Bautista de Anza's defeat of the Comanches under Cuerno Verde, turned the tide in the Spaniards' favor. Before that time a new approach to Indian affairs was developing on the viceregal level in Mexico City that Governor Vélez Cachupín put into effect in New Mexico. This new policy laid the groundwork for Anza's effective Indian policy. Some scholars have failed to recognize Vélez Cachupín's skill in achieving peace with the Comanches and other hostile groups decades before Anza accomplished the same long-sought-after goal.[35]

Lacking knowledge of conditions on the ground in remote northern New Mexico, Viceroy Juan Francisco Güemes y Horcasitas, the first Conde de Revillagigedo, asked his auditor general of war to report to him about the Comanche threat to New Mexico. In October 1746 Viceroy Revillagigedo received a sobering report on the Comanches, which undoubtedly came to the attention of Tomás Vélez Cachupín, a member of the viceroy's household. The Comanches, noted the report, "were a most intimidating and feared nation...because of the atrocities [committed] upon the [Pueblo] Indians and the Spanish residents."[36] In an attack on Pecos in June 1746, the Comanches killed twelve inhabitants, including two women, three boys, and three Jicarilla Apaches who were at peace. They also carried off a seven-year-old Christian Indian boy who was later found killed by hatchet blows. When Spanish troops with their Indian allies engaged the Comanches after this raid, they lost nine soldiers and killed sixty Comanches. The Comanches killed so many of the Spaniards' horses that the Indians were able to retreat without being pursued. The battle was a standoff, an example of another warning in the auditor general's report that the Comanches were "so numerous and so disciplined with their arms that they have been victorious [over the Pueblos]," and were willing to lose one hundred of their own warriors in order to kill one Spanish soldier.[37]

Another example of Comanche daring took place in June 1746 when they tried to set fire to the Pecos church and priest's lodging with a burning log but were stopped by some Pecos Indians. The auditor general recommended that the Spaniards wage all-out war against the Comanches "to instill fear in them and maintain the reputation and terror of our [Spanish] arms."[38] Although the auditor general cited Spanish laws and the reading of the *requerimiento* (the notification of the Indians of Spaniards' intent to bring Christianity to them, giving them the option of swearing loyalty to the king to avoid the attack), the end result the Spaniards sought was nothing less than the extermination of the Comanches.[39] Viceroy Revillagigedo adopted his auditor's report and ordered Governor Codallos y Rabal's strict compliance. In response, Governor Codallos undertook a major—but unsuccessful—campaign against the Comanches that did little to change anything on the ground in Abiquiu. Vélez Cachupín, in contrast, took the auditor general's advice about the Comanches to heart and applied it successfully when he became governor of New Mexico. Moreover, Vélez Cachupín added flexibility and a willingness to negotiate to the ironfist policy the viceroy recommended.[40]

Vélez Cachupín doubtless learned about the Indian problems in New Mexico as part of Viceroy Revillagigedo's household and apparently prepared himself for a radically different approach to dealing with Comanche, Ute, and Navajo raids. Key to Governor Vélez Cachupín's strategy was the establishment of a pueblo of Genízaro Indians at Abiquiu to help defend nearby Spanish settlements from attack. These Genízaros included representatives of most Plains groups, some Eastern Pueblos, and Hopis. Placed in the middle ground between the Spaniards and their nomadic Indian enemies, these Genízaro Indians needed all their physical and spiritual strength to withstand the pressures of life on the Abiquiu frontier.

The fear instilled in the Spaniards and the Pueblos by the Comanches must have seeped into the Abiquiu Genízaros as well, since word of Comanche atrocities spread fast. Spaniards considered scalping to be a cruel outrage when they suffered what ethnohistorian James Axtell has called "the unkindest cut," but it was a sign of honor and a means of acquiring power among Plains Indians.[41] In a particularly gruesome example of Comanche cruelty, the Comanches forced an enemy captive to dig a hole in the ground, then tied him up, made him get in the hole and covered him with dirt except for his head. Before leaving him to die a slow death, the Comanches scalped the prisoner and cut off his ears, nose, eyelids, and lips. Similar eyewitness accounts from settlers in the Abiquiu area led to the climate of fear that resulted in the temporary abandonment of Abiquiu in 1747.[42]

A similar abandonment of Ojo Caliente in the mid-1760s was contemporaneous with the Abiquiu witchcraft trial. Testimony of Spanish settlers reluctant to return to Ojo Caliente because of Comanche atrocities provides a sense of how formidable were the Comanches as an enemy and how Spaniards, Pueblos, and Genízaros alike regarded them. In 1769 Governor Pedro Fermín de Mendinueta (1767–78) noted that Ojo Caliente had been temporarily abandoned by Spanish settlers "filled with a fearful panic caused by the Comanches, owing to past battles with said nation."[43] Ordered to resettle, the Spaniards refused because of "the great warfare that the enemy [Comanches] has waged at Ojo Caliente, causing some deaths, the sorrow of which the heart does not forget, nor dries the tears of the soul."[44] One settler, Gregorio Sandoval, was more specific about his reasons for refusing to resettle, "having seen with his own eyes that first the Comanches had killed fourteen of his cattle and carried off the few horses he had...and second that they had killed one of his young men, and scalped another, and that going to resettle would cause great difficulty for his family...for they do not want to see their wives [taken] captive."[45]

A few months before the October 1747 Ute/Comanche attack on Abiquiu, Governor Codallos y Rabal took part as judge in a criminal case against a Genízaro named Pedro de la Cruz, accused of conspiring to leave the service of his master to join the Comanches and of then returning to attack New Mexico settlements. This case demonstrates the fear that possessed northern New Mexico settlers in the summer and fall of 1747. Mere mention of a plot by a marginalized Genízaro to join the Comanches and return with them to attack the Spanish and scalp the villagers was enough to convict Pedro de la Cruz. As De la Cruz alleged, the story was incredible on its face, a fabrication of Antonio Martín, an elite Spaniard, whose other servants were the only witnesses. It was just this kind of accusation connected with the Comanches—almost like the charge of witchcraft—that could inflame a court of law and be accepted with little proof. Governor Codallos y Rabal convicted De la Cruz and sent him to Socorro to serve a new master there, but the Comanche threat did not abate; instead, it increased in intensity.[46]

Near panic in the Abiquiu settlements was so palpable that it must be seen as one of the main contributing factors to the witchcraft outbreak from 1756 to 1766. During his first term, Governor Vélez Cachupín succeeded in bringing a semblance of calm to agitated frontier communities such as Abiquiu. Yet, from 1754 to 1762, the period between Vélez Cachupín's two terms as governor of New Mexico, new hostilities shattered that calm. This eruption of violence resulted in the main from the inept policies of the three governors who served during that hiatus.[47] Abiquiu again became a war zone.

The close association between fear and violence and an outbreak of witchcraft echoed similar events in other places. During the European witch-craze trials and resulting hangings and burnings at the stake, manipulation of fear generated by the uncertainty and terror that were part of life in medieval and early modern Europe, led to scapegoating of marginalized minorities such as older women, lepers, Jews, and Muslims. What was different about the Abiquiu witchcraft outbreak was the climate of fear generated by the constant threat of attack by Comanches, Utes, and Navajos. Many Abiquiu families still have stories about family members who were captured by Plains Indians or Navajos.[48]

Active warfare around Abiquiu spawned a siege mentality, particularly in the period before Vélez Cachupín's first term began in 1749 and again in the interregnum between his two terms, which lasted from 1754 to 1762. This situation probably had more to do with the Abiquiu witch craze than did any other single factor. The circumstances in Abiquiu in the 1760s were much like those in Salem, Massachusetts, in 1692. Pervasive fear characterized the mind-set of Puritan New Englanders in the period leading up to the Salem witchcraft outbreak and convinced them they were in the Devil's snare. Mary Beth Norton has convincingly demonstrated that random attacks by Wabanaki Indians so frightened these New Englanders that they equated the Indians with the Devil. Many Salem residents were refugees from the Indian wars on Maine's frontier. Like Abiquiu inhabitants, Salem residents saw themselves as antagonists to the "Devil worshipping" Indians whose shamans they considered to be witches. Puritan ministers such as Cotton Mather fanned the flames of this fear in their sermons, in which the presence of the Devil among the citizens of Salem was vividly described.[49] In Abiquiu, as in Salem, priests such as Toledo and probably Ordóñez before him, bore a large share of the responsibility for creating an atmosphere of fear that led to the wide-scale demonic possessions and exorcisms at Abiquiu. Although the content of

Father Toledo's sermons is unknown, they may well have followed a similar pattern. He considered Abiquiu Genízaros to be Devil worshippers, and Indians such as Miguel (El Cojo) Ontiveros were singled out as Satanic cult leaders.

Figure 3
Genízaro dances at Abiquiu. *Drawing by Glen Strock.*

CHAPTER TWO

The Genízaros

Genízaros are the least understood of all the population groups in colonial New Mexico.[1] The Abiquiu Genízaros were a mixed group of Plains Indians, Hopis, and probably some Pueblos displaced from their home communities. Their religious beliefs were different from the Christian worldview and included a mixture of beliefs from groups such as Pawnees, Kiowas, Apaches, Navajos, Utes, Comanches, and Hopis. There are hints throughout the Abiquiu witchcraft documents that what Father Toledo was describing as witchcraft was actually native religious ceremonials considered Devil-worship by the European worldview. Because these ceremonies, such as the Turtle Dance, were foreign and unfamiliar to Toledo, he demonized the participants. An examination of the makeup of some Genízaro communities in New Mexico makes possible an exploration of the nature of the Genízaros and their religious ceremonies.

The first-known group of Genízaros in New Mexico lived in the Analco barrio of Santa Fe, south of the Santa Fe River. These people replaced the

Indians who were the first occupants of Analco before the Pueblo Revolt, mostly Tlascalans from central New Spain. These first Genízaros may have been established as part of the hermitage of San Miguel south of the Santa Fe River even before Governor Pedro de Peralta (1610–14) moved the capitol from San Gabriel to Santa Fe in 1610. During the 1680 Pueblo Revolt, the Pueblos almost wiped out the Analco settlement on the first day of the revolt, having unleashed a particular fury there. This may have occurred due to Pueblo Indian jealousy over the special treatment the Spaniards accorded these Indians from New Spain, some of whom had Pueblo servants.[2]

At the time of the Reconquest of New Mexico in 1693, the Spaniards in El Paso requested that some of the few surviving refugees from Analco be allowed to return with them to Santa Fe. One of the returning Indians was Juan de León Brito, who in 1728 received a grant in the Analco area of lands that had belonged to his father. In 1742 Brito received a second grant from Governor Gaspar Domingo de Mendoza (1739–43). Most other new settlers at Analco after the Reconquest were also Genízaros.[3] Some of these Analco Genízaros acted as servants for the Spaniards in Santa Fe and were scouts and allies in Spanish retaliatory expeditions against the Plains Indians.[4]

Genízaros often spent most of their lives as purchased servants in New Mexico households but were not considered slaves because—at least theoretically—when their term of servitude was completed, they became free.[5] It was not always clear, however, how long this term lasted. Many Genízaro owners tried to keep the length of service vague and continue to reap the benefit of Genízaro labor without paying them. It was often the case that a Genízaro's status was close to slavery because they were physically abused and accorded few rights. Technically Genízaros were not slaves, although the subtle distinction was surely lost on them. Spanish law differentiated between the purchase of captives for servants who would eventually be freed, and outright slavery, which was prohibited in the Americas largely because of the influence of fray Bartolomé de las Casas.[6]

In 1733 a group of one hundred mostly Plains Indians, who identified themselves as "Los Genízaros," filed a petition with the strict, conservative New Mexico governor, Gervasio Cruzat y Góngora (1731–36), asking for their own land grant at the abandoned site of Sandia Pueblo.[7] This was the first time in New Mexico history that Genízaros had the temerity to ask for land of their own. Speaking through an anonymous advocate, "Los Genízaros" informed Governor Cruzat y Góngora that they had all been baptized and did not include any servants of Spaniards among their number. Still, Cruzat y Góngora was unimpressed and demanded that all these Plains Indians identify themselves by name and "nation."[8] The response listed far fewer than a hundred men; in fact, only twenty-five responded: seventeen heads of families, and eight single men. Their names and tribes give us a sense of who made up this group that referred to itself as Los Genízaros:

1. Francisco Baca I	Pawnee	14. Andrés Martín	Ute
2. Francisco Baca II	Apache	15. Domingo Martínez	Aa
3. Pablo Chávez	Kiowa	16. Rafael Montoya	Kiowa
4. Francisco Chávez	Tano	17. Antonio Padilla I	Pawnee
5. Agustín Fernández	Jumano	18. Antonio Padilla II	Pawnee
6. José Fernández.	Jumano	19. Cristóbal Romero	Apache
7. Agustín García	Aa	20. Francisco Sedillo	Pawnee
8. Francisco García	Jumano	21. Antonio Tagle	Jumano
9. Sebastián Gallegos	Jumano	22. Juan de Ulibarrí	Apache
10. Antonio Gurulé		23. Juan Antonio	Apache
11. Juan Antonio Gurulé	Pawnee	24. Bernardo	
12. Antonio Jaramillo	Kiowa	25. Joseph	Jumano[9]
13. Cristóbal Luján	Pawnee		

Of those who identified their tribes, Pawnees were the most numerous (six),[10] then Jumanos (five),[11] Apaches (four),[12] Kiowas (three),[13] the mysterious Aas (two),[14] one Ute,[15] and one Tano.[16] These mostly Plains Indians all had nomadic lifestyles and similar religious beliefs, although there were variations in important details. This is the most complete description of Genízaros by name and group affiliation from the first half of the eighteenth century.[17]

For these twenty-four individuals to have identified themselves by name may have placed them in some jeopardy. Governor Cruzat y Góngora showed little sympathy for the plight of these landless Genízaros in his final order, which abruptly ended the proceedings. He denied their petition without giving a reason, showing little enthusiasm for the idea of a separate Genízaro land grant.[18] Although the petition was not granted, the proceedings provide quite a bit of information about Genízaros in the 1730s. The petitioners were scattered throughout the Rio Abajo, some living in Spanish settlements, some in pueblos. There must have been an unusual cohesion among this group for them to come together, hire an advocate (who remained anonymous), and request a grant of this prime tract of land. It seems likely that the core petitioners did not really number a hundred but expected to enlist more once they got the grant. That possibility is strongly suggested by later events.[19]

The 1733 proceedings also demonstrate a change in attitude and power among the Genízaros and other groups on the fringe of colonial New Mexico society. To have sought improvement of their economic situation through their own land grant would have been unthinkable for a similar dispersed group of marginalized Indians two decades earlier. Even though they did not get the land grant, some of the 1733 petitioners eventually found land within Hispanic land grants. Three of them (two Pawnees) established themselves at the Plaza de los Genízaros in Belen by 1750.[20] By the 1750s Genízaros had begun to achieve recognition of their own property rights. The 1751 Las Trampas grant was settled with a group of twelve families from the Analco barrio, several of whom were Genízaros, eventually proving themselves to be hardy and law-abiding settlers, "who settled whatever difficulties they had among themselves."[21] Genízaros were also at least partially responsible for the settlement of other frontier outposts such as Ojo Caliente, San Miguel del Bado, Sabinal, Tome, Belen, and San Gabriel de las Nutrias. By 1776 Genízaros made up at least 14 percent of the population of Santa Fe.[22] In 1754 they received their own land grant at Abiquiu.[23]

The traditional definition of Genízaro includes Indian captives sold to Spaniards who then became household servants. Most Genízaros in New Mexico were Plains Indians captured as slaves by another Plains tribe and then sold to Hispanos or Pueblos. The legal basis for this arrangement is found in the laws in the *Recopilación*, which justified the purchase of captives under the Christian obligation to ransom captive Indians.[24] The practice was given further sanction after a group of Navajos brought some Pawnee children to New Mexico to sell. When the Spaniards refused to purchase the captives, the Navajos beheaded the children. Henceforth, the king ordered that, if necessary, royal funds be used to purchase captives to avoid such an outcome.[25] Traffic in Genízaros was originally sanctioned by the government as a method of Christianizing Indian captives, but teaching one's servants Christian doctrine was often ignored by Spaniards. More emphasis was placed on the amount of work Genízaros performed. The value of Genízaro servants varied from the eighty pesos paid for Pedro de la Cruz to the equivalent in pesos of fifteen mares (about one hundred fifty pesos) paid for an

Apache captive in 1731. A 1732 order from Governor Cruzat y Góngora prohibited the sale of Apaches to the Pueblos by Spaniards and provided a hun-
dred-peso fine for Spaniards and two hundred lashes for Pueblos who violated
the order.[26]

Once the process of Christianization was completed, and they had earned
enough to pay off the amount of their ransom, Genízaros were supposed to
be freed. The standard wage for a Genízaro was three to five pesos per month,
depending on the length of service.[27] Genízaros were purchased at annual
trade fairs held at Pecos, Taos, and Abiquiu, where they were considered one
of the most profitable commodities, the "richest treasure for the governor,"
in the words of Franciscan provincial fray Pedro Serrano.[28] Generally
Genízaros had a low social status because they were neither Spanish nor
Indian; thus, it was difficult for them to obtain the land, livestock, or other
property required to make a living. Some Genízaros, however, were able to
use their contacts in the Hispanic and Native American worlds to their advantage, acquiring land, livestock, and a substantial amount of material goods,
even though they retained their Genízaro status.

The Genízaro classification in mid-eighteenth-century New Mexico varied depending on the classifier. In 1764 a group of families from the Río Arriba
area asked for a land grant at San Gabriel de Las Nutrias south of Belen. When
Governor Vélez Cachupín ordered Alcalde Miguel Lucero to investigate and
learn something about the petitioners, Lucero conducted a census of the
group, counting twenty-four individuals, including four Genízaros, two *coyotes* (generalized term referring to the offspring of a Spaniard and an Indian
or mestizo), and one Apache. Vélez Cachupín subsequently made his own
census of the same group of settlers without employing the Genízaro classification. He referred to some individuals as *indio-genízaros* but changed
the designation Lucero had given to certain people from Genízaro to Indian
and from coyote to mestizo. Several individuals whom Lucero called
Spaniards received the designation "mestizo" from Vélez Cachupín.[29]

The two Las Nutrias censuses demonstrate that the Genízaro classification was flexible and varied depending on who recorded the census. When
Alcalde Lucero made his count, he wrote down the designation of *calidad*
(class) reported to him by the Nutrias settlers. Vélez Cachupín, by contrast, made his own determination of the status of each settler. The governor found almost half of the settlers to be Spaniards, but instead of using
the designation "Spaniard" as Lucero had done, Vélez Cachupín counted

the first fourteen settlers and then noted, "all of these fourteen families are reputed to be white." The governor was relying not only on how the settlers classified themselves but also on his own classification and their reputed calidad.[30]

In the 1730s, a Kiowa Genízaro named Ventura, who was instrumental in determining the perpetrators of the 1747 raid on Abiquiu, was captured by Comanches and then sold to an Indian from Senecu in the El Paso juris-diction. He was subsequently sold to several other masters, including Carlos Fernández and Diego Torres, before he went to live with the Navajos for a year and a half. He then went to Taos where he joined a military campaign against the Utes.[31] Although some scholars specializing in the study of iden-tity among captives and servants would designate Ventura as a slave from the time he was captured by Comanches until he went to live with the Navajos, others would use the term slave up to the point Ventura was pur-chased by the Senecu Indian.[32] From then on he would be termed a Genízaro.[33] Still other scholars would consider Ventura a servant until he left his last master and went to live with the Navajos, at which point he would become a Genízaro.[34] Since the definition of Genízaro varied during the eighteenth century and continues to vary today from scholar to scholar, it is useful to examine the common factors involved in considering an indi-vidual to be a Genízaro, coyote, or mestizo.

The primary elements of Genízaro status were servitude or captivity and Indian blood. Within these two factors there were numerous variations, the defining characteristics being quite elastic. Some Genízaros were considered to be Spaniards in the community in which they lived but were seen as Genízaros by people with whom they interacted elsewhere.[35] Genízaro ser-vants were found in pueblos such as Taos, San Juan, Santa Clara, and Nambe where they were acting as domestic servants for Pueblo families.[36] Genízaros were known to be purchased by and to serve other Genízaros, as well as Pueblos.[37] Even after being released from service to a master and given land in a frontier community, most Genízaros retained their status when they remained in Genízaro communities, such as Santo Tomás de Abiquiú, or the plaza at Belen called Nuestra Señora de los Genízaros.[38] Instead of growing, the population of Genízaro plazas such as Santo Tomás de Abiquiú, remained relatively constant, as many former Genízaros assimilated into sur-rounding plazas and became full-fledged Spanish citizens through marriage to Spaniards.[39] Some Genízaros maintained contact with their original tribe or pueblo, a connection they used to their advantage in trade with those tribes outside the authorized trade fairs.

When the Genízaro category is expanded to include mestizos who were captives of Indians and then lived as Spaniards after their release, received land grants, and owned substantial estates while retaining their mestizo status, additional permutations of what constituted a Genízaro emerge. One such individual was Juana Hurtado, also known as La Galvana. She fit the Genízaro classification because she was part Zia and was a captive of the Navajos during the Pueblo Revolt.

In 1680 Juana Hurtado was living on the rancho of Andrés Hurtado as his daughter by a woman from Zia Pueblo who was probably his domestic servant. Andrés Hurtado held Santa Ana Pueblo in encomienda, making him an elite member of pre-Revolt Spanish society entitled to collect tribute from that pueblo.[40] This meant that Juana occupied a semiprivileged niche in this society, although she was still considered a coyota, mestiza, or Genízara. A few months before the Pueblo Revolt erupted in August 1680, Juana was taken captive by a band of Navajos during a raid on Hurtado's rancho. Juana was only seven then, but by the time she was ransomed twelve years later by her half-brother in 1692, she had borne one or two children with Navajo father(s).[41] Instead of being stigmatized by her experience, Juana used her connections with Spanish, Pueblo, and Navajo society to make trading contacts that allowed her to acquire a substantial amount of property. When she died in 1753, Juana Hurtado owned a rancho with three houses and managed extensive herds of cattle and flocks of sheep. Juana also successfully petitioned for her own land grant at the northwest corner of Zia Pueblo lands near the community known today as San Isidro.[42]

Not only did Juana bear children during her captivity, she may have been adopted into a Navajo clan. Whatever ties she established there stood her in good stead, as evidenced by the frequent trading visits by Navajos to her rancho. She got her nickname "La Galvana" from a liaison with a man from Zia Pueblo presumably named Galván. This relationship resulted in four more children and even closer ties with the Zia people. The Zias demonstrated their loyalty to Juana in 1727 when Alcalde Ramón García charged her with scandalous behavior and threatened to put her in the stocks. The alcalde was deterred from carrying out this threat, however, when the Zias "threatened that the whole pueblo would move to the mesa tops, rather than have her [Juana Hurtado] mistreated."[43]

When Juana died, Alcalde Antonio Baca appointed himself to go to her home with two witnesses and inventory her property. The livestock alone was substantial: 333 goats, ewes, and rams; forty-two large cows; three oxen; three bulls; thirty-eight calves; thirty-one horses; one mule; and two jackasses. Alcalde Baca noted that the funeral expenses had already been paid to the priest at Zia, fray Pedro Montaño. Baca's accounting shows the following in-kind payment to Father Montaño: four cows with calves (one hundred pesos), several goats with kids and several sheep (seventy-two pesos), one fine mare (thirty pesos), one horse (fifteen pesos), one embroidered manta (eight pesos), and one cotton manta (four pesos), for a total of 229 pesos. Father Montaño was paid handsomely for the funeral mass and an additional novena. Even though Juana, la Galvana, was referred to as a *coyota* in these proceedings, the size of her estate and the amount of her funeral expenses place her in the same category as other women of property in eighteenth-century New Mexico. Yet Juana was a Genízara by virtue of her status as a Hispanicized Indian.[44]

Juana, La Galvana, provided for each of her four sons, but her favorite was Lorenzo Galván, whom she referred to as her legitimate son and heir. The value of his share of the estate was 1,222 pesos, including a house and agricultural lands at Zia Pueblo. The shares of the other sons were: Matías Galván, 1,101 pesos; Diego Galván, 823 pesos; and Juan Galván, 480 pesos. The balance of the estate came to 1,855 pesos, which was given to unnamed creditors. The share of Juan Galván, a fifteen-year-old minor, was to be held for him by his brother Diego, who was charged with teaching Juan the rudiments of Christian doctrine. It appears that all of Juana's sons were tied more closely to Zia Pueblo than they were to Spanish society, which would explain the need to teach the boy the elements of Christian doctrine. It would also explain the alcalde's admonition to the *caciques* of the pueblo "not to order or employ this boy for the time being but to leave him to care for his inheritance."[45]

It is clear from her will that Juana Galván Hurtado was a woman with one foot in the world of her father, the Spanish conquistador, and the other foot in the Indian world of the Navajos and Zias, two quite different cultures. A century later, Pedro León Luján maintained a similar ambiguous connection between the Utes and the Spanish citizens of Abiquiu. In both cases the Indian contacts of these two entrepreneurs-traders served to empower rather than marginalize them.[46]

Another Genízaro who defies easy classification was Antonio Casados, a Kiowa who attempted to establish an independent Genízaro pueblo within the Belen grant. Casados's story contains several additional variations from the usual definitions of Genízaro. Casados was a Kiowa Apache purchased when he was twelve years old by Miguelito, a Genízaro servant of Sebastián Martín living at Ojo Caliente. Baptized while working for Miguelito, Antonio was soon sold to Alonso Rael de Aguilar, the younger, and then to Francisco Casados of Santa Fe.[47] Eventually Antonio ran away from Francisco and married an Indian woman "he stole from the house of Juan de Naranjo of Chihuahua." Casados married the Indian from Chihuahua and was living in Santa Fe in 1745 when, along with several other Genízaros, he was ordered to the Belen land grant of Diego Torres.[48]

In June 1745 Antonio Casados traveled all the way to Mexico City to present a petition to the viceroy of New Spain. Casados claimed to be the captain of a pueblo of Genízaros at Belen and asked the viceroy to protect the rights of this pueblo by measuring its lands and evicting all Spaniards living within the pueblo. Casados must have been aware of the success that New Mexico pueblos had achieved in having their lands measured so they could obtain some protection from the Spanish government for their four square leagues. With the help of a lawyer in Mexico City, Casados was able to persuade the viceroy that he was a Pueblo Indian, not a Genízaro.[49] The viceroy, the Conde de Fuenclara, believing that Casados was captain of the natives of the "Pueblo of Belen," ordered the governor of New Mexico to investigate. Should the allegations contained in the Casados petition prove true, the governor was to relieve Casados of the "annoyances and oppressions that may have been caused by the Spaniards mentioned," in other words, he was to evict the Spaniards.[50]

Casados then returned to New Mexico to take part in the trial the viceroy had ordered, meanwhile gaining the support of numerous Pueblos. On the day set for the trial, Casados appeared in Santa Fe with an escort of seventy Pueblo Indians, a substantial, potentially rebellious, presence. This display so angered Governor Codallos y Rabal that he immediately placed Casados in jail for the duration of the trial. Under these circumstances, the hearing was certainly not fair. The proceedings were eventually sent back to Mexico City for decision by the viceroy. The case's outcome is unknown to contemporary scholars, but it is known that no Genízaro pueblo was ever established within the Belen land grant, although there was a Genízaro plaza there.[51]

Antonio Casados was purchased by another Genízaro and sold several times before obtaining his freedom. Whether he was adequately instructed in the Christian doctrine is questionable, but like Juana Hurtado Galván, Casados was able to use his contacts with the pueblo world to his advantage.

One of the best ways of assessing how Genízaros were defined and treated in mid-eighteenth-century New Mexico is to study the lawsuits in which they were involved. There was a dramatic shift in the attitude of the Spanish government toward Genízaros in 1749 when Tomás Vélez Cachupín replaced Joaquín Codallos y Rabal as governor of New Mexico. Before Vélez Cachupín the judicial climate was not favorable to Pueblos or Genízaros. During Codallos y Rabal's term, criminal charges were brought against Indians from Cochiti, Tesuque, and San Juan for conspiring with Utes and Plains Indians to incite an uprising. By contrast, Pueblos or Genízaros brought few cases on their own behalf seeking recognition of their land and water rights because the negative judicial climate did not favor such claims. In cases that were brought by and against Genízaros, Codallos y Rabal was far less sympathetic to the Genízaro point of view than was his successor, Governor Vélez Cachupín. One case that demonstrates Codallos y Rabal's bias and the skewed judicial system he oversaw involved criminal charges against Pedro de la Cruz.[52]

De la Cruz was a Genízaro from Isleta Pueblo, who, in 1747 while serving Antonio Martín, was accused of conspiring to leave Martín's house with another servant to join the Comanches. Martín charged that De la Cruz and other servants (particularly the Indian María de la Luz) planned to seek out the Comanches and return with them to attack the Spaniards and "to take [them] by their hair" (scalp them). Most of the witnesses against De la Cruz were also Martín's servants who dutifully corroborated their master's charge. Yet, when Miguel de Moya was appointed as attorney for De la Cruz, the other side of the story emerged. Moya argued that Martín had concocted the entire story so that he would not have to pay De la Cruz for his work, and that Martín coerced his other servants through beatings and other forms of intimidation to give false testimony. It appears that De la Cruz had completed his term of service to Martín and would either have to be given his freedom or be paid for future service.[53]

Criminal procedure in New Mexico in the eighteenth century "placed the accused at a distinct disadvantage," because the procedures were inquisitorial rather than accusative.[54] Under the accusative procedure, the aggrieved party brought charges against the accused, whereas the local magistrate filed the charges under the inquisitorial procedure. In this case, Teniente Alcalde Pedro Martín, a relative of Antonio Martín, filed the charges and conducted the initial investigation (the *sumaria*). Pedro took statements from Antonio and from the witnesses, most of whom were his servants. The formulaic quality of these statements, in which each witness was asked the same set of questions and gave similar answers, was filtered through the alcalde's summary of their testimony and was not calculated at arriving at the truth. Not until this preliminary investigation was completed was De la Cruz allowed to make his initial statement.[55]

Governor Codallos y Rabal personally questioned Pedro de la Cruz, indicating the importance of the case. At this point in the proceedings, another filter was inserted. The governor appointed Francisco Rendón to interpret for the defendant, even though it was acknowledged that De la Cruz was fluent in Spanish. De la Cruz told the governor, through the interpreter, that he was born at Isleta Pueblo, and that his father, Agustín de la Cruz, was a Genízaro Indian. This might explain why Pedro is called an Indian at some points in the proceedings and at other times a Genízaro. De la Cruz denied the charges Antonio Martín had brought, while admitting at one point that he had told Antonio Jorge that he wanted to go to the Comanches when he got angry at Jorge for refusing to sell him arrows.[56] This must be where the story got started, but De la Cruz later told the court through his attorney that Martín took his words, perhaps uttered in jest, and invented the charges against the Genízaro. According to De la Cruz, Martín "was the author of everything."[57]

Codallos y Rabal handed down the sentence without commenting on the conflicting testimony, stating only that the defendant's guilt was established "with ample proof of the witnesses."[58] The governor was acting as judge and prosecuting attorney when he announced the sentence, which served to extend De la Cruz's period of servitude for another five years. He was to be taken to the presidio of El Paso del Norte and from there delivered into the service of Antonio Tiburcio de Ortega, the *teniente alcalde* of the pueblo of Nuestra Señora del Socorro.[59] Ortega was to pay De la Cruz three *reales* per month to be applied to the fees and expenses of this case, which Codallos y Rabal determined to be 180 pesos. The governor also arrived at the sum of 180 pesos as the value of De la Cruz's services for five years, which was to be paid in advance to the court. In effect Tiburcio de Ortega was purchasing De la Cruz's services by paying the expenses of his criminal case. Thus De la Cruz ended end up serving both Martín and Tiburcio de Ortega without pay.[60]

Pedro de la Cruz did not receive a fair trial. The charge against him was patently ridiculous. At a time when Comanche and Ute raids struck fear in the hearts of Spanish settlers, the charge that a fellow Spaniard might be involved in fomenting such an attack was calculated to inflame the passions of everyone connected with the case. Barely a month after the De la Cruz case, a large number of Indians, at the time thought to be Comanches but later determined to be primarily Utes, fell upon Abiquiu.[61]

De la Cruz was never able to state his side of the case directly. Although he was fluent in Spanish he was assigned the same interpreter, Francisco Rendón, appointed for Antonio Casados a year earlier in the Belen case. He was also assigned an attorney but was unable to present his version of the charges against him until the investigation phase of the case was complete. By that time the charge that De la Cruz planned to flee to the Comanches had been repeated over and over and gained a measure of credibility. When De la Cruz's lawyer finally put forth the claim that Martín had fabricated the entire story, the damage had been done. Despite the lack of evidence of the conspiracy of which De la Cruz was accused, Governor Codallos y Rabal seems to have made up his mind to send him to another master irrespective of evidence. The case shows dramatically why Genízaros were often rebellious; with a few strokes of his pen Governor Codallos y Rabal consigned Pedro de la Cruz, who by rights should have been a free man, to years of continued servitude.

In a real sense, the empowerment of Genízaros in New Mexico began with Governor Vélez Cachupín's arrival in 1749. He found a frontier province surrounded by mostly hostile Utes, Apaches, Comanches, and Navajos. His response was to expand Spanish settlements onto the periphery of the settled areas, making peace with friendly Indians when possible and fighting the hostile ones when necessary. Once the governor had achieved peaceful relations with the surrounding indigenous peoples, he was able to turn his attention to the Genízaros who were complaining of mistreatment at the hands of their Spanish masters and seeking independence and land of their own. Vélez Cachupín's approach to lawsuits involving Genízaros was generally sympathetic to their complaints, often giving them precisely the relief requested. Vélez Cachupín was much more concerned with the treatment of Genízaros than had been previous governors and in particular with their instruction in the Christian faith.[62]

In an early case during his first term, the governor found Bernabé and Baltasar Baca guilty of disobeying an order prohibiting the employment of Indians for personal service and fined them. This was not an outcome that would have been expected from any of Vélez Cachupín's predecessors.[63] During his second term Vélez Cachupín dealt with several cases of reported mistreatment of Genízaros. In 1763 two Genízara servants of different masters complained to the governor that their Spanish masters had neglected to instruct them in the Catholic faith and had assigned them duties inappropriate to their sex. The two women had been required to help tend sheep, and one of them had been raped while in the fields performing this duty. Governor Vélez Cachupín ordered an investigation, directing that the two Genízaras be examined (probably by a priest), regarding their knowledge of Christian doctrine. They failed the test. Since the investigation found the charges to be true, Vélez Cachupín removed the Genízaras from the homes of their masters, Tomás and Isabel Chávez, and placed them in other homes "where they might be instructed in the Christian doctrine and customs and be fed and clothed through household chores appropriate to their sex."[64]

Governor Vélez Cachupín found ways to bring more Genízaros into frontier settlements such as Abiquiu, while resolving Genízaro complaints that were frequently brought before him. Gertrudes de Cuellar and José María Montaño complained to the governor about mistreatment by Juan Bautista Montaño, in whose house they were serving. The judgment in this case stands in sharp contrast to the Pedro de la Cruz case.[65] In May 1766 Gertrudes and her husband José, both Genízaros, rode horseback from the Belen area to Santa Fe to file a complaint with Governor Vélez Cachupín. They informed the governor that their master would not allow them to leave his employment unless they agreed to pay him one hundred pesos or agreed to serve him for five more years. They claimed that they had already served Montaño for ten years and that he should pay them a salary if he wanted

the couple to continue to serve him. Gertrudes also complained of other conduct by Montaño that was so egregious she did not want to serve in Montaño's
house under any circumstances. Gertrudes told Vélez Cachupín that
Montaño had forced himself on her on two occasions. In addition, Montaño
beat her and would not allow either of them to plant a single corn plant.
Even the horse they rode to Santa Fe to present their petition cost them five
pesos in rental from Montaño.[66] Not only was Montaño abusing the two
Genízaros, he was also neglecting to instruct them in Christian doctrine, or,
as Gertrudes put it, "instead of providing us with the [Christian] doctrine
he has us in Hell."[67]

   This testimony was enough to convince Vélez Cachupín. He did not even
ask to hear Montaño's side of the story. Instead he investigated independently and found that Montaño had paid about eighty pesos for José María
nine years before when the Genízaro was about thirteen. As part of the
inquiry, Vélez Cachupín ordered Nicolás Ortiz and Carlos Fernández to carry
out an investigation, which provided a detailed analysis of the value of a
Genízaro's services. The two experts found that a Genízaro servant should
be paid three pesos per month for the first three years, four pesos per month
for the following three years, and five pesos per month for the last three
years.[68] This assessment of the value of a Genízaro's services was "in accordance with the customs and practices of this country [of New Mexico]," but
it is not likely that everyone paid their Genízaro servants this well. Vélez
Cachupín requested this information to determine if José María had
worked off the amount that had been paid for him. When the calculation
was made, José María Montaño had a credit of 352 pesos (432 pesos less 80
pesos). Accordingly, Governor Vélez Cachupín rendered the following judgment: "I declare [the Genízaros] free from the services that are being compelled by Juan Bautista Montaño."[69]

   Freeing the two Genízaros was just the beginning for Vélez Cachupín.
Concerned with the welfare of Gertrudes and her husband and with the
precarious nature of frontier settlements like Abiquiu, the governor
ordered José María "to go to the said pueblo [of Abiquiu] with his wife where
they will be assigned lands to farm and a lot for a house so that with his
labor and industry they will feed themselves and be enumerated with the
rest of the individuals of the pueblo." Thus Vélez Cachupín, in marked contrast with his predecessors' practice, changed the status of José María
Montaño and Gertrudes Cuellar from Genízaro servants subject to the whim

of their master, to free landholders and members of a land grant community, which individually and collectively owned all the resources necessary for survival.[70]

The governor realized, however, that it might take more than a written decree to effect this change. Vélez Cachupín understood that the nomadic lifestyle of the Genízaros left them "totally free and restless because they do not have possessions or a proper place to live." José María and Gertrudes had complained that their master would not allow them to plant any corn, so perhaps they would embrace the opportunity to be farmers and landowners.[71]

Genízaros were often caught between two worlds, unable to fully participate in either Spanish society or pueblo society. They were supposed to be given their freedom after they worked off the amount paid to "ransom" them, but as can be seen from the case of *Antonio Martín v. Pedro de la Cruz*, the courts before Vélez Cachupín did not always protect Genízaros or grant them a fair trial. Governor Vélez Cachupín was the first New Mexico governor to give Genízaros and other oppressed minorities a fair hearing in court.[72]

Genízaros were also locked in a struggle with the Franciscans over two competing value systems. Spanish policy sought to convert the Genízaros to Catholicism, restructure their beliefs and religious practices, and make them productive members of Spanish society. Genízaro resistance to this goal and their desire to maintain their ceremonies and belief systems set up a tension between conflicting goals and worldviews that was difficult to reconcile. Some individuals navigated successfully in both worlds before eventually leaving behind the lower status of Genízaro.

Manuel Mestas served for many years as a Ute interpreter. In the 1789 Abiquiu census he was listed as a Genízaro. Mestas led several expeditions into Ute country to recover livestock stolen from him and from his neighbors. Prior to July 1805, Mestas, a man of about seventy, traveled alone to Ute country and succeeded in recovering eight horses the Utes had stolen from him. Then, in July 1805, Mestas returned to Ute country for a month to recover more livestock. In the area of Utah Lake he retook eleven animals that had been stolen from him, as well as twenty mules and eight horses taken from other New Mexicans. Mestas lost most of the livestock on his way back to New Mexico to "marauding bands, possibly Kiowas who were at war with the Yutas (Utes)." By 1808 Mestas was a private landowner at La Cuchilla, no longer a Genízaro, having achieved *vecino* status.[73]

Andrés and Lucrecio Muñiz accompanied the Domínguez-Escalante expedition to Utah in 1775–76 and performed important services, while causing the friars much grief by trading with the Utes. Andrés was hired as the Ute interpreter and Lucrecio, who was also a landowner at Ojo Caliente, came along uninvited.[74] Fathers Domínguez and Vélez de Escalante described the Muñiz brothers as Genízaros and wrote disparagingly of them in the expedition journal. Father Vélez de Escalante noted that Andrés and Lucrecio had joined the expedition solely to trade with Utes, not as had the priests: "For the glory of God and the salvation of souls."[75] Normally it was illegal to trade with the Utes without a license, so the Muñiz brothers must have believed they were immune from prosecution as long as they were traveling with the good fathers. The members of the expedition were told not to bring any merchandise to trade with the Indians, but the Muñiz brothers apparently disobeyed, and as Vélez de Escalante facetiously reported, "[They] proved themselves to be such obedient, loyal, and faithful Christians that they peddled what they secretly brought along, and most greedily sought weapons from the infidels." Apparently, the priests brought some trade goods themselves, such as glass beads, to trade for food such as buffalo meat. Andrés Muñiz had been listed as a mulatto in the church records and his wife, María Chávez, was listed as a coyota. Later, both were listed as Spaniards, providing another example of Genízaros who achieved vecino status.[76]

Pedro León Luján came from Abiquiu, a village steeped in the tradition of Indian trade, whose Genízaro parentage led historian Sondra Jones to assume that Luján was probably a Genízaro. To Luján the trade in Indian captives was profitable, customary, and socially acceptable so long as the Genízaros were humanely treated, for Genízaros were always in demand by Indians and Hispanic New Mexicans. Luján was born in Abiquiu on 8 April 1794, the son of Juan Antonio Luján, a child of the [Genízaro] pueblo, and María Isadora Romero (widow of José Antonio Chávez). Luján married at least three times, although only one child was recorded as his, a son named José Agapito, christened in 1828. At least four Ute or Paiute Indians were christened with Luján acting as godfather, and all of them lived in his home. Other children, possibly offspring of his second and third wives, were also living there. Luján became a veteran of the Navajo and Apache Indian wars and was an established trader stationed in Abiquiu.[77]

Luján first appeared in the Mexican records in the militia muster rolls for an 1836 Navajo campaign. By 1839 he had risen to a position of leadership, submitting a report to the governor on militia troop strength in Abiquiu. In December 1839 Captain don Pedro León Luján led a campaign against the Navajos; his troops attacked a small rancheria where they killed two warriors and a woman and captured "six little slaves of both sexes" along with other plunder. This is an example of how Genízaros were acquired during military campaigns.[78]

The practice of trading in Indian captives, who were sold to Spaniards and Indians to serve as Genízaro servants, was closely connected to Indian warfare and Hispanic raiding. Slave-raiding perpetuated the Indian wars. Slaving caused the friction leading to hostilities, and the wars were used as a cover for the purpose of "harvesting" new crops of slaves.[79] Manuel Mestas, Andrés and Lucrecio Muñiz, and Pedro Luján eventually acquired vecino status largely through their trading—often for Indian captives—with Utes. The facility of Mestas and the Muñiz brothers with the Ute language indicates that they may have been part Ute themselves. Like La Galvana, they were able to use their Genízaro status to their advantage, acquiring some property and the respect that went along with vecino status. The fact that Luján began to be referred to as don Pedro León Luján is an indication of that respect.[80]

Andrés and Lucrecio Muñiz illustrate another way in which they used their Ute connections to their advantage. Both received land as part of the Ojo Caliente grant. Even though the brothers were classified as Genízaros in the Domínguez-Escalante journal of 1776, at Ojo Caliente they were designated as Spaniards. There was a purely Genízaro settlement on one side of the river at Ojo Caliente, but the Muñiz brothers received allotments on the Spanish side of the river. Most of the Spaniards at Ojo Caliente abandoned their holdings in the face of devastating Ute and Comanche raids as Governors Vélez Cachupín and Mendinueta repeatedly ordered these Spaniards to return. Most replied that they would resettle only if all the settlers resettled. Governor Mendinueta was so angered by the statements of the settlers who refused to return to Ojo Caliente that he sentenced two of them to serve a month in the militia detachment and delayed the resettlement of Ojo Caliente. Mendinueta became so frustrated that he decided to go to Ojo Caliente with Alcalde Antonio José Ortiz and inspect the community.[81]

When Alcalde Ortiz inspected the Genízaros and the Spaniards to determine who was still living at the vulnerable outpost of Ojo Caliente

and what they had planted, Andrés Muñiz was the only Spaniard living
in his house with his family. He had one of the largest gardens in Ojo
Caliente, having planted corn, peas, chile, and onions. Alcalde Ortiz
found only three Genízaros had planted, and only two had their families with them.[82]

The only way the small community of Ojo Caliente could hold out
against the Utes and Comanches was to trade with them. Muñiz had assimilated sufficiently into Spanish society so that he could act as an interme-
diary between these Indians and the Spaniards who wanted to trade. Thus,
he was not targeted by either group, as Utes and Comanches found it more
in their interest to trade than to fight. Ojo Caliente in the 1760s and 1770s
was similar to southern Colorado almost a century later; the only way to
settle peacefully along the Ute frontier was at the sufferance of the Utes
when they found it to be in their interest.[83]

These brief histories have several common threads that reveal more
about what it meant to be a Genízaro. All of these people, except perhaps
the illiterate Pedro León Luján, were fluent in the Ute language and used
that skill to their advantage as interpreters and traders. These well-connected Genízaros became acculturated and assimilated into Hispanic society while retaining ties to the Utes and other groups. Although there is
sufficient information to create such biographical sketches of these
notable individuals, comparatively much less is known of the Genízaro
community of Abiquiu during the witch scare of the 1760s. Governor Vélez
Cachupín provided the best description of the Abiquiu Genízaros in his
report to the viceroy as part of the witchcraft trial. Speaking of Genízaros
in general, the governor did not mince words. His description was based
on firsthand experience and helps explain why the Abiquiu sorcerers were
so intractable. Vélez Cachupín described the Genízaros as:

> perverse, lazy, and with such serious vices, that they
> are most difficult to regulate and subdue, because they
> and their families love the life of the vagabond. They
> move from one place to another within these areas,
> causing much damage to the planted fields and live-
> stock, living by theft without respect of justice. They
> are quarrelsome and stubborn in their ways, especially
> in their love of gambling.[84]

The governor's harsh opinion was ameliorated by his judgment that Genízaros were the best Indian fighters, whether they served as auxiliaries to Spanish troops or lived in frontier settlements such as Abiquiu, Ojo Caliente, or San Miguel del Bado. Vélez Cachupín believed that the negative character traits of the Genízaros were due not to any "innate propensity," but to a lack of proper training by their masters, who typically employed them as shepherds and wood gatherers and failed to teach them the Christian doctrine. Vélez Cachupín knew this was true because of the many complaints he received from Genízaros regarding this kind of treatment. Often he removed complaining Genízaros from abusive masters, assigning them to other households, emancipating them, or sending them to be part of the Abiquiu Genízaro grant.

The Genízaros who settled on land Governor Vélez Cachupín granted them at Abiquiu were primarily Hopis, Plains Indians, and some Tewas from nearby pueblos. The Hopis had been living at Abiquiu in the house of the Montoya family, who were dislodged and forced to retreat to the Rio Abajo as a result of the devastating Ute/Comanche raid of 1747. At the time of the resettlement of Abiquiu in 1750, only the Montoya Genízaros were left, and thirteen of them were settled at the former house of Miguel de Montoya.[85] These Hopis living in the Montoya house formed the nucleus of the Genízaro grant, although there were many Genízaros scattered throughout the surrounding settlements who probably participated in the Abiquiu land grant. An indication of the number of Genízaros kept by individual families is found in the Santa Clara Pueblo church records. In 1743 seventeen Hopis were brought to Santa Clara for baptism by the Montoya family.[86] The Martín Serrano family owned even more Genízaros. Between 1754 and the 1840s, members of this extended family from various settlements in the Abiquiu area baptized more than two hundred Indian children listed as Ute, Comanche, or Genízaro, into their family. Many of these Genízaros and some in the category "Indian of unknown parentage" were probably Hopis.[87]

The Hopis living in the Montoya house at Abiquiu could well have been descendants of original inhabitants of the Abiquiu area. More than twenty Chama Valley pueblos dotted the mesa tops above Abiquiu in prehistoric times. The present-day Tewa pueblos south of Abiquiu are inhabited by descendants of these prehistoric pueblos. Some of these Tewas fled to Hopi country at the time of the Vargas Reconquest and established a Tewa-speaking pueblo named Hano on First Mesa.[88]

Figure 4
Dances at the feast day of
Santo Tomás Apóstal de
Abiquiú, November 7, 2004.
Photograph by Isabel Trujillo.

The Abiquiu Genízaros were similar to all New Mexico Genízaros. They were, as Benito Cordova optimistically put it, "special individuals, with two cultures, Indian and Hispano. [They] are a living bridge between two people."[89] At the time of the Abiquiu witch trials more than two cultures were involved in the makeup of the Abiquiu Genízaro. Besides the Hopi, Hispanic, and Pueblo influence, the cultures of Plains Indians, and Ute, Navajo, Kiowa, Pawnee, Apache, and Comanche customs were also passed on to the Genízaros. Soon, however, tribal affiliations became lost among the Genízaros. They would simply be identified as Genízaros or "Indians of unknown parentage," as was true among the Martín Serrano servants. Beginning in the early nineteenth century, many individuals would cease to call themselves Genízaros but would eventually refer to themselves as Spaniards, especially after they were freed and had married. The term "Genízaro" gradually disappeared as a designation of casta, although the

practice of Hispanic households keeping such Indian servants continued
into the late nineteenth century.

In more recent years, individuals of Genízaro ancestry from Abiquiu
would consider themselves Hispanic throughout the year except on the
Abiquiu feast day of Santo Tomás in late November, at which time they would
be Indians.[90] Among the most solemn dances performed at the Abiquiu feast
day in November were El Nanillé and Los Cánticos del Cementerio, performed
in front of the cemetery of the church. The Nanillé is danced to the cadence
of the tombé, or hand drum, and includes mysterious words such as "nanillé"
that no one recognizes. To some the nanillé song sounds Navajo, to others it
is similar to the Tewa eagle dance from Jemez. The origins of the Abiquiu
songs, dances, and pantomimes, still performed on the November feast day,
remain a mystery. A recent book, *Nuevo México Profundo*, summarizes the
Genízaro feast-day festivities at Abiquiu: "The Indo-Hispano heritage has a
dark side that stems from the historical struggle that molded it, but
here . . . satire and burlesque minimize the pain of such memories."[91]

One of the pantomimes performed at the Abiquiu feast day directly con-
fronts the experience of captivity that is at the heart of the Genízaro experience. As described in *Nuevo México Profundo*, "A cautivo is taken prisoner
from the crowd and presented to the people with a shout of '¿Quién lo
conoce?'—'Who knows this person?' Someone comes forward with the
desempeño [ransom], which is paid to the singers. If nobody claims the captive, the person remains the 'property' of the singers." This pantomime beau-
tifully encapsulates the nature of the Genízaro experience as being in the
middle, living in two worlds. Genízaro territory was a place where their fate—
to be ransomed and freed, or to remain a captive or a servant—was often
in someone else's hands: their Hispanic master, a priest, or a governor.[92]

Figure 5
Father Toledo attacked by Vicente in the shape of a wolf. *Drawing by Glen Strock.*

CHAPTER THREE

The Priest

Fray Juan José Toledo

F ray Juan José Toledo must have felt completely isolated when he was assigned to Abiquiu as parish priest in 1756. Toledo had the difficult task of converting the Genízaros and training them in the rites of Catholicism. In spite of the magnitude of this challenge, fray Juan José initially thought he was up to the task. His faith, courage, and physical endurance were beyond question. Father Toledo had demonstrated this many times in his forty-one years. The story of the priest's life shows it to have been an adventurous one. He had a close call with death at Hopi in 1749, but nothing prepared him for his long encounter with the Abiquiu Genízaro sorcerers. This is his story.

On 3 June 1714, Manuel Toledo and Paula Mejía de Vera, Father Toledo's parents, underwent prenuptial investigations in Mexico City.[1] Manuel was a native of Seville in southern Spain where he had been born to Juan Toledo and Isabel de León. At the time he was preparing to wed Paula, Manuel had been a citizen of Mexico City for eight years. His intended was an orphan, whose parents' names are unknown. Also unknown is exactly when they married, because the records for those years have not survived. Presumably the celebration of their marriage took place soon after the investigations were completed, since within a year Manuel and Paula had a child. On 31 May 1715, they presented Juan José Felipe de Toledo for baptism in the cathedral of Mexico City. In a foreshadowing of the boy's future as a priest, a Franciscan, fray Juan Muñiz, baptized him. According to church records, Juan José had been born six days earlier, on 25 May. The godfather was Captain Cristóbal de Avendaño, *alcalde ordinario* of the viceregal capital. The participation of this local official in the baptism of Manuel's son would seem to indicate that Juan José's father moved in circles that offered him the opportunity to know personally some of the city's leading citizens.[2]

Nothing specific is known of Juan José's youth up to age sixteen, although it can be concluded that he must have heeded a genuine vocation to enter the Franciscan order. Vocations were not in short supply, and the sincerity of an applicant's vocation had to be examined before being admitted into the novitiate, the year-long probationary period. Juan José must also have acquired a good basic education, including knowledge of Latin, before entering his novitiate at the Convento Grande de San Francisco in the summer of 1731. As a novice, Juan José spent his probationary year learning the Franciscan Rule and "the rules of norms of religious education based on [St. Bonaventure's] *Speculum Disciplinae* and other standard works, the rules of ascesis, the recitation of the Divine Office, and the Order's ceremonial."[3] The young novitiate also received instruction in the proper way to sing in church.

The instruction in morals and personal discipline, with its emphasis on duty and practice, was complemented by a more spiritual teaching—including, but not limited to, mysticism—that informed the prayer life of the novice and inspired him to lead a virtuous existence.[4] On 14 July 1732, he made his profession, taking vows as a full-fledged member of the order.[5] After his profession, fray Juan José continued similar studies for the next few years. During this time he also would have completed his study of Latin grammar and logic. At some point in his studies, Toledo became familiar with a book that was standard reading fare for missionaries in training, Alonso de la Peña Montenegro's *Itinerario para párrocos de indios*.[6] The *Itinerario* was a manual for priests ministering to Indians and contained sections on idolatry, witchcraft, and the Devil's Pact, which Toledo quoted or paraphrased at length. Although no record remains of the books fray Juan José might have had in his possession, his citations from the *Itinerario* were at least as accurate as his quotations from his Vulgate Bible, so he certainly had access to a copy for consultation.[7] It is known that multiple copies of the *Itinerario* existed in the Franciscan library in Santo Domingo Pueblo, and certain clergymen in New Mexico at the same time as Father Toledo had copies of the *Itinerario*.[8]

As a young friar Toledo performed his share of the many menial tasks required to keep a large institution like the Convento Grande running, all under the watchful eyes of his teachers. At age twenty-one, having shown an aptitude for scholarship, fray Juan José began the study of philosophy and theology, both moral and mystical, the latter to foster the contemplative aspect of Franciscan life. In this period of study, Toledo would have become familiar with the medieval philosopher theologians Thomas Aquinas (c.1225–74) and John Duns Scotus (c. 1266–1308), the latter a Franciscan himself, and a favorite of fellow members of the Order. In addition to these universally recognizable figures, fray Juan José would doubtless have read such works by Spanish theologians as fray Enrique de Villalobos's *Summa de la teología moral* (Salamanca, 1662) and fray Jaime de Corella's *Suma de la teología moral* (Barcelona, 1690).[9] His writings in New Mexico demonstrate that he was sufficiently familiar with the works of Antonio Ruiz de Montoya's *La conquista espiritual del Paraguay* (1639) and St. Jerome's literary works to cite them chapter and verse.[10] Finally, at age twenty-four, the successful seminarian would have been ordained a priest.[11]

There is nothing to indicate that Father Toledo had a mission posting before being assigned to New Mexico, so it seems likely, assuming he stayed on track as a student from novitiate to ordination, that he spent a few years at the missionary training center at Santiago Tlatelolco near the viceregal capital.[12] There the young priest and future missionary had an opportunity to refine his preaching skills and study Indian languages, although it is doubtful if anything offered there, typically Nahuatl, Otomí, and Tarascan, would have helped Toledo in New Mexico.

While at Tlatelolco, Father Toledo may well have consulted a primer or catechism in Keres and met its author. Fray Antonio de Miranda wrote but never had printed such a work, and Father Toledo might have had an opportunity to consult the manuscript version and thus have some exposure to that language. That might explain, in part, why his first two postings in New Mexico were to Keresan-speaking Acoma and Laguna.[13]

In the early centuries of Spain's New World enterprise, Franciscans with a missionary vocation were seldom lacking. The desire for martyrdom and strict observance of the Rule were the hallmarks of those friars who prepared for the often-dangerous life of a missionary. By fray Juan José's day, however, mission service may well have lost much of its appeal. Indeed, by the late eighteenth century there is clear evidence of Franciscans being sent to the far northern frontier against their will, but there is nothing to suggest that Father Toledo was compelled to serve in New Mexico.[14] He must have gotten his assignment very soon after the completion of his studies, which probably concluded early in 1743. In addition to his formal study, the young Franciscan would have been steeped in the history the Order, especially of its activities in New Spain. Therefore he would have known of the emphasis early Christian evangelists placed on the notion of Indians as children.[15] Implicit in this view was the need to punish the Indians as though they were children and the Franciscans were their fathers. Father Toledo likely would have also believed that the natural docility of the Indians made them particularly vulnerable to the Devil. Toledo's close reading of De la Peña Montenegro would have reinforced this concept. In the prologue to libro 2, tratado 1 of the *Itinerario*, De la Peña Montenegro describes the Indians as "poor unfortunates, wretches if anyone ever deserved the name".[16] At the same time, Toledo doubtless knew the glorious history of his martyred brethren who fell in the New Mexico mission field during the Pueblo Revolt of 1680 at the hands of Indians, which was surely the work of Satan. If he pondered his future in light of the past of members of his Order in New Mexico, fray Juan José may well have been prepared to meet the Devil and his minions in the far north before he departed the Valley of Mexico, probably in early spring of 1743.

It is likely that Father Toledo accompanied the governor-elect of New Mexico, Joaquín Codallos y Rabal, from Mexico City as far as Durango in Nueva Vizcaya. Traveling with a new governor's retinue on the long journey north had a long tradition among the Franciscans destined for the New Mexican mission field.[17] The change in administrations from Governor Gaspar Domingo de Mendoza to Governor Codallos y Rabal coincided with the movement of Franciscans in and out of New Mexico. In all, the exchange of priests involved ten Franciscans: four leaving, six arriving. Fray Pedro Díaz de Aguilar, fray José de Eguía de Lumbre, fray José Antonio Guerrero, and fray Juan Antonio Sánchez departed New Mexico.[18] Fray José Blanco, fray Ángel García, fray Francisco Javier Guzmán, fray Agustín de Iniesta, father Toledo, and fray José Manuel Trigo went to New Mexico. Five of the incoming priests were *criollos*; that is, they had been born in New Spain; Father García was a Spaniard. Three of the four departing Franciscans were criollos; the origin of Father Eguía de Lumbre is unknown.

This maintained an equilibrium. Governor Codillos y Rabal tarried in Durango to make certain arrangements, which included the right to farm the tithes in Santa Fe, until late September 1743.[19] By that time, the Franciscans had completed their journey to New Mexico.

A new reality greeted these new arrivals, a different missionary experience than their brethren had faced in the colony for most of the history of their order in New Mexico. In the 127 years from 1598 to 1725, the Franciscans had a monopoly on leading the struggle for the spiritual well-being of the residents of the colony, Indian and Spaniard alike. In 1725, the bishop of Durango, Benito Crespo y Monroy traveled as far as El Paso on an official tour of his diocese. That year Antonio de Valverde Cosío, former governor of New Mexico and the wealthiest landowner in El Paso, requested of the bishop that a mission for the Suma Indians be established near his hacienda of San Antonio. Valverde's desire for a solution to the Suma problem gave Bishop Crespo a chance to further the diocese's claim to jurisdiction over the province of New Mexico. On a number of occasions since the early seventeenth century, bishops in Durango had made halfhearted attempts to assert their authority over New Mexico and had always met with Franciscan resistance, but Bishop Crespo began to pursue the matter in earnest. In 1728 he placed native New Mexican Santiago Roybal in Santa Fe as vicar. A royal cedula issued in Madrid on 7 December 1729 seemed to resolve the matter; it mandated that Durango be recognized as diocesan authority over New Mexico. This brought a stinging rejoinder from the Franciscan commissary general in Mexico City. Recalling the martyrs of 1680, he stated that twenty-three missionaries had already fallen in that province and no bishop had. He added that were it not for the Franciscans those regions would have already been lost. This opposition notwithstanding, Bishop Crespo named fray Salvador López vicar and ecclesiastical judge in El Paso on the basis of the 1729 cedula. The other Franciscans refused to recognize him as such, and he had to leave the province. Bishop Crespo then informed the *custos*, fray Andrés Varo, that he intended to conduct a second visitation of the province, which he initiated in July 1730. The visit did not settle matters, however, and a viceregal decree in 1731 revoked Roybal's appointment. Another viceregal decree in 1733 upheld Durango's diocesan jurisdiction over New Mexico, and the struggle continued.

El Paso emerged as the focal point in the struggle between the bishop of Durango and the Franciscan order in New Mexico for spiritual control of the colony, as the diocesan see pushed the transition from missions to secular parishes, and the Franciscans insisted that the predominance of Indian populations created mitigating circumstances. As a matter of fact (rather than mere jurisdiction), the people of the riverine communities of the Paso del Norte area were frequently under the control of both secular officials who reported directly to Durango and regular, Franciscan Church officials who responded to the provincial in Mexico City. Even though the bishop of Durango had placed a diocesan priest in New Mexico's capital during this period, the situation in El Paso made it a logical site for diocesan priests from Durango to establish a firm foothold in formerly Franciscan territory, and the experiment there was more complex. In 1731, with the approval of the viceroy of New Spain, the Marqués de Casafuerte (1722–34), Bishop Crespo established a curacy in the El Paso area and named Santiago Roybal to serve it.[20] For more than a decade, Father Roybal served either as curate in Las Caldas (1731–36) or as vicar and ecclesiastical judge in Santa Fe.[21]

The first written evidence of fray Juan José Toledo in New Mexico was an entry in the mission books at Acoma Pueblo recorded on 14 July 1743, the eleventh anniversary of his profession in the Franciscan order.[22] Toledo served at Acoma until 14 March 1745. While there, he briefly ministered to nearby Laguna Pueblo until handing that post off to fray Caetano Otero on 13 August 1743, and occasionally at more distant Zuni, a pueblo that evidently was of abiding interest for fray Juan José.[23]

Father Toledo had arrived in New Mexico at a time when Franciscan hegemony was also being challenged by the Jesuit order. From their missions in Sonora, Jesuits had begun to press their claims to Hopi country as an expanded mission field. This met strong resistance on the part of both Franciscans in New Mexico and the leaders of the order in Mexico City who expressed renewed interest in the lands and peoples to the west of the Rio Grande Pueblos. It was in the context of this jurisdictional fight that the Franciscan commissary general, fray Pedro Navarrete, ordered a mission to the Navajos in March 1744.[24]

To establish this mission, an expedition under the leadership of Father Carlos Delgado departed Isleta on 21 April 1745.[25] After spending six days among the Navajos at a settlement called Los Coyotes, Fathers Delgado, José Irigoyen, and Pedro Ignacio Pino and company returned to Isleta. In June Fathers Miguel Menchero, Delgado, Irigoyen, and Pino traveled to Navajo country with Lieutenant General Bernardo Antonio de Bustamente y Tagle and an escort of twelve soldiers. They moved among various Navajo settlements, distributing gifts and calling on the Indians to become Christians. While this activity was taking place, Toledo was at the Zuni pueblo of Halona. At Zuni, Father Toledo often performed multiple baptisms of twenty or more Indians at a time.[26] From Zuni he petitioned in 1745 for permission to travel to the Hopi pueblos with Fathers Delgado and Irigoyen later that year.[27]

The venerable Father Delgado aspired to evangelize the Hopis and fulfill the wishes of higher authorities in the Franciscan order. Governor Joaquín Codallas y Rabal granted Father Delgado permission to lead an expedition to Hopi on 14 September 1745.[28] Two days later, Fathers Delgado, Irigoyen, and Toledo departed with an escort consisting of eighty Pueblo Indians. After a journey of two weeks duration, they arrived in Hopi country on 29 September. While in the area, the Franciscans and their escorts reportedly visited six Hopi pueblos.[29] According to a census the priests conducted, there were 10,846 individuals living in the various pueblos.[30] Fray Carlos informed his superiors in Mexico City that his mission had been well received and that he had told the Hopis that they should send word when they were ready for the Franciscans to return to baptize them. Since he was the junior cleric, almost nothing was recorded about Toledo's activities among the Hopis. Whether he participated in delivering sermons to the Hopis or whether the vastly more experienced Fathers Delgado and Irigoyen handled this is unknown. Doubtless Toledo assisted in the census taking. For a young priest only recently arrived in the New Mexico mission field, the trip to Hopi country and the promise of such a rich bounty of souls for the faith must have been very heady stuff. Surely fray Juan José felt some sense of disillusionment when what appeared to be an early success came to naught when Abiquiu exploded with witchcraft.

After returning from Hopi country, Toledo served at Isleta Pueblo from November 1745 to April 1746.[31] He made another brief trip to Zuni in June 1746. From July 1746 to May 1749, fray Juan José served at Jemez. At Jemez he occasionally gave his surname to individuals he baptized, a practice not uncommon among Franciscans in colonial New Mexico.[32] The sacramental records from Jemez contain a curious entry related to Father Toledo. Clearly written under four of his signatures in a different hand is the word *catatumba*.[33] In contemporary Spanish, this word is considered to be of Mexican origin with the usual meaning being "somersault."[34] In the context of a book of marriage records, this meaning makes no sense. Another possible understanding of the word, however, makes a good deal of sense. The verb *catatar*, which means to bewitch, comes from the Qechua verb *katiti*, to drag. Perhaps some priest who served at Jemez and was familiar with the word catatar scribbled this word in later, confusing the meaning of the noun with the verb, as an indication of what subsequently befell Toledo at Abiquiu.[35]

In the fall of 1748, Governor Codallos y Rabal ordered the alcalde of Laguna, Pedro Romero, to Navajo country to help select mission sites in the Cebolleta Mountains.[36] Fathers Menchero, Juan José de Padilla, and Toledo, accompanied by Fernando de Horcasitas, the captain general of the Navajo people, traveled under escort provided by Juan Felipe de Rivera, lieutenant of the Santa Fe presidio; ten regular soldiers; ten militiamen; and twenty-five Pueblo warriors. They departed Laguna in early November 1748 and journeyed to Cebolleta Canyon. There, the Franciscans baptized a hundred Navajo children and scouted out four possible mission sites. Since Father Menchero was a practical realist, after his experience with the Navajos he recommended abandoning the idea of penetrating deep into Navajo county, opting instead for the establishment of Navajo missions in the Cebolleta area. New Mexico governor Tomás Vélez Cachupín approved this change in May 1749, and viceregal authorities in Mexico City agreed in October but approved the establishment of only two missions.[37] As it happened, Toledo had no further involvement in the ultimately unsuccessful Navajo missions.

Soon after Governor Vélez Cachupín had replaced outgoing governor Codallos y Rabal in April 1749, a mysterious stranger arrived in Santa Fe.[38] Little is known of José Ornedal y Maza. According to the Franciscans, especially fray Andrés Varo, Ornedal y Maza was a member of Viceroy Revillagigedo's family.[39] Both surnames are rare, especially the first one, but Maza is toponymic in the province of Santander (and elsewhere in Spain) in the Laredo area. At the time Ornedal y Maza was named inspector of the presidio of Nueva Vizcaya and New Mexico, he was a *subteniente*, or second-lieutenant, in the Regimiento de Infantería de España.[40] This regiment was dispatched to Spain's overseas empire in 1741. It is also possible that the two men crossed paths earlier in their careers when the future viceroy was Inspector de la Infantería Española y Extranjera de los Reinos de Aragón, Navarra, y Guipúzocoa. Ornedal's assignment included the presidios of El Gallo, Cerrogordo, Valle de San Bartolomé, and Conchos in Nueva Vizcaya and El Paso and Santa Fe in New Mexico. He was also to conduct the *residencia* of Governor Codallos y Rabal. That such a low-ranking officer garnered such a commission is further testament to his influence in the viceregal palace.

In May 1749 fray Juan José made yet another trip to Zuni and Hopi country. On this trip, Father Toledo once again accompanied Father Delgado. Another Franciscan companion was fray Juan Sanz de Lezaun, who recorded the details of their expedition. The aged Father Delgado fell ill, which meant that Fathers Toledo and Sanz de Lezaun played more active roles than they might have. At a gathering of Hopis, fray Juan José had a violent encounter with the leader of Gualpi. After listening to the Franciscan exhort the Hopis to become Christians and seeing the priests offer his people presents, the Hopi leader attacked Father Toledo, shoving him to the ground and threatening the Indians that they should not accept anything from the priests. The Franciscans managed to avoid an escalation of this tense situation and withdrew with promises to return.[41]

By June the peripatetic friar was back in the New Mexico heartland, and in July Ornedal was on his way out of New Mexico. Father Toledo had managed to miss most of the curious inspector's stay in the north. Ornedal was in El Paso during the period 13–16 July 1749, but Lieutenant Governor Alonso Victores Rubín de Celis conducted the actual inspection in his stead.[42] Ordenal's report hardly seemed like an examination of the workings of the Presidio of El Paso. It consisted in the main of information collected from the local clergymen. This method of operation suggests that Ornedal's true agenda was to find out what he could about the activities of the Church in New Mexico and he was not really interested in the presidios. Ornedal's report on the state of upriver New Mexico was dated 26 July 1749 at the El Paso Presidio.

Juan José Toledo was assigned to Pecos from August 1750 to March 1753. Much of that time he ministered to Galisteo as well.[43] As an apparent result of Father Toledo's contact with Hopis and Navajos, he was said to have some knowledge of their languages.[44] The policy of frequently moving priests from pueblo to pueblo usually meant that few learned more than a smattering of any Indian language, and there is no evidence that fray Juan José's apparent skill with Hopi and Navajo was ever put to any further use.[45] Some evidence of Toledo's continued intellectual curiosity with regard to language is evidenced by the fact that while he served at Pecos he attempted to transliterate Pecos names.[46] Fray Juan José's concern with indigenous languages may also reflect De la Peña Montenegro's influence.

In libro 1, tratado 10, sección 6 of the *Itinerario*, the bishop stressed the care that must be taken when attempting to translate the concepts of the Mysteries of the Faith to the Indians and the serious risks presented by preaching and teaching with an imperfect knowledge of their language.[47]

At Pecos Father Toledo also got a taste of international relations. Although nothing much is made of his participation, fray Juan José was at Pecos in November 1750 when a party of four Frenchmen appeared. Among the intruders was Pierre Mallet, who had been apprehended in New Mexico back in 1739 and allowed to leave.[48] Father Toledo played a much more important role when two more Frenchmen arrived at Pecos on 6 August 1752.[49] According to fray Juan José, the two men were dressed in rags, and one was holding a stick to which was affixed a piece of white linen with a cross on it, a crude French flag. The Franciscan knew no French, but he clearly had a good ear for languages. He rendered Jean Chapuis as Xanxapy and Louis Feuilli as Luis Fuixy, actually fairly close Spanish approximations of the French pronunciation. Father Toledo ordered their nine pack horses, which were laden with trade goods, unloaded and the goods stored in the *convento*. He then dutifully notified Governor Vélez Cachupín of what had transpired in Pecos.

While Father Toledo was dealing with the French intruders, fray Andrés Varo was crafting a point-by-point response to Inspector Ornedal's scathing critique. Varo's response covered ninety points and ran to some fifty folios.[50] In refuting Ornedal's numerous charges, Father Toledo merited several mentions by Varo in relation to his missionary efforts among the Western Pueblos.[51] Toledo might well have been cited as an example of a Franciscan with a facility for indigenous languages, since much of the criticism leveled at the Franciscan missionary program revolved around the language issue. Ornedal had made much of the Franciscan's inability to speak indigenous languages, and Varo countered that this was unnecessary and unwise. Most Indians could communicate in Spanish, and attempting to teach Christian doctrine in a poorly understood language was an invitation to commit heresy. Varo not only denied the Ordenal charges, he also accused Ordenal of being "a mouthpiece for Vélez Cachupín whose 'well known hatred of the priests' was acknowledged in New Mexico."[52]

Several New Mexican friars, not including Father Toledo, wrote rebuttals that bolstered the claims of Varo's report, charging that the presidial soldiers were ill equipped and harshly treated by the governor. These reports also contained the familiar charges that the Pueblos were required to work without pay and that their woven goods and agricultural products were taken by the civil authorities without compensation. The Franciscans also collected affidavits from prominent Spaniards, including former alcaldes and presidio officers, support- ing the missionaries. Both the charges and countercharges were undoubtedly exaggerated for each side was trying to protect and expand its jurisdiction, and the Franciscans were losing ground since the focus of the charges was the Pueblo Indians. The governor and the alcaldes charged that the Franciscans were fail- ing in their task of Christianizing the Indians, and the Franciscans said the gov- ernor and his alcaldes were mistreating the Indians and profiting from their labor. There was some truth in both of these allegations, but no one seemed to care about improving the conditions under which the Indians were living, until Governor Vélez Cachupín arrived in New Mexico.[53]

The specific charges against the civil officials that the Franciscans made did not really apply to Vélez Cachupín but to his predecessors. The 1751 Varo report included charges against an earlier governor, presumably Codallos y Rabal, such as the forced labor without pay of eight to ten Indians a week on his ranch. When Vélez Cachupín was named and attacked, it was always per- sonal, such as Father Varo's statement that the governor was "childish, with- out maturity, knowledge, or experience."[54] Varo also leveled an ad hominem attack at Vélez Cachupín by questioning his honor and going so far as to sug- gest that he was less than a real man. He further charged Vélez Cachupín with usurping the *Patronato Real*, acting as vice-patron of the New Mexico Church by moving Franciscan clergy form mission to mission as he saw fit. This author- ity to assign priests was jealously guarded by the Franciscan leadership in New Mexico and became a major point of contention with eighteenth-century gov- ernors from Vélez Cachupín on.[55]

Governor Vélez Cachupín viewed the controversy among the Franciscans over the Ordenal report as a major distraction from the Comanche, Ute, and Apache threat to New Mexico. Priests and civil officials played important roles in the welfare of the frontier province of New Mexico, and neither group could prosper if there was continual warfare with the nomadic tribes. What upset Father Varo and the Franciscans who were trying to get their side of the story to the viceroy, was Governor Vélez Cachupín's decree forbidding alcaldes, pre- sidial soldiers, or other government officials from testifying either for or against the Ordenal report or certifying any Franciscan report. To enforce his order, Vélez Cachupín decreed that no Franciscan mail, except correspondence per- taining to the Inquisition, could leave New Mexico without his approval. Any violation was punishable by a two-hundred-peso fine. Because of this action, the volume of Franciscan mail leaving the province diminished dramatically. The only way a non-Inquisition-related Franciscan document could leave New Mexico was with Vélez Cachupín's approval.[56]

Feeling stymied, the Franciscans attempted to bring to bear their strongest weapon against the young governor, the Holy Office of the Inquisition. Custos Andrés Varo asked fray Pedro Montaño, the local commissary of the Inquisition, to investigate the governor. Such an investigation could have intimidated Vélez Cachupín or even led to his removal from office. Yet, Montaño, apparently a supporter of the governor, refused to open the investigation. Then the vice custos, Manuel de San Juan Nepomuceno y Trigo, demanded that Father Montaño expel Vélez Cachupín from New Mexico. This attempt also failed because Montaño instead ordered Nepomuceno y Trigo into seclusion.[57]

There is no evidence that fray Juan José was actively involved in the raging Church-State controversy that swirled about him. Toledo labored at Nambe Pueblo from October 1753 to October 1755, and in 1754 also took up the post at Abiquiu, succeeding the late Father Félix (Isidro) Ordóñez y Machado.[58] Father Ordóñez's death in 1756 in Laguna Pueblo was reputed to have been caused by witchcraft.[59] During Phase Two of the witchcraft proceedings it was established that Vicente Trujillo, who had been governor of the Genízaro pueblo while Ordóñez was its priest, was responsible for his death. Soon after he was assigned to Abiquiu, Toledo himself was the subject of numerous attacks causing illness, also perpetrated by Trujillo and his wife María. Father Toledo must have been relatively healthy and vigorous during the ten-year period of the Abiquiu witch craze (he was forty-one when it began in 1756, fifty-one when it terminated in 1766), for he survived the attacks and had enough energy to engage in multiple marathon exorcisms in the winter of 1763–64.

When the bishop of Durango, Pedro Tamarón y Romeral, was conducting his official visitation of New Mexico in 1760, Father Toledo came to meet him on 14 June at the villa of Santa Cruz de la Cañada and presented the books of sacramental records for inspection. Bishop Tamarón noted that among the Abiquiu books he "found a guide to confession and catechism in the Tewa and Spanish languages."[60] The record of the bishop's visitation indicates that the book in question was quite long, but that he was told it was not used.[61] Interestingly, given the fact that diligent research has failed to turn up this work, the notation indicated that copies of it were to be made.

The bishop was disappointed to learn during his travels in New Mexico that few priests had mastered a Pueblo language, and the discovery of this guide

Figure 6
Abiquiu vista with Cerro del Pedernal in the background. *Photograph by Malcolm Ebright.*

led him to take to task Toledo and other Franciscans who were present in Santa Cruz.[62] Given fray Juan José's interest in languages, one wonders whether he tried to use the Tewa guide and found it lacking or whether the residents of Abiquiu were predominately Spanish speakers. There is evidence that at least the latter condition was true. During the ecclesiastical visitation of fray Jacobo de Castro in 1755, the Franciscan noted that the inhabitants of Abiquiu had above-average Spanish-language ability.[63] He further observed that of the individual New Mexico pueblos two had either above-average or average Spanish-language ability, nine had average ability, and only five had below-average skills. In 1760 Bishop Tamarón y Romeral did not actually visit Abiquiu and thus made no observation about the language ability of the people living there.

Adams and Chávez place Father Toledo at the Guadalupe mission in La Junta de los Ríos in 1760,[64] but close examination of the sacramental records at Abiquiu clearly establishes that this was impossible; fray Juan José was present in Abiquiu during every month of that year.[65] Apparently Father Toledo's superiors in Mexico City did select him to serve at La Junta de los Ríos some time in the 1760s. His name appears in a *nómina*, or list of projected appointments, prepared by provincial authorities in Mexico City, which was undated but probably for 1760 or 1765.[66] Such listings were frequently at variance with the actual assignments individual Franciscans held. For a variety of reasons they remained in a previous post or failed to take up a new one. Perhaps Father Toledo had been tapped for a new assignment before word of the impending transfer of the presidio from La Junta upriver to Julimes was received. That move took place in 1766 and might have resulted in the cancellation of his new posting. For whatever reason, fray Juan José remained in Abiquiu until at least September 1770.[67]

The historical record has little to say about Father Toledo after his presence at center stage in Abiquiu, battling the Devil in the winter of 1763–64, but he seems to have mellowed in the decade before his death. First, Father Toledo's own ailments were cured, not by prayer alone, although he would have believed this must have helped, but by the assistance of a folk healer, or *curandera*. Such healers were among the individual defendants who got caught in the web of witchcraft accusations in Abiquiu. The contradiction must have softened the priest's ardor to eradicate all semblance of Indian culture and identity at Abiquiu.[68]

At some point during 1771, Father Toledo found himself in serious difficulty with the Holy Office of the Inquisition for having remarked "that fornication was not a sin because God had created man and woman to multiply humankind." When this accusation, lodged by an individual named José Marco, was examined in Mexico City, fray Juan José was still referred to as the priest of Abiquiu. According to what he informed the vicar and ecclesiastical judge in Santa Fe, Father Santiago Roybal, José Marco was in Abiquiu in November 1769, when he chanced to have a fateful conversation with the militia alferez, Ignacio Gallego. Gallego told José Marco that he heard the shocking statement about permissible fornication directly from fray Juan José Toledo's lips. Father Toledo's accuser was so scandalized by the priest's words that he decided to keep them secret and only decided to tell Father Roybal about the situation to unburden his conscience.[69]

Father Santiago Roybal forwarded José Marco's accusation in a file containing a marriage investigation to the Secret Chamber of the Inquisition in Mexico City. The Tribunal of the Inquisition in the viceregal capital instructed Father Roybal to investigate the matter in September 1771. The vicar and ecclesiastical judge was asked to investigate: whether Father Toledo was in the habit of abusing strong drink, whether he was inebriated when he allegedly made the statement in question, and whether anyone else was a witness. Roybal was also instructed to locate Alferez Gallegos and take his statement, but time and distance apparently conspired to delay Father Roybal's response. In 1772 Father Toledo was assigned to the villa of Santa Cruz de la

Cañada. A gap in the documentation makes it impossible to pinpoint his death, but it had taken place before 1774.[70] A follow-up to Father Roybal's communications came from the Inquisition in September 1774 and indicated that no word on the matter had reached Mexico City; finally, a note in the file dated 6 February 1776 indicated that since Father Toledo had died, the case was closed.[71]

In contrast to the numerous priests killed by Indians resisting forced Christianization, Father Toledo survived. He fought to protect his flock from what he thought were attacks by the Devil, and the people in his pastoral care seem to have accepted him during and after the witchcraft proceedings. Toledo seems saintly when compared to some priests, such as the greedy fray Teodoro Alcina, who tried to acquire land from the Genízaros fifty years later and then verbally damned them, bringing hailstorms and plagues of locusts upon the Genízaros. Father Toledo's ability to withstand the rigors of life at Abiquiu and to overcome the onslaughts of the *hechiceros* who were trying to kill him was due in large part to the support of the governor who had installed him at Abiquiu, Tomás Vélez Cachupín.

Figure 7
Governor Vélez Cachupín at the Battle of San Diego Pond. *Drawing by Glen Strock.*

CHAPTER FOUR

The Governor

Tomás Vélez Cachupín

I n late August 1752, Alcalde Juan José Lobato reported to Governor
Tomás Vélez Cachupín that the Comanche chiefs wanted to make peace
with the Spaniards after their stunning defeat by Spanish troops under
the young Vélez Cachupín, whom the Comanches praised as "the captain
who amazes":

> Because they had the memory of many years of hos-
> tility toward this province [of New Mexico] in
> which they had committed robberies, murders, and
> attacks, they said: How much have our triumphs
> amounted to when we have suffered the punishment
> which this "boy captain" had heaped upon us?
> Whatever undertaking they might attempt, it would

have to come out badly because of the timidity with
which [the Comanches] would enter upon it as well
as because of the courage of the "captain who
amazes." This title . . . is what all the Comanches give
to [Vélez Cachupín].[1]

Vélez Cachupín was one of the most effective of New Mexico's eighteenth-century governors in his understanding and dealing with Genízaros,
Pueblos, and the nomadic tribes, such as Comanches, Utes, and Apaches.
This knowledge stood the governor in good stead when he was called upon
to help resolve the Abiquiu witchcraft dispute. He enjoyed a reputation among
all the tribes surrounding New Mexico as a courageous warrior who treated
the Indians fairly and kept his word in peace negotiations. He dealt with the
Plains Indians by meeting them at their camps and treating them as equals.
Vélez Cachupín achieved peace with the Apaches, Comanches, and Utes as
well as a virtual cessation of their raids on Spanish and Indian settlements,
which threatened the very existence of the colony. He established new communities composed primarily of Genízaros and made land grants that
resulted in some of the most enduring communities in New Mexico, such
as Las Trampas, Truchas, and Abiquiu.[2] He was a man of intellect whose legal
decisions reveal a remarkable grasp of Spanish New Mexican law and custom. Vélez Cachupín's decisions exhibited a sense of compassion and fair-
ness in upholding the rights of Genízaros and other minorities. His decrees
and official reports on a wide range of matters demonstrated practicality
and resourcefulness. When it came to dealing with the witchcraft accusations and litigation that rocked the Abiquiu Genízaro pueblo for more than
six years, Vélez Cachupín's understanding of Genízaros made him uniquely
suited to the task as did his ability to deal effectively with the Franciscans.
He appreciated the Genízaro's worldview and also embraced the Catholic
worldview he grew up with in Spain.[3]

Vélez Cachupín was one of the few New Mexico governors to serve two
full terms (1749–54 and 1762–67), and he was one of the most competent men
to have occupied that office. Governors Diego de Vargas and Juan Bautista
de Anza have received much more attention than he has, but Vélez Cachupín
deserves to rank in their company.[4] The prevailing view of his career in New
Mexico, however, is rather dismissive. Historians such as Hubert Howe
Bancroft minimized Vélez Cachupín's contribution to eighteenth-century New

Mexico by dealing with him and his two terms as governor in a few short paragraphs.[5] Other historians, echoing his Franciscan contemporaries, called him "young and brash and full of ambition and not a little impetuous,"[6] and pugnacious.[7] Even recent works about eighteenth-century New Mexico understate or ignore Vélez Cachupín's importance.[8] By contrast, Alfred Barnaby Thomas recognized Vélez Cachupín as the most effective of New Mexico's eighteenth-century governors before Anza.[9] A reexamination of Governor Vélez Cachupín, the records of his Indian campaigns, his legal and land grant decisions, and especially his response to the Abiquiu witchcraft proceedings, demonstrates that Vélez Cachupín's two terms as governor of New Mexico marked a turning point in Spanish interactions with the Comanches, Utes, Navajos, and Genízaros. It was also a watershed in Church-State relations.

Tomás Vélez Cachupín was a *montanés*, the name given to natives of the province of Santander in northwestern Spain. He was born in the seaport of Laredo to don Francisco Vélez Cachupín and doña María de la Quintana. His parents were locally well connected, partly because of their interest in the Casas Cachupinas, houses in Laredo and surrounding communities where members of the Vélez Cachupín extended family lived. The institution of the Casas Cachupinas was also a *mayorazgo,* or entailed estate, that was theoretically inherited by the eldest son in a family line in each generation under the law of primogeniture.[10] The purpose of a mayorazgo was to preserve the fame, renown, and wealth of a family by tying together its assets into an unalienable whole that was passed from first-born son to first-born son. The institution of the Casas Cachupinas has been in existence since the seventeenth century and still exists in Laredo, where one of the Casas Cachupinas is now occupied by descendants of the Vélez Cachupín family.[11] It appears that Tomás was the second of Francisco Vélez Cachupín's two sons, an accident of birth that strongly influenced Tomás for the rest of his life. The doctrine of primogeniture placed second-born sons such as Tomás in a decidedly inferior economic position, requiring them to fend for themselves without an inheritance. Yet, when he returned to Spain after serving two terms as governor of New Mexico, Vélez Cachupín reversed the rules of primogeniture in regard to the estate he had acquired in New Spain, providing that the income from his property in the Casas Cachupinas mayorazgo would go to the second son of his heirs rather than the first.[12] As did many other second sons of well-to-do families, Tomás made his career in the New World, but unlike most of them, it was not wealth or noble status that Vélez Cachupín sought; rather, he pursued distinction through great and enduring deeds that would add luster to an already famous family name.[13]

The Cachupines of Laredo were so well known that they are immortalized in Miguel de Cervantes's *Don Quixote*. In chapter 13 of the first book, don Quixote is asked by Vivaldo, a gentleman he meets on the road, to describe Dulcinea, the lady he serves. When Quixote says she is a princess, Vivaldo asks, with some skepticism, about Dulcinea's family and lineage. Quixote lists several of the leading families of Spain and then says that Dulcinea is of a modern lineage: "El Toboso of La Mancha." Vivaldo replies, "Although I am descended from the Cachopines of Laredo... I shall not dare to compare my family with the El Toboso of La Mancha; though, to tell you the truth, such a surname had never reached my ears till now." There appears to be no irony intended in Cervantes's reference to Cachopín as a famous family, and the Cachopín family mentioned in *Don Quixote* seems to be the same as the Vélez Cachupín family.[14]

Tomás began life in the New World as a cadet in the permanent regiment of Havana in the 1740s. His service in Cuba coincided with that of Juan Francisco de Güemes y Horcasitas, the first Conde de Rivellagigedo, the future viceroy of New Spain. Güemes y Horcasitas was related to Vélez Cachupín either directly or through his wife and may have known him before coming to the Americas. The future viceroy was born in Reinosa, in the Spanish province of Santander, some forty-five miles as the crow flies from Vélez Cachupín's hometown of Laredo. Whether he knew Vélez Cachupín personally before coming to the New World, he probably knew he had a relative under his command in Cuba, where Güemes y Horcasitas held the post of captain general from 1734 to 1746, a period during which Vélez Cachupín was also in Havana. Upon his appointment as viceroy, the Conde de Rivellagigedo probably took Vélez Cachupín with him to Mexico City to serve in his household. Vélez Cachupín was appointed the viceroy's equerry, an official in charge of the horses in the viceregal stable, but Vélez Cachupín undoubtedly had additional responsibilities. It is likely that in the viceroy's household Vélez Cachupín began to learn the intricacies of colonial administration. By the time he received an interim appointment as governor of New Mexico in 1749, Vélez Cachupín had absorbed a great deal of information about Spanish colonial law and practice. At the court in Mexico City, he was able to closely observe colonial administration. He may also have had the opportunity to study books of Spanish law applicable to the New World in the viceroy's library, including the *Recopilación de leyes de las Indias*, which he sometimes cited almost verbatim in his decrees as governor of New Mexico. What Vélez Cachupín lacked was experience, and the job of governing what the Franciscans called "this miserable kingdom" of New Mexico would soon provide an abundance of that.[15]

Vélez Cachupín took possession of the governorship of New Mexico ad interim on 6 April 1749.[16] His arrival landed him squarely in the middle of a renewed battle between the Franciscans and civil-military officials that had been waged periodically since before the Pueblo Revolt. During such controversies, Franciscans typically took every opportunity to embarrass the governors in their reports to the viceroy; the governors responded in kind. As it happened, young Vélez Cachupín got caught in the crossfire over events that occurred during the administration of his predecessor, Joaquín Codallos y Rabal. The battle between Codallos y Rabal and some Franciscans was bitterly personal and mutually unprofessional. The priests condemned the governor as a Franciscan-hater; he damned them for meddling in his personal affairs. When the new governor took over, the Franciscans soon tarred Vélez Cachupín with the same brush.

In many respects, from the Franciscan point of view, this administration was a continuation of an irksome trend that had begun on Governor Juan Domingo de Bustamante's (1722–31) watch. Governor Bustamante enraged the Franciscans by reporting unfavorably to the bishop of Durango, Benito Crespo y Monroy, on conditions in New Mexico. Former governor Antonio de Valverde Cosío (1717–22), who was Bustamante's uncle and whom he had served as lieutenant governor in El Paso, further provoked Franciscan ire by requesting in 1725, coincident with the Bishop Crespo's ecclesiastical visitation of the El Paso area, the erection of a curacy to minister to Suma Indians at his Hacienda de San Antonio. Following Crespo's second visit to New Mexico in 1730, the curacy of Santa María de las Caldas was established near El Paso. Diocesan priests from Durango staffed it during most of its life. The establishment of Las Caldas gave the See of Durango a toehold in what had been an exclusively Franciscan ministry in New Mexico. To this was added the irritating presence of diocesans in the role of vicar and ecclesiastical judge in Santa Fe and the El Paso area. Finally, Durango began to exercise control of the collection of tithes.

Continuity from Governor Bustamante's administration through Codallos y Rabal to Vélez Cachupín came in the person of Bernardo Antonio de Bustamante y Tagle. Bernardo Antonio was a relative of Governor Bustamante and served all three governors as their lieutenant. During the Bustamante administration, he had emerged as an enemy of the Franciscans. Another element that linked Valverde y Cosío, the Bustamantes, and Vélez Cachupín was their common origin: all were montañeses who hailed from the province of Santander, Spain, as was the sitting viceroy, the Conde de Revillagigedo. As if that were not enough, a new nemesis was also a son of Santander, Bishop Dr. Pedro Anselmo de Tagle (1747–58), a native of Santillana.[17]

The peculiar attraction to the *patria chica*, that is, the love of a particular geography, manner of speaking, and folkways of the place where one was born and grew up was a defining characteristic of many Spaniards in the New World. From this shared love of place came an almost instinctive solidarity among people from the same environment. That this was important to Vélez Cachupín is readily apparent from correspondence written soon after his arrival in Santa Fe.

In June 1749 Vélez Cachupín penned a personal letter to Juan Manuel Díaz de Tagle, the government secretary in Durango.[18] The governor was responding to a letter from Díaz de Tagle, to whom Vélez Cachupín professed to be his "most loyal, affectionate servant and true friend... with the sincerity of a good montañés." The letter from his friend and paisano had been delivered by another paisano, fray Francisco de la Concepción.[19] The bearer of Vélez Cachupín's response was his lieutenant governor, Bernardo Antonio de Bustamante y Tagle, who was traveling to Mexico City on crown business. In recommending Bustamante y Tagle to his friend and fellow montañés Díaz de Tagle, Vélez Cachupín stated that Bustamante y Tagle was an individual whose comportment was in accord with the circumstances of his birth; the "esteem for him and his merits were warranted because of his proven qualities and that he had complete confidence in him." Vélez Cachupín entrusted to Díaz de Tagle his power of attorney to act in the matter of the farming the New Mexico tithes for 1748 and 1749 and to secure them for the next four years as well, at the rate of 1,650 pesos a year.

Soon after his arrival in Santa Fe, the new governor had successfully nego-
tiated with Juan José Moreno to take over his interest in the collection of
tithes for the next two years. Vélez Cachupín's financial agent in Mexico City,
José González Calderón, would handle the payments, except for the three
hundred pesos owed to the vicar in Santa Fe.[20] The governor would take care
of that payment personally. From the Franciscans' perspective, Vélez
Cachupín could hardly have gotten off to a worse beginning. He befriended
a hated Bustamante and kept him in royal service, he arranged to farm the
tithes, and he paid the bishop's man in Santa Fe out of his own pocket, all
in just over two months. Another relative of Lieutenant Governor Bustamante
y Tagle was the captain of the El Paso Presidio and alcalde mayor of El Paso,
Francisco Antonio Tagle Bustamante.[21] When he died in 1753, Governor Vélez
Cachupín took a hand in the settlement of Tagle Bustamante's estate. The
proceedings were administered by one of Tagle Bustamante's relatives,
Francisco Joaquín Sánchez de Tagle, who was living in the El Paso area.

The new governor soon gained an undeserved reputation for exaggeration as well. Early in his first term Vélez Cachupín sent a report to the viceroy
in which he noted that 150 Pecos Indians were killed between 1743 and 1749
during Governor Codallos y Rabal's administration. This number was almost
certainly an exaggeration that Vélez Cachupín picked up from secondhand
sources, since he was not living in New Mexico during this period. The true
figure of Pecos Indians killed during the six-year period was likely less than
one-third of the number reported killed, but a report by fray Juan Sanz de
Lezaun and fray Manuel Vermejo soon compounded the governor's error.
The two priests took the governor's figure and manufactured a story of a
Comanche ambush at Pecos with 150 Indians killed *in one encounter*. Later
writers repeated this mistake, some even citing it as the cause of the even-
tual abandonment of Pecos Pueblo, and thus, Governor Vélez Cachupín's
error was magnified. Franciscans and historians relying on this material as
a source unfairly accused Vélez Cachupín of exaggeration.[22]

Historians, such as Thomas, uncritically accepted the Franciscan complaints against Vélez Cachupín. Thomas took note of charges against Vélez
Cachupín and other governors before him of "inventing expeditions that he
did not make." Thomas gave credence to the allegation that Vélez embellished his account of the Battle of San Diego Pond, although he admitted
that "the details of the battle are too numerous to be entirely discounted [and]
supporting evidence is found in the report of Juan José Lobato."[23]

Thomas missed a great deal of other supporting evidence favoring the accuracy of the governor's report and labeled his failure to provide specific directions and other geographical details typical of such accounts "as disconcerting." In fact Vélez Cachupín provided quite a bit of detail about the land he was traversing as he chased the Comanches in November 1751, particularly in view of the fact that he was undertaking a forced march with only two to three hours of sleep for his troops and rest for their horses. Governor Vélez Cachupín did not have time to keep a detailed journal of each day's march, but there is sufficient information in his report to generally locate the route he traveled. The most important indication of the veracity of the governor's report is that the reputation of the Comanche defeat at San Diego Pond, where more than a hundred Indians were killed, lived on in the memory of Comanches and Utes for decades.[24]

Vélez Cachupín became ever more deeply involved in the Church-State debate that had been going on throughout the seventeenth and the first half of the eighteenth centuries, a debate so vituperative that it weakened New Mexico both militarily and spiritually. Vélez Cachupín realized this and was able to take charge of the situation so he could make decisions affecting frontier defense and even spiritual matters regarding the effectiveness of the Franciscans in converting the Indians. Resultant Franciscan criticism of Vélez Cachupín was scarcely justified and has influenced how such historians as John Kessell, Warren Beck, and Ross Frank viewed Vélez Cachupín.[25] These scholars give scant recognition of his significant role in achieving peace with Comanches, Utes, and Navajos for the first time in New Mexico's history.[26]

The Franciscans vilified Vélez Cachupín over his treatment of Indians even though the governor demonstrated unusual sympathy and understanding of the plight of Pueblos and Genízaros. When he criticized the priests it was not over alleged excesses in the use of Indian labor but because of their failure to learn the Indian languages to properly teach Christian doctrine.[27] In particular, Vélez Cachupín was concerned that the sacraments could not be administered properly through an interpreter, stating in a 1754 report that "they [the Indians] do not receive Penance until they are at death's door, confessing through an interpreter, and this is not very adequate for such a venerable act."[28] Moreover, Franciscan charges of economic exploitation or physical abuse of Indians were unfounded; there is no evidence that Governor Vélez Cachupín engaged in these practices.

When it came to the governor's treatment of certain priests, however, critics such as fray Andrés Varo could hardly contain their righteous indignation. Still, it took two sides to have a good argument. The governor's unseemly threat to send fray Pedro Ignacio del Pino and fray Andrés García to Mexico City thrown across a mule and in shackles was the sort of hyperbole that might be expected from a brash military man whose authority had been challenged; it begged for a Franciscan rejoinder. Vélez Cachupín had apparently had the priests transferred to other missions for some unstated offense, although Father Varo insisted they were innocent.[29]

In 1764 the governor received a decree from the viceroy, the Marqués de Cruillas, regarding the conversion of the Indians in New Mexico. The viceroy referred to an earlier inspection by Felipe de Luna, attorney for the audiencia, during which it was determined that Franciscan missionaries who did not know the native languages were to be replaced by priests who spoke and understood these languages, or if there were none with that ability, then by priests who were zealous and capable and would apply themselves to the art of writing and understanding the native languages so that they could teach their successors.[30] This decree provided some authority for Vélez Cachupín to transfer priests.

Vélez Cachupín believed he already had sufficient authority to transfer Fathers García and Del Pino under his exercise of the Patronato Real. Certainly Vélez Cachupín was not expelling the two priests as the Franciscans alleged, and his action was generally in accord with a policy of the Franciscan authorities to rotate priests from one pueblo mission to another rather frequently, although they jealously guarded their rights regarding mission assigments.[31]

The other specific charge Father Pedro Serrano made against Governor Vélez Cachupín was that he interfered with communications between the Franciscans and their superiors in Mexico City. There is no doubt that this occurred, but the governor had strong justification for his actions. He was in the middle of a power struggle between the Franciscans and the civil government of New Mexico that affected his ability to implement an effective policy regarding the threat of Apache, Ute, and Comanche raids on the province. He had to act forcefully. In the end, Governor Vélez Cachupín was able to turn his complete attention to bringing a stop to the incessant Plains Indian raids on the embattled New Mexican settlements, both Spanish and Pueblo Indian communities.[32]

Governor Vélez Cachupín's relations with the Franciscans were contentious from the outset. In the military sphere he soon realized that the Comanches and other Plains Indians would test him "to see whether he was vigorous, strong for war, and capable of putting up with the inconveniences of it."[33] Vélez Cachupín passed the test during his first term, earning respect from the Comanches that lasted into his second term. Comanches, Utes, and other nomadic Indians had been mercilessly raiding Spanish settlements throughout the early eighteenth century, especially during the late 1740s. Vélez Cachupín began making peace overtures to the Comanches in the early 1750s, but in November 1751 he felt betrayed when three hundred Comanche warriors attacked Pecos and Galisteo a few months after accepting his offers of peace. The governor personally led a retaliatory expedition, telling the viceroy "my heart leapt with the ardent desire to give them [the Comanches] a taste of our arms."[34] The story of Vélez Cachupín's first major Indian campaign bears repeating in some detail, for it was highly successful, and the account of his victory was repeated over and over, even reaching the attention of the king of Spain. This battle more than any other single event increased the glory associated with the Vélez Cachupín name.

Vélez Cachupín caught up with the Comanche raiders after six days of riding nonstop, except for a few hours at night to pasture the horses and permit his soldiers a little sleep. On the evening of the sixth day the Spanish took the band of Comanches completely by surprise near a shallow pond covered with tall reeds. As the sun went down the Comanches retreated to the center of the pond, a difficult position to defend because of the freezing temperatures. Vélez Cachupín ordered fires built on the edge of the pond to observe the Indians' movements. When the Spaniards saw the Comanches hiding in water up to their waists, the governor ordered his men to set fire to the reeds in the pond and then to shoot at the Comanches revealed by the flames. On hearing the cries of some women and children, Vélez ordered the shooting stopped and notified the Indians through an interpreter that he would spare their lives if they surrendered. If not, "by the time the sun came up he would finish them off without pardoning anyone," according to a battle report. No one accepted the offer until about midnight, when a sixteen-year-old boy, wounded in the foot, came out holding a cross made of reeds, asking for mercy. Vélez Cachupín seated him by the fire, and when the others saw how he was treated, most of them came out of the water and surrendered. Only the chief and seven of his warriors remained in the thicket.

Vélez Cachupín kept watch all night as he reported, "astride my horse with my arms [weapons] in my hands."[35] At about three o'clock in the morning, the remaining Indians "in the light of the moon, uttered a war whoop" and attacked. The Spaniards fired on them, killing the chief and wounding most of the others, who soon surrendered.[36]

The governor and his troops scored an impressive victory that Comanches and other Indians would long remember. As a result of the Battle of San Diego Pond, as the event came to be called, the Comanches agreed to peace. Because of his courage in that battle and the mercy he showed the captives, the Comanches called Vélez Cachupín "the captain who amazes."[37] The Comanches agreed to a peace that lasted throughout the governor's first term, was broken in the interim between Vélez Cachupín's two terms, and resumed again during his second term.[38]

Although historian John Kessell believed that Vélez Cachupín was "in the habit of exaggerating his own merits and the faults of others," he agreed that Vélez Cachupín, "like Vargas before him and Anza after him, seemed to grasp intuitively the key to peace with the raiders: an active personal diplomacy backed by proven prowess in battle and a supply of gifts or trading opportunities."[39] Vélez Cachupín was effective in dealing with Indians because he met them face to face and treated them with respect.

At the Battle of San Diego Pond more than a hundred Comanches died and forty-four men, six women, and three children were taken prisoner. Most of the men were wounded, and sixteen of them died of their wounds the day after the battle. Eight Spaniards were wounded, one of whom died later. Vélez Cachupín told the surviving Comanche captives that he would release most of them, asking them to persuade their leaders to establish a permanent peace in return for which they would be permitted to trade at Taos. As a condition of this offer, the Comanches were to return the Spanish captives carried off in the 1747 raid on Abiquiu. If this was unacceptable to the Comanches, Vélez Cachupín told them "they would be persecuted until they were destroyed completely."[40] Vélez Cachupín took four Comanches to Santa Fe as "hostages . . . to oblige their people to fulfill their promise of delivering the captive women and boys [from the Abiquiu raid]," and released the rest.

The governor took two of the least seriously wounded hostages to convalesce in his home in Santa Fe. Whereas other governors were unwilling even to talk to Comanches, Vélez Cachupín lived with these two in the Palace of the Governors.[41] The Comanches would agree to Vélez Cachupín's peace terms, saying that they knew of two Spanish women and a boy held captive at the rancheria of another chief beyond the Arkansas River and would work to return them. They would also "inform the whole tribe of the great charity of the Spaniards, who after having conquered them, had kept their promise to them."[42] Governor Vélez Cachupín was said to have treated the two Comanche boys housed in the governor's palace so well that word spread among the Comanche bands that this governor could be trusted. Alcalde Juan José Lobato interviewed a Comanche Genízara who had been captured by Utes and sold to Antonio Martín about the Comanche hostages. She said their names were Antonio and Cristóbal, and they praised Vélez Cachupín for his good treatment of them, "giving them something to eat at all hours to their satisfaction; visiting with them and giving them hats each time to play with to amuse themselves," and providing them "with pelts, glass beads, ribbons, and other trinkets."[43]

The governor learned about the ways of the peaceful Comanches through these visits, just as he learned about the warlike Comanches in the campaign that ended in the Battle of San Diego Pond. In turn, the Comanches learned about Vélez Cachupín. Alcalde Lobato said that Vélez Cachupín's reputation was well established in that battle "and the Comanche chiefs agreed to make peace because their triumphs in raids against the Spanish were insignificant compared to the punishment which this 'boy captain' has heaped upon us."[44]

After the battle, the chiefs of the various Comanche bands met to consider Vélez Cachupín's peace offers. Chief Nimiricante, "the most peevish chief," was zealous to carry out the promise to bring in the three Spanish women and the two little Spanish boys."[45] They were kept in the rancheria of Nimiricante's brother, El Oso, who had quarreled with Nimiricante because the latter wanted to purchase one of the Spanish women in return for an Apache woman. Evidently the captive women were so highly prized that the chiefs of the respective bands kept them, making it doubtful that Nimiricante could persuade El Oso to surrender the female Spanish captive. It is not even clear that the Spanish captive wanted to be rescued, for "not all Spanish captives chose to return to Spanish settlement and society."[46] In most cases of return of captives a ransom was paid, but here it was the return of the two Comanche hostages that was the inducement for the return of the Spanish captives.

A Comanche peace was declared as a result of Vélez Cachupín's victory at San Diego Pond, but the fate of all the Spanish and Comanche captives is unknown. In 1754 one of the 1747 captives was returned, perhaps in return for one of Vélez Cachupín's Comanche captives.[47] In April 1752 Vélez Cachupín returned all the Comanche hostages save one before the Comanches sent any captives back. Governor Vélez Cachupín reported to the viceroy, the Conde de Revillagigedo, that not all Comanche hostages were returned because "one of the four is still with me having refused to return to his people, a fact that I reported to the Comanches so that they would understand that it was his free will to remain here."[48] Just as some Hispanic captives preferred their new lives among their Indian captors, some Native American captives preferred to live in Spanish households.

The story of Vélez Cachupín's November 1751 Comanche campaign at San Diego Pond reveals much about the governor's attitude toward Indians and provides ample evidence with which to assess some of the Franciscan charges against him. Ten years later, the Franciscan provincial in Mexico City, fray Pedro Serrano, filed a lengthy report to the viceroy, the Marqués de Cruillas. Serrano echoed Father Varo's charges made just before Vélez Cachupín began his second term in 1762.[49]

Father Serrano's complaints mostly involve the charge of interference by the governors in the Franciscans' exclusive jurisdiction in the Christianization of the Indians. Any criticism of priests was seen as meddling in the affairs of the Church. Yet, Father Serrano did not limit himself to spiritual matters and saw fit to complain about many matters in the secular realm, including such civil-military matters as military training and the strategy employed on Indian campaigns.[50] The Franciscan complaints Varo had expressed, which Father Serrano also aired, were mostly general observations that could have applied to almost any New Mexico governor in the seventeenth or eighteenth century and involved the charge that the governors were deficient in military training. Instead they "come from the ease of their own homes, or from trading at the counter of a shop or warehouse and attempt to order everything."[51] Since the governors "think more of their own advantage, fortunes, and property than of the fulfillment of the obligation of their offices...they do not seek capable men for military service, but for their own interests."[52] As a consequence, according to Father Serrano, Plains Indian attacks were decimating the province, which was headed for destruction at the hands of the barbarians. Not only did the governors fail to deal with the Comanche and other Indian attacks, according to Serrano, but also they interfered with the Franciscans in their mission, indulging the Pueblos "in their vices, dances, *estufas* [kivas], superstitions, witchcraft, and idolatries in the mountains," and blocking the priests when they tried "to compel the vicious and rebellious [Indians] to receive their instruction and catechism."[53] Serrano implied that because of the governors' actions, the Pueblos might form secret alliances with Plains tribes.

A charge leveled specifically at Vélez Cachupín was that of exaggerating or falsifying reports of military campaigns: "Although it is true that they fulfill their duty by going out on various campaigns, it is also true that they lie, for as soon as they go out they return again. This is the truth and not the lies that they report, the deeds that they pretend, and the enterprises that they exaggerate."[54] A dispassionate review of the events of the Battle of San Diego Pond does not support Father Serrano's criticism when applied to Vélez Cachupín. With a relatively small force Governor Vélez Cachupín scored a stunning victory at San Diego Pond that was passed on as oral history among the Comanche bands. With a group of only 164 men (compared to Governor Anza's force of 747 soldiers and Indian allies that defeated Cuerno Verde in the more famous 1779 Comanche battle), Vélez Cachupín demonstrated his courage and skill in battle, as well as his compassion in dealing with the Indians who surrendered. The evidence also suggests that the governor prepared for such an encounter even before he came to New Mexico.

Vélez Cachupín was on the staff of the viceroy when Revillagigedo sent a dispatch to Governor Codallos y Rabal in 1746 with recommendations for the pacification of the Comanches. The strategy Vélez Cachupín subsequently employed was similar to what the viceroy proposed.[55] When he first arrived in Santa Fe, Vélez began training the soldiers and citizen militia in military tactics and strategy.[56] Because of his military background, he realized that such formal training and frequent military drills were necessary. In the summer of 1752 Vélez Cachupín reported that he had organized 150 settlers "designated and equipped, and am instructing them in the use of arms and the necessary movements and evaluations of cavalry in which they are reasonably well informed. Formerly the settlers and soldiers were totally ignorant of such matters."[57]

Governor Vélez Cachupín considered Comanches to be treacherous and untrustworthy, so even when they were at peace "it is a prudent measure to deal with them with the left hand and keep the sword unsheathed in the right."[58] To respond quickly if attacked, the governor frequently sent out reconnaissance parties to observe the approaches to New Mexico's settlements while also "keeping two hundred men armed and equipped for a month who within a day can be on the march."[59] Such preparedness paid off, and Comanche attacks soon stopped until the term of Vélez Cachupín's successor, Francisco Antonio Marín del Valle.

Vélez Cachupín also made peace with the Utes by taking advantage of a clever Navajo stratagem.[60] In the early 1750s the Utes attacked a group of Navajos in Navajo country, surrounding them and driving them to the top of a mesa. Believing defeat inevitable, the Navajos put down their arms and approached the Utes with a wooden cross and what appeared to the Utes to be a letter but was in fact a calendar/almanac. The Navajos shrewdly announced to the Utes, "The great chief of the Spaniards sent you this letter and the cross and ordered you to be friends."[61] The Ute chiefs agreed to peace because they were aware that Vélez Cachupín had "punished the Comanches severely and afterward pardoned them benignly when they sought peace carrying another similar cross."[62] Word of the Battle of San Diego Pond had reached the Navajos and Utes, which made the Utes susceptible to the Navajo's ruse. The Utes did not want to displease the governor and feared that if they angered him, he would go to war against them.

When Governor Vélez Cachupín was notified of the incident, he went to meet with three Ute Chiefs at their rancheria sixteen leagues from Santa Fe. The governor told the Ute chiefs that the calendar/almanac was indeed his, as the Navajos had told them, and peace with the Utes was established on the strength of the governor's defeat of the Comanches at San Diego Pond in early November 1751. Vélez Cachupín stayed two days with the Ute bands, trading pelts with them after the peace agreement "from which all parties derived much pleasure and satisfaction."[63]

Viceroy Revillagigedo reported Governor Vélez Cachupín's first-term accomplishments in achieving peace with the Comanches and Utes to the king and recommended that the governor be continued for a second term. The viceroy repeated some of the details of the November 1751 Battle of San Diego Pond but embellished the account when it came to the number of Comanches killed. Instead of the one hundred dead Vélez Cachupín reported, the viceroy described a battle where more than three hundred Comanches lay slain after a powerful assault. This exaggeration was the viceroy's, not Vélez Cachupín's, but the gist of the report was still accurate.[64] The king, through his representative, the Marqués de Ensenada, ordered Vélez Cachupín to continue in office for a second term, but by the time the decree was received in Mexico City, Vélez Cachupín had set sail for Spain, and governor-elect Marín del Valle was on his way to New Mexico.[65]

Before departing Vélez Cachupín prepared an extensive set of well-thought-out recommendations for dealing with the Plains Indians that his successors proceeded to ignore. As a result, the network of alliances that Vélez Cachupín had so carefully crafted soon began to unravel. The outgoing governor told his immediate successor that he should "be very humane in your contacts with [the Utes]. You should show them the greatest kindness... treating them with generosity and simpleness of spirit, with some show of pleasure... without revealing fastidiousness or repugnance at their rude clownishness and manners."[66] The governor recommended that the Comanches and Utes should be treated fairly when they came to Taos to trade, without allowing the Spaniards or Pueblos to take advantage of them. It was important, said Vélez Cachupín, for the governor to attend the Taos trade fair and visit the rancherias of the assembled Comanches, Utes, and other Plains Indians "observing that any appeal for justice is met at once."[67] This was a duty that the governor must perform himself, "for there is no subject to delegate this duty to who would discharge the trust with the zeal equal to that of the governor himself."[68]

Unfortunately, neither Marín del Valle nor the two governors who succeeded him had Vélez Cachupín's charisma or his desire to meet the Plains Indians in their own camps. Vélez Cachupín avoided potential problems before they escalated into violence by holding such meetings, but Marín del Valle did not deign to engage in this kind of diplomacy. Soon the Comanches started raiding again, and in early August 1760, three thousand Comanches were reported to have descended into Taos Valley intent on attacking Taos Pueblo. The Comanches were outraged by "the spectacle of Taos [Indians] dancing with two dozen Comanche scalps before their very eyes," and started to attack Taos Pueblo but were diverted to a Spanish settlement along the Rio Fernando.[69] As the Comanches approached a Hispanic *torreón* (watch tower), fourteen well-armed men holed up along with their families in Pablo de Villalpando's fortified house. They were no match for the Comanches, however, who outnumbered them and killed all the men. Bernardo de Miera y Pacheco included the story of this battle on his 1779 map of New Mexico, describing the aftermath: "They all perished and sixty-four persons, large and small of both sexes, were carried off. Of the enemy, more than eighty died."[70] In the aftermath of the Villalpando massacre, it was clear that the cycle of violence between the Plains Indians and New Mexico settlements had resumed.

During his first term, Vélez Cachupín realized and tried unsuccessfully to convey to his successors the importance of captives, both Spanish and Indian, to the delicate balance between war and peace with Plains tribes. After Marín del Valle's term as governor expired, two short-term governors followed, Mateo Antonio de Mendoza (1760) and Manuel del Portillo y Urrisola (1760–62). The latter had serious Comanche problems related to the issue of Spanish captives.

In 1761 a band of Comanches came to Taos to negotiate with Portillo y Urrisola over Spanish captives from the Villalpando raid. Portillo met with the Comanche captains, who told him they had seven Spanish captives, three women and four boys, who they were willing to return if trade with the Spanish could be resumed. Instead of offering a proportionate response to this offer, Portillo demanded that all the captives from the Villalpando raid be returned. When the Comanche chiefs refused, the governor took the Comanche negotiators hostage, a serious violation of the code of honor between the two negotiating parties.[71]

What happened next is unclear from Governor Portillo's report, but it certainly was not the glorious victory that he claimed. Portillo left the ten Comanche captains under guard and had Lieutenant Tomás Madrid and his troops surround the Comanche encampment of sixty-eight tipis. The Comanches who had come to return captives and trade at the Taos trade fair were under siege. After a night of standoff, a Comanche emissary came out with a cross and a white banner seeking peace, asking that their captains be returned and that they be permitted to trade. Portillo could not have complied with this request had he wanted to, for one of the Comanche captains had been killed, and most of the rest were wounded. Portillo y Urrisola did not tell this to the main body of Comanches but instead demanded that all the Comanches "must hand over their horses to me and remain on foot; after the fair and after we had reached an agreement, I would return them so that they might depart."[72] This was an outrageous demand, especially since

Portillo had just demonstrated he could not be trusted. When the Comanches refused, Portillo fired on them with a field cannon and muskets until all the Comanches, including women and children, fled. Not only were there an estimated four hundred Comanche deaths, but the Utes, who had also come to Taos to trade, took more than a thousand horses and three Comanche women from the Comanche encampment. Governor Portillo had misjudged the Utes and had thrown away all hope of peace with the Comanches.

Vélez Cachupín's second term began in February 1762, a few weeks after Portillo's debacle at Taos. As the Comanches held war councils, word soon reached them that the new governor was the same one they had sat and smoked the pipe with eight years earlier, when a mutually beneficial peace had been established. Vélez Cachupín had often repeated his opinion that peace with the Comanches was the only rational policy, for they far outnumbered the Spaniards and Pueblos combined and could make life impossible in the scattered and exposed New Mexico settlements.[73]

One of Vélez Cachupín's first acts on moving into the Palace of the Governors for his second term was to free six female Comanche captives and return them to the Comanche nation as a goodwill gesture. The Comanches in kind sent nine warriors and six women to Taos to negotiate with Vélez Cachupín and to see with their own eyes if this was the same governor they had dealt with earlier, the one they called "the captain who amazes." Vélez ordered this delegation escorted to Santa Fe by fourteen Puebloans, and when they arrived he reported, "I made special efforts to entertain them. Because I had known them during my previous term of office, they extended on their part congratulations on these new visits."[74] The Comanche delegation told Vélez Cachupín that "they had discord with the governors that had succeeded [him]" and in particular with Governor Portillo, who had "killed their people in Taos and captured their families when they had come with their hearts full of kindness to establish peace."[75] Instead, "[they] suffered great punishment at the hands of that governor, *who never wished to hear them speak directly to him.*"[76] The latter complaint underscores the differing approach to Indian relations between Vélez Cachupín and the intervening governors. Vélez Cachupín was sensitive to the protocols of negotiation and peace making and realized the importance of personal diplomacy. He was not afraid to speak directly to Comanche leaders.

Vélez Cachupín told the Comanches he was sympathetic to their complaints against Governor Portillo and their "well-founded resentment," but he let them know that their actions at the time of the Villalpando raid were inexcusable.[77] Vélez Cachupín diplomatically noted, however, that "the total discord between Spaniards and Comanches did not arise from mutual general acts but from particular ones committed by very pernicious individuals, who exist in all republics."[78] The governor suggested that the solution was for each side to punish the offending parties "so that the evil of the delinquents on both sides might be corrected and rooted out."[79] Vélez Cachupín suggested that the Comanches and Spaniards should make peace, resume trade, and exchange captives. The Comanche delegation agreed, promising to return by July all the captives taken since 1760, the year of the Villapando raid, and to place the peace proposal before their chiefs for a final decision.

Before the July deadline another Comanche delegation consisting of four chiefs, seven warriors, five women, and three children in three tipis reached Santa Fe on 10 June. As with the earlier group of Comanches, Vélez Cachupín "fed them and presented them with tobacco to smoke while they rested until the next day."[80] When negotiations began, the delegation explained that they had been sent to verify again that the governor was the same person they had known during his first term and to bring back further assurances to that effect. The Comanches were still smarting from Portillo's ill-advised attack of 22 December 1761. Vélez Cachupín suggested that the Comanche delegation tell him what signs of his good faith they required. The oldest of the four chiefs asked that each of the four be given one of the Comanche captives, or Genízaros, held by the Spaniards to take back with them, preferably "some relative or his own woman."[81]

Governor Vélez Cachupín was prepared for this request. He realized that the exchange of captives was one of the things the Comanches most desired. Soon after he took office in February 1762, the governor issued a decree prohibiting the sale and purchase of Comanche Genízaros, ordering instead that any captives be divided among the settlers living near Santa Fe, with the proviso that, if notified, the settlers would be required to return the Genízaros to Vélez Cachupín for possible repatriation as part of an exchange of captives. Lists were kept of the homes to which these Genízaros were assigned so that the Spaniards who housed them could be notified.[82] The plan worked so well that Vélez Cachupín was able to gather thirty-one Comanche Genízaros, all women and children, among whom each of the chiefs found a relative. This second release of Comanche Genízaros so pleased the chiefs in the delegation that they embraced the governor and thanked him profusely. Vélez Cachupín sent the delegation on its way with "sufficient tobacco for their return, gave them another portion to present to the chiefs, principal men, and elders and said good-bye to them."[83] The governor provided the Comanches with an escort of thirty Pueblo warriors to prevent any unfortunate encounter with the Utes. As a result of these peace overtures, Vélez Cachupín concluded another treaty with the Comanches that lasted throughout his second term. When the Marqués de Rubí made his inspection of New Mexico at the end of Vélez Cachupín's second term, he noted that the Comanches were still at peace and were keeping to their obligations.[84]

Vélez Cachupín conducted these peace negotiations in a masterful manner, putting the lie to the prediction of Governor Portillo, who already knew of Vélez Cachupín's captive release plan: "He seems to have the intention of summoning the Comanches, [and] sending them some of their captive women."[85] Portillo, who had been the cause of Comanche distrust of the Spaniards, forecast that Vélez Cachupín's peace plan would not work, suggesting instead that "[the Comanches] will destroy the kingdom on one of these occasions when they come to trade, for experience has shown that all the wicked things which this bellicose and false tribe has committed have always occurred when they were at peace."[86] Vélez Cachupín was aware of this problem. In his report to the viceroy he noted specific precautions: "I have taken measures to protect the frontier settlements from any malicious attacks, have garrisoned them with the troop of this presidio and have kept advance parties posted to explore the approaches . . . [and] if they wish to follow the road of vengeance, I have sufficient justification to make war upon them."[87]

Governor Vélez Cachupín was not soft on the Comanches. He was a practical man who understood them as did no other governor. He saw Comanches and other Plains Indians, indeed all indigenous peoples, as human beings deserving of respect. As a good Catholic, the governor spoke ill of Plains Indian religious practices as "false religions and diabolical misconceptions."[88] In spite of this Vélez Cachupín was convinced that the Comanches would continue to engage in peaceful trade with the Spaniards if they were treated with "the measures which the rules of religion, respect for humanity, and the rights of people dictate."[89]

Vélez Cachupín established peace with Comanches, Utes, and to some extent, Apaches but feared his successor would lose all his gains by undertaking a policy of all-out warfare against the Comanches and other Plains Indians. Vélez Cachupín warned that such an approach was folly because these Indians outnumbered the Spaniards and could increase their advantage through alliances with Utes or Apaches. To Governor Vélez Cachupín the only sane policy entailed a combination of peace with the Comanches giving them the opportunity to engage in peaceful trade and providing additional training of Spanish troops to increase preparedness.[90]

For this policy to be successful, the governor, as chief military strategist, had to understand Indians. Although his predecessor and his successors did not fully trust the Pueblos as allies, Vélez Cachupín had nothing but praise for them. They had given him no cause to question their loyalty for "they have always been very prompt to serve the king in war."[91] He knew the Pueblos' capabilities, their strengths and their weaknesses, and assigned them duties accordingly. As a first line of defense, Vélez Cachupín had Pueblos familiar with the terrain guard the approaches the Comanches customarily used during their attacks on New Mexico settlements. To the north and east he sent scouts from Taos, Picuris, Pecos, and Galisteo to watch routes Comanches traveled when entering the Rio Grande Valley. He assigned Picuris and Taos scouts to patrol the vulnerable gaps in the mountains near Mora and reconnoiter the mountain slopes as far as the Canadian River.[92]

Governor Vélez Cachupín urged these Pueblos to be ever vigilant to prevent Comanche surprise attacks. In the Rio Abajo, he maintained a continuous summer patrol from the six Keres pueblos to protect settlements around Albuquerque, as well as Santo Domingo and San Felipe. Pueblo scouts were advised that if they met a hostile force in numbers too great to be overcome, they were to report to their pueblos so that a larger force could be gathered to repel the attackers.[93]

Because of his readiness, Vélez Cachupín could respond quickly to any attack, as he did in November 1751. This readiness and his decisive defeat of the Comanches at the Battle of San Diego Pond meant that New Mexico achieved a period of peace, relatively free from Indian raids for the rest of his first term and all of his second term as governor. This was in sharp contrast to the decade of intense warfare with Comanches that followed Vélez Cachupín's second term as governor.[94]

Within six months after he terminated the Abiquiu witchcraft proceedings in September 1766, Tomás Vélez Cachupín relinquished the governorship of New Mexico to his successor Pedro Fermín de Mendinueta on 1 March

1767. Still at the height of his powers after completing his second term as
governor of New Mexico, Vélez Cachupín remained in Santa Fe awaiting further orders from the viceroy and the king. There is no evidence that Vélez
Cachupín ever underwent a formal *residencia*. Instead the former governor
met with Mendinueta, passing on some of the knowledge and experience
he had acquired as governor. Unfortunately, Mendinueta did not take this
to heart and did not continue Vélez Cachupín's policy of making peace with
Utes, Comanches, and Navajos. Instead almost constant Indian raiding characterized Mendinueta's administration. This resulted in part from an
aggressive new policy the Spanish crown adopted in 1772 to strengthen frontier presidial garrisons so as to carry the war to the hostile Indians.[95]

   By August 1767 Vélez Cachupín was eager to obtain a new assignment
worthy of his experience and his background. After counseling Mendinueta
for five months, Vélez Cachupín returned to Mexico City to appear before
the viceroy, who finally gave him leave to depart New Spain as soon as he
received permission from the king. Vélez Cachupín still did not have a new
job and was therefore in a state of uncertainty as he sailed back to Spain on
the warship *La Castilla*. In the vicinity of the Island of Terceira in the Azores,
Vélez became extremely ill from an unknown ailment that was never
described in any detail.[96]

   On 25 January 1769, almost two years after delivering the governorship
of New Mexico to Mendinueta, Vélez Cachupín found himself in Madrid,
Spain, in the words of his will, "ill in bed with the illness that God Our Lord
has seen fit to give me."[97] He had arrived in the southern port of Cadiz a
few months earlier and had written the king, asking for a new position. He
told the Spanish monarch that he had not come immediately to Madrid
because "having suffered a great decline in my health . . . [on board ship] I
disembarked in such a weak condition [and] had such a lengthy convales-
cence, that I was prevented from going to place myself at your excellency's
feet."[98] Vélez Cachupín finally arrived in Madrid but apparently suffered a
relapse. He called an *escribano*, Lorenzo de Terreros, to his bedside to prepare his last will and testament because "the hour of my death is unknown
[and] I do not want to be caught unprepared when it comes."[99]

   It seems likely that Vélez Cachupín received medical attention at two
hospitals in Madrid before his death. In his will he made a bequest to the
royal Hospital General and the Hospital de la Pasión in the Spanish capital, a one-time gift of thirty reales. The stated reason for the bequest was to

forestall any future claim against his estate. The exact date of his death has not come to light, but it was probably not long after he signed his will in late January 1769. Vélez Cachupín's signature and especially his rubric were feeble, indicating his frail health, but he was strong enough to write the last paragraph of the will in his own hand. It was not at all unusual for a dying man to add a note to his will on his deathbed and this was certainly in character for a man who had drafted countless legal documents, knew the proper legal language, and preferred to do things himself. He was also extremely proud of the Vélez Cachupín name, and an important clause in his will provided that the person receiving the income from the Casas Cachupinas must "always use the name Vélez Cachupín so that for all time the fame and glory of the family will not be lost."[100]

Tomás Vélez Cachupín had done much to polish the luster of the family name during his tenure as governor of New Mexico. He calmed the feud between Church and State that had continued off and on for 150 years, thus strengthening a divided colony; he achieved peace with the Comanches, Utes, and Navajos, who had been attacking New Mexico settlements with devastating results; he provided personal and property rights to marginalized mestizos and Genízaros who asked him to adjudicate their lawsuits, and he established the first true community land grants in New Mexico, often using these mestizos and Genízaros as the core of these settlements. One of the jewels in the crown of these land grants was the Abiquiu Genízaro land grant.

Figure 8
Governor Vélez Cachupín signs order freeing Gertudes Cuellar and Juan Bautista Montaño and assigning them land at Abiquiu. *Drawing by Glen Strock.*

CHAPTER FIVE

The Abiquiu
Genízaro Land Grant

Its Settlement and Early History

T he Abiquiu Genízaro grant is the only grant made exclusively to Genízaro Indians. Numerous land grants were made in the Abiquiu area to members of the Salazar, Martín Serrano, Torres, Trujillo, and other elite families, who often received land more as a reward for military service than for purposes of settlement, farming, and raising livestock. These elites frequently used their tracts solely for grazing large flocks of sheep and herds of cattle, but early eighteenth-century governors were strict about enforcing the requirements that grantees live and labor on the land for four years before they could receive full title. Grantees commonly used Genízaros to settle and farm the land for them without giving them any rights to the land.[1]

Among the early grants made in the Abiquiu area was the 1734 grant to
Bartolomé Trujillo and nine other interrelated families. These early Hispanic
settlers formed a plaza around the church of Santa Rosa de Lima, then under
construction. The bishop of Durango granted permission to build the Santa
Rosa church in 1737, but by 1746 the chapel was still unfinished. When Father
Miguel Menchero made his visitation in 1744, he listed twenty-four fami-
lies of Spaniards living at Santa Rosa under the jurisdiction of the priest at
San Ildefonso.[2]

The devastating August 1747 Ute/Comanche attack on the Abiquiu settlements led to the abandonment of Santa Rosa de Lima. Father Juan José
Pérez Mirabal of San Juan Pueblo reported the raid to Governor Codallos
y Rabal, but by the time the governor dispatched troops to apprehend the
raiders four days later, they could not find enough tracks to trail them.
The Santa Rosa de Lima settlers then organized their own party to pursue the Indians, picked up their trail, and came upon the dead bodies of
three women and a newborn child. Still, the settler's militia was unable
to overtake the Ute/Comanche raiders.[3]

The 1747 attack was so destructive and punishing that the exposed settlers at Santa Rosa de Abiquiú asked Governor Codallos y Rabal for permission to abandon their settlement. The governor approved the
temporary abandonment, without loss of property rights, until it was safe
to return. In fact, Codallos y Rabal ordered the Abiquiu settlers to evac-
uate their lands on pain of a five-hundred-peso fine. Utes and Comanches
thus achieved an impressive victory as the Spaniards retreated to San José
de Chama and Santa Cruz de la Cañada to take up residence with their
relatives. Then Ute and Comanche raiders were able to penetrate as far
as San José de Chama, after protection of the settlers at Santa Rosa de
Abiquiú melted away.[4] When Viceroy Revillagigedo learned of the abandonment of Abiquiu and several other communities in 1750, he ordered
those settlements resettled.

In accordance with the viceroy's order, Vélez Cachupín commanded
that Abiquiu and other Río Chama settlements be resettled, and he provided a small detachment of soldiers from the Santa Fe presidio to protect the returning settlers. Vélez Cachupín did not make new grants but
ordered settlers who came back to abandoned settlements to establish and
live in fortified plazas. Seven Spanish heads of families and thirteen
Genízaros resettled in Abiquiu. Among the returning families were those

of Miguel and Jerónimo Martín Serrano; Ignacio, Juan, and Rosalía Valdés; and Juan José de la Cerda. Thirteen Genízaros assigned to the abandoned house of Miguel de Montoya were also resettled in 1750. They probably formed the nucleus of the 1754 Abiquiu Genízaro land grant.[5]

Alcalde Juan José Lobato led the settlers back to Santa Rosa and laid out a closed defensive plaza in accordance with Vélez Cachupín's orders. Similar to the earlier decree of Codallos y Rabal that provided a fine for failing to abandon Abiquiu, the governor's strict decree imposed a two-hundred-peso fine and four months in jail for settlers who failed to resettle. Nevertheless, Juan, Pablo, and Bartolomé Trujillo and Pablo Martín decided to give up their lands rather than return to Abiquiu. Members of the Valdés family—Ignacio, Juan, and Rosalía—who received a grant in 1739, filed a petition in protest of resettlement, which Vélez Cachupín denied. The Valdés clan accordingly changed their minds, gathered their livestock and scant possessions, and resettled their lands.[6] By 1752 Bartolomé Trujillo resettled his lands as he finally became convinced that the defenses were strong enough to assure reasonable safety to his family. Nonetheless, he had to pay sixty pesos to recertify his title.[7]

Resettlement of Spaniards on their old land grants and the assignment of presidial troops at Abiquiu set the stage for the Genízaro grant of 1754. Governor Vélez Cachupín was probably working with local alcaldes to assemble a list of eligible Genízaro families. No such list has survived, but the governor noted in the witchcraft trial documents that he settled sixty families at Abiquiu in 1754. The 1754 Abiquiu Genízaro grant must have been profoundly disconcerting to the surrounding elite Spanish landowners, unaccustomed as they were to respecting Genízaro land and water rights. Likewise, the Genízaros sometimes reacted to their Spanish neighbors in strange ways. A summary of the history of the Abiquiu Genízaro grant demonstrates the give and take that developed between the Genízaros and their neighbors.

In the 1754 Genízaro grant documents Governor Vélez Cachupín referred to Viceroy Revillagigedo's order to resettle Abiquiu and to the orders of the *fiscal*, the viceroy's legal advisor, and the auditor general of war in Mexico City. The fiscal specified that the Genízaros must be given sufficient land in accordance with book 6, title 3, law 8 of the *Recopilación de leyes de los reynos de las Indias*, which provided that Indians have the advantage of sufficient water and woodlands, and an *ejido*, or commons, one league long.[8] Governor Vélez Cachupín went to the site of the new pueblo, to be called Santo Tomás Apóstol de Abiquiú after the governor's patron saint, with Father Ordóñez, who was under the jurisdiction of the prelate and vice custos of New Mexico, fray Tomás Murciano de la Cruz. The viceroy had appointed fray Félix José Ordóñez y Machado as priest and *doctrinero*, or teacher of Christian doctrine, at the Genízaro pueblo.[9] The governor examined the area and found it to be endowed with rich lands of fine quality and an abundance of water, pasture lands, and woodlands. With the assistance of Alcalde Juan José Lobato, the measurement of the grant was made as follows: 2,400 varas to the north, 2,550 to the east and west, and five thousand varas to the south. Much of this property was said to be agricultural land under irrigation. In addition, an ejido to the south was measured as follows: north, the pueblo boundary; south, the road that goes to the Navajo; east, the arroyo that descends along the edge of the pueblo; and west, the height of the Río de los Frijoles. Governor Vélez Cachupín noted that toward the western boundary, the high ground of the Río de los Frijoles, the pastures were of excellent quality because of the superabundance of grama grass.

Governor Vélez Cachupín later noted that he had placed sixty families in possession of the Abiquiu grant in a document related to the witchcraft trial, but by 1776 there were only forty-six families totaling 136 persons at the pueblo.[10] Abiquiu Pueblo was abandoned just prior to 1770 when Governor Pedro Fermín de Mendinueta (1767–78) again ordered it resettled.[11] Governor Mendinueta directed the new settlers to build compact settlements near the homes of either militia sergeant Francisco Valdez or Alferez Ignacio Gallegos.[12] Governor Mendinueta subsequently ordered a copy of the grant made at the request of leaders of the pueblo.[13] Governor Mendinueta's land grant policies were not as favorable to indigenous peoples as were those of Governor Vélez Cachupín, nor was his military policy as effective in achieving peace with Utes, Comanches, and Navajos, who continued to terrorize frontier settlements such as Abiquiu.[14]

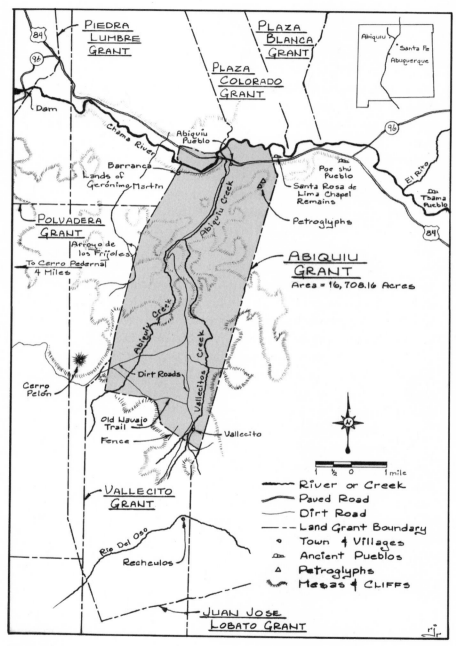

Figure 9
Map showing the Abiquiu grant and surrounding land grants. *Courtesy of Robert Wittwer.*

In any case, after its second abandonment Abiquiu was again resettled, this time for good. The 1770s were a difficult time for all frontier settlements as the Comanches and Utes stepped up their attacks. The Spanish
settlements in and around Taos moved into Taos Pueblo for protection,
and Ojo Caliente was almost abandoned many times before it was resettled permanently in 1793. Mendinueta blamed the Spanish settlers for refusing to return to Ojo Caliente, calling them "churlish types" and threatening
them with jail and fines of up to two hundred pesos.[15] Although the
Spaniards refused to resettle Ojo Caliente, the Genízaros stayed, continued to plant gardens, and traded with Utes and Comanches. This was probably the case for Abiquiu as well. When Abiquiu was said to have been
abandoned after the 1747 Comanche/Ute raid, some Genízaro families must
have remained, while the Spaniards moved in with their extended families at Santa Cruz and San José de Chama.[16]

During the latter part of the eighteenth century, the Genízaro population at Abiquiu fluctuated, sometimes dipping below the sixty families originally settled on the grant. In 1760 Bishop Tamarón counted 57 Genízaro
families totaling 166 persons and 104 Hispanic families totaling 617 persons.[17]
In 1776 when Father Domínguez made his visitation and census he counted
46 Genízaro families with 136 persons and 49 Spanish families with 254 persons. Domínguez noted that both groups had fields irrigated by the Chama
River in separate areas and that the Spaniards' fields produced more and better crops because they applied themselves more assiduously. In contrast
Domínguez said that the Genízaros were "sterile in their labor and cultivation so they do not yield what they might with attention and as a result so
little is harvested that the Indians are always dying."[18] Father Domínguez further noted that Abiquiu Genízaros spoke a form of Spanish similar to that
of Santa Fe Genízaros, but as to their customs (and probably their religious
practices), the chatty and censorious priest said that the Genízaros were
"examples of what happens when idleness becomes the den of evils."[19]

By the early 1800s, Indian raids were less of a threat to Abiquiu Genízaros
than were land sales by individual Indians to Hispanic elites. The decline

in farming at Abiquiu and the 1812 laws of the Spanish Cortes allowing privatization of unused pueblo lands created a situation that was ripe for exploitation by Hispanic citizens, including the priest at Abiquiu, fray Teodoro Alcina.

During this period Hispanic elites treated Abiquiu as an Indian pueblo, moved by the desire to privatize unused land and acquire as much of it as possible from the pueblo. Fray Teodoro Alcina, more an enemy of the Genízaro pueblo than a source of friendly guidance, was one of the worst offenders in the practice of wresting land from the Abiquiu Genízaros. The situation got so bad that the pueblo took the unprecedented step of filing a lawsuit against their priest. Not only was he acquiring their land, but he and José García de la Mora were bringing biblical-style disasters upon the pueblo. On one occasion Father Alcina cursed and damned all the Genízaros in the pueblo in a public meeting.

In 1820, after a series of abuses by Father Alcina that stretched over the past several years (including his refusal to perform the last rites and bury the deceased in the Abiquiu cemetery), a group of people from the Genízaro pueblo and surrounding communities met with the *ayuntamiento,* or town council, of Abiquiu to see what could be done to rectify the situation. Members of the Genízaro community were in agreement with Hispanos from nearby plazas that the situation was serious, and many of these people attended the meeting. They charged that Father Alcina was not performing his "obligations of preaching and teaching...the doctrine or the Holy Gospel as is ordered by the Council of Trent."[20] The reference to the Council of Trent shows that both the vecinos from nearby plazas and the Abiquiu Genízaros were familiar with and supportive of official Church doctrine and wanted Alcina to perform the services required by that doctrine.[21] In the ayuntamiento's petition, Alcalde Santiago Salazar reported what happened next. As the meeting was being convened, "the said minister (Father Alcina) entered without being summoned and without any reason yelled at everyone congregated there in a threatening voice that the ayuntamiento was intervening in something in which they had no right to intervene," and if they persisted, "he swore to bury them all and finish them off, cursing and damning all of them."[22] As if this were not bad enough, Alcina's crony, José García de la Mora, stood up and said three times, "Damned be this district [of Abiquiu]. Damned be this district [of Abiquiu]. Damned be this district [of

Abiquiu]." That afternoon a severe hailstorm destroyed the crops in the Abiquiu area. A plague of locusts soon totally wiped out what little remained. It seemed that the curse of García de la Mora and Father Alcina had come to fruition. Neither the Genízaros nor the Hispanic vecinos would soon forget that day.[23] This incident profoundly shocked the members of the Genízaro pueblo.

After cursing Abiquiu Pueblo, Father Alcina attempted to force a sale of its common lands in order to facilitate collection on some unspecified debt that the pueblo was said to owe him. Again the Genízaro Indians of Abiquiu protested, this time to the territorial deputation of New Mexico. Governor Facundo Melgares, president of the deputation, reported on 26 April 1822 that "the sale [or payment] of lands was null, and the land was to be returned to the community."[24] If the transaction had not been reversed, Father Alcina would have taken over most of the common lands of the Genízaro pueblo. Irrespective of the governor's ruling, Alcina retained several private tracts of land within the boundaries of Abiquiu Pueblo; a tract claimed by Teresa Cortés was bounded on one side by Father Alcina's land. In addition to taking land from Abiquiu Pueblo, Father Alcina admitted to stealing at least two sacks of corn from Abiquiu Pueblo. The Genízaro pueblo had to sue the priest in order to obtain this admission. In so doing, it reasserted its identity as a pueblo that would not put up with theft of its lands and other property, even by its priest.[25] The charges and testimony against Father Alcina were referred to Custos José Pedro Rubín de Celis, who unfortunately took no action. It would have helped to clear the air if the custos had rendered a decision. Father Alcina was not as tolerant as Toledo had been, yet he remained at Abiquiu as biblical catastrophes continued to afflict the community.[26]

Another catastrophe Abiquiu faced was the sale of its lands by individual Indians of the pueblo, as well as sales by Father Teodoro Alcina himself. It was unclear whether individual Indians had the power to sell community or private land of the pueblo, but while government officials debated the question, Indian land sales continued. In 1812 Teresa Cortés sold lands she had acquired from Abiquiu Pueblo to José Velarde, but three years later in 1815 Governor Alberto Máynez (1814–16) revoked the sale when the pueblo protested, stating that "no one can sell pueblo land, and if any has been sold the sale is null and void."[27]

Abiquiu Pueblo spent more than a decade fighting illegal land sales to elite New Mexicans in courts as high as the commandant general's in Chihuahua and Durango. These elites included Governor Bartolomé Baca and acting Governor Juan Esteban Pino, who both coveted pueblo land in general; Manuel Martínez, the successful petitioner for the Tierra Amarilla grant; and José García de la Mora, the largest purchaser of Abiquiu Pueblo land.[28] García de la Mora was a prime mover in the litigation, representing Father Alcina and other individuals who had purchased land from Teresa Cortés. García de la Mora acted as alcalde at a time when he was one of the largest purchasers of Abiquiu Pueblo land, which presented a clear conflict of interest. In March 1823 he petitioned Governor José Antonio Viscarra (1823) on the purchasers' behalf, asking the governor to validate sales that previous governors had held null and void. Instead, Vizcarra, on behalf of the provincial deputation, ordered the sales rescinded and the purchase prices refunded.[29]

José García de la Mora was not happy with Governor Vizcarra's decision favoring Abiquiu Pueblo, and his response to the governor and to the commandant general showed how deeply he was involved in Abiquiu Pueblo land and how far he was willing to go in challenging the very identity of the Genízaro pueblo. First, he complained that if the Indians of Abiquiu Pueblo were to refund the purchase price to him, he should receive not two hundred pesos but one thousand pesos and would accept nothing less. His attitude demonstrates the value García de la Mora placed on the land he purchased, although it does not appear that he paid that much for it. Second, García traveled to Chihuahua, about four hundred miles south of Santa Fe, to present his case directly to the commandant general.[30]

After Mexican independence in 1821, the commandant general of the interior provinces continued to act in some of the same areas of his jurisdiction as before independence, including hearing appeals from decisions of the governors. This official often knew very little about the conditions of New Mexico Indians and even less about the Abiquiu Genízaros. His decisions were generally legalistic, vague, and sometimes ambiguous. Since no lawyer or agent represented the Abiquiu Genízaros in Chihuahua, it was a perfect opportunity for García de la Mora to attempt to mislead the court and have the Abiquiu Pueblo land sales approved. García de la Mora informed Commandant General Gaspar de Ochoa that the Indians had

only four years to object to the sales made to Spaniards and, most important, he implied that they lacked standing to object because they were not
even from Abiquiu but were Genízaros or coyotes.[31]

This argument was similar to García's earlier attempt in 1820 to alter
the nature of the Genízaro pueblo. Even before Mexican independence,
García de la Mora, in his capacity as alcalde of Abiquiu, asked Governor
Melgares (1818–22) for clarification of the status of the Abiquiu Genízaros.
He told the governor that the viceroy and the commandant general had
notified him of the total elimination of the former status of the mission
of Abiquiu as a settlement of Genízaros, which had been established, protected, and assisted by the king. To García de la Mora this meant that the
common lands of Abiquiu were subject to partition and that the people
of Abiquiu were no longer Indians deserving protection. García explained
to Governor Melgares, "I must see this pueblo not as it was, but as a plaza
of vecinos subject to the tithe, first fruits, and other obligations and consequently. . . . I should proceed to partition the common lands into equal
parts [subject to acquisition by] poor vecinos who lack land." The pueblo
later claimed García de la Mora was planning its destruction.[32]

This challenge to the very identity of the Abiquiu Genízaro pueblo was
not accepted either in 1820 or in 1823 by the lawyer for the commandant
general who considered the Abiquiu Genízaros to be Indians subject to the
jurisdiction of that court, ruling that local authorities should decide the
dispute after making an attempt at conciliation. In the meantime, the
Spanish purchasers should retain possession of the land in question.[33]

Following the commandant general's decision, both sides interpreted
the ruling according to their own interests. García de la Mora took the
language about leaving the purchasers in possession to mean that the commandant had ruled in his favor. The Genízaro pueblo, however, focused
on the language allowing local officials to decide the case. Accordingly,
on 20 April 1824, Alcalde Francisco Jaramillo ruled that "the lands within
said community [of Abiquiu] cannot be acquired or purchased by any individual of another race [that is, non-Indians]."[34]

The delay caused by an appeal to Chihuahua gave García de la Mora
and others the opportunity to take additional land belonging to the
pueblo and begin farming it. Abiquiu Pueblo filed numerous petitions
with Governor Baca, pointing out these injustices and attaching
decrees of former governors decreeing sales of pueblo land to be void.

Yet, Governor Baca, who was interested in privatizing as much pueblo land as possible so he and his allies could acquire it, continued to rule in favor of the purchasers.[35]

Abiquiu Pueblo was slow to respond to García de la Mora's attempt to circumvent the series of decisions voiding sales of Abiquiu Pueblo land. When the pueblo's response came in April and May 1824, it was two-pronged. Acting on the pueblo's behalf, Francisco Márquez, Francisco Trujillo, and Miguel Antonio García brought suit before Governor Baca seeking the anticipated return of the lands sold to García de la Mora and restraining him from occupying additional Abiquiu Pueblo land. Francisco Trujillo [a different Trujillo from the petitioner with the same name] ruled on 18 May 1824 that "the land [sold to Hispanos] be restored to the natives of the Pueblo."[36] Similar rulings had been handed down before without compliance by the authorities, so former Protector of Indians Ignacio Sánchez Vergara was appointed to present the pueblo's case as its attorney.

A less consistent Indian advocate than Sánchez Vergara would be hard to find. In this case, he made a forceful argument for the inability of the pueblos to sell their land without permission of their attorney or a judge. He asserted that the pueblo lands Cortés and García sold should be returned to the pueblo with the pair refunding the purchase price. Sánchez Vergara argued convincingly that any sale of the lands of the pueblo of Abiquiu damaged the subsistence base of the Genízaro Indians, stating that the pueblo was dwindling in area because of the land sales "leaving only a few families at the pueblo who are in complete misery, with not even a piece of land to farm and cultivate in order to make a living."[37]

The April 1824 petition filed by Abiquiu Pueblo provided an opportunity for the pueblo to assert its identity and set the record straight on several matters. First, the petition mentioned the 1754 Vélez Cachupín grant that legally established the pueblo with definite boundaries, "leaving the pueblo fully satisfied." Then Abiquiu Pueblo pointed out that Teresa Cortés was a founding member of the Genízaro pueblo, having equal rights with the other pueblo members to use the grant lands but not to sell them. Finally, Father Alcina, who had been claiming a right to lands of Abiquiu Pueblo for more than a decade, was described as being in league with the alcaldes who "instead of protecting and advising us as to our rights were planning our destruction."[38]

Father Alcina had several tracts of Abiquiu Pueblo land, but the main one he acquired was given him in trust to farm with Genízaro Indian labor, using the harvest for the upkeep of the church and as payment for administering the sacraments. Instead, Alcina appropriated the land for himself and continued to overcharge the Genízaros for his services. In spite of the charges against him, Father Alcina remained at Abiquiu until 1823. Since there was no resolution of the charges against Alcina by the Genízaros, and since Alcina became custos, some scholars have considered his record to be primarily positive, ignoring some of the more sensational charges against him.[39]

In addition to these struggles over land within the pueblo, the Abiquiu Genízaros were actively involved in another aspect of the protection of their lands, the measurement of their ejido to the south of the grant.[40] The southern boundary of the Abiquiu ejido, which was considered to be part of the Abiquiu grant, was disputed by neighboring Hispanic settlers from Vallecitos between 1829 and 1831. Unlike the Pecos pueblo, whose common lands began to be partitioned and privatized under the authority of Governor Bartolomé Baca, Abiquiu Pueblo fiercely defended its ejido against attack. Although pueblo members sold some land to local Spaniards, much of the Abiquiu ejido remained in Genízaro hands, and to this very day, the community still owns and uses it.[41]

In 1807 José García de la Mora and twelve associates received a land grant known as the Vallecitos de San Antonio grant. The northern boundary of the Vallecitos grant was Abiquiu Pueblo, but the exact location of that boundary became the subject of a heated dispute. Soon after the Vallecitos grant was made, Abiquiu residents complained that livestock of the Vallecitos settlement had wandered onto their planted fields and caused damage.[42] As with other grants to Spaniards that were adjacent to Indian pueblos, the exact location of the boundary of the pueblo was often not determined and marked with accuracy until after an encroachment on the pueblo's lands made the boundary issue important. Often the measurement of the pueblo league was a first step in the resolution of such disputes.[43] Since the southern boundary of the Abiquiu grant was the northern boundary of the Abiquiu ejido, the question arose as to whether the pueblo owned the ejido or shared it with adjoining landowners. Other cases of ejidos attached to grants made to Spaniards answered this question in different ways. Although the ejido concept implied

common usage of land by the community receiving the land grant (usually for grazing cattle), in some cases several communities shared an ejido,
and in others the ejido was for the exclusive use of the community to
which it was attached.

The *Recopilación* law under which the grant to Abiquiu Pueblo was
made implied that the latter interpretation was meant for indigenous pueblos such as Abiquiu. *Recopilación* book 6, title 3, law 8 states that the one
league ejido given to Indian pueblos must be a place "where the Indians
can have their cattle without mixing with those of the Spaniards."[44]
Governor Vélez Cachupín repeated this provision almost verbatim in the
1754 Abiquiu grant and made this interpretation when he granted the
adjoining Polvadera grant to Juan Pablo Martín. In the Polvadera grant,
west of Abiquiu Pueblo, Vélez Cachupín provided that the grant "shall be
without prejudice to the Indians of Abiquiu, their farmlands and ejidos."[45]
If only the Indians' cattle was to be kept on the Abiquiu ejido, it would
appear to be an ejido that was part of the land grant to the pueblo.[46]

While the status of the Abiquiu ejido seemed clear in 1766, by 1826
the Mexican government's views about common land had changed somewhat. The Spanish Cortes had encouraged the privatization of unused
and unneeded pueblo common land in 1812 and 1813, and those laws were
still in effect in the early 1820s. In 1825 lands of pueblos like Pecos, whose
members had dwindled to only a handful, were privatized and either
allotted to Spaniards or purchased by them from neighboring Indians.
During this period a dispute broke out over the southern boundary of
the Abiquiu Pueblo grant with the Vallecitos de San Antonio grant to
the south.[47]

At the time of the partition of private farmlands at Abiquiu in 1825,
the southern boundary of Abiquiu Pueblo was recognized as "the road of
the Tewas that goes to Navajo."[48] This was also the south boundary of the
ejido, but no landmarks remained to mark the location of that boundary. Accordingly, a new measurement of the southern boundary of the
Abiquiu grant was ordered. It was not always clear how many varas should
be measured, but most everyone agreed that the landmark on the south
was the road to Navajo country.

In 1829 Governor Manuel Armijo directed Alcalde Miguel Quintana
to establish Abiquiu's southern boundary after examining the Vallecito and
Polvadera grants. He noted that the Polvadera grant was made "without

prejudice to the five-thousand-vara [ejido] of said pueblo." Alcalde Quintana then introduced serious confusion into the proceedings when he stated that the Abiquiu grant called for a "measurement of five thousand varas south from the center of the pueblo to the Camino Real of the Tewas which goes to Navajo, which bounds the front of the pueblo."[49] The Abiquiu grant actually called for a measurement of the agricultural lands as five thousand varas south from the plaza of Abiquiu Pueblo to a landmark, from which the ejido of five thousand varas was to be measured south to the road to Navajo country. Thus the distance from the plaza of Abiquiu to the road to Navajo country should have been ten thousand varas. A look at the later survey of the Abiquiu grant shows the village of Abiquiu to be on the north side of the grant. This confusion over the proper distance from the pueblo to the road to Navajo country almost led to violence when the location of Abiquiu's southern boundary became the subject of a lawsuit between the residents of the Vallecitos grant and the Abiquiu Genízaros.[50]

In August 1831 the matter came to a head when an attempt was made to find the Vallecitos grant in the Santa Fe archives. Governor José Antonio Chávez stated that the land grant could not be found because "it is not easy to find old documents in an archive as old as this particularly when the date in not given."[51] Apparently the Santa Fe archives were not well organized and the grant was not found. At the same time the Vallecitos settlers had little information about their own grant to go on.

Finally, in October 1831, Alcalde José Francisco Vigil attempted to locate the south boundary of the Abiquiu grant. He appointed "two of the oldest men of the jurisdiction who have been raised from childhood as shepherds in Vallecitos so they might point out to me the road of the Tewas that goes to Navajo."[52] In addition, each side was to name an arbitrator, and Alcalde Vigil was to name a third in case the other two did not agree. The focus would be on locating the road and then checking its location through a measurement, to determine the boundary between the Vallecitos grant and the Abiquiu grant. If the boundary was further north the Vallecitos settlers would not be trespassing.

The Abiquiu Genízaros did not like this procedure because there were so many old roads in the area, any one of them could be the road in question. The Genízaros refused to participate in the proceedings, which caused the alcalde to rail against them: "Indeed these Genízaros only try to disturb the order of the proceedings."[53] The Genízaros were wise to boycott the proceedings, for the road that Alcalde Vigil identified was only 5,704 varas from the church on the north side of the pueblo, not the 10,000 varas claimed by the Genízaros.[54]

Because the Abiquiu Genízaros were dissatisfied with the October 1831 measurement and had not participated in the procedure, Alcalde Vigil decided to make one more attempt to satisfy them and the Spaniards of the Vallecitos grant. It took almost a year, however, before he could get both sides to go to the land. Even so, the situation was so volatile that Alcalde Vigil had to appoint "fifteen of the principal citizens of the jurisdiction to assist me in the delivery of the said lands."[55] Undoubtedly, these principal citizens did not include any Genízaros, for this alcalde's posse was insufficient to keep the peace. As soon as Alcalde Vigil tried to again measure the land of Abiquiu Pueblo as he had done the year before, he was attacked by two of the Genízaro leaders stirring up the rest of the pueblo "with a tumult of the whole pueblo of old men, young men, and women trying to take the documents from my hands... [and] shaking the bridle reins of my horse with his hand after several ignominies and insolent arguments with which they insulted me."[56] Initially, Alcalde Vigil had intended to measure only five thousand varas south from the pueblo and then measure "the surplus until he reached the road to Navajo."[57] Referring to the Abiquiu ejido as surplus land was not what the Genízaro pueblo had in mind, and after the forcible display of their displeasure, Alcalde Vigil quickly reversed himself. He ordered that the lands should be measured south from the pueblo five thousand Castilian varas, and immediately thereafter there should be measured for commons another five thousand varas, where the alcalde found "the road of the Tewas that goes to Navajo and an old landmark."[58] This landmark does not appear to be the one erected during the 1829 proceedings and was probably established at the time Vélez Cachupín made the grant in 1754. Miraculously, through their resistance and rebellious conduct the Abiquiu Genízaros retained the full extent of the land granted them by Governor Vélez Cachupín in 1754. This was the end of the litigation of Abiquiu's southern boundary, but the northern boundary remained a matter of controversy sixty years later before the Court of Private Land Claims.

The Abiquiu grant was submitted to the Court of Private Land Claims in 1892 and confirmed in 1894. Chief Justice Joseph R. Reed's decision

Figure 10
The Plaza of the Pueblo of Abiquiu with the Santo Tomás Church in the center viewed from Abiquiu mesa. *Photograph by Malcolm Ebright.*

upholding the grant specifically mentioned Vélez Cachupín's 1754 grant to a group of "converted half-breed Indians," and confirmed the grant with the following boundaries: "On the north, the Chama River; on the south, the highway formerly called the Teguas Road, leading to Navajo; on the east, the source (*nacimiento*) of the arroyo, which descends along the border of the pueblo (or lands of the Plaza de la Capilla); and on the west, the hill (*alto*) of the Rio de las Frijoles, and the lands formerly of Geronimo Martín."[59] When Deputy Surveyor Sherrard Coleman surveyed it, the grant was found to contain a little more than 16,500 acres, about 1,000 acres short of four square leagues (17,712 acres) allotted to all Indian pueblos under Spanish law and practice. The claimants protested the location of the northern boundary at the Chama River, arguing that the line should be established along the Chama River as it flowed in 1754. The Land Claims Court overruled the protest and a patent was finally issued to the Abiquiu Board of Grant Commissioners on 11 November 1909.[60]

The board of commissioners of the Abiquiu land grant still administers the common lands of the grant, mostly for grazing purposes. The Genízaros of Abiquiu had to fight for their land, just as they fought the Devil and Father Toledo in the witchcraft proceedings.

Figure 11
Mauricio with his obsidian-edged sword expelling flames from his mouth and ears as he sits on the coals of a fire. *Drawing by Glen Strock.*

CHAPTER SIX

Witchcraft Trials in Colonial New Mexico and on the Northern Frontier

E arly witchcraft trials in colonial New Mexico often involved the dreaded Inquisition. Not only were Indians initially subject to capital punishment by the Inquisition, *conversos* or "converted Jews were the first to receive the formal sentence of burning at the stake." Later the Inquisition did not have jurisdiction over Indians after the uproar over the execution of the Indian leader Don Carlos in 1539, so cases involving Indian witchcraft were tried as criminal prosecutions by the governors and their alcaldes.[1] The Inquisition cases often dealt with a mixture of native religious practices and witchcraft activities similar to those carried out at Abiquiu. The

Abiquiu witchcraft proceedings involved both the criminal justice system of New Mexico and the Inquisition, so it is important to distinguish the two.

The Inquisition, which was introduced into the Americas in 1517, was "aimed at maintaining moral censorship and purity of the Catholic faith."[2] There was a broad group of offenses that came under its jurisdiction, such as bigamy, blasphemy, quackery, and sexual immorality. Any belief that ran counter to Catholic theology was considered heresy subject to the wide reach of the Inquisition. Thus, Catholics who followed the teachings of Calvin, Erasmus, or Luther, and converted Jews found practicing their own rites, were all subject to punishment by the Inquisition. In addition sorcery, superstition, and *curandismo* (folk healing) were offenses falling under the rubric of witchcraft prosecuted by the Inquisition.

One of the earliest Inquisition cases in New Mexico involved one Luis de Rivera, who in 1630 was the subject of an investigation into allegations that he had made a pact with the Devil.[3] The following year, Juan de la Cruz and his wife underwent an Inquisition investigation of her superstitious behavior.[4] Another early New Mexico case was against Bernardo Gruber from 1668–70. It will be examined in detail because it illustrates the operation of the Inquisition at this time.

Bernardo Gruber was a member of the colonial elite who was the victim of the inefficiencies and cumbersome procedures of the Inquisition in the latter part of the seventeenth century. Gruber was a prosperous German trader who arrived in the mission settlement at Quarai and Abo in 1668 with a pack train loaded with merchandise. Gruber, known by the Spaniards simply as El Alemán (the German), brought "fine stockings, gloves, embroidered cloth, buckskins, iron tools, and weapons" to trade in the New Mexican settlements. Little is known about Gruber before he appeared in the church of Nuestra Señora de la Purísima Concepción at Quarai Pueblo on Christmas Day. Just as Father Francisco Salazar began to sing the Gospel Acclamation, Gruber and his friend Juan Martín Serrano climbed up the ladder to the choir loft and began whispering to the members of the chorus. Later testimony disclosed that Gruber pulled several *papelitos* (strips of paper) from his pocket and wrote the following spell on each one: +ABNA+ADNA+. Then he whispered to the choir members, as he offered them the papelitos that whoever ate one would be rendered impervious to physical harm for twenty-four hours, so that "neither the arrows of Apaches, nor bullets, nor swords, would wound him."[5]

Juan Nieto, an Indian from Quarai, took one of the papelitos and later swallowed it in front of several Indian men gathered at the kiva at Quarai. The Indians were amazed when Nieto tested his invulnerability by stabbing himself with a sharp awl and failed to draw blood. Later Juan Nieto thought better of engaging in such practices and told the whole story to Father José Paredes of the mission at San Buenaventura. Father Paredas began an investigation but soon turned the case over to fray Juan de Paz, the agent for the Inquisition, since the activities charged against Gruber smacked of witchcraft and sorcery. Gruber was arrested and held in a small cell at Abo Pueblo, while his property was inventoried. The cell was too small so Gruber was transferred to a room with barred windows at the nearby estancia of Francisco Ortega. Little did Gruber know that he would languish there for more than two years while Father Paz and his successor Father Juan Bernal made excuses to the Inquisition authorities in Mexico City about why they could not bring Bernardo Gruber there for trial. Gruber had asked for a speedy trial, confident that he would be exonerated since he had harmed no one. As he told the investigators, he learned the spell in Germany where it was customary to use such spells for protection when they went to war.

Although the Holy Office in Mexico City sent letters of harsh criticism to Father Paz and Father Bernal for their delay, Gruber's cattle were dying and he was becoming impatient, so he began to plot his escape. With the aid of his Apache servant and one of his guards, Gruber escaped and then eluded his pursuers. He and his servant reached the Jornada del Muerto, as far as Las Peñuelas, but Gruber could travel no further. He disappeared while his servant was getting water, and his bones were discovered three weeks after the escape, scattered near the remains of his roan horse.[6] There was no doubt that the bones and skull were Gruber's for near the spot where the horse was found was "a doublet or coat of blue cloth lined with otter-skin . . . [and] and pair of trousers of the same material."[7]

Bernardo Gruber suffered a fate similar to the Genízaros of Abiquiu who were imprisoned in the Santa Fe jail for more than two years. Instead of escaping, several of them died in prison. But at least they had received a trial of sorts; Gruber never did. The Gruber case caused Father Paz and Bernal to be criticized severely, and the miscarriage of justice that resulted "had significant consequences for the history of the Inquisition in New Mexico and other similar frontier areas. In condemning Father Paz's conduct, characterized as 'gross ignorance and lack of attention to the obligations of his office,' the Holy Tribunal in Mexico City decreed that the local commissaries of [the Holy Office] in New Mexico and other areas no longer had authority to make arrests without express orders from the Holy Office of the Inquisition. Consequently, only one other Inquisition case was prosecuted in New Mexico during the decade prior to the Pueblo Revolt of 1680."[8]

Another early witchcraft case involved the criminal justice system of New
Mexico and not the Inquisition.

In early July 1715, Antonia Luján summoned the alcalde of Santa Fe to her house,
telling him she was ill and feared she would die. Serving as alcalde at that time was
Juan Páez Hurtado, an elite Spaniard who had occupied or would occupy almost
every important government post in New Mexico.[9] Luján told Páez Hurtado that
one day when she was at home she struck up a conversation with her neighbor's
wife, an Indian woman from San Juan. Suddenly, out of the blue, the Indian asked
Luján if she wanted to be rich and have an abundance of everything.[10] When Luján
questioned how that was possible, the woman told her to drink a certain herb and
rub part of it into her hands. In addition the Indian scraped a powder from a large
shell (*un caracol grande*) and told Luján to drink part of it with warm water and
rub the rest on her hands. The San Juan Indian then told Luján that if she followed
these instructions she would not only have an abundance of everything, "she would
not lack important people in her house." When Luján was skeptical and refused,
the Indian left without saying a word.[11]

Soon Antonia Luján began to suffer great pain throughout her body with sores
covering her torso and left thigh. Believing that witchcraft had caused her illness, Luján
confronted the San Juan woman and demanded a cure. Although Luján paid in
advance with a colored blanket and four deerskins for the treatment, the Indian failed
to cure her. Luján then went to the Indian's house and took back the blanket but was
unable to get her deerskins. Then Antonia Luján sought help from another Indian
curandera, who gave her an herb she had sent for from Galisteo. Still Luján was not
cured from the effects of the witchcraft practiced against her. This is why she had
sought out Alcalde Páez Hurtado. Almost as an afterthought Luján told Páez Hurtado
that her husband, Mateo de Ortega, was having an illicit relationship with a woman
from San Juan (Francisca Caza), thus adding a whole new dimension to her story.[12]

With a possible motive established, Páez Hurtado proceeded to question the
San Juan Indian who had since been imprisoned. She said her name was Francisca
Caza and that she was married to a Jumano Indian named Francisco Cuervo. There
then followed a question reminiscent of the Inquisition: instead of directly confronting Caza with the charges against her, the alcalde asked her if she knew why
she had been imprisoned, admonishing her to tell the truth. It is unclear whether
Caza saw a copy of the charges, but she was skillful in admitting some charges while
denying that she practiced witchcraft against Antonia Luján.[13]

Francisca Caza may have realized the distinction the religious authorities
drew between idolatry and the less serious charge of superstition when confronted

by native belief systems.[14] The use of herbs fell into the category of superstition and was freely admitted in all details, but the powdered shell involved a power object used to effect a desired outcome by supernatural means. Since Caza must have known that use of the shell fell into the more serious category, she said that its use would only have the desired effect with divine intervention. Later in her testimony she brought up another exculpatory stratagem used by defendants in these cases when she said that "the Devil had tricked her and put the idea [of the use of the shell] in her head." Upon hearing the Devil mentioned, Caza's questioners asked her whether the Devil himself had spoken to her. She quickly responded that no, she did not see the Devil and never talked to him.[15] This question was commonly included in manuals for priests attempting to extirpate native beliefs.[16]

The resolution of the case of *Antonia Luján v. Francisca Caza* is unknown. Nor is it known whether Caza was punished or Luján cured and reconciled with her husband. The activities involved in the case, coming under the heading of witchcraft, are known, however, and are typical of many seventeenth- and eighteenth-century witchcraft cases. Often the motive for causing harm through witchcraft was a love triangle, as was the case with Antonia Luján, her husband, Mateo de Ortega, and Francisca Caza. Either it was the wife of an unfaithful husband who sought to regain his affections, or as here, the husband and his lover sought to do away with the betrayed wife. Such a scenario was not uncommon in colonial New Mexico, and usually the defendant suffered only light punishment unless the victim died.

The use of herbs to harm someone or achieve a magical goal (to become rich, to attract famous people or a lover) was difficult to separate from a curandera's legitimate use of herbs to heal people. New Mexicans on all levels of society consulted curanderas, and such practices were often winked at, even though technically they fell into the prohibited category of superstition.[17] Even Father Toledo appreciated the curing power of a curandera, although he knew that a priest should not be involved with folk medicine, and that such conduct, even if successful in effecting a cure, would be frowned on by his superiors. That is why in his petition to Governor Marín del Valle, Father Toledo would make no mention of the fact that during the three-year period during which El Cojo was said to be running the School for the Devil and causing harm to people through witchcraft, Toledo suffered from a serious illness he believed was also caused by witchcraft. In colonial New Mexico it was widely believed that witchcraft brought about many illnesses, and a dearth of information about the medical causes of diseases led the sick to seek help from the only medical practitioners: Indian (and sometimes Hispanic) curanderas.

To Spanish authorities curanderas were a contradiction. They offered a solution to the health problems of people in remote areas where doctors were unavailable, but their healing practices were squarely in the realm of superstition because they commonly involved the use of hallucinogens and ceremonies employing prayers and sacred relics. Spanish curanderas argued that they healed people "through the grace of God," while mestizos and Indians often involved their own religious practices in aid of a cure. When the use of herbs was intended to achieve magical ends like attracting people and becoming rich, then the practice was considered superstitious. The Inquisition prosecuted many curanderas, but few were severely punished unless they committed a second offense. After prosecuting numerous curanderos in Spain for relatively minor offenses, the Inquisition became more lenient. When it began to see that the curandera served an important function by healing through traditional medicine, the Holy Office ceased to prosecute individuals for the use of herbs alone.[18]

In the case of Antonia Luján, the curandera from San Juan Pueblo sought her out with the offer of riches and important friends. After she became ill, she "presumed she had been bewitched."[19] Luján's supposition was based on the general belief system of Hispanic New Mexicans of that time as well as the specific contact she had with Francisca Caza, the San Juan Indian. When Luján became so ill that she could not tolerate the pain and thought she was about to die, Francisca offered to cure her. Francisca then admitted she was the cause of Antonia's suffering and apparently took pity on her. As was true of the Abiquiu Genízara whom Governor Vélez Cachupín would tie to a gun-carriage wheel, the curandera causing the illness usually knew the herb that would effect a cure.[20] But generally in New Mexico, the use of herbs by itself did not result in severe punishment even when the purpose was to kill the victim.

The Inquisition in New Mexico and particularly its commissaries, or agents, were skeptical about charges of bewitchment through the use of herbs. This was due in part to the difficulty of sorting out who was telling the truth in witchcraft trials. In some cases, charges of witchcraft made against curanderos were determined to be entirely fabricated.[21] One such case, again handled by the criminal justice system of New Mexico, took place in Santa Fe in 1707.

Leonor Domínguez accused three Indian women from San Juan Pueblo of causing her severe illness through witchcraft. Doña Leonor, as she was called throughout the trial, informed Governor José Chacón Medina Salazar y

Villaseñor, the Marqués de Peñuela (1707–12), that she was suffering from severe maladies for which she had been given numerous remedies by "persons practiced and intelligent in medicine." Instead of curing her, however, these medicines worsened her condition. Leonor Domínguez told Governor Chacón that although she was a Catholic Christian and presumably had no direct contact with witches, she did know of several women who were witches and she was not shy about naming names. The reputed witches were San Juan Indians Catarina Luján, Angelina Puma-zho, and Catarina Rosa, wife of Zhiconqueto. Having established the existence of witchcraft and unleashing a barb against her sister-in-law María Luján as a known witch, Domínguez asked the governor to investigate her charges against the San Juan women.[22]

As Governor Chacón ordered, Alcalde Juan García de las Rivas appeared at doña Leonor's house on 13 May 1708 with a notary, where he found her in bed ill and suffering.[23] Her testimony provided only flimsy and unsubstantiated evidence against the accused. On Holy Thursday, as she was praying at the Santa Cruz de la Cañada church, Leonor Domínguez found the Indian Catarina Luján praying beside her. A little further off she saw Angelina Puma-zho, the wife of the painter, Zhiconqueto. There ensued a colloquy between the two that had an ominous ring in Domínguez's ears. Luján asked Angelina, "Is this the wife of Miguel Martín?" "Yes, it is," she replied. Without further warning, she heard Puma-zho say, "Now." Catarina quickly replied, "Not yet." Domínguez told the alcalde that she immediately moved away from Luján, and was terrified when she heard Puma-zho say, "It would be better now." Suddenly Angelina Puma-zho moved in close behind Domínguez and put her hand on doña Leonor's back near her heart. According to her testimony, Domínguez's entire body immediately began to itch and she claimed to be unable to lift her head ever since.[24]

On the strength of this testimony, Governor Chacón ordered Alcalde García de las Rivas to go to San Juan Pueblo and arrest the three Indian women Domínguez had accused: Catarina Luján, Angelina Puma-zho, and Catarina Rosa, wife of Zhiconqueto. Civil authorities handled the matter expeditiously as a criminal complaint without any Church involvement, a marked departure from the practice generally followed in eighteenth-century New Mexico.[25] Having moved so quickly to imprison the Indian women solely on Domínguez's word, Alcalde García de las Rivas began to have second thoughts. He wondered how it was possible for Leonor Domínguez to understand the San Juan Indians, who presumably were speaking their native Tewa language. Even if they were bilingual, he could not understand why they would have spoken Spanish within her earshot while plotting an attack on Domínguez. When the alcalde asked her about this the day after the arrest, she simply stated that they spoke Spanish and offered no further explanation.[26]

When the alcalde questioned the first two Indian women, both denied being in church on Holy Thursday but admitted attending church on Palm Sunday, when they saw Leonor Domínguez on that day. Most importantly, both Indians vehemently denied that any of the other events described by Domínguez had taken place. What did take place, according to Catarina Rosa, wife of Zhiconqueto, was that Domínguez was suffering from some malady in church, and Catarina Rosa had wanted to relieve her suffering.[27]

After collecting testimony, Leonor Domínguez's case seemed weak. Questions remained, however, and Governor Chacón appointed another official, Sergeant Major Juan de Ulibarrí, to complete the investigation.[28] Ulibarrí asked Domínguez for additional proof, and she named several more witnesses who she claimed would corroborate her story. Upon interrogation, however, these witnesses also contradicted her testimony. The only thing they agreed on was that Domínguez had told them the same story about the San Juan Indians that she told the Spanish civil authorities.[29]

The real motive for Domínguez's complaint, it appears, was that her husband was having sexual relations with the daughter of one of the Indian women. Leonor Domínguez was jealous and looking for a way to end the affair. Nobody disputed her illness, which gave her an excuse to blame it on the witchcraft of the two San Juan women, and the daughter who was her husband's mistress. When Ulibarrí questioned Domínguez, he asked her if she had heard any rumors about the defendants being witches. She replied that she had not known them to be witches, but presumed they were because the daughter was her husband's mistress.[30]

Leonor Domínguez assumed that her husband would have sexual relations with the Indian woman only if he was under some kind of love spell. There was a widespread belief in seventeenth- and eighteenth-century New Mexico in love spells, and numerous love potions were used to counteract such sorcery.[31] In another attempt to bolster her case, Domínguez added that there were real witches in San Juan, although she did not know their names. She knew this because San Juan Indians had bewitched her sister-in-law, María Luján (the wife of Sebastián Martín), and Agustina Romero, (the wife of Miguel Tenorio de Alba). Another Indian named Juanchillo, and his wife Chepa, had cured them.[32]

To track down this last bit of evidence, Ulibarrí went to San Juan and took a statement from Juanchillo and his wife. Juanchillo readily admitted curing Luján and Romero. Although he said he heard that a Spanish-speaking woman from San Juan had bewitched the two women, he and his wife had cured them with healing herbs and not through the use of dark arts. Asked whether he knew if Catarina Rosa or Catarina Luján had cast an evil spell on doña Leonor Domínguez, Juanchillo answered that he did not know. Nor did he know whether there were any "persons [at San Juan] who may bewitch or harm people."[33]

Juanchillo's testimony provided no incriminating evidence against the defendants, or much general information about witchcraft. In essence, Juanchillo admitted to being a curandero, a fact that failed to arouse any concern either on the part of Ulibarrí or Governor Chacón. Even when the Indian women themselves were questioned, their strong denials of the accusations seemed credible. Catarina Rosa suggested that most Spanish women believed that witchcraft brought on all illnesses. Ulibarrí must have believed her testimony, for he immediately freed Rosa and placed her in the house of Captain Antonio Isasi. Besides the veracity of Catarina's statement, Ulibarrí sympathized with her condition because she had "crippled legs and could not move herself with the weight of the irons with which she was confined."[34]

Ulibarrí forwarded the proceedings to Governor Chacón on 27 May 1708, and within days the governor rendered his decision. He noted that even the witnesses Domínguez named had failed to corroborate her story, calling her testimony "false, futile, and despicable." Accordingly, Governor Chacón released the three Indian women, declaring them innocent of having harmed Domínguez through witchcraft."[35]

The case of doña Leonor Domínguez and the San Juan Indians shows that New Mexico's judicial system could operate efficiently to expose false testimony against accused witches and achieve a just result. Much of the credit for the exoneration of the San Juan Indians rested with Juan de Ulibarrí. Before he replaced Alcalde García de las Rivas in the investigation, it was Domínguez's word against that of the three Indian women. Early in the eighteenth century the testimony of an Indian was not given as much weight as that of a Spaniard. Domínguez's elite status, evidenced by the honorific "doña," implied that her testimony carried more weight than that of the San Juan Indian women. In another situation the Indian women could easily have been convicted simply because they were from San Juan, a pueblo suspected of being a hotbed of witchcraft.[36]

Other witchcraft cases throughout New Mexico reveal a similar pattern. In the 1730s and 1740s in the greater El Paso area, the Holy Office prosecuted several women for practicing love magic, among other things. Micaela de Contreras was seen by witnesses to practice bilocation; that is, she could be in two places at once.[37] She was said to have rendered one fellow, a local merchant named Felipe de Aguado, impotent when he tried to perform sexually with anyone but Micaela. On various occasions Micaela took the form of a dog or a cat. Once she made a woman so ill that her brains began to come out through her nose. In another El Paso case, Beatriz de la Cabrera was denounced to the Inquisition because she had the power to make a man do whatever she wanted him to, even against his will.[38] Beatriz managed this feat through the use of an herb she baked into a cake made of wheat flour, and then gave to the unsuspecting man to eat.

Similar investigations took place in the northern part of the colony. In Santa Fe in 1734, María Domínguez was denounced to the Inquisition as a witch because she gave men intoxicating drinks made with peyote that caused them to be able to see the future.[39] In 1743 Getrudis Sánchez, the widow of Pedro Chávez, was accused of having used an herb to make fray Pedro Montaño of Isleta fall deeply in love with her.[40] In Santa Cruz de la Cañada in 1748, Magdalena Sánchez came to the attention of the Inquisition after she boasted that she knew how to make a man love a woman, even if she was not sufficiently beautiful.[41]

One of the last Inquisition cases in the region took place in San Elizario in 1800. Juana María Apodaca or Venegas was accused by numerous citizens of having performed what seemed to be almost miraculous cures when all the folk ministrations known to the people of the community had failed. In one celebrated case, La Cáliz (chalice, or bitter cup), as María Apodaca was more commonly known, cured both the mother-in-law and the wife of Bernardo Bustillos, a soldier in the presidial company of San Elizario.[42] Bustillos's wife, Elena Holguín, was suffering from a tumor on her knee and others in both breasts. After performing the cure, La Cáliz informed Bustillos that his wife had been bewitched but refused to inform on the witch.

In Monclova, Coahuila, and surrounding communities and haciendas, a serious witch hunt took place during the period 1748 to 1751.[43] In a number of respects, the outbreak of witchcraft there was similar to the events in Abiquiu a decade later, though it was different in other ways. The entire episode revolved around the discovery of a bag in the middle of a street in Monclova, which contained objects associated with love magic.[44] The bag belonged to a Spanish woman named María Inojosa (Hinojosa), who was responsible for most of the magic objects in the bag. Another woman identified as India Frigenia prepared others. The witchcraft at issue all related to various instances in which witches worked to control the love lives of men and women in the area around Coahuila, although some of the bewitchments were intended to cause death. The accused witches were said to have pacts with the Devil.[45] They utilized certain spaces for their activities that were known to all the accused, such as a meeting place outside Monclova, a nearby cave, and an old, dilapidated church.[46] Such locations were used as gathering places to meet Lucifer and to fly around the countryside.

The Holy Office probably became involved in the Monclova case because some of the principal accused witches were Spaniards. As a frontier region, Coahuila was ethnically diverse, a diversity reflected in the composition of the actors in the witch hunt in the region. There were twenty-seven individuals directly involved in witchcraft and eighty-one more who were related in some indirect way to the activities.[47] Most were women. Although the ethnic identity of a good number of those involved in the witch hunt is unknown, sufficient information exists to draw some conclusions. The single largest category was Tlaxcaltecans, but there were also other Indians, Spaniards, mulattos, and meztizos.[48] They ranged in age from eighteen to fifty. Most of those directly implicated in witchcraft activities were between twenty-eight and thirty-five years old.[49] The ethnic diversity of colonial Coahuila on evidence in this witch hunt is strikingly similar to Abiquiu. The cultural and racial mixing that took place in that environment is reminiscent of the Genízaro pueblo. It is also interesting to note that the response of the Inquisition in Coahuila was characterized by a certain restraint, as was the case with Governor Vélez Cachupín's response to the Abiquiu witch craze.

The sampling of witchcraft cases in New Mexico and beyond reveals how different the Abiquiu witchcraft case was from anything in New Mexico before or after. The Coahuila case was similar in that it took place in a similar frontier society, but none of these earlier cases would have prepared Father Toledo or Governor Vélez Cachupín for what was in store for them at the Abiquiu Genízaro pueblo.

Figure 12
Father Toledo whips Atole Caliente for disrupting his celebration of the mass. *Drawing by Glen Strock.*

CHAPTER SEVEN

The Witchcraft Proceedings

Phase One: El Cojo

I n July 1760 Father Juan José Toledo fired off the first of many petitions that exposed for the first time the shocking events that had been occurring at Abiquiu ever since he took over there in 1756. New Mexico at midcentury was a world polarized between Spaniards and Indians and their mutually exclusive worldviews. The Spaniards understood little of the indigenous worldview, rejecting most of it—except some healing and sorcery practices individual Spaniards found to be helpful. Likewise the Indians found most of the Spanish worldview objectionable because it held little room for an autonomous and prosperous indigenous population. Indians were to be exploited, and they resisted exploitation and forced Christianization with what may well have been their strongest weapons: sorcery and witchcraft.

With the Spanish and Indian belief systems being polar opposites, except for a common belief in magic and sorcery, it is no wonder that mid-eighteenth-century Abiquiu was ripe for an outbreak of witchcraft when Father Toledo arrived there.[1]

As the sole representative of Christianity in the Genízaro settlement where a variety of other belief systems prevailed, Toledo must have felt completely isolated at Abiquiu. He had the difficult task of converting diverse indigenous people and training them in the rites of Catholicism. A small group of Genízaro sorcerers who directly challenged his religious authority posed an even greater test for Father Toledo. These Genízaros were a blending of Hopis, Pueblos, Kiowas, Pawnees, Comanches, and other Plains Indians, all assembled in this remote settlement on the rim of Spanish hegemony in New Mexico.

Despite the magnitude of this challenge, Father Toledo initially thought he was up to the task. He had demonstrated his faith, courage, and physical endurance many times in his forty-one years: at Acoma, at Zuni, and at Picuris, and especially when he traveled to the Hopi villages to bring back a group of Hopis who eventually settled at Abiquiu. Yet in 1756 Father Toledo faced the biggest challenge of his life at a time of wrenching change in the Spanish-Pueblo world. The relationship between Spaniards and Pueblos had changed fundamentally since the 1680 Pueblo Revolt, one of the most successful indigenous uprisings ever staged against Spanish rule in the New World. It roughly coincided with other native rebellions in the Americas and changed the dynamics in New Mexico regarding the extent to which native belief systems could exist side by side with Spanish Catholicism. After the revolt, Pueblos were no longer required to pay tribute, submit for long periods to Spanish levies of forced labor, or abandon all vestiges of their ceremonies and belief systems. To be sure Spanish oppression of the Pueblos was slow to die out in eighteenth-century New Mexico, but by midcentury it was clear that there would be an accommodation by which Spaniards allowed some forms of Pueblo religious expression, and the Pueblos accepted at least the trappings of Christianity.[2]

During the first half of the eighteenth century the balance was still weighted toward Spanish oppression of the Pueblos. Usurpation of Pueblo land and water, repression of native ceremonies, and destruction of their kivas were still common occurrences. By midcentury, during the first administration of Governor Tomás Vélez Cachupín, the balance began to shift. This

was due to several factors. In lawsuits between Spaniards and Pueblos or
Genízaros, courts began to rule for the latter, and participation of the Pueblos
and Genízaros in alliances with the Spanish against the *indios bárbaros* (un-
Christianized nomadic Indians), gave the pueblos more leverage with the
Spaniards. Most important, Governor Vélez Cachupín began to recognize
indigenous rights. Vélez Cachupín recommended in a report to his successor, Governor Francisco Antonio Marín del Valle, that his policy of treating
the Pueblos well should be continued so that they might live comfortably
and contentedly.[3]

Governor Marín del Valle was less of an activist than his predecessor in
matters of frontier defense and with regard to religious conflict, so it was
unfortunate that Father Toledo directed his first complaint in the drawn-
out Abiquiu witchcraft proceedings to Marín del Valle. Father Toledo was
hoping for a sympathetic hearing because he badly needed help. As he told
it, a sect of Devil worshippers under the leadership of a powerful sorcerer
named Miguel Ontiveras, alias El Cojo (the Cripple), was thwarting his
attempts to convert the Abiquiu Genízaros. Father Toledo told Governor
Marín del Valle that Abiquiu witchcraft had become so notorious that it was
common knowledge to "those who live here [and] experience it [directly]
and [to] those who come to this place on business or for pleasure [who] confirm it according to what they observe."[4]

Father Toledo was not known for brevity in his writings. He admitted
as much at the beginning of his petition to Governor Marín del Valle when
he said, "To say much with few words is conceded to only a few."[5] Toledo's
lengthy petition tended to ramble, almost as if it was the text for a sermon,
but it contained several core charges centering on the Genízaro known as
El Cojo. Father Toledo told Governor Marín del Valle that "the entire pueblo
is complaining to the *teniente* [*alcalde*] Juan Trujillo about an Indian named
Miguel, El Cojo, and about the damages and deaths known to have origi-
nated with his explicit Pact with the Devil."[6]

The specifics of the witchcraft El Cojo allegedly performed constitute
a bizarre catalog of how the Abiquiu Genízaros settled their disputes with
one another. In most cases the methods used were sympathetic magic (sticking pins or thorns in an image of the victim), the Evil Eye, or causing the
victim to ingest poison or an herb causing illness or death. Father Toledo
placed all of El Cojo's conduct, as well as other non-Christian ceremonies
and observances, under the theologically accepted rubric of a Pact with the

Devil. This meant that Toledo and the other Franciscans considered legitimate Native American ceremonies that were also found at Abiquiu, to be Devil worship.

Very little is known about El Cojo, although one of the charges against him in the second phase of the witchcraft proceedings may shed some light on his nickname. El Cojo was the leader of a group of men from Abiquiu who formed a hunt society. The usual procedure was for the hunting party to surround the game and then slowly tighten the circle, so it was important that no one allow an animal to escape through his part of the circle. Before starting the hunt, El Cojo performed a ceremony to bring each member of the group success. After the ceremony each hunter received one lash from El Cojo as they were told the punishment to expect if they allowed an animal to escape. El Cojo informed each member of the party that if he let an animal get through his part of the circle, he would become lame.[7] Possibly El Cojo learned about this method of penalizing unlucky hunters when he allowed an animal to escape.[8]

El Cojo may have been following traditional Native American hunting ceremonies at times (similar to those Antonio, known as El Chimayó, practiced in Phase Two), but in the charges Father Toledo leveled, El Cojo was accused of numerous acts of witchcraft. Witchcraft existed in Abiquiu, as it did throughout New Mexico during the seventeenth and eighteenth centuries, alongside Native American spirituality and ceremonialism.[9] What confused Father Toledo and civil and ecclesiastic officials as well, was where to draw the line between witchcraft (unacceptable to both Church and State), and native belief systems that both religious and secular authorities were beginning to tolerate.

Father Toledo was quite specific in his many charges against El Cojo, although his side of the story is not presented in Phase One of the witchcraft proceedings. Toledo accused El Cojo of killing an Indian named Dionista by giving her a little piece of curd cheese (*un pedacillo de cuajada*). The cheese gave her a stomachache that soon became so painful that Dionista could not sleep. She suffered from continual thirst and internal burning, and her thirst continued no matter how much water she drank. Her symptoms quickly worsened, and soon Dionista died a horrible death from an illness similar to what other Pueblo members were experiencing at the time. Dionista's teeth became dark, she bled through her mouth and nose, and suffered the same symptom that Father Toledo endured, although he miraculously survived.

Her stomach became swollen and "so massive, that the body could not be held to be buried."[10]

As terrible as this description of Dionista's death is, it was not the whole story, since others were dying in the same way without being bewitched. Father Toledo ignored this minor plague in Abiquiu until the second phase of the witchcraft proceedings in 1763, although he mentioned the extent of the illness obliquely. In Phase One Father Toledo focused almost single-mindedly on his efforts and those of medicine men and curanderas from other indigenous groups to stop El Cojo. Perhaps because he feared the reaction of the Church to his own healing by a curandera, which he revealed in Phase Two, Father Toledo kept the emphasis on El Cojo and the deaths and injuries he allegedly caused.

On her deathbed, Dionista asked Father Toledo to give her the Last Rites and hear her confession. When she named El Cojo as the cause of her suffering, Toledo called two witnesses and the teniente alcalde so that she could repeat her story in their presence, but she died before the witnesses arrived. Although these officials were not able to get Dionista's statement in writing, Father Toledo took pains to name other Spaniards who had witnessed more awful events blamed on El Cojo. In addition, Father Toledo conducted his own investigation throughout the Abiquiu Genízaro pueblo, looking for other victims of El Cojo's malevolence.[11]

Toledo found an Indian who had hired El Cojo to kill his wife so that he could "enjoy his mistress more freely."[12] The wife became ill, but after a year and a half she still had not died. The husband finally felt sorry for his wife, for when El Cojo came to him offering to "finish her off," the husband instead went to Father Toledo with his story.[13] The priest heard his confession and made him ask forgiveness of his wife. The couple reconciled, and Father Toledo "placed the wife in peace with the husband."[14] This account shows how deeply Father Toledo was involved with what must be seen as a rivalry with El Cojo. Toledo had his hands full with his spiritual duties, including hearing confessions and performing other Church rites. He also apparently acted as a marriage counselor and mediator in serious domestic disputes as he looked after the social and spiritual well-being of the pueblo. This was normal for a parish priest in mid-eighteenth-century New Mexico, but Father Toledo's energies were taxed far beyond those of the average priest.[15]

Father Toledo confronted El Cojo on numerous occasions concerning the deaths and injuries charged against the Genízaro. On one occasion Toledo called El Cojo before the pueblo officials and victims who claimed to have been injured through his witchcraft. In the face of these complaints El Cojo finally admitted everything. According to Toledo, "El Cojo affirmed to me that said pact [with the Devil] was true."[16]

This so-called Pact with the Devil was central to the accusations against El Cojo. Father Toledo, like many priests of his day, was obsessed with the idea of the Devil's Pact. Toledo was a product of the late medieval Christian worldview that had been influenced as much by St. Thomas Aquinas as by Dante's *Divine Comedy*. Within this cosmology there was a clear division between virtue and vice, good and evil, light and darkness. Toledo and his fellow servants of God were on the side of virtue, good, and light and saw themselves as warriors against vice, evil, and darkness. God personified the light, and the Devil was the incarnation of darkness and evil. Priests such as Toledo, whose mission was to convert the Indians to Christianity, saw all indigenous beliefs as Devil worship. Accordingly, Toledo and his fellow evangelists found the Devil behind every rock and tree. From equating the Devil with native gods it was but a short step to seeing all practitioners of native religions as witches who had made a Pact with the Devil.[17]

The Devil was present from the time of the founding of New Mexico in the writings of the Franciscan priests and the secondhand testimony of Pueblos who habitually told their Spanish interrogators what they wanted to hear. Spaniards and Pueblos had the same answer to the question of why the Indians followed practices the Franciscans considered idolatrous or why they revolted in 1680. The answer was: the Devil made them do it.[18] The dramatic events described in these witchcraft documents show us the conditions of life in an eighteenth-century frontier community in a remote province of New Spain where two vastly different cultures and religions existed side by side. The isolation of New Mexico meant that its inhabitants were living in two worlds, influenced as much by the mind-set of late medieval Europe as by the Enlightenment.[19]

The demonic pact was present in witchcraft folklore and witchcraft trials from Europe to Salem, Massachusetts, whether Catholic or Protestant. It was fundamental to the Christian doctrine of heresy and witchcraft, implying an entire ritual of evil (including the Devil's Sabbath), antithetical to all the Church's teachings. Under rules for some witchcraft trials, involvement with the Devil was necessary to convict a defendant of witchcraft.[20] Such a concept was alien to native belief systems, and, as Marc Simmons has pointed out, "a strict division of the universe into opposing forces of good and evil was incomprehensible [to them]."[21] Neither Pueblos nor Plains Indians had a figure like the Devil in their myths.[22] In contrast, Native American religious worldviews tended to see all life forms as interconnected.[23] El Cojo probably told his questioners what they wanted to hear, especially about the Devil, as so often happened in the Salem trials and the idolatry proceedings in Spanish colonial Peru.[24]

Beyond making a Pact with the Devil, El Cojo was accused of running the School of the Devil (*escuela del Demonio*). News of the school emerged in an unusual way. An eight-year-old boy who worked at the mission as a door-keeper was overheard talking in his sleep about the school while napping before dinner. When he awoke and was told what he had said, he replied, "It was a lie that his uncle, El Cojo, taught him to harm people [in the school]."[25] The boy was brought before Father Toledo, who questioned him. The boy admitted attending meetings of the School of the Devil in a nearby cave, where he was shown images of people in the pueblo whom El Cojo wanted to harm and was told whom the images represented. Some of them had already died.

Father Toledo tried to correct the situation himself. He gathered the entire pueblo together with its officers and the witnesses and brought the eight year old before them. Again the boy denied everything. Toledo may have gotten the boy to confess to him privately, but in front of the entire pueblo, it was a different story. Other "students" in El Cojo's School of the Devil had also confessed to Father Toledo, asking to be pardoned because they had renounced their Pact with the Devil. In the case of the unnamed eight-year-old boy and El Cojo, however, Father Toledo had to resort to physical and spiritual coercion. Father Toledo asked the boy to show him the cave he had described in his confession. When the boy was evasive and refused to lead the priest to the place, Toledo whipped him, to no avail.

El Cojo's punishment for his recalcitrance was to be placed in the stocks until he agreed to forsake his Devil's Pact and turn over the power objects with which he performed his witchcraft. Although he promised to do so, each time he was released from the stocks he refused, saying that he was not the only sorcerer in the pueblo. El Cojo had been Christianized to the extent that Father Toledo had heard his confession and allowed him to take communion, but these rites were denied El Cojo after he appeared before the entire pueblo and admitted his diabolic pact. Father Toledo told Governor Marín del Valle that this spiritual punishment was in accordance with the laws of the Holy Councils of the Indies.[26]

Withdrawal of Church rites had little effect on El Cojo. If anything he seemed emboldened by his struggle with Father Toledo. Not only did he admit to being the main sorcerer in the pueblo, El Cojo also confessed to killing the Indian Dionista. The only excuse he gave was that others were guilty of similar acts. In particular, El Cojo named the Indian Vicente and his wife as the ones who had taken the life of Toledo's predecessor, fray Félix Ordóñez. Perhaps one reason for El Cojo's arrogance was his knowledge that Vicente and his wife were, at that very moment, trying to kill Father Toledo himself. Toledo may have known this too, which would explain his failure to mention his own illness. For a priest such as Toledo to admit that he was succumbing to witchcraft might be an admission that his spiritual power was no match for a sorcerer using diabolical power.[27] Father Toledo was clearly at his wit's end with Miguel, El Cojo, and said as much to Governor Marín del Valle: "I wrack my brains not being able to explain [the events] ... that are noted and observed with amazement in this pueblo."[28]

When Father Toledo's efforts alone were not enough to suppress or convert El Cojo, Toledo decided to consult the Utes for help. The Abiquiu settlers and the Utes had an uneasy relationship built primarily on trade and familial ties, although Ute raids on Spanish settlements continued intermittently. The Spanish government tried to regulate this trade by limiting it to the annual trade fairs held in late September and early October, but it was too profitable to stop all together. The Abiquiu settlers obtained dressed hides to sell in Chihuahua and Indian captives for the New Mexico market, and the Utes got highly prized Spanish horses, as well as foodstuffs such as corn and flour. Abiquiu officials were particularly lenient in their enforcement of the trade regulations, and some well-connected families like the Martín Serranos traded with the same Ute families year after year with impunity. As a side effect of their contact through trade, it was inevitable that Spanish settlers would also consult Ute curanderas when they needed herbs, expertise in healing, and even love potions.[29]

So it was that Father Toledo consulted a Ute curandera or medicine woman about the witchcraft in Abiquiu. Toledo stated that she told him that El Cojo was responsible for many of the deaths that had taken place in the pueblo over the past two years. The curandera offered to confront El Cojo in front of the Abiquiu Genízaros. Father Toledo arranged the confrontation, but once again El Cojo prevailed, this time with his power of the Evil Eye. "El Cojo looked at the Ute with very angry eyes [causing her to] return to her nearby home deathly ill, bleeding from her mouth and nose. Then she dropped dead."[30] Although the Ute curandera presumably had more power to withstand the Evil Eye than did the average Genízaro at Abiquiu, she was no match for El Cojo. Father Toledo put it in theological terms reminiscent of De la Peña Montenegro, "The Devil of El Cojo being more powerful ... [nevertheless] the Indian [the Ute curandera also] had a Pact with the Devil and [therefore] died in sin."[31]

This was a strange statement for Toledo to make; he had asked the Ute for help, and now she was a Devil worshipper. Father Toledo's ambivalence toward the Ute is apparent from his attempt to justify his having contacted the curandera in the first place. Since he had involved her in the confrontation with El Cojo, he must have felt somewhat responsible for her death. Father Toledo attempted to relieve himself of this responsibility, however, by citing De la Peña Montenegro's *Itinerario para párrocos de Indios*. Fray Juan José referred to this work frequently as he sought to justify his actions in dealing with witchcraft at Abiquiu.[32]

Bishop De la Peña Montenegro liberally sprinkled specific examples of witchcraft practices throughout his manual and cited a plethora of authorities. The detail of the examples in the *Itinerario* clarifies the Church's views on witchcraft, and the care with which guidance is provided to priests testifies to the seriousness of the problem of witchcraft in the Church's eyes throughout the Americas in the seventeenth and eighteenth centuries.[33] One section of the *Itinerario* lists four situations in which a priest may be called on to remove a curse and the proper methods for doing so. The most accepted method recommended was to rely on God, using the sacraments of confession, the Eucharist, and the Mass; prayer and fasting; or the power inherent in the Cross and the reliquaries of the saints. If that did not work, the priest could use exorcism to remove a sorcerer's curse. Father Toledo had tried the first method with El Cojo to no avail, and he had probably tried most of the others except exorcism. He eventually made extensive use of the rite of exorcism in Phase Three of the proceedings. The use of herbs and medicines was not recommended for removing a curse, not because they were bad in and of themselves, but because the Devil had the power to block their effect.[34]

De la Peña Montenegro suggested that if Church rites were ineffective, the parish priest might have to consult a sorcerer. If the sorcerer knew the cause of the bewitchment and was not afraid of the witch who brought it on, the priest could ally himself with the sorcerer. Otherwise it was a sin to proceed, for if the allied sorcerer was afraid, he would be forced to use witchcraft himself, which was unacceptable. Or the sorcerer might feel compelled to consult the Devil to find the cause of the bewitchment, which was also disapproved of by the Church.[35]

Father Toledo was attempting to walk a fine line in his description of the death of the Ute curandera and his application of the principles found in the *Itinerario*. Although it was generally not theologically correct for a priest to fight the power of one sorcerer with the help of another, De la Peña Montenegro provided an exception to this general rule. If a sorcerer knew how to cure a victim of bewitchment, he could be asked to remove the spell out of desperation when there was no proper or moral way to cure the victim. The *Itinerario* mentions several analogous situations in which a greater evil can be eliminated with the help of a lesser evil. If the sorcerer knew how to rid the victim of bewitchment, either through *maleficio* or without it, he might be asked to remove the spell. Then if the sorcerer used witchcraft or a Pact with the Devil, the priest was not to blame since the sorcerer himself chose to use illicit methods. These were cases where the end justified the means, where the hair-splitting distinctions would put a lawyer to shame, and where the priest would rather not know too much about the means.[36]

De la Peña Montenegro gave an example of the approved method of working with a sorcerer. His illustration involved the confession of a sorcerer who placed a curse on the victim. This occurred when a woman living in Quito was near death because she had been bewitched. The offending sorcerer confessed that he had caused the woman's pains by placing numerous thorns in a wax figure, presumably in her likeness. As each thorn was stuck in the statue, the woman suffered pain, but when the sorcerer removed the thorns in the woman's presence, she was completely cured. Because he knew how he had made her ill, the sorcerer knew how to cure her and was the best person to do it.[37]

Father Toledo must have realized he was on shaky ground in his alliance with the Ute curandera even with De la Peña Montenegro to back him up.[38] Toledo would appear weak in the eyes of the Genízaros and his Church ineffective were he incapable of doing what a superstitious curandera could do. Yet, the Ute curandera failed and lost her life in the process. Had she succeeded, Toledo would probably have been grateful to see the pueblo rid of the cause of so much misery. Because of the Ute curandera's failure, Father

Toledo elected to emphasize her sins, telling the governor that her devil was less powerful than El Cojo's.[39] Had the Ute curandera defeated El Cojo, it is unlikely that Father Toledo would have given the Devil the credit.[40]

Father Toledo had dealt with another curandero/medicine man when he was first assigned to Abiquiu in 1756. An Apache medicine man had been working at Abiquiu, trying to cure the illness that was spreading throughout the community. Unlike the nameless Ute curandera, the Apache was referred to as the son of El Canoso (the Gray-Headed One). Apparently he was a recognized healer who had met with some success in the past and had been summoned to help solve the problem of the illness in the pueblo. The son of El Canoso told Father Toledo that he was unable or unwilling to end the plague sweeping the pueblo because it was not caused by El Cojo alone. "A magic poisonous snake that El Cojo had, alive and concealed, was partially responsible."[41] This snake was as much to blame for the problems at Abiquiu as was El Cojo, according to the Apache medicine man. As El Cojo had so often said, he was not the only evil sorcerer.[42]

When he realized that the snake El Cojo and his followers worshipped might have caused much of the suffering at Abiquiu, Father Toledo treated the problem in the way the *Itinerario* advised priests to deal with any form of idolatry: destroy it. This was in accordance with Church doctrine and had the added advantage of helping Father Toledo acquire allies within the pueblo in his battle against the illness. Although most members of the pueblo feared the snake as well as El Cojo, the snake was less formidable. The Abiquiu Genízaros were finally able to kill the magic snake by attacking and beating it with sticks. They hung it up on a post, but it took an unusually long time to die.[43]

Soon Father Toledo realized that killing the magic snake had not cured the illnesses throughout the pueblo, so he again focused on El Cojo. In his report to Governor Marín del Valle, Toledo apparently felt the need to justify his involvement with the Apache medicine man and the magic snake, just as he had with the Ute curandera and the Evil Eye. Fray Juan José informed the governor that his actions concerning the magic snake were governed not only by De la Peña Montenegro's book but also by advice he had received from a priest named Father Mariano.[44] Father Mariano had apparently approved of several actions that Father Toledo took or planned to take beyond slaying the magic snake, including a form of torture by fire seen both as a punishment and a way of discovering what other means El Cojo used to accomplish his nefarious ends.

Father Toledo had more to contend with than magic, it seemed. He informed Governor Marín del Valle that the sorcerers in Abiquiu were using toads and other snakes in furtherance of their Devil's Pact. Once the pact was sealed, according to Father Toledo, "these animals respond to what is asked of the Devil."[45] Father Toledo realized that these matters might better be handled by the Inquisition, but he told Governor Marín del Valle that he had not filed a complaint with the Holy Office because though the snake had caused a lot of the harm, Toledo knew that the Inquisition could not proceed against a snake. Instead, said Toledo, "I have proceeded in the aforesaid matter with prudence, observing actions, notwithstanding that all the Indians recognize and admit that the snake is an evil thing."[46]

The snake was a potent symbol for both Christians and the indigenous inhabitants of the Americas. For Christians the serpent embodied evil as well as being an emissary for the Devil. In Genesis it is the serpent who convinces Eve to eat of the fruit of the tree of knowledge of good and evil and therefore is cursed by God "upon thy belly shalt thou go and dust shalt thou eat all the days of your life."[47] For indigenous peoples the snake was often a symbol of revitalization and rebirth due in part to the belief that when the snake shed its skin it was rejuvenated. In the Andes the snake represented *amaru*, "a destructive force erupting from beneath the earth in an attempt to recreate balance when relations of equilibrium were not maintained in the social and natural universe."[48] In the Pueblo world of New Mexico, the snake was also a fertility symbol found in petroglyphs and kiva mural art, especially in the Abiquiu area.[49]

The Hopi snake dance, in which the dancers carry live snakes, including rattlesnakes, in their mouths, could have some relation to the snake imagery at Abiquiu since so many Hopis came to Abiquiu. The elaborate Hopi snake dance, which is celebrated over several days, had counterparts at Zia and Laguna, although in these pueblos the snakes were carried in the hand rather than in the mouth. As with other Native American ceremonies, the Hopi snake dance is now largely secret and performed only for the Hopis.[50]

These differing interpretations of the snake as a symbol help explain the conflicts between Father Toledo and the Abiquiu Genízaros. Father Toledo's beliefs were governed by the biblical view of the serpent, whereas Native Americans of the southwest saw the snake as a complex symbol embodying both dark and light forces, like Quetzalcoatl, the protean plumed serpent of Mesoamerican mythology.[51] Father Toledo returned to El Cojo's magic snake over and over again in his first petition, but in the second phase of the witchcraft proceedings the snake is barely mentioned. Undoubtedly, the meaning of the snake for the Abiquiu Genízaros was closer to Quetzalcoatl and a fertility symbol than to the biblical serpent.[52]

Faced with magical snakes and El Cojo's School for the Devil, Father Toledo knew he needed help. His enemy, in what seemed to him as an epic battle between Good and Evil, was all pervasive, using animals and other sorcerers as allies and eliminating the priest's potential allies (other priests, sorcerers, and governors of the Genízaro pueblo). When Father Toledo tried to enlist the assistance of sorcerers or curanderos he was again thwarted by the powerful sorcerer, El Cojo. So Father Toledo decided to use someone within the Genízaro pueblo to ferret out other sorcerers. Father Toledo authorized a Genízaro named Joaquinillo to act as El Descubridor (the Discoverer, or Finder), what in modern parlance would be an informer. As he would today, Joaquinillo probably received some form of leniency, for Joaquinillo was also a sorcerer.

Joaquinillo, El Descubridor, promised Father Toledo that he would capture El Cojo either as a human sorcerer or as a cat. Apparently other members of the pueblo had seen El Cojo running around the pueblo at midnight in the form of either a dog or a cat. One time when El Cojo was seen in the form of a dog, some of the Genízaros realized it was not an ordinary dog and shot at it with arrows but were unable to hit the animal form of El Cojo.

Father Toledo knew that his position with Governor Marín del Valle was tenuous because the primary thrust of his petition was to obtain the governor's permission to torture El Cojo. Father Toledo had already put El Cojo in the stocks and administered lashings, but he then suggested subjecting El Cojo to more public whippings to induce him to reveal the instruments he used in his sorcery. Failing that, Toledo sought permission for a more severe punishment: that El Cojo be tied to a stake over a fire until he confessed. Father Mariano had reluctantly approved this ultimate measure, saying that it would be a new experience for him even though he had been a priest of the Indians and the Spaniards for many years, as well as serving as commissary of the Holy Office (the Inquisition). This recommendation seems to refer to something short of a full-scale witch burning, more like holding El Cojo's feet to the fire and depriving him of water until he confessed. Either way, Father Toledo was talking about torture. Fortunately for Miguel, El Cojo, Toledo's recommendation of torture by fire was not carried out.[53]

In his response to Father Toledo's petition, Governor Marín del Valle barely mentioned El Cojo, saying only that Father Toledo should continue his investigation and send any prisoners suspected of witchcraft to Santa Fe with Alcalde Nicolás Ortiz. Instead of being tortured, El Cojo was to be placed in shackles and imprisoned in the Santa Fe jail. In the Third Phase of the witchcraft proceedings, Governor Vélez Cachupín used a relatively mild form of torture on the Genízara María Trujillo to learn the particulars of Father Toledo's latest affliction—how it was done and how it could be cured. In 1760, however, it was clear that Governor Marín del Valle wanted nothing to do with Father Toledo's problems with the witches of Abiquiu.

Toledo's ambivalence, frustration, and doubt reflected his lack of knowledge of what was really going on with the Abiquiu Genízaros. He did not know that it was not El Cojo who had caused the stomach affliction from which Toledo suffered; rather, sorcerers barely mentioned in his 1760 petition had brought it on Vicente Trujillo and his wife, María. Neither did Father Toledo know that the methods the couple used against him were similar to the ones Toledo had so graphically described previously: sticking pins in dolls resembling the priest and putting unwholesome matter in his food. Most of all, Father Toledo was unaware that not all the unfamiliar practices at the Abiquiu Genízaro pueblo were witchcraft. Some were legitimate Native American curing and religious ceremonials that the priest did not comprehend, even though Father Mariano told him that not all sorcerers used poisonous herbs. Some knew how to heal with roots and herbs; they were curanderos/medicine men. Toledo was blinded to the true significance of the events at Abiquiu because he had little basis for understanding these Indians beyond guidebooks such as De la Peña Montenegro's *Itinerario* treatise. In contrast to priests in central New Spain and Peru, who studied the language and belief systems of the Aztec, Maya, and Inca peoples, De la Peña Montenegro had never been to New Mexico or met a Genízaro or Pueblo Indian. Often Father Toledo's day-to-day experience conflicted with the rather limited view of indigenous people found in the *Itinerario*, a conflict that increased the longer Father Toledo stayed at Abiquiu.[54]

In De la Peña Montenegro's view, all native religious practice was superstition and idolatry. Native religious leaders were sorcerers and must be given the choice of abandoning their own religion and following Christianity or being branded a sorcerer. Unwilling to forego their traditional beliefs, many native practitioners adopted a defiant stance toward priests such as Toledo, using witchcraft as a means of resistance.[55] Faced with open defiance and outright attack, Father Toledo's frustration led him to propose the radical alternative of torture as a method of learning the truth from El Cojo. His failure to see clearly the meaning of the events at Abiquiu meant he may have suggested the wrong person to be tortured by fire. It was not El Cojo, but Vicente Trujillo and his wife, María, who were responsible for the greatest number of deaths by witchcraft in Abiquiu. Indeed, they were trying to kill Father Toledo by putting various herbs in his food, crafting a doll that resembled him, and sticking pins in it. Although there are hints in the first phase of the witchcraft proceedings of Vicente and María Trujillo's involvement in witchcraft, it is not until the second phase that the full story begins to emerge about them and other sorcerers in Abiquiu.

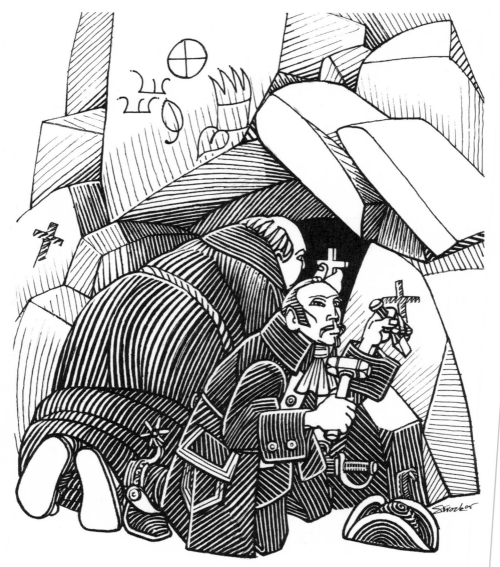

Figure 13
Petroglyphs on a cave near Abiquiu exorcised by Father Toledo and Alcalde Carlos Fernández.
Drawing by Glen Strock.

CHAPTER EIGHT

The Witchcraft Proceedings

Phase Two: Joaquinillo, El Descubridor

The witchcraft proceedings that started with fray Juan José Toledo's lengthy petition to Governor Marín del Valle of July 1760 languished for three years before an investigation began. There was no real inquiry after Father Toledo's convoluted petition, although he had been led to believe that Governor Marín del Valle had taken some interest in the matter. The Abiquiu Genízaros had complained to Alcalde Juan Trujillo a few years before Father Toledo's 1760 complaint, and Alcalde Trujillo had contacted Marín del Valle directly. The governor had suggested that Toledo conduct an investigation, take corrective measures, and if that failed, summarize the matter in a report. When Governor Marín del Valle received Toledo's 1760 report, however, he simply ordered Alcalde Nicolás

Ortiz to go to the pueblo and give Father Toledo all the help he needed. This dismissive reply was not what Father Toledo had hoped for: he wanted Indians such as El Cojo, punished more severely so that all vestiges of witchcraft could be eradicated from the Genízaro pueblo. Whether Alcalde Ortiz ever went to Abiquiu to help Father Toledo with his witchcraft problems during the three years between Phase One and Phase Two of the witchcraft proceedings is doubtful. In any case, nothing seems to have changed during that period.

Then, in April 1763, a woman from the Genízaro pueblo complained to Alcalde Juan Pablo Martín that she was ill because an Abiquiu Genízaro named Joaquinillo had bewitched her. Thus began Phase Two of the witchcraft proceedings. The alcaldes and eventually the governor finally began to take Toledo's complaints seriously and commenced an investigation into his charges. The emphasis shifted, however, so that instead of centering on El Cojo, the investigation broadened to include every suspected sorcerer and witch in Abiquiu and beyond. Instead of focusing on the School of the Devil and the Devil's Pact, attention was devoted to the mechanics of how each instance of witchcraft was accomplished. Accusations included stories of love magic; sorcerers turning into cats, dogs, and owls; and one who tried to fly to the Cerro Pedernal in the shape of a woodpecker. Although El Cojo was still involved, there were so many other charges of witchcraft that the investigation soon turned into a witch hunt, reminiscent of Salem, Massachusetts, in 1692, as a series of charges and countercharges through the criminal justice system of New Mexico spun out of control.[1]

When Alcalde Martín questioned Joaquinillo as a result of the unnamed Genízara's complaint, Joaquinillo first pointed his finger at Antonio Menchero of Sandia Pueblo, saying that he could prove Menchero was a sorcerer with the help of Juan Largo of Santa Ana Pueblo, who happened to be his brother. Alcalde Martín summoned Juan Largo and Joaquinillo to appear before him (together with Father Toledo and two witnesses), and the two brothers became the chief investigators or informers charged with naming other sorcerers in the pueblo; Joaquinillo was the lead informer.

One of the first sorcerers named was someone Father Toledo had not previously mentioned, Agustín Tagle. Agustín was said to be the most powerful sorcerer of all because he "followed the Laws of Montezuma and never went to confession or communion."[2] When Agustín denied engaging in witchcraft, Juan Largo suddenly grabbed his hand and, using a practice common to medicine men, he sucked out of the man's palm a small piece of iron wrapped in buckskin. Agustín denied that the iron was his, but Juan Largo said that Agustín's heart was as hard as that iron and for that reason he was feared in the pueblo and was able to recruit many followers. As Alcalde Martín looked on, Juan Largo then announced that Agustín wore colored beads on his wrist to give him luck. Largo said Agustín wore two blue beads to give him luck at gambling and two green ones so he would be lucky at love. When the alcalde examined Agustín's wrist he found the beads, just as Juan Largo had said, and confiscated them.[3]

Plains Indians in Abiquiu probably considered the use of these colored beads a harmless form of love magic rather than sorcery.[4] The Inquisition did not consider the use of love magic to be that serious either, although several seventeenth-century New Mexico cases reported on activities concerning the attraction of both love and riches. In Spain and in New Mexico this fell into the category of superstition, which was not as serious as idolatry and resulted in relatively mild punishment by the Inquisition, or no punishment at all. The piece of iron wrapped in buckskin, however, was definitely a different matter.[5]

Alcalde Martín then revealed the other sorcerers who had been responsible for the wave of witchcraft at Abiquiu: Miguel, El Cojo, and Vicente Trujillo. For the first time it became clear that El Cojo was not the only sorcerer, as he had said throughout the first phase of the investigation. El Cojo had already confessed to Father Toledo, and in Alcalde Martín's presence he confessed again, admitting that he had learned his art in his homeland in Pawnee country, but he denied that he had ever bewitched anyone. This was too much for Joaquinillo to stomach, and he challenged El Cojo to display his power. When El Cojo said he had lost it, Joaquinillo sucked a heart-shaped flint from El Cojo's back, which Joaquinillo said El Cojo used to bewitch people. As with Agustín's piece of metal wrapped in buckskin, this was undoubtedly similar to the bundle that many sorcerers carried under their clothes, and the sucking performed by El Descubridor was similar to Apache and Navajo shooting sorcery. The closeness between witches and curanderas or medicine men is seen in the sucking cure of the medicine man who sucks out of the victim's body what the witch has sent into it.[6]

In the face of this concrete evidence that El Cojo was a sorcerer, El Cojo sought to shift attention to someone else. Cojo named Pedro Trujillo as a sorcerer who had bewitched people in the form of a cat. Joaquinillo named four people whom Trujillo had bewitched, including Joaquinillo's brother, Vicente, and Vicente's wife, María. Having completed his investigation, Alcalde Martín ordered that all the new people named be arrested and brought before him for questioning.

At this point, Alcalde Carlos Fernández started carrying out the investigation since the Abiquiu Genízaros requested that he, rather than Alcalde Martín, investigate the witchcraft that was beginning to be uncovered. Apparently the Genízaros of Abiquiu were more comfortable testifying in front of Alcalde Fernández, who, as one of the governor's most trusted officials, played a major role in the entire witchcraft proceedings. As alcalde of Santa Cruz de la Cañada, Fernández was further removed from the pueblo than was Alcalde Martín and perhaps for that reason a more detached observer.

Before Fernández began his investigation he took custody of the three main sorcerers, El Cojo, Agustín Tagle, and Vicente Trujillo, and sent them to Governor Vélez Cachupín in Santa Fe to be incarcerated. With this triumvirate out of action, details began to emerge of another level of witchcraft. Women were the primary actors, and herbs the primary means employed, indicating that some of what was going on in Abiquiu was not witchcraft but healing by curanderas. In addition, more information began to surface about the victims of El Cojo, Agustín, and Vicente Trujillo and how they were killed or injured. With the three most powerful sorcerers in jail in Santa Fe, there was less fear of retaliation and less concern that knowledge of witchcraft activities would brand the informant as a witch.[7]

Phase Two of the witchcraft proceedings contains Alcalde Fernández's matter-of-fact account of all the victims of Abiquiu witchcraft and a description of the methods the sorcerers used to harm them. The alcalde seemed completely detached from the horrific details he recounted. As he listed the names of the victims in the text of his report, Fernández often kept track in the margin of the numbers of victims each sorcerer killed: for example, "Agustín, El Viejo, five killed by this defendant."[8]

The Genízaros' trust of Alcalde Fernández is evident from the detailed information he was able to elicit from the accused sorcerers and their victims. In addition to placing tallies of victims in the margin of his report, Fernández gleaned more details about the sorcerers' methods, which indicate a shamanic belief system independent of the acknowledged sorcery occurring at Abiquiu. In a particularly intriguing passage, Alcalde Fernández learned from Joaquinillo, El Descubridor, that Agustín Tagle, El Viejo, was the most dangerous sorcerer. He described a cave where Agustín and his followers met, including the drawings on the wall of the cave. In the margin of his report, Fernández reproduced the drawings as he spelled out his interpretation of them.

The cave drawings that Alcalde Fernández reproduced in the margin of his report contained symbols reminiscent of Aztec motifs at Teotihuacán and other sites in central Mexico; some of these motifs are also present in New Mexico petroglyphs. As the alcalde described it, the circle divided into four parts was the world held by the Devil and his lords. The Devil was offering the world and all that was in it, including the four winds, to those who would give him their hearts. Included in this cave drawing, which probably still exists somewhere in the Abiquiu vicinity, are symbols meant to protect the images on the cave wall. This is how Alcalde Carlos Fernández interpreted the images he found in the cave and on the side of a nearby rock face, but they were probably rock art representations the Spaniards did not understand. It is difficult to know exactly what appeared to Alcalde Fernández, Father Toledo, and the others because they looked at what seemed to them strange images smacking of witchcraft. It is known that the circle divided into four parts was a common image in the Southwest and in Mesoamerica.[9] In Aztec belief systems the four-part circle represented the underworld: Tlalocan. It was the land of darkness, with each of the four sides connected to one of the four directions. "The image had decorated the Mexican world since the time of Teotihuacan ... in ancient codices and on crumbling temple walls." The association of the sorcerer Agustín with "the laws of Montezuma" makes this similarity between these two symbols even more compelling.[10]

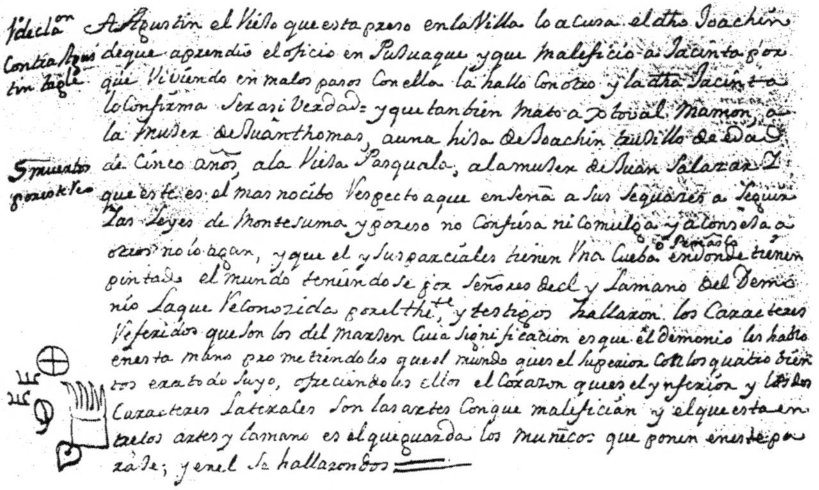

Ydecla.on Contra Agustin Ingle.

Agustin el Viejo que esta preso en la Villa lo acusa el dho Joachin de que aprendio el oficio en Pusuaque y que malefició a Jacinto por que viviendo en malos pasos con ella la hallo con otro y la dha Jacinta lo confirma ser asi verdad = y que tanbien mato a Xptoval Mamon, a la muger de Juan thomas, auna hija de Joachin Trujillo de edad de cinco años, ala Vieja Pasquala, ala muger de Juan Salazar Y que este es el mas nocibo respecto a que enseña a sus sequaces a seguir las leyes de Montesuma y por eso no confiesa ni comulga y a los demas a otros no lo agan, y que el y sus parciales tienen una cueba o peñasco en donde tienen pintado el mundo teniendose por señores del y llamano del Demonio la que reconozida por el the.te y testigos hallaron los caracteres referidos que son los del margen cuia significacion es que el demonio les habla en esta mano prometiendoles que el mundo que es el superior con los quatro vientos estara suyo, ofreciendoles ellos el Corazon que es el ynfierno y los dos caracteres laterales son las artes con que malefician y el que esta entre las artes y llamano es el que guarda los muñecos que ponen en este paraje; y en el se hallaron dos =

5 muertos

Figure 14
Notation by Alcalde Carlos Fernández in the margin of his report depicting the drawings/pictographs. ***Courtesy of Bancroft Library, Berkeley, California.***

Several of the practices Alcalde Fernández described as witchcraft involved folk medicine, not witchcraft.[11] Some materials used in those activities appear to have been benign indigenous ceremonial objects, such as an arrow with eagle feathers. The difference between the picture of Abiquiu that Father Toledo painted in Phase One and the picture that emerged from Fernández's investigation is striking. A description of belief systems different from Christian Catholicism began to form in Phase Two and is more completely described in Phase Three. Father Toledo, by contrast, considered every practice other than Church-sanctioned ritual as Devil worship. Toledo believed that the witchcraft problem at Abiquiu was the fault of El Cojo's School of the Devil and of Satan himself, in sharp contrast to the picture painted as a result of Fernández's investigation.

On 30 April 1763 Alcalde Fernández began to interrogate the Genízara Paula, beginning a long series of statements and confessions by the Genízaros recorded in front of a witness. Each statement yielded specific information about individual sorcerers and acts of witchcraft they were alleged to have performed. As new suspects were named, Fernández questioned them, and they in turn accused others of being witches. Joaquinillo, El Descubridor, aided the alcalde. Joaquinillo was a Kiowa whom

Comanches had captured and then sold to a Spaniard in Taos. He became part of the Genízaro settlement of Abiquiu, and when he was accused of witchcraft on 6 April 1763, he agreed to help the alcalde identify all the other witches. By this means Joaquinillo received special treatment. In Phase Three of the witchcraft proceedings, he named numerous witches, many from other pueblos.[12]

Paula was one of the most helpful of all the witnesses Fernández queried. She was fifteen years old when her own parents died, and she was placed in the home of Vicente Trujillo and his wife María Tagle, two of the most powerful sorcerers in Abiquiu. With Trujillo in jail in Santa Fe, Paula may have felt more secure about describing witchcraft practices going on in Abiquiu and naming the witches engaged in them, especially Vicente Trujillo. Although much of what she described seems to fall into the category of witchcraft rather than native religious practices, it must be remembered that everything was reported through the eyes of Spaniards who were being told what they wanted to hear.[13]

A good example of the blurred line between Native American spirituality and actual witchcraft is Paula's description of some of the activities that took place in the cave mentioned earlier. When Vicente and María took Paula to the cave for the first time (possibly the same cave where El Cojo conducted his School for the Devil), she was greeted by various animals, including snakes and toads. Paula was told to remove the cross from around her neck and kiss the snakes and toads and then enter through a circular opening so she could learn to fly. She turned into a woodpecker and tried three times to fly to the Cerro del Pedernal. Each time she was unable to do so because her arms and legs became tired, causing her great pain. Then the animals turned into Indian men and a Spaniard. When asked to kiss the snakes and toads again on the mouth, she became afraid and started to praise the Holy Sacrament. This relapse into Christian beliefs and sacraments caused Vicente and his wife great pain, and they started howling and ordered Paula not to mention God or the Virgin Mary, but she persisted. Vicente and María were so angered that they threw her out of the cave and the next day made her leave their house.[14]

This fantastic story has some counterparts in the testimony in the Basque witchcraft trials the Spanish Inquisition conducted in the early seventeenth century. There accused witches confessed to using an ointment made from toads that allowed them to fly to the Witches' Sabbath.

Figure 15
Part of the community of Abiquiu looking west from Abiquiu mesa with the Cerro del Pedernal in the distance. *Photograph by Malcolm Ebright.*

These confessed witches were asked whether it was necessary to anoint themselves with flying ointment to go to the Sabbath. Most responded that it was and even provided a recipe for the ointment.[15] One wonders whether there was a connection between Paula's experience of flying toward the Pedernal and kissing toads. Shapeshifting, or nagualism, as found in Aztec religion, was a common theme in most native religions. The god Tezcatlipoca (or Smoking Mirror) was famed for his ability to assume the form of a wide variety of animals. In present-day Huichol culture, shamans who can take the form of spirit animals with whom they have formed special relationships are considered to have reached "an exalted level of shamanic completion."[16]

Juan Largo and Isabel, La Pastora, leveled other accusations of shapeshifting at Vicente (Paula's erstwhile teacher). Isabel stated that she saw Vicente in the form of an owl, and Juan Largo saw him in the form of an unidentified animal from the waist up. Other Abiquiu Genízaros were said to have assumed the shape of a dog. Juan Tagle had an owl's claw he used for doing evil, and he was accused of killing Felipe Roybal's wife with such an owl's claw.[17] There is a long tradition, especially in New Mexico, of witches assuming the shape of a *tecolote*, or owl.[18]

Vicente Trujillo and his wife were also said to be responsible for the death of fray Félix Ordóñez, the first priest assigned to the Abiquiu Genízaro mission. Ordóñez left his post under suspicious circumstances and died soon afterward at Laguna Pueblo.[19] It had been rumored that witchcraft caused his death, and Paula's statement corroborated that rumor. Paula said that Trujillo and his wife María killed Father Ordóñez by witchcraft. Later, another María, El Cojo's wife, confirmed that accusation, stating that her husband had told her that Trujillo and his wife killed the Franciscan. Joaquinillo, El Descubridor, also corroborated this testimony.[20]

Paula added seventeen more names to the list of victims of Vicente's witchcraft and five more victims of Vicente and his wife. Accordingly, Alcalde Fernández noted in the margin of Paula's testimony that Vicente had caused twenty-two deaths. After this list of individuals killed by witchcraft, Paula named those who had been made ill but had not yet died. This list included only two names, but it was the most important information revealed so far in the investigation. First on the list was Miguel Luján, "who is alive although ill," followed by "the father minister fray Juan José Toledo." Almost offhandedly, Paula disclosed that Vicente Trujillo and his wife María had caused all of Father Toledo's suffering by "putting various herbs in his food and forming a doll that resembled him." Most sinister of all, the couple was reported to have said that they would eventually kill the priest.[21]

Vicente Trujillo may have borne a grudge against Father Toledo for having shoved him to the ground. This incident and a general resistance against Christianization probably account for Trujillo's antipathy toward Father Toledo. Most of those Trujillo and his wife killed, however, were Abiquiu Genízaros. Many of these acts are inexplicable as either native ceremonialism or resistance to Christianization and can only be ascribed to witchcraft. As details began to emerge of how the victims died, the use of herbs, hallucinogens, and poisons explained many of the deaths.[22]

More benign practices that Alcalde Fernández's investigation uncovered, although condemned by the Inquisition, were what has been termed love (or erotic) magic.[23] These were rituals and procedures used to attract members of the opposite sex to make husbands or wives hate their spouses and desire the person invoking the amorous spell. These practices were condemned because of their misuse of the sacred liturgy, as well as their invocation of the Devil and lesser evil spirits. In Abiquiu, Trujillo's wife María was accused of engaging in a ritual involving fire and making signs with smoke through the use of a rag. María's accuser, Isabel, La Pastora, interpreted the rituals as signifying that a "man shall hate his wife and have no pleasure with her, but only have pleasure with María's client."[24]

Other instances of love magic among the Abiquiu Genízaros involved Agustín Tagle, one of the most powerful sorcerers. Tagle wore blue and green beads on his wrist to make him lucky at gambling and love. Alcalde Juan Pablo Martín examined Tagle, found the beads, and confiscated them. Diego Tagle used an owl's claw as a charm for making women fall in love with him, and Diego's brother, Juan, used peyote for the same purpose. Joaquinillo, El Descubridor, singled out Pedro, El Paseño (meaning from El Paso), for using a kennel of corn wrapped in a cloth along with some peyote, to make women fall in love with him and to help him run faster.[25]

These accusations of using witchcraft to cast love spells were relatively harmless when compared to the charges of causing intentional deaths and illness, although fatalities and illnesses were often inflicted on the third member of a love triangle. The use of love magic was common in seventeenth-century New Mexico and was one of the chief accusations the Inquisition investigated. Many Spanish soldier-citizens were unfaithful to their wives, who often resorted to love potions acquired from their Indian servants to win back their husbands' affection and loyalty. When the Inquisition was reinstated in New Mexico in 1631, the Franciscans informed the population that such practices were banned. Father Esteban Perea, the new commissary of the Holy Office, took testimony from fifty people concerning love magic and similar practices, but most of the accusations regarding love potions were not taken seriously or acted on.[26] Among the love charms described was a paste made of certain herbs or of maize that was either put in the husband's food or rubbed on his body, causing his love to be renewed toward his wife. If applied during sexual intercourse, this anointing of the body was said to be even more effective. Other recipes for love potions involved a certain kind of worm that was either fried or mashed up and cooked in a kind of gruel. Other potions and powders of various kinds were also used.[27]

In Spain, testimony before the Inquisition regarding love magic revealed three kinds of procedures, usually performed by women: divination procedures to learn the intentions of the beloved person; procedures with an underlying erotic content to attract the desired one and achieve sexual intercourse with him; and chants and invocation of spirits to appease a suitor and regain his love. The chants and rituals reveal that the women who invoked them usually wanted more than the ability to attract a lover; they wanted total control over their beloved's will for they needed "masculine support at all costs so as not to be socially devalued." Nevertheless, as in the Abiquiu witchcraft trial, the authorities did not take seriously the charges of engaging in love magic, for even in the most egregious cases, the defendants' penalties were usually limited to whipping and sometimes to exile.[28]

By the mid-eighteenth century, the Inquisition was even less interested in punishing the use of love magic; nor was it interested in demonic possession, which formed the core of the third phase of the witchcraft proceedings.[29] This helps explain why many of the accused Abiquiu sorcerers received such light sentences at the conclusion of the proceedings. Sentencing the confessed Abiquiu witches rested entirely in the hands of Governor Vélez Cachupín, a pragmatic military man, who wanted the Genízaro pueblo to remain as a buffer against attacks from hostile Indians.

As Alcalde Fernández took down the testimony of the Abiquiu Genízaros, more surprising revelations surfaced, often with the assistance of Joaquinillo, El Descubridor. One of the most intriguing statements came from Antonio Ulibarrí, a former teniente alcalde. He stated that when he was alcalde he punished Vicente Trujillo for some offense, and to get revenge Vicente hexed him. Ulibarrí spent two years ill in bed as a result. His wife also became ill and was "still alive, but very ill and still under his [Vicente's] spell."[30] A different Antonio Ulibarrí was imprisoned with the other sorcerers and was one of those who "died of illness during their imprisonment."

Fernández's investigation revealed numerous instances of sucking to reveal a witch or to cure the victim of witchcraft. Sorcerers were also able to shoot objects, such as bits of wood, pebbles, beads, small arrowheads, and strands of hair, over great distances into the body of victims who would become ill after being struck. The shooting was either carried out by means of a tube, or the objects were placed on a cloth or piece of buckskin and made to travel through the air by incantation. The objects were propelled at such great speeds that they were said to be invisible. The special cure for this type of witchcraft was sucking out the object that the sorcerer had shot into his victim.[31]

This kind of sorcery was much in evidence during the Abiquiu witch-craft trials. María Salvia Trujillo testified that when she was ill in bed in extreme pain, Isabel, La Pastora offered to cure her. La Pastora sucked var-ious things from María's temples, but said she did not get everything out. She told María to have her husband there when she came back the next day to complete the cure. The following day, La Pastora, holding an arrow with eagle feathers in her hand, sucked out more things from María. La Pastora showed María everything she had extracted except what she took from the crown of her head. That object, a small white stone, she swal-lowed, making many grimaces and gestures, thus healing the patient. El Descubridor then placed Isabel, La Pastora next to a tub of water and after performing certain ceremonies, sucked out from La Pastora the small white stone she had removed from María.

In a series of declarations against Vicente Trujillo, Prudencia Trujillo said that when she became ill, not knowing the cause, she asked Juan Largo to cure her. Largo, one of the sorcerers who seems to have escaped pun-ishment, sucked out a number of small shells and pieces of hair from Prudencia's body. Largo told her to leave these items in front of Vicente's house: if Vicente were the sorcerer who caused her illness, he would become ill. It was commonly believed that articles a sorcerer used to bewitch some-one could also be used to determine who the sorcerer was. This seems to have worked in the case of Vicente, who became ill when the items taken from Prudencia's body were placed at his doorstep.[32]

Belief in witchcraft was so pervasive in seventeenth- and eighteenth-century New Mexico that when someone became ill and did not get well, witchcraft was immediately suspected.[33] The belief in witchcraft was a pop-ular folk tradition, and to the extent that it involved a Pact with the Devil, it also became a tenet of the Catholic Church. Father Toledo pointed this out in his next report to Governor Vélez Cachupín. This report came at the conclusion of the marathon series of declarations in which one sor-cerer after another confessed to some of the charges against him and then pointed his finger at another sorcerer. This series of charges and coun-tercharges revealed that the witchcraft conspiracy was far deeper and wider in the Abiquiu Genízaro community than Father Toledo had indicated in his initial petition of 26 July 1760.[34]

With all the declarations completed, Alcalde Fernández asked Father Toledo to report on the proceedings to clarify and aid in the understanding

of these strange events. Toledo's report was to be attached to the file delivered to Governor Vélez Cachupín. True to form, Father Toledo's report was
verbose, disorganized, and in sharp contrast to Governor Vélez Cachupín's
tightly organized and practical style. Whereas Toledo was abstract and theological, Vélez Cachupín was concrete and pragmatic. Father Toledo, who perhaps felt guilty because he had not been able to deal with the witchcraft
outbreak himself, tended toward a theological approach to problems at
Abiquiu that were, in the end, his responsibility.[35]

Father Toledo began his report with characteristic self-deprecation,
saying that he would respond to Fernández's request "in my limited ability and lack of words to explain the many things that happen in this
pueblo." He proceeded with a lengthy theological discussion of witchcraft
from a priest's perspective, with few specific details about the Abiquiu sorcerers.[36] Toledo described sorcery as the power to do evil to others with
the aid of the Devil. Sorcerers, according to Toledo, made a Pact with the
Devil, worshipped him, and gave him their souls. As he did in his first petition, Toledo emphasized the Devil's Pact and described some of the Devil's
attributes, adding some illustrations from recent cases. First, Toledo tack-
led the old theological debate on the nature of evil. He stated that the Devil
acted only with the permission of God and did not represent a force of
evil independent of God. This followed the teachings of the early
Christian theologians, particularly St. Augustine. According to these
thinkers, God allows the Devil to do evil either to punish us or to aid us
in reforming our lives.[37] Toledo alluded specifically to Job, who was tested
when God allowed the Devil to visit innumerable hardships upon him to
see if Job would keep his faith and remain a devout Christian.[38] Father
Toledo himself was suffering from the effects of a witchcraft attack and
must have wondered whether God was permitting these attacks to punish or reform him. Toledo became much less orthodox in his Catholic views
and more tolerant of Native American beliefs near the end of his tenure
as resident priest at the Abiquiu Genízaro pueblo. Perhaps he was being
tested himself and would be found to be flexible enough to embody the
new syncretism that would include both native beliefs and traditional
Catholic beliefs under one spiritual worldview.[39]

Father Toledo noted that while most witchcraft was accomplished with
the aid of the Devil, Satan did not have the power to change sorcerers into
animals, "rather with their [the sorcerers'] artifices they do *appear* as

domestic animals, most of the time as cats."[40] To illustrate his point, Toledo alluded to the recent case of Joaquín Mestas, who was able to capture an animal that was apparently attacking him inside his house. Mestas killed and burned the animal and the next day "in the bosque of San Juan when the sun came up, there was a certain Indian dead and singed."[41]

Father Toledo believed that the Devil was responsible for the entire outbreak of witchcraft at Abiquiu and saw himself in direct combat with Satan, who he characterized as unhappy that the Christian faith was taking root at the pueblo. It is unclear how effective Toledo had been in Christianizing the Genízaros, but it appears that some form of native ceremonialism, such as the Turtle Dance, was still being practiced at the pueblo. Father Toledo did his best to justify his effectiveness in the face of mounting evidence to the contrary.

As an illustration of how the Devil was impeding his work, Toledo reported that when he traveled to someone's house to hear their confession, he would suffer terrible pains in his feet so that he could barely walk, an affliction he attributed to the Devil. He could only make the trip with the help of his parishioners, "who, by the force of their supporting me with their hands on my chest and back, gave me the will to arrive." When he finished hearing the confession and returned to the Genízaro pueblo, his pains ceased. What Toledo attributed to the Devil, however, could just as likely have been the result of witchcraft that one of the Abiquiu sorcerers practiced on the priest. Although Father Toledo was willing to blame the problems facing the Abiquiu Genízaro pueblo on the Devil, he was reluctant to name a specific Genízaro who might be attacking him through witchcraft, until someone admitted doing just that.[42]

One of Toledo's strongest demonstrations that the Devil was working through the Abiquiu witches and sorcerers was an incident involving Father Manuel Sopeña and Vicente Trujillo that took place during the time that Father Ordóñez, Toledo's predecessor, was at the pueblo. When Father Sopeña and Father Miguel Campos were at the pueblo on other business, a delegation from the pueblo of Abiquiu headed by Vicente Trujillo, the pueblo governor, including two other Indians, visited Toledo and the other two priests. Trujillo told the priests that they should leave the pueblo immediately and that in any case the Genízaros would not respond if the priests summoned them. Vicente's demand was so unexpected and was delivered with "such daring [and] boldness that the prudence and gray hair of Father Sopeña prevented him from answering," and he was unable to speak.[43] The shock to Father Sopeña was so great that within twenty-four hours "he fell dead so suddenly that when [Toledo] lifted his head from the ground, he was already dead."[44] Toledo blamed the Devil, for only a man imbued with the Devil would show such disrespect to these priests, and he considered it obvious that Trujillo intended to take Father Sopeña's life. It does seem certain that the Abiquiu Genízaros were resisting Christianization even before Toledo arrived and that Father Félix Ordóñez's death, about the time Father Toledo assumed his duties at Abiquiu, was part of this pattern of resistance.

Resistance to Christianization and unwillingness to surrender their traditional belief system moved other Indians to attack the Catholic clergy in New Mexico and throughout the Southwest. In New Mexico such attacks, often resulting in the death of the priest, were more frequent before the Pueblo Revolt. In California, attacks on the missions and attempts to poison the Franciscan priests there continued into the late eighteenth-and early nineteenth-centuries.[45] In a kind of circular self-fulfilling prophecy, the Franciscans viewed native religious ceremonies as witchcraft, and the Indians used witchcraft against the Franciscans as a form of resistance to Christianization. Father Toledo and his Franciscan brethren saw activities that were part of Native American religious ceremonies as witchcraft because they involved what they called idolatry: the veneration of non-Christian symbols. One example involved Antonio Ulibarrí, El Chimayó, and his use of bird feathers in a hunting ceremony.

Father Toledo reported that he intercepted Antonio "very oddly adorned with many feathers of eagles, hawks, *gernicalo*, magpies, and other unknown birds, which he worshipped and had others worship when he went with them to hunt."[46] El Chimayó was engaged in a hunting ritual that was common to Plains Indians and Pueblos. The ritual included a sacrifice involving rain and was connected to an upcoming deer hunt. Antonio, El Chimayó, was the hunt chief using his shamanic powers to bring the deer to the hunters. El Chimayó told Toledo how he used eagle and magpie feathers to aid him in the hunt. Antonio, El Chimayó, gave Father Toledo two of each kind of feather, explaining that he used the eagle feathers to create an atmosphere in which the deer would be trapped, and the magpie feathers to "advise him where the deer are," since the magpie lives off meat.[47]

Father Toledo was given eagle and magpie feathers and told of their use in hunting rituals, which surely smacked of paganism to him. Doubtless more disturbing was El Chimayó's statement of how he would bring the deer back to the hunters. Antonio advised the other hunters "not to shoot the one that came on point as a guide," implying that *he* had become that lead deer.[48] In a manner similar to the idolatry trials in Mesoamerica and the Andes, Antonio, El Chimayó, did not admit to shapeshifting, but instead told Father Toledo what he wanted to hear, or the priest interpreted what he heard to mean that "the Devil would take that form [the deer] because the said Antonio could not transform into [a deer]."[49]

From Father Toledo's description it is apparent that Antonio, El Chimayó, was engaged in a hunting ritual not unlike the rituals of other Plains Indians, who made up a sizable portion of the Genízaros at the pueblo of Santo Tomás Apóstol de Abiquiú. This was not witchcraft but native ceremonialism at the core of the indigenous worldview, which was challenged by Catholic doctrine. The contrast between these two world-views is immense. In the indigenous view human beings are connected to everything, especially to animals. Because of this interconnectedness all animals were considered sacred. By contrast, the Church demonized animals that Indians worshipped, especially snakes, wolves, coyotes, and so forth, viewing them as manifestations of the Devil.

The usual form of communal hunting of Plains Indians involved a cooperative effort to drive a herd of deer into a brush corral where they could be shot with arrows, sometimes with poison tips, or to ambush the deer as they were driven along a narrow trail. In either case, the hunters divided the important functions of driver and bowman. Key to the success of such a hunt was the hunt chief-shaman, who was expert in bringing the deer to the point where the herders could begin their job.[50] Among the Western Shoshone the shaman "acquired the power to capture the antelope's souls through dreams, songs, and other ritual activities, charming the animals into the center of the corral."[51] Among the Washoe the leader of the hunting party was "an admired hunter or one who had dreamed of deer."[52] The pattern of reliance on medicine persons and ritual processes when engaged in communal hunting was widespread among the Northern Plains Indians.[53] This shamanic tradition of the hunt chief is not unlike what Father Toledo described for Antonio, El Chimayó. The connection with native spirituality is reinforced by rock art found in the Great Basin where Paiutes and some Utes resided. There petroglyphs often occurred at sites "propitious for game-taking: at points where animals coming to drink could be ambushed . . . [or] along game trails over which animals moved during migrations or in changing foraging grounds."[54] By making these petroglyphs, hunters hoped to acquire the power of the animal and to predict their whereabouts.

Although Father Toledo revealed much new information in his 6 May 1763 report, there was much he did not disclose. Toledo was trying to provide a single explanation that would cover the entire witch craze in Abiquiu up to that point and lead to a resolution that Governor Vélez Cachupín could put into effect. In contrast to his 1760 petition to Governor Marín del Valle which singled out Miguel, El Cojo, as the leader of the School of the Devil, in 1763 Toledo named more names. He could hardly do otherwise, having just sat through numerous Genízaro declarations and confessions made to Alcalde Carlos Fernández.[55]

Father Toledo said that the Devil had revealed those who were in league with other demons, as sorcerers: Vicente Trujillo and his wife, María; Agustín Tagle, and his sons, Diego and Juan Tagle; and Miguel, El Cojo. Antonio, El Chimayó, was not listed among the sorcerers the Devil named, but his earlier mention was sufficient to cause his arrest and imprisonment. Even though Toledo was suffering the effects of Vicente and María Trujillo's attacks on him revealed by Paula's testimony, he was at first silent about his own afflictions. A week later, however, Toledo would file another declaration in which he finally mentioned the large ball growing in his stomach (or intestines), the result of Vicente and María's witchcraft. Once Father Toledo had named the main sorcerers, it was a simple matter for Governor Vélez Cachupín to arrest and imprison them, as he did. Vélez Cachupín also made an independent assessment about who the most powerful witches were. Later lists prepared by the governor included La Come Gallinas and Isabel, La Pastora, names not on Toledo's first list.[56] Vélez Cachupín later released from jail Juan Largo, against whom witchcraft allegations were made, as well as Vicente Trujillo and El Cojo, without punishment other than time served and the restriction that they never return to Abiquiu.

Father Toledo was not content with his 6 May 1763 report and followed it with another long report on 15 May 1763. This rambling document veered between long theological discourses liberally sprinkled with biblical references, to graphic descriptions of the physical ailments Father Toledo had been suffering. It must have been extremely confusing to Governor Vélez Cachupín as he tried to understand just what the good father was recommending. The document reads more like a sermon than a report, but it adds some important information to earlier documents. Father Toledo took as his text the biblical story of the field of wheat being invaded by a weed called the bearded darnel. The weed was a metaphor for the idolaters at Abiquiu. The weed and the sorcerers both needed to be extirpated, according to Father Toledo. But the moral question St. Jerome had posed and Toledo made relevant to Abiquiu was whether to punish all the suspected sorcerers in the Genízaro pueblo before charges were proven against them, as a good gardener would "pull out [the weeds in his field before they can spread], making room for the wheat to grow more healthily."[57] The alternative—to wait until charges could be proven against all the suspected sorcerers—is what Father Toledo had been doing all along, and the results had been disastrous.

Father Toledo mentioned idolatry trials in Mesoamerica and the Andes that Franciscans had carried out, and he suggested to Vélez Cachupín that Genízaro idolatry was so pervasive at Abiquiu that all suspected idolaters must be vigorously extirpated. Furthermore, Father Toledo said that he and the governor were the ones to do it: "Indeed, your honor, with your permission and your pleasure, we, said servants of the Divine Father of families, shall pull the weeds out."[58] Of course, this was not to be. As much as Father Toledo visualized himself as single-handedly leading a battle against the Devil, the conditions in New Mexico in the mid-eighteenth century were radically different from the mid-sixteenth-century Yucatán of Bishop Landa or the late seventeenth-century Peru of the Andean idolatry trials.[59] For one thing, the Pueblo Revolt had altered the balance of power between Spaniards and Indians, leading to an accommodation that allowed the continued practice of native ceremonies alongside Catholic religious observances.[60] Moreover, Governor Vélez Cachupín was not about to give the Franciscans the power to conduct an idolatry trial just when he had succeeded in curbing them. The governor handled the matter himself, in his characteristically hands-on manner.

Even if an idolatry trial had been the way to rid Abiquiu of witchcraft, Father Toledo was not the man to lead the effort. Toledo had failed to control the witchcraft outbreak that had been simmering ever since he moved to Abiquiu in 1755. He had tried to get Governor Marín del Valle to authorize the burning of El Cojo at the stake or the threat to do so. He had attended the interrogations by Alcaldes Martín and Fernández of the wider circle of sorcerers, who were now confessing to more serious charges than Toledo had imagined in 1760. Now he suggested to Governor Vélez Cachupín that *he* was the man to lead an even more extensive and militant investigation into every corner of the Genízaro pueblo, where Toledo suspected more sorcerers were hiding. Actually Toledo was ambivalent about the next stage of the witchcraft proceedings because he was unwilling to assume responsibility for his failure to achieve the complete Christianization of the Genízaro pueblo (implying that it was Vélez Cachupín's responsibility). Even though he was still suffering the effects of the witchcraft attack on his own person, Toledo implied that he alone understood the nature of the sorcery the Genízaros practiced. Yet he was powerless to stop it when it was directed at him.[61]

Fellow Franciscans shared fray Juan José's dilemma, because their worldview did not include an understanding of the indigenous people they were trying to convert.

> The Franciscans were convinced that their labours would be aided by God himself. They lacked all recognition of the profound and systematic otherness of others [the Indians]. They had no sense of the intricate interrelationships between different aspects of Indian life, rather seeing here the hand of the Devil, there the tender intervention of Christ, and so they could have no sense of the difficulties in the way of the reception and understanding of their message.[62]

Vélez Cachupín, in contrast, had a much deeper understanding of Pueblos, Genízaros, and nomadic Indian groups gained through direct contact with them. He fought them in the field, parlayed and made agreements with them, and even took some into the Palace of the Governors to live with him.[63] It is revealing to compare the different responses of Father Toledo and Governor Vélez Cachupín to the charge that Toledo was suffering from a witchcraft attack brought about by Vicente Trujillo and María. Where Toledo went into vivid detail about his illness and pondered the abstract question of which devil was aiding the witches, Vélez Cachupín simply arrested them when he learned that it was María who had hexed Father Toledo, and later he took extreme measures to induce María to confess.[64]

In his 15 May 1763 report Father Toledo fully revealed for the first time the afflictions he had been suffering as a result of the witchcraft of Vicente and María. The illness began on 30 July 1757 at one o'clock in the afternoon when Father Toledo began to cough and choke. He was suffering from what he described as dropsy of the phlegm and fully expected to die. Father Toledo began to feel a moveable ball growing in his belly that caused him great pain. His suffering continued for years until late December 1760 when the pain increased until, as he told Vélez Cachupín, he was beset with unimaginable pain that nearly killed him. Toledo took medicine to alleviate the pain, but it did not work, and the pain increased. Having suffered with this affliction for more than three years, Toledo was at the end of his rope. On the last day of December 1760, when those assisting him had all gone to sleep, something close to a miracle occurred. "A woman appeared before me dressed as a Spaniard, lying on the side of my bed, hiding her face from me."[65] She was a curandera who began to help Father Toledo by massaging him so that he was finally able to expel the ball, to his great relief.

At this point Father Toledo's health improved, but soon his stomach began to swell again, and another ball began to form. This time Father Toledo contacted a different curandera from outside the pueblo of Abiquiu who also massaged him and gave him herbs, including *estafiate*.[66] Again the ball, which the curandera told him was coagulated phlegm, disappeared. Father Toledo continued to suffer, however, from choking, coughing, and a great heaviness in his legs. He also developed an eye problem, which he did not discuss in any detail. As with his 1760 petition, there was still much that Father Toledo did not reveal.[67]

Father Toledo demonstrated great fortitude and courage as he continued his spiritual duties, even as he was suffering from these horrible afflictions. As a Franciscan he was bound to adhere to the practice of self-abnegation characteristic of "the largest order in Spain, and arguably the most vigorous."[68] The virtues of poverty, humility, and simplicity were encouraged for the Franciscans through a life of celibacy, fasting, and prayer. Beyond the strictures of the Rule, Father Toledo suffered afflictions of the flesh inflicted by the Abiquiu Genízaro sorcerers, an additional burden not visited on most other priests. Yet he did not complain. In fact, he seemed eager to take on the new challenge of leading a wider witchcraft investigation at Abiquiu.

Although courageous, Father Toledo was also confused about the cause and remedy for the Abiquiu witch craze in general and for the attack visited on him in particular. In his 1760 petition Toledo made only passing reference to his afflictions, stating in a marginal notation, "I had a swollen belly for such a long time, with a great loss of appetite."[69] Yet, by 20 July 1760, the date of Father Toledo's first petition, it had been three years almost to the day that his afflictions began. Toledo knew that one of the Abiquiu Genízaro sorcerers was assailing him, but in 1760 he thought it was El Cojo. Toledo believed that if El Cojo could be induced to break his Pact with the Devil, the priest's illness would be cured. By May 1763, however, Toledo realized that it was Vicente and María who were causing his afflictions.

Instead of focusing on what caused his illness, Father Toledo speculated as to which devil had a pact with Vicente and María. Toledo determined, after studying his Bible carefully, that the devil aligned with Vicente and María was Asmodeus, whom Toledo called "the prince of injustice, the third from Lucifer down."[70] Asmodeus is mentioned only once in the Bible and is thus a rather obscure devil, yet Father Toledo felt it was important to identify him. By his emphasis on the Devil or on lesser devils, Toledo revealed his limited understanding of the Abiquiu Genízaros and of Pueblo Indians in general. Toledo was blinded to the possible motives of a Genízaro such as Vicente Trujillo (who was once governor of the Genízaro pueblo) for attacking him. Father Toledo could not fathom that such a personal attack could be an act of resistance. This mind-set meant that the efforts of Father Toledo and other priests like him had only limited success in converting Indians, a situation that existed throughout the Americas.[71]

Governor Vélez Cachupín was not interested in the name of the devil with whom Vicente and María had a pact. He was a pragmatist concerned about the agent María used to cause Toledo's illness, while Father Toledo was more interested in finding justification for consulting a curandera who he believed could cure him. According to De la Peña Montenegro, it was permissible to consult a curandera only if she was not afraid of the sorcerer who bewitched the victim and thought she could remove the curse. If the devil with whom Vicente had a pact was less powerful than Satan, it was more likely that a curandera would be unafraid of him and willing to attempt to cure Father Toledo.[72]

Fray Juan José closed his 15 May 1763 report with a sustained diatribe against Vicente, whom he now believed to be his sole tormentor. Toledo reported that when two old women came to him and reported they were dying because of a curse Vicente had placed on them, Father Toledo had the two confess in front of the entire pueblo, revealing that Vicente and his wife were the cause of their illnesses. Father Toledo began to exorcise the two women to rid them of Vicente's curse, but when this seemed ineffective, the Franciscan terminated the exorcism and told the women to file a complaint with the civil justice. This so angered Vicente that, having taken the form of a wolf, he attacked Father Toledo as the priest was returning from hearing confession. The ensuing description of the encounter vividly depicts the priest and Vicente in the form of a wolf struggling in a life or death battle:

> He arrived in a small swirling of dust (and apparently turned into a wolf). He attacked me, and I stopped him many times with my hands. He fought with great force, punches, and bites, although I kept him down [and] remained firmer in the saddle, holding on to the mane between both ears.[73]

Father Toledo hit his head on a branch and lost consciousness. He was caught in the stirrups, as his horse fell with him to the ground. When he came to, he and the horse were able to get up. Whether Vicente was aided by Satan or Asmodeus is unclear, but Governor Vélez Cachupín did not take this fantastic story of Vicente's shapeshifting and attacking Toledo

very seriously, for the incident was never mentioned again in the ensuing reports. From the proceedings that took place in Phase Four, it seems
clear that the governor and other priests whom he asked for advice considered Toledo's reports unreliable, not only because of his rambling style
and content, but also because of the outlandish nature of the events he
related. The more fantastic the events described, the more the priest's credibility was called into question.

As a postscript, Father Toledo noted that he had just heard Gregorio
Trujillo's confession. Trujillo had been named to escort the last group of
sorcerers arrested by Alcalde Fernández to Santa Fe, either to be imprisoned or placed in the houses of Spaniards as servants. Included in the group
were Juana Pacheco and Vicente Trujillo's wife, María. María later was placed
in José Maldonado's house where she again tried to bewitch Father Toledo,
but now she and Juana Pacheco attempted to bewitch their escort,
Gregorio Trujillo. It seems that María was one of the boldest of all the
accused, having no scruples about trying to bewitch anyone she considered an enemy. In this particular incident, however, it is unclear whether
witchcraft, food poisoning, or a combination of the two, was involved. As
Father Toledo told it, the prisoners and their escort stopped on the road
to eat and Gregorio Trujillo was given a piece of tortilla and some cooked
meat. When he returned to the Genízaro pueblo, Trujillo became so ill with
choking and vomiting that Father Toledo thought he would soon die.[74]

Fray Juan José's description of the cause of Gregorio's bewitching is
confusing, partly because of Toledo's style and partly because the story
came from Trujillo's confession.[75] Toledo noted that María and Juana
Pacheco also ate some meat and tortilla, so the food itself was not the cause
of Trujillo's illness. Father Toledo revealed that when vomiting, Trujillo
failed to disgorge a small rock from an anthill (*piedracita de hormiguero*).
Apparently Trujillo was aware of the practices of witchcraft and knew that
such a stone could bewitch him and that one of these small rocks had been
given him in the tortilla with a piece of meat. That Gregorio Trujillo was
connected to the sorcerers of Abiquiu and was the enemy of Vicente and
María is suggested by the fact that Gregorio's daughter had been
bewitched by Vicente and Pedro Trujillo, El Paseño.[76]

This episode also reveals the power of the confessional in Father
Toledo's war against the witches of Abiquiu. Through the confessions
of the victims of the Abiquiu sorcerers, Toledo learned the methods the

sorcerers used to injure and eventually kill them. This, taken with the declarations that Alcalde Fernández recorded, helped Toledo learn the methods that Vicente and María used to attack him. The information from the confessions was not kept secret, however, as Toledo was bound to do. This was one of the things that angered Vicente when he attacked Father Toledo in the form of a wolf. Beyond that, the confessions had the effect of wiping away the Indian identities of the Abiquiu Genízaros and, since their Christianization was failing to take effect, giving them nothing with which to replace their old identities. This helps explain why there was such a hysterical reaction in the third phase of witchcraft proceedings—similar to what happened in 1692–93 in Salem—and why neither Governor Vélez Cachupín nor the Inquisition in Mexico City wanted anything to do with the numerous cases of demonic possession that Father Toledo reported during the 1763 Christmas season.

Toledo's worldview dealt obsessively with the Devil; all the evils he described came from Satan. As Toledo put it, the Devil's great power in Abiquiu was well known. Beyond that, Father Toledo longed to do battle with the Devil in order to uproot the idolatrous practices he saw overrunning the Abiquiu Genízaro pueblo like weeds in an untended garden. Toledo saw his challenge as a direct confrontation with Satan:

> Judges must engage the Devil man-to-man to take from his bloody claws so many souls and deprive Him of the ancient worship that many of these sorcerers offer Him. [Those who confront the Devil] must have ardor in their breast and on occasion know how to convert themselves into a flaming volcano. Spiritual resolve, rectitude, faithfulness, prudence, impartiality, skill, and knowledge are the weapons for so arduous an enterprise. An undertaking such as the present one is a field and material for many feats. What began as a battle will thus be a triumph of great difficulty.[77]

Even after his long bout with the afflictions that Vicente and his wife visited upon him, Father Toledo was not only willing but also eager for the opportunity to go head-to-head with the Devil. Toledo got his chance.

In Phase Three of the witchcraft proceedings the Devil possessed a group of Abiquiu Genízaros who called on Father Toledo to exorcise them. This was the most extraordinary part of the Abiquiu witch craze.

Vélez Cachupín thought he had halted the witchcraft outbreak in Abiquiu, but as Phase Three of the proceedings shows, the Devil was still lurking in the austere hills and arroyos of Abiquiu. Father Toledo got his wish to confront the Devil, and Governor Vélez Cachupín tried to mediate between a priest, who some thought had lost his mind, and the feared Inquisition. Both governor and priest faced the greatest challenge of their respective careers and the embodiment of that challenge was the Devil.[78]

Figure 16
The Devil hiding in the bushes. *Drawing by Glen Strock.*

CHAPTER NINE

The Devil

When Father Juan José Toledo sat down in January 1764 to write a report to the governor of New Mexico about the strange doings that had taxed his energies for a month during the past Christmas season, he knew that he had been involved in a battle with the Devil. Toledo recounted a story of demonic possession and exorcism, an epic spiritual combat of good versus evil, and a contest between belief systems. Father Toledo explained to Governor Vélez Cachupín why he could not avoid this conflict: "I am at a loss how to begin my own declaration, for it [contains] a contest with the Devil [*el Demonio*], from which, as a minister of God, I cannot excuse myself. It is within my jurisdiction and at my doorstep."[1] Father Toledo saw this as his personal challenge, a battle with the Devil within the framework of the conversion of the Indians to Christianity. Since native religion was seen as Devil worship, stamping out native belief systems meant interposing the power of the Catholic Church against the power of the Devil. The Devil Toledo was dealing with was a somewhat different entity from the

Devil encountered by the first Franciscan missionaries in the Americas. The Devil Father Toledo encountered in Abiquiu inhabited the same philosophical territory as did the Genízaros: the no-man's-land called nepantla, the middle ground.

The Devil, or Satan, made his first appearance in the New Testament gospels written in the first century B.C.E. Early Christians used the concept of the Devil, the personification of evil, to demonize competing religions and religious ideas. As Elaine Pagels points out:

> Because Christians as they read the gospels have characteristically identified themselves with the disciples, for some two thousand years they have also identified their opponents, whether Jews, pagans, or heretics, with forces of evil, and so with Satan.[2]

In the New World the Franciscans' opponents were native religious leaders, who they considered devils, and their indigenous ceremonies, which they considered to be acts of Devil worshipping.

Early Christian thinkers such as St. Augustine of Hippo and St. Thomas Aquinas saw the Devil as subordinate to God's will, without the power to make men sin against their will. Under this way of thinking, in contrast to the biblical view of Satan, evil had no independent existence.[3] The so-called problem of evil resulted in these contradictory perspectives, but during the Abiquiu witchcraft proceedings the latter view prevailed. Father Toledo and Governor Vélez Cachupín were careful to point out that the many forms of witchcraft they encountered occurred with God's permission. This was the central viewpoint of the famous 1486 witch-hunting handbook, the *Malleus Maleficarum*, by Heinrich Kramer and James Sprenger. Pope Innocent VIII commissioned Dominicans Kramer and Sprenger as Inquisitors to hunt and punish witches in northern Germany. The 1484 papal bull making those appointments implied the papal approval of the *Malleus Maleficarum*. Although it is unclear whether there were copies of this book in seventeenth- and eighteenth-century New Mexico, the work probably influenced Bishop De la Peña Montenegro's *Itinerario*, which contains many of the same ideas as the *Malleus Maleficarum*.[4]

When it came to witch hunting and witchcraft trials, the *Malleus Maleficarum* was "the ultimate, irrefutable, unarguable authority" for nearly three centuries.[5] This explains the importance of part I of the *Malleus Maleficarum*, which treated "of the three necessary concomitants of witchcraft, which are the evil, a witch, and permission of almighty God."[6] After a long discussion of the arguments on both sides of these theological questions, the two Dominicans held that not to believe in witches, the Devil, or the permission of almighty God "manifestly savours of heresy."[7] This is why God's permission for the existence of sin, evil, and witchcraft is often mentioned in the Abiquiu witchcraft proceedings.

The extent of the Devil's participation in native beliefs and religious practices was the subject of heated debate in sixteenth-century Spain between theologians Bartolomé de las Casas and Juan Ginés de Sepúlveda. Las Casas argued that the Indians were basically good and could become Christians through persuasion and patience. Sepúlveda saw the Indians as evil by nature and their religious practices as superstition or worse—as Devil worship.[8] Other theologians, such as the Jesuit missionary José de Acosta in Peru, viewed native beliefs as idolatry and wrote that "the cause of idolatry has been the pride and envy of the Devil."[9] Acosta noted that native Andean religious practices had a diabolical origin and that honoring idols was the same as honoring the Devil.

In the early 1500s, priests in the Americas looked for similarities between Christian and indigenous beliefs with the idea of converting the Indians through gentle persuasion, allowing them to keep much of their own belief systems. Hard-liners such as Acosta won the debate about the best method of converting the Indians, dwelling on the role of the Devil in manipulating the native religious practitioner. Acosta thought the Indians "received instruction from Satan himself." In Acosta's writings about the Devil and Andean religion, "one can feel the heat of the fire, smell the smoke, and savor the brimstone."[10] If the Devil inspired native religion, the Franciscans had no choice but to wipe out that religion.

In Peru and in Mexico other theologians studied the Inca and Aztec religions with the explicit goal of eradicating these belief systems so that Christianity could supplant them. The Jesuit José Pablo de Arriaga wrote a manual to be used by priests in the extirpation of Andean religious beliefs. Arriaga used the term "hechicero" as a generic name applied to all religious practitioners even though a hechicero was usually considered a sorcerer who caused harm through maleficio. In the extirpation trials that followed in Peru, no distinction was made between those charged with *hechicería maléfica,* or witchcraft, and those charged with the practice of indigenous religious beliefs through the worship of the Andean gods. Thus evidence of one activity was often used to convict individual defendants of the other.[11] The confusing use of the term hechicero to define all religious specialists in Peru meant that the sorcerer was confused with the shaman, the healer, and the indigenous priest, and all of these beneficent occupations were associated with the Devil. Christian theologians were skeptical of the powers of native priests, believing that the effects attributed to these practitioners (bringing rain, locating water sources, defeating one's enemies) were illusions. In the same way sorcerers were seen as lying tricksters who were not able to heal or bring the rain but only created the illusion of doing so with the Devil's help.[12] This ambivalence about the Devil's power, which mirrored the theological debate over the existence of evil in a world created by a benevolent God, placed the Devil at center stage.[13] Whether the effects or the beliefs were credible, they were all the Devil's work, and whatever power the religious specialist or sorcerer had was due to his Devil's Pact. Thus Arriaga's manual, which was used to interrogate suspected sorcerers, contained the important and frequently asked question, "Have you spoken to the Devil, and in what form did he appear?"[14]

In New Spain, the first missionaries attempted to understand Nahua belief systems in order to convert the Nahuas to Christianity.[15] These early friars, who were preaching in Nahuatl, used the names of Nahua gods and places in the Nahua cosmology to convey the Christian message. The missionaries were steeped in the late medieval worldview where creation was divided into the light, associated with Christians who served God, and the dark, connected with pagans who served the Devil.[16] Within this cosmology there was no middle ground. Since priests saw indigenous beliefs as Devil worship, they accordingly found the Devil behind every rock and tree. From equating the Devil with native gods, it was just a short step to seeing all practitioners of native religions as witches who had made a Devil's Pact.[17]

Missionaries learned to depict Hell in vivid detail, since the most frequent argument for conversion was salvation, and it was easier and more persuasive to describe the fires of Hell than the beauty of heaven. Fray Bernardino de Sahagún described the torments of Hell and the devils that inhabit the place in one of his sermons:

> They have mouths like huts, they have gaping mouths. They have metal bars for teeth, they have curved teeth, they have tongues of flame, their eyes are big burning embers. They have faces on both sides. Their molars are sacrificial stones. Everywhere they eat people, everywhere they bite people, everywhere they gulp people down. They have mouths on all their joints like monsters with which they chew.[18]

The Augustinian fray Antonio de Roa felt that words alone could not convey the torments of Hell as well as example, so he depicted that suffering by walking on hot coals and having his Indian assistants choke him, whip him, and drip burning pitch on his wounds. The Franciscan fray Luis Caldera took it one step further by burning small animals alive in front of his converts: "Their [the animals] cries of pain were to represent the anguish of sinners in Hell." These images, which combined the worst features of the indigenous Devil-like gods and the Christian Hell, "seemed to have stepped right out of a converted Nahua's nightmare."

The Nahua cosmology contained an underworld where all but exceptional individuals journeyed after they died. It was called *mictlan*, and it was not a pleasant place since it represented the dark and disorderly side of things, but neither was it the same as the Hell of the medieval Christian where the Devil presided.[19] The identification by the Franciscans of native deities with the Devil was designed to induce the Indians to reject their traditional religious practices. Instead, indigenous people from Peru to Mexico to New Mexico told the priests who converted them that they believed in both the Christian God and their own gods, which may have included Devil-like figures.[20] Although there was some similarity between Christian and Nahua beliefs regarding Hell and the Devil, there were fundamental differences between the two worldviews. As with native religious beliefs throughout the Americas, the Nahua believed in a cosmos that was animate. "Mountains, bodies of water, the wind, the moon, stars, and the heavens, as well as the earth itself, were animate beings... [accordingly] a people's place in [this] cosmos differs fundamentally from a world where human beings rule over a passive creation. . . . Human beings were a part of the world; the world was not something to be rejected or striven against."[21] The Nahua did not understand Christian ideas of sin and salvation. They saw the world as a dangerous place simply because of the nature of things. It was easy to fall into immoral ways, not because of the temptations of the Devil or the weakness of the flesh, but simply because of the slippery nature of the earth. One must live according to the guidelines established by one's ancestors and focus on the core indigenous beliefs dealing with the collective preservation of the cosmic order. Otherwise one would continually fall in the mud, or worse, tumble over the abyss.[22]

Likewise, the Nahua had no word for evil, although concepts of good and bad did exist. But the Nahuatl words for these ideas were expressed in terms of order and disorder, growth and decay. The Christian concept of sin was replaced by the word for damage. Instead of sin as the cause of universal guilt, the Nahuas accepted the ideas of disorder, damage, and chaos as part of the cosmic process. The Nahuas had nothing in their belief system analogous to the Christian belief in the central importance of sin and salvation. Nahuatl words dealt with the concrete more than the abstract. The word for a bad person, for example, connoted a person with a disorderly emotional state, or a condition of uncontrolled anger, not a person with an evil nature. The Nahua word for good did have moral implications for the Indians, but it had the concrete meaning of something finished or completed.[23] The friars preaching to the Indians in Nahuatl were forced to express the Christian categories of good and evil in terms of order and disorder. Thus the Christian concepts became "Nahuatalized" as the only way to express them in a meaningful way to the Nahuas.[24]

The Nahua god Tlatlacatecolo and the mythical figure of Quetzalcoatl were both equated with the Devil. The mythical figure of Quetzalcoatl, known to the Nahuas as well as the Olmecs, Toltecs, Zapotecs, and Mayans, combined the destructive powers of the earth with the fertile and ordering forces of the heavens. The name Quetzalcoatl combined the Nahua word for serpent, *coatl* (symbolizing the powers of the earth), with *quetzalli*, the word for feather (signifying bird/forces of the heavens).[25] Since the figure of Quetzalcoatl, the feathered serpent, embodied both order and disorder, the Nahua devil was diminished to the status of a sorcerer, not a god.[26] Similarly, in the Andes, the serpent did not embody the forces of evil as it did for

Christians. It was amaru, "a destructive force erupting from beneath the earth in an attempt to re-create balance when relations of equilibrium had not been maintained."[27] So in the Andean world the pre-Inca god Pachacamac was a two-faced deity who "on the one hand created and sustained human beings, made the corn grow, and cured disease, but on the other hand, brought disease and caused earthquakes and the overflowing of the sea."[28] The indigenous people of Peru worshipped Pachacamac for his healing powers, but the Spaniards under Pizarro saw this god as the Devil and destroyed his shrine, replacing the image of the god with a cross.

The Christian belief in the Devil would not allow the possibility that light and dark powers, the power to create and destroy, could exist in one god. The attempt to eliminate native gods and replace them with Christian images was repeated all over the Americas.

Franciscan priests such as Juan José Toledo were taken by civil officials to indigenous religious sites, as happened in 1763 when Alcalde Carlos Fernández went to the location of a stone lion near the Abiquiu Genízaro pueblo where the Indians had offered sacrifices. Toledo removed what he called a stone idol and erased some nearby drawings. He then proceeded to another site on the side north of the pueblo where petroglyphs were drawn on a cliff face, which Fernández reproduced in the margin of his report. These rock art sites were also destroyed, crosses were drawn on the cliffs nearby, and Father Toledo exorcised both these places.[29] Such activities embodied a confrontation of two religious belief systems on a concrete level. The Spaniards soon learned that all the activities directed at physical destruction of a shrine or piece of rock art did not change native religious views. Indigenous people either accommodated the Christian beliefs to fit their system or continued to worship at the site where the shrine once stood because it was site itself that was sacred, not merely the shrine.[30]

These contradictions and contrasts between Christian and indigenous worldviews seen elsewhere in the Americas also existed among Spaniards, Pueblos, and Abiquiu Genízaros in New Mexico. It is striking how similar the Pueblo worldview is to that of the Nahuas and the Andean people. Such

similarities to the Nahuas may have come about in part because of trade contact between the groups before Spanish conquest.[31] In addition, defectors
from the thirteen hundred Indians from New Spain in Coronado's expedition settled throughout the Southwest and would have brought their religious beliefs with them.[32] Pueblo anthropologist Alfonso Ortiz noted a basic
similarity in worldview among all agricultural societies. He also observed
the dualities in Pueblo mythology and ritual drama that are both cosmic and
concrete. The dualities of good and evil are realized in concrete form in the
priest and the witch. Other dualities, such as ripe and unripe, cooked and
raw, are used to describe the good versus evil duality. Deviant behavior, especially in the uninitiated young, is dismissed as raw, unripe, or simply uninitiated and therefore not fully human, rather than evil.[33]

As Franciscan missionaries and colonists traveled from Mexico City to
New Mexico their ideas about the Devil traveled with them. Also making
the journey from Mexico City to Santa Fe were procedures followed by the
Inquisition and the Andean extirpators in rooting out superstition and heresy.
Indian defendants in extirpation trials in Peru or before the Inquisition in
Mexico City learned to mold their answers to their accusers' worldview. For
instance, they would admit to involvement in a Devil's Pact, which allowed
them to effect a healing. Since the sorcerer's accusers did not believe he had
done the things to which he confessed, the defendants received relatively light
punishment compared to those who were accused of heresy. Suspected
Protestants or Jews accused of holding non-Catholic beliefs received
harsher sentences, including being burned at the stake, while sorcerers who
confessed to trying to cure people, admitting that they did not believe they
could achieve the result they claimed, received light sentences.[34] Later, the
simple act of confessing, even if it involved a Devil's Pact and *maleficium*,
or causing harm to people, merited a light sentence.[35] The case of Luis Rivera
illustrates how the idea of the Devil's Pact was viewed in New Mexico.[36]

Two years after the Inquisition was established in New Mexico with the
appointment of fray Alonso de Benavides as commissary of the Holy Office,
Luis Rivera hired on as a muleteer in the caravan that brought the custos,
fray Esteban Perea, back to New Mexico after a stay in Mexico City. Perea
had appeared before the Inquisition in the trial of Governor Juan de Eulate
(1618–25) and was undoubtedly hypersensitive to any occurrences that could
be viewed as heresy. Such an occurrence took place in the valley of Santa
Bárbara on the northward journey. When the mules and the cattle stampeded,

rumors passed among the people in the caravan that only the presence of someone with a Devil's Pact could explain the event. The Devil had obviously caused the stampede. In this witch-hunting atmosphere Luis Rivera soon confessed to having made such a Devil's Pact in his younger days when he offered the Devil his soul. When the caravan reached Santa Fe, two of the friars denounced Rivera to the Inquisition, testifying that he had admitted speaking with the Devil more than once and calling on him for aid, especially in rounding up cattle. Rivera confessed his involvement in a Devil's Pact to Father Benavides, who convinced the young man to go to Mexico City with the returning caravan to face the Inquisition there and beg for mercy. Events were escalating quickly, and Rivera's life was now in jeopardy, all because of the general belief that only the Devil could have caused a cattle stampede.[37]

Although he had undertaken the journey voluntarily, when Rivera reached Mexico City he was arrested and placed in irons. From the public jail, Rivera was led before the Inquisition to respond to the charge that he had made a pact and sold his soul to the Devil. In his confession, Rivera admitted using an herb he received from an Indian in order to attract women. When the herb failed to achieve the promised results, he threw the herb away and had no more contact with the Indian. About the same time, Rivera, who was only about fourteen at the time, met a Black slave who convinced him that if he made a pact with the Devil he could improve his skills in rounding up cattle, come out successfully in a bull fight, or even catch a mustang on foot. The Black slave sold Rivera a book in which he had drawn pictures of demons, assuring him that if he signed his name in blood in the book, making a pact with the Devil and offering him his soul, the Devil would always help him. Rivera drew blood from his nose with which he signed the book, and the pact was made. Within a few weeks Rivera destroyed the book, fearing that he might be committing a sin.[38]

Rivera had once been in the service of an inquisitor from Seville, his birthplace in Spain, and thus may have gained some understanding of the workings of the Holy Office. Yet nothing could have prepared him for the intense questions his examiners posed to him in Mexico City. The focus of the examination was Rivera's intent when he used the herb and when he made his pact with the Devil. His inquisitors wanted to know whether the herb had the power in itself to attract women, or if it was through the Devil's Pact that he hoped to achieve that result. Pressing him on the pact with the Devil, they asked Rivera whether, when he made his bargain with the Devil, he acted in the belief that the Devil was more powerful than God and with the intent to separate himself from the Church. Rivera answered truthfully that he was only about fourteen when these events occurred and at the time was ignorant of these theological questions, although he understood and believed that God was all powerful and the Devil was his creature. He insisted that in no way had he intended to separate himself from the Church.[39]

Rivera's denials were for naught, however, when the formal accusation was presented. He was charged with cutting himself off from the Church, "giving over to the Devil his soul...adoring him (the Devil), and regarding him [as] more powerful than God...giving to him de facto the adoration and worship owed to God alone."[40] If the tribunal did not believe these charges had been proved, the Inquisition's attorneys asked that Luis Rivera be tortured until he admitted them. Fortunately for Rivera the theologians and jurists who advised the Inquisition on matters of heresy believed him when he said he did not intend to separate himself from the Church. Rivera had testified that even when he had the book in his possession, he had continued to pray the Pater Noster and Ave María before retiring at night. The jurists and theologians decided that it was theoretically possible to engage in a pact with the Devil "and at the same time preserve a true belief in God."[41] Rivera was convicted of use of the herb and making a pact with the Devil, among other crimes, and sentenced to a two-month confinement in the Jesuit convent in Mexico City. There he was to confess his sins and abjure his errors, and for at least a year he was to fast on Fridays, and confess and take communion at least once a month.

Rivera escaped severe punishment out of luck and because his answers to the questions of the inquisitors followed the formula defendants used in heresy and witchcraft trials from Peru to Mexico to New Mexico. Rivera told his questioners that he was a practicing Christian, even during the time he had made a pact with the Devil and was carrying the Book of the Devil in which his name was written in blood. Rivera testified that the Black slave tricked him and that he always believed that God was more powerful than the Devil. The Inquisition judges agreed that this was possible, partly because "his tender age could not give him full appreciation [of his act]."[42] Such a position was similar to the belief by some Franciscans in New Mexico that the Genízaros could keep aspects of their religious beliefs and still remain good Christians.

The belief in a Devil's Pact has persisted to this day in Central and South America, especially among Indians working in the economic system their conquerors established. Michael Taussig has documented contemporary Devil's Pacts in the sugarcane fields of Colombia and the tin mines of Bolivia. By making such a contract with the Devil, these workers hoped to increase their production and make more money. Although it is believed that a Devil's Pact will earn short-term gains, one who enters into such a pact suffers in the long term, experiencing calamities such as serious illness, unexplained accidents, or early death. The belief is that the Devil is the true owner of the mines and minerals but is seen as a greedy spirit "bent on destruction and death. As he is on the Colombian sugar plantation, the devil is a mainstay... of increasing production, but this production is believed to be ultimately destructive of life."[43] In other words, the short-term gain of increased production is offset when the land becomes sterile. These beliefs are remarkably similar to those of seventeenth-century New Mexico, where a stampede was blamed on the Devil, and a muleteer named Luis Rivera took responsibility because he accepted the notion that a deal with the Devil required payment at some point, even if the promised benefits never materialized.

As missionaries in New Spain fought the Devil in their struggle to convert the Indians, Satan and his minions manifested themselves physically in the world of the Franciscan priests, especially in Querétaro. The Franciscans' view of the Devil as the personification of evil who tempted and harmed people by attacking and possessing their bodies became a reality when Indians suffering from unexplained illnesses and convulsions appeared at the doorstep of the church for exorcism. As a result of several fantastic cases of exorcism which Franciscans reported to the Inquisition, the Holy Office became suspicious of these head-to-head battles with the Devil and eventually told the Franciscans to stop reporting them and to cease practicing the rite of exorcism altogether.

The most notorious case of exorcism of the Devil involved the demoniacs (those possessed by devils) of Querétaro.[44] A group of women in Querétaro who frequented the Franciscan missions and had taken Franciscan habits showed signs of being possessed." The Inquisition in Mexico City was notified but became skeptical, as were other religious orders such as the Carmelites, Jesuits, and Dominicans. On 2 January 1692, to justify the Franciscan position in the face of this skepticism, fray Pablo Sarmiento of the Franciscan College of Santa Cruz de Querétaro wrote a long letter to the

Inquisition describing the possession of several women and his attempts to exorcise them. The events described are much akin to the Abiquiu exorcisms fray Juan José described in 1764.[45]

In one Querétaro case the victim's belly grew to an unnaturally large size; in another, after successful exorcism the afflicted one expelled four avocado stones, a half pound of river pebbles resembling small nuts, a cow bone, a small toad, and a snake that came out of her ear.[46] In the process of many exorcisms, fray Pablo Sarmiento claimed that many devils entered and left the victims' bodies and that he engaged the demons in a dialogue. One devil said that a group of witches led by La Chuparratones (the Mice Sucker) placed him and his fellow devils in the victims' bodies. At times the devils would submit to the exorcisms only temporarily, saying they were controlled by the witches. The Franciscans were baffled but kept up the battle "working fervently every evening for up to eight hours in their attempts to drive out the devils."[47] Finally, when one of the afflicted women became pregnant, allegedly from a devil, the Holy Office acted. The Inquisition accused the three afflicted women of pretending to be possessed, reprimanded the priests for being gullible, and forbade them from mentioning the possessions or practicing the rite of exorcism again. The Inquisition ordered the cessation of all exorcisms and all discussion about them either public or private.[48]

The Inquisition found it easier to blame the "ignorant women" of Querétaro for activities contrary to the Church's traditional concept of the Devil, than to attack the Franciscans, which would have brought reprisals. The Franciscans were making a valid point, for they supported the reality that their parishioners were indeed possessed by the Devil. Soon, however, the possession of apparently innocent citizens of Querétaro began to increase. It became something of a scandal involving the entire city, causing the municipal magistrate to write to the Inquisition arguing that it was not the Devil who was causing the problem, "but rather the effects of some spell or frenzy."[49] Querétaro was getting a bad reputation and the citizens were being scandalized, not only by the demoniacs, but also by the Franciscans.

In some of the exorcisms the Devil expressed himself in a way that went beyond the traditional concept of the Devil as the embodiment of evil but subordinate to God. God was more powerful than the Devil in the medieval belief, and the Devil acted independently to test people. In Querétaro, by contrast, the Devil spoke through one of the possessed saying, "I Lucifer, Prince of Hell, swear to Almighty God . . . that it is the will of the Most High, my creator... that I say what I am about to say for His greater glory."[50] Lucifer went on to say that he entered the body of Francisca de la Serna because God willed it. After this statement by the Devil himself, it was clear that God was using the Devil as his agent, "in a way a tyrant might employ a cruel chief of police," as Fernando Cervantes expressed it.[51] The Devil made this crystal clear when he said that he was no vile petty devil, but Lucifer himself. "God had put me here for the justification of his cause, [f]or God is very irritated with the world.... How long is it since Lucifer came out of Hell? God has now sent me so that you may realize that he is just."[52] The Devil that the Franciscans of Querétaro were conversing with had lost all responsibility for his evil actions and was simply a messenger of God.

This, of course, was unacceptable to the Inquisition. The Holy Office was concerned that the demoniacs of Querétaro threatened to take the powerful Christian concept of the Devil, as the embodiment of evil and the ruler of Hell—heretofore useful in the Church's attack on idolatry and heresy—and turn it into an incredible and ridiculous idea.[53]

The Querétaro case marked a change in the Inquisition's attitude toward the Devil and demonic possession. Instead of taking pains to find evidence that the demonic activities reported to them were real, the Inquisition hoped that no such evidence would be found so that the idea of the Devil would retain its credibility. Even when the concept of the Devil was not threatened, by the early 1700s the Inquisition had largely refused to deal with accusations or confessions regarding the Devil and the Devil's Pact. When the mulatto Baltasar de Monroy claimed to have talked to the Devil in 1704, the Inquisition called it one of the "superstitions very widespread among the vulgar folk."[54] When the Indian Tomás de Aquino told a Franciscan a few years later that he was possessed by the Devil, the Inquisition sentenced him to twenty-five lashes for misleading a priest.[55] In 1723 and in 1727 the Inquisition responded to reports that Antonio Rodríguez had the Devil "locked in his pantry," and that the mestiza Maritata had made a Devil's Pact, that these were matters lacking substance.[56]

The case that best illustrates the Inquisition's skeptical attitude toward the Devil and diabolical possession was reported to the Holy Tribunal in 1748 by Francisco Javier Gómez de Cervantes, the vicar-general and ecclesiastic judge of the Archbishopric of Mexico City. The mestiza Josefa de Saldaña claimed to be possessed by the Devil, having been bewitched by her former lover, Juan de Cadena. After doctors failed to cure her, the chaplain at the hospital exorcised her, expelling "mice, snakes, frogs, scorpions, worms, and even an occasional bird."[57] Saldaña's priest persuaded the exorcist to address the Devil in Latin. The Devil confessed, in Spanish, that Saldaña's former lover had bewitched her. The Devil continued that even though he spoke Latin well, he would not speak it until he was allowed to confront Cadena in person.

The vicar-general included a report by master surgeon Apolinario Antonio de Gálvez about his many failed attempts to cure Saldaña through the use of available treatments. Gálvez praised the use of exorcism in Saldaña's case because "it now seems clear that her ailments result from malefice and have not been caused by natural humours."[58] Included in the packet of materials submitted to the Inquisition to persuade them to look into Saldaña's demonic possession and Cadena's pact with the Devil was a letter from Saldaña's protector, Nicolás Fernando de Tapia, regarding the evidence that she was indeed possessed by the Devil. Tapia, along with Bachiller Juan de Cordero, both university graduates in canon law, argued that demonic possession was not a light matter. Although they were not positive that the Devil was responsible for Saldaña's expelling such foul things as snakes and frogs, they believed that this was a more likely explanation than natural causes. Tapia and Cordero cited numerous ecclesiastic authorities, including the *Malleus Maleficarum*, stating that the Devil was perfectly capable of creating these "foul things," "either [by] forming them out of aerial bodies," or by "proposing them to the imagination by directly exciting the humours."[59] The Inquisition, reticent to become involved in cases of diabolical possession, again ordered the priest to stop further exorcisms under pain of excommunication. The priests were showing too much credulity in the Inquisition's view, and the Holy Office simply ignored Saldaña's complaint.

Inquisition records contain many other examples of people who admitted having pacts with the Devil. Often these were marginalized individuals such as free Blacks or slaves during the seventeenth and eighteenth centuries who felt they had no other option for improving their circumstances than to petition the Devil. In a recent study of several Inquisition cases involving Devil's Pacts with those of African descent, the hoped-for outcomes of these bargains with the Devil differed between men and women. Most defendants were at the most productive time of their lives and desired to surpass the limits their marginalized circumstances placed on them. Women wanted the mobility and freedom that men, especially cowhands, had. Some female defendants dressed like men and asked the Devil for help when they were breaking horses, bullfighting, or fighting other cowhands. María de Rojas, who dressed in men's clothing, asked for increased competence in lancing, for the stable love of a man, and the possibility of having a family.[60] Men accused of entering into a Devil's Pact wanted their freedom if they were slaves, property usually denied them because of their status, access to all the women they desired, luck in lancing, protection against bulls, and other skills associated with a competent cowhand.[61]

The Inquisitors always asked how the Devil appeared to these defendants, and they got various answers. Men often saw the Devil as an attractive female figure with whom they had sexual relations, or in the form of a man riding a horse, or as a bull. To women such as Antonia de Soto, the Devil was a white man, one time riding a horse with a machete, another time dressed in black with a judge's collar, hugging her around the neck.[62]

One of the most powerful of the sorcerers studied was Juan de Santiago. He was believed to be capable of killing his enemies through witchcraft, could interrupt their dreams, and provoke pain and hallucinations. He learned the technique of making wax replicas of his enemies and burying them on the road where the adversary would pass. Then he would fast to the Devil for three Thursdays and be avenged. Santiago made many of his enemies ill, thus obligating them to seek his power to heal them. In one such cure of Francisco Izaquirre, Juan de Santiago used estafiate (wormwood or black sage), the same herb the second curandera used to cure Father Toledo. The Devil in the form of a woman also used *sahumario de copal* to cure Izaquirre and completed the cure by taking a small whitish worm with a gray head from the patient's buttocks. Juan de Santiago practiced witchcraft to make people ill and then cured them in a manner similar to the Abiquiu sorcerers.[63]

Some of the elements of these Devil's Pact cases had other similarities with Abiquiu. Often the defendant was required to abandon the practices of Catholicism, including missing mass and confession; to offer obeisance to the Devil; and to carry the Devil's image close to the body. The use of peyote merited special mention since priests believed it was one of the most common methods for communicating with the Devil. Peyote cactus played a major role in the religious rites of the Chichimecas before the Spanish Conquest and was expanded to practically all of New Spain, including Abiquiu, during the sixteenth to eighteenth centuries.[64]

Another similarity between these Devil's Pact cases and those of Abiquiu is the use of caves and snakes in sealing the Devil's Pact. In 1691 María de Rojos, a brown-skinned slave, and her female companion went to an empty cave where they sat on a large live snake. María also sat on a lizard, and the Devil appeared seeking to bring them into his service and offering them the love of men. This description is reminiscent of Father Toledo's depiction of the cave where El Cojo had his School of the Devil and the cave used by Vicente and María Trujillo and of the snakes and toads said to have been kept there.[65]

Many defendants in these Inquisition cases denounced themselves to the Holy Office in an attempt to reestablish themselves in the Catholic community. It is likely that, as in Abiquiu, some of these cases dealt with indigenous religious practices and not witchcraft, especially the cases in which peyote was involved. The defendants who sought forgiveness for the sin of entering into a pact with the Devil had to go to confession, but only a bishop could pardon the sin of entering into a Devil's Pact. Most defendants were pardoned and given some penance to perform.[66]

The 1748 Saldaña case has several interesting parallels with the Abiquiu witchcraft trials. Less than a decade after the Saldaña case, Father Toledo suffered ailments believed to result from witchcraft and a pact with the Devil. As far as is known, Toledo never sought to be exorcised himself but later exorcised others in his parish who were thought to be possessed by the Devil. The Abiquiu Genízaros sought help from Father Toledo when they began suffering strange ailments, convulsions, bloated stomachs, and the like. Father Toledo seized the opportunity to join with the Genízaros in battling the demons they believed were causing their illness. The priest was on their side, and the opponent was the Devil himself.

The traditional way of dealing with the Christianization of the Genízaros did not work in Abiquiu. First, the Inquisition did not favor extended exorcisms, stretching out over days and weeks and sometimes years, and made it clear that it did not want to hear about them. Second, such exorcisms were ineffective because the Devil kept popping up in new places as soon as he was made to abandon his possession of the Genízaro who was being exorcised. If there was a solution to the witchcraft craze in Abiquiu, then it lay in the middle ground between the traditional polarities of virtue and vice, good and evil, and light and dark. This middle ground, whose existence was denied in the medieval worldview, was where the Genízaros lived. It was the same territory the Mesoamerican Nahuas called nepantla, meaning "in the middle." It was also the ground inhabited by the indigenous Andeans, a place described by Nicholas Griffiths as "an uneasy no-man's-land," between lost traditional belief systems and a new religion not fully assimilated or understood.[67] "The intense spiritual unease that it provoked was a highly unstable condition; ... the tension had to be resolved at the communal level."[68] The Abiquiu Genízaros may have been particularly prone to resolving this tension by resorting to witchcraft. As former nomads they once had the option of resolving spiritual as well as social conflict by moving to another location. When they became sedentary, the tension of being in the middle was intensified to the breaking point. As was true of some African pastoral tribes that moved from a nomadic to a sedentary lifestyle, the initial period of settlement of these former nomads was often accompanied by accusations of witchcraft.[69]

The Abiquiu Genízaros, a group of Indians each with different religious beliefs based on their individual tribe, group, or pueblo, were in the middle ground of transition between the old and the new. New Mexico in the middle of the eighteenth century was also in a transitional stage. It was a time of danger and opportunity. Father Toledo and Governor Vélez Cachupín were spiritual and political leaders who had to seize the opportunities provided by the middle ground to lead the Abiquiu Genízaros into a new world that involved a form of acculturation different from any other community in New Mexico.

The Devil was central to the Abiquiu witchcraft proceedings, especially the third phase, the exorcisms. During the winter of 1763–64, Satan showed himself in multiple ways at Abiquiu. In a general, theological way fray Juan José saw all Genízaros as manifestations of the Devil. Father Toledo encountered the Devil and lesser demons in a more concrete way, however, as he conversed with them, usually in Latin. He also exorcised them and struggled with them physically as they possessed the bodies of the Abiquiu Genízaros. The contradictions of the opposing realities of Catholic dogma and Genízaro witchcraft almost tore Father Toledo apart as he placed himself in the midst of sorcerers, witches, and possessed women during the Abiquiu witch craze.

Figure 17
María Trujillo hung from a gun carriage wheel until she confesses. *Drawing by Glen Strock.*

CHAPTER TEN

The Witchcraft Proceedings

Phase Three: The Exorcisms

The third phase of the Abiquiu witchcraft proceedings began with another long and convoluted letter from Father Juan José Toledo to Alcalde Carlos Fernández recounting in detail the priest's long anticipated battle with the Devil. Father Toledo told the story of a series of afflictions his parishioners suffered during the previous year, culminating in an outbreak of demonic possessions and exorcisms by Father Toledo between December 1763 and January 1764. Fray Juan José also reported an earlier case in May 1763 of demonic possession and exorcism at Ojo Caliente in a separate document. In that case Toledo was more successful in healing the afflicted and expelling their demons than he was at Abiquiu, or so he said.

Toledo went to Ojo Caliente in late May 1763 with Joaquinillo, El Descubridor, when he was notified about several possible cases of demonic possession there. Toledo was unsure whether the afflictions suffered were the result of witchcraft or possession by the Devil. If it was demonic possession, Father Toledo was authorized to administer the rite of exorcism, but if the afflicted suffered from the effects of witchcraft, he might need Joaquinillo's help. Toledo doubtless turned to De la Peña Montenegro's *Itinerario* for guidance.

When they arrived at Ojo Caliente, it turned out that several people needed assistance. One was an "Indian man who had been bewitched for a long time, even though he was said to be a good man." The priest gave Joaquinillo permission to treat the man "on the condition that Joaquinillo neither touch nor massage the ill person, much less take anything out of him."[1] This treatment was apparently successful, but Toledo's conditions were soon broken when Mauricio, a coyote Genízaro from Ojo Caliente, requested their assistance. When Father Toledo placed his hands on Mauricio's head and began reading from the Gospel of John, the priest's body began to shake uncontrollably, a circumstance that led Toledo to believe that Mauricio was possessed by the Devil or a powerful demon. As Father Toledo started to exorcise him, Mauricio made an insolent remark, and Toledo discovered a *macana,* or obsidian-edged wooden club, under Mauricio's clothes. Far from being exorcised, Mauricio then demonstrated his shamanic powers by sitting "naked in the burning coals without burning himself, with the flames rising all around him. Then he took some coals and put them in his mouth and began to expel sparks and flames from his mouth and eyes."[2]

This spectacular scene persuaded Father Toledo in dramatic fashion that Mauricio had not given up his shamanic ways. Later, however, after staying with him all night, Father Toledo reported that Mauricio knelt before him asking forgiveness and permission for Joaquinillo to remove something from his body. After repeated requests, Father Toledo finally relented, and Joaquinillo was able to suck a stone from Mauricio's body.

The stone was sent to Alcalde Fernández with the suggestion that it be forwarded to Governor Vélez Cachupín as proof of the things that were going on at Ojo Caliente.[3] It must have been difficult for Governor Vélez Cachupín to decide whether to believe Father Toledo, and even more difficult to decide what to do about it. Whether Vélez Cachupín ever received the stone sucked from Mauricio's body is unclear, but the governor was put on notice that strange things were occurring in Ojo Caliente and other parts of northern New Mexico at the same time as the Abiquiu witchcraft outbreak.

Before Father Toledo left Ojo Caliente on 13 May 1763, he was asked to exorcise a man whose wife complained that he continually beat her, especially when she told him that she wanted to confess and receive communion. When Father Toledo questioned him, the husband said that a powerful sorcerer named Cascabel had set upon him "a devil so that he would hate his wife because she did not want to consent to the act [with Cascabel]."[4] Toledo proceeded to give the Indian a drink of the water of San Ignacio after which the man came to his senses, and Toledo exorcised him. By this time husband and wife had reconciled, and as Toledo reported, "The sorcerer Cascabel did not achieve his pleasure."[5]

The next report the governor received from Father Toledo concerned the Christmas season possessions and exorcisms in 1763; it was even more bewildering. This epidemic of possessions at Abiquiu began with a María Trujillo—not the same María Trujillo who was married to Vicente and was responsible for Toledo's illness. This other María Trujillo's symptoms began in June 1763 when she fainted in church "at the moment of the prayer of exorcism."[6] She was covered with purple spots on her right shoulder, elbow, knee, and on the palm of her hand, but as soon as Father Toledo exorcised her, these symptoms were alleviated. Later, however, Trujillo suffered new symptoms when she began experiencing headaches, indigestion, and severe depression. Her afflictions worsened on 14 November, the Feast of the Immaculate Conception, when she fell asleep in church and did not participate in the ceremonies of the fiesta. A month later Trujillo's symptoms worsened further when she fainted and "instead of coming to started tearing at herself [as if possessed] by unnatural forces."[7] On 17 December 1763, Trujillo came to Father Toledo and begged him in the name of God to exorcise her. Toledo did so, apparently with some success, although Trujillo was soon possessed again before the Devil departed Abiquiu.

The day after this incident, an eighteen-year-old girl named Francisca Varela also became possessed but with symptoms more serious than Trujillo's. Varela began to realize that something out of the ordinary was happening when she was drawing water at a spring near her house. As she was getting the water "her body shook with great fear and terror, without [her] knowing the source."[8] She heard a strange noise that sounded like a pig, and when she returned again to the spring for water and heard the same noise, she became afraid and hurried home. She fainted as soon as she arrived at her house, and when her brother tried to lift her up, "she started giving out frightening and furious cries to which the neighbors responded." They "were all amazed and agreed to bring her to [Father Toledo's] mission."[9] Varela then suffered some very strange symptoms, such as the sensation of ants crawling all over inside her, but when she reached the Abiquiu mission and saw Father Toledo her situation quickly deteriorated. As Father Toledo reported: "When she arrived and saw me she let out some unbelievable screams, [began] flailing her arms and legs, [and] moving her eyes wildly... undoubtedly wearing out the people holding her [down]... as she punched them, tried to bite them, and grabbed at their hair."[10] As Francisca Varela was being held down in front of Father Toledo, he observed her "vividly imitate pigs, cows, burros, owls, and other animals" and decided it was time to act.[11]

Father Toledo gathered his stole, his cross, and the Gospel of St. John and began to pray over Varela, asking whether what was occurring was God's will or something else. Fray Juan José was unsure whether he was actually dealing with demonic possession, but what happened next persuaded him that the Devil had again appeared in Abiquiu. "On hearing the words of the Holy Gospel, [Varela] went into another seizure with convulsions, screams, and howls," whereupon Father Toledo immediately grabbed his Book of Exorcisms. But before he could proceed, Varela began calling him names such as "insolent, kid goat, Mulatto."[12] As Father Toledo began to exorcise the demon from Varela, she interrupted the rite of exorcism with her loud cries and more insults. Varela seemed possessed of superhuman strength as four men tried to hold her down with only partial success. She tried to escape "by arching her body in all directions and slipping out of her shoes with such violence [that] it was almost impossible to hold her."[13] Varela's convulsions and her exorcism continued all night, as Father Toledo reported, "until dawn when she finally relaxed, falling on the floor still howling in [a] loud voice from time to time, just like the Indians of this land."[14]

As Father Toledo began to relax as well, the sun came up on 19 December 1763, and a third girl was brought before the priest with symptoms of possession even more severe than Trujillo's and Varela's. María Chávez, a twelve-year-old girl, reported severe pain on her right side and suffered such violent convulsions that Father Toledo called Joaquinillo, the alcalde, and two witnesses to observe her affliction. El Descubridor reported that Chávez had eaten a *bollito* (small bun) that contained an evil spirit that made her ill, an indication that what Toledo thought was demonic possession may have been witchcraft-induced food poisoning.

There was also an indication that Father Toledo knew something more was going on with Chávez than had been the case with Trujillo and Varela. That something was a pair of witches: Jacinta, who was the head baker at the pueblo, and her mother, "an Indian woman scornfully called Atole Caliente."[15] Soon both of them, joined by Varela and her sister, were writhing in pain whenever Father Toledo tried to say Mass in church. The scene that developed was reminiscent of the trials and torments of the afflicted girls and women in Salem Village in 1692.[16]

Father Toledo brought Chávez, Jacinta, and Atole Caliente to the Abiquiu church of Santo Tomás to be exorcised while he was celebrating Mass before the congregation. As Toledo began the Introit, "they all fell to the floor together, becoming irritated and falling to pieces when people rushed to restrain them. Seeing that they were pinned down they began an uproar, giving out loud Indian howls and war chants, like they do when they are grinding corn, and flailing their hands all about, and when their crazed actions came to a halt, they would sing like owls, foxes, pigs, cows, and so forth."[17] Incredibly, Father Toledo still attempted to celebrate Mass during this disturbance, but the afflicted ones made so much noise that neither Toledo nor the choir could be heard. Just as everyone began to quiet down, Varela, who was sitting amongst the congregation, "started shouting loudly from her chair at the beginning of the Gloria and it was necessary to eject her from the church."[18] This did not resolve the problem, however, for Jacinta and Atole Caliente became even more defiant and unruly. By now, fray Juan José was certain he was dealing with the Devil. When he began the exorcism again, in the priest's words, it "pained the Devil greatly since he was in the bodies of the ill persons."[19] Toledo's confrontation with the Devil soon reached the point where he was conversing with the Evil One in Latin, and the scene in the Abiquiu church of Santo Tomás was destined to become even more violent.

As Father Toledo moved into the second day of another exorcism marathon, the priest began to wonder whether he should have ejected Jacinta and Atole Caliente from the church, just as Jesus had driven the money lenders from the temple. Later he *did* eject them, punishing Atole Caliente for her insolent acts. Joaquinillo considered Atole Caliente one of the most powerful witches in Abiquiu but had never mentioned or challenged her because she was his teacher.

What infuriated Father Toledo most was the arrogance with which Atole Caliente tried to control the twelve-year-old María Chávez. Atole Caliente told Father Toledo that she had ordered Chávez not to attend Mass. When Toledo told her he would take Chávez to Mass by force if necessary, Atole Caliente brazenly replied that the priest would not govern her. These disturbances continued until near dawn on 21 December 1763 when things finally calmed down at the Abiquiu mission church and everyone got some rest.

The next day, however, matters again got out of control. As Toledo was preparing for another day of exorcisms, he saw Atole Caliente trying to suffocate Chávez by stuffing the end of her shawl in María's mouth. Chávez was yelling that Jacinta and Atole Caliente were choking her to prevent her from telling Toledo anything. Infuriated, Father Toledo "went into the middle [of everyone] to remove the said Indian [Atole Caliente] whose insolence caused [him] great distress."[20] This time Father Toledo completely lost his patience. He took Atole Caliente outside the church and "in view of many [people] gathered there, whipped her in punishment for the disrespect she showed in church."[21]

Before Atole Caliente and Jacinta were removed from Abiquiu, they caused fray Juan José Toledo even more trouble as they led the group of afflicted ones in what Father Toledo thought was Satanic possession, but what can also be seen as resistance to Christianization.[22] The afflicted women of Abiquiu went to church and left in a body, often escorted by a group of crows. Father Toledo reported that observers present at the proceedings "have seen crows flying around their heads and escorting them in front and behind their bodies every time they [the afflicted] go out."[23]

Besides María Chávez, Atole Caliente, Francisca Varela and her sister, and Jacinta, other young women soon joined the group of afflicted ones. The group was especially active on 21 December 1763 when Father Toledo began to say Mass and continue the exorcisms. He reported that "they were quiet until I started to sing the first verses of the Gospel, when they started one after another, making grimaces, tremblings, fainting spells, violent acts and other strange actions accompanied by great cackling and vulgarities, and so forth."[24] A new girl joined the group of the afflicted, someone who had been tormented since September 1763. She was unnamed, but her strength impressed Father Toledo, who reported that "fury was unleashed with greater maleficio that would overcome four to six men. Her tongue was also unleashed in its evil when she started to speak."[25] The similarity between the afflicted ones in Salem Village and those of Abiquiu, at least on the surface, is striking. At Salem, "the girls seemed to be bitten and pinched by invisible agents. In visible and audible agony, the victims twisted their arms and backs and contorted their faces. Sometimes they could not speak; other times they could not stop speaking."[26]

By the middle of January 1764, the demonic possessions at Abiquiu were showing no sign of abating; they were actually increasing to a point of hysteria reminiscent of Salem in 1692 and Querétaro of 1691–92. Father Toledo tried to exorcise as many as five or more young women at a time, all of whom the priest thought were possessed by the Devil. Part of the Roman Ritual of Exorcism is an "Exorcism Addressed to the Evil Spirit," which includes a direct address to Satan and the lesser devils. Father Toledo's exorcism may have been similar to this:

> I exorcise you, Most Unclean Spirit! Invading Enemy!
> All Spirits! Every one of you! In the name of Our Lord
> Jesus Christ: Be uprooted and expelled from this
> Creature of God. He who commands you is He who
> ordered you to be thrown down from the highest
> Heaven into the depths of Hell. He who commands

you is He who dominated the sea, wind, and the
storms. Hear, therefore, and fear, Satan! Enemy of the
Faith! Enemy of the human race! Source of death!
Robber of life! Twister of justice! Root of evil! Warp
of vices! Seducer of men! Traitor of nations! Inciter
of jealousy! Originator of greed! Cause of discord!
Creator of agony![27]

As Father Toledo performed the Rite of Exorcism, the afflicted often
responded in Latin. Toledo reported, "All of them as they answered demonstrated knowledge of Latin, which is the most certain sign of possession [by
the Devil]. When the words of the greater mysteries [were spoken] they would
laugh and start howling and go into vulgarities as I said *in nomine patri*, and
shaking their heads in denial as I referred to the Trinity. When I asked the
spirit possessing Francisca Varela, in Latin, why he was afflicting her, he
answered [again in Latin] that all this came from on high."[28]

Father Toledo received more than he bargained for as the exorcisms continued, and the priest engaged the Devil one on one. One of the devils afflicting the girls and women told Toledo that at the end of twenty-eight days of
exorcisms, all the devils would depart from the afflicted. Nevertheless, the
priest persistently continued his exorcisms, no matter what the demons said
because he thought they were heading toward their inevitable defeat. Whether
the Devil was defeated decisively in Father Toledo's terms is unclear.
Nevertheless, Father Toledo continued with the exorcisms (although he was
tempted to hand the task over to other priests) because his parishioners
begged him on their knees to free them from this oppression.

For Father Toledo to declare victory over the Devil in the short term,
the possessions had to cease, which would mean that the Devil/devils had
departed. In the long term, however, only when Father Toledo and the other
Franciscans succeeded in converting the Genízaros and Pueblo Indians to
Christianity was the Devil, in the form of indigenous religious belief systems, truly conquered. But that was not to be. Native American religions continued to exist side by side with Catholicism throughout the eighteenth,
nineteenth, and twentieth centuries, down to the present day.[29] This was not
the case for Abiquiu, however, as native beliefs and ceremonies were gradually replaced with Christian ones. In this sense, Father Toledo's influence
was greater than he could have imagined. This was due more to the failings

of the priests who followed him at Abiquiu—particularly Father Alcina—than with anything Father Toledo did.

Father Toledo's image of defeating the Devil became murky and lost its sharp outlines of good versus evil when the devils he was exorcising and speaking to became lesser devils, not *the* Devil, also known as Satan or Lucifer. Some of these lesser devils had names; others did not give their names. Asmodeus, with whom Father Toledo said Vicente Trujillo had a pact, was a lesser devil, said to be the third down from Satan. Another lesser devil whom Father Toledo exorcised was named Diablo Cojuelo, who was afflicting María Agueda, the sister of Francisca Varela. Diablo Cojuelo told Father Toledo that he had entered María Agueda "in Chimayo in order to mistreat her and [to] finish off the community."[30] Father Toledo drove Diablo Cojuelo out of María Agueda's body only to have him enter and possess three others. At that point, the Abiquiu possessions were becoming contagious, as had been the case earlier in Querétaro in 1691–92. Instead of beating the Devil, Father Toledo was losing ground.

In mid-January 1764 Satan was also still afflicting Genízaros such as María Trujillo at Abiquiu. At one point Trujillo was said to have summoned the Devil to her because of a dispute she was having with her husband, "and the Devil hastened to her call, making the house tremble as a sign, as witnessed by those present."[31] Trujillo was in a private house at the time, and Toledo was celebrating Mass at the Abiquiu church. When he was called to assist her with an exorcism, Father Toledo was initially unwilling to go, because he mistrusted the Devil's wiles. Eventually, the priest again exorcised Trujillo but must have had misgivings about helping her since she had called the Devil to her. Earlier, Lucifer had possessed Trujillo in the Abiquiu church where she fainted. Then as Father Toledo was exorcising Trujillo, "she spit out a horse's tooth with so much difficulty that it was necessary to strike her on the back several times with [his] stole."[32]

As Father Toledo concluded his report, it seemed clear that he was growing tired. He had been at the center of an epidemic of demonic possessions that had been going on for more than a month. Fray Juan José was justified in feeling weary: many exorcisms stretched well into the night. Although the afflicted ones had all the signs of demonic possession described in the manuals of exorcism, the Devil/devils were not departing as a result of Toledo's exorcisms. Instead of the clear-cut battle with Satan in which he would be victorious, as Toledo had imagined, the number of evil spirits was proliferating in Abiquiu. Toledo could not keep up with the outbreak and was beginning to have doubts about what was taking place in the Abiquiu Genízaro pueblo. At one point, when one of the lesser devils entered María Trujillo's body in a field near her house, she reported that "at said spot and house, there were legions [of] devils." Not only was there an increase in the number of evil spirits, but also the clear bright line Toledo had drawn between good and evil was beginning to blur.

As Father Toledo examined his spiritual power to stand up to the Devil/devils, his view of the witch craze became more nuanced. He even began to think there might be some good in the outbreak, since it made it possible to witness the torments that lay ahead for those who failed to repent their sins. In other words, the afflictions visited upon the Abiquiu Genízaros gave them a taste of what it would be like in Hell if they did not show contrition. This is probably the kind of argument Father Toledo would begin to weave into his sermons as another inducement for the Genízaros to convert to Christianity, just as Father Sahagún had done in the sixteenth century.[33] Thus the Devil became an ally instead of an enemy. First, he gave the Genízaros a taste of what Hell would be like, then he helped point out the unrepentant Devil-worshippers still among them. Genízaras, such as María Trujillo, promised to identify, with the help of the Devil, all the idolaters who had not been converted. She would help "cleanse the land of so much impurity... [because] it is the will of the Creator that so much adoration of the Devil should stop."[34] Trujillo, with the help of the Devil, would become like Joaquinillo, an informer who pointed out those who had made a Devil's Pact.

Father Toledo made no specific recommendation for solving the Abiquiu witchcraft and demonic possession outbreak, but did provide a list of suspected sorcerers who had not been questioned (see Appendix A).[35] The list, most of which Joaquinillo prepared, contained quite a bit of descriptive information about accused witches from all over New Mexico and beyond, even when names were lacking. But the list of accused sorcerers failed to name many important Abiquiu sorcerers. Only five were listed for Abiquiu: Atole Caliente; her daughter, Jacinta; Miguel, El Cojo; Isabel, La Pastora; and Pedro Trujillo. Missing from the list were Agustín Tagle and his sons, Diego and Juan; Vicente Trujillo, and his wife María; and Ambrosio Janisco, the latter said to be, along with the Tagle and Trujillo families among the leading sorcerers of Abiquiu. Since Joaquinillo had intimate knowledge of the accused sorcerers of the other pueblos, it is surprising that he did not list all the Abiquiu sorcerers, many of whom he had pointed out himself. The answer may lie in the most telling omission from the list: Joaquinillo himself.[36]

Joaquinillo was able to use his position as informer to avoid being listed (and possibly jailed) as a sorcerer. He may also have feared repercussions such as being denounced and imprisoned from the powerful sorcerers he failed to name. In fact, María Trujillo had already suggested that she should be allowed to identify the unconverted idolaters. One of those sorcerers might have been Joaquinillo.[37]

Joaquinillo's list of accused sorcerers includes much information that reveals quite a bit about himself and also his intimate knowledge of a network of Native American sorcerers throughout the pueblos of northern New Mexico and south as far as Sonora, Mexico City, and Oaxaca. By the time Joaquinillo provided this list to the Spanish authorities he had become adept at negotiating the interstices between the dominant Hispanic culture and the subservient Genízaro and Pueblo cultures. This space could be used to perform the contradictory feat of telling both sides what they wanted to hear. He told the Spanish officials about those who had invoked the Devil in prison (Miguel, El Cojo, and Pedro, El Paseño), and named or described more than one hundred accused sorcerers. Joaquinillo knew that the quantity of names or descriptions would impress the Spanish civil authorities. Yet, when it came to identifying particular individuals, Joaquinillo's descriptions were often so general they could fit any number of people.[38]

Joaquinillo listed 107 sorcerers, not including those listed in more than one pueblo (Bárbara Canosa and her son, Antonio, were listed both in Sandia and Isleta; they are counted under Isleta in Appendix A). Taos Pueblo had the most sorcerers with twenty-four; next came Chimayo with twenty; Isleta with fifteen; Nambe with eight; Sandia with seven; followed by Abiquiu, San Juan, Picuris, and San Ildefonso with five; Pojoaque and Tesuque with four; Belen with three; and Galisteo and Laguna with one each.[39]

Of the twenty-four sorcerers listed at Taos, seven were not named but only described, and three descriptions were so general they could apply to any number of people. Also included were individuals identified by name with a telling piece of information added that could be highly incriminating. Examples are Quiteria from San Juan, "head cook who took Father Mirabal's life"; Isabel from Taos who "resembles Atole Caliente and in one night goes to and returns from Mexico City"; Cascabel, Genízaro from Chimayo who was "imprisoned and had his art in a small black stone and is very powerful"; and Getrona who had a "wrinkled face and sometimes wears a snakeskin for a belt."[40] Knowledge about these accused sorcerers must have come from Joaquinillo, who learned the information either directly or through the testimony taken by Alcalde Carlos Fernández.

The accusation that Quiteria from San Juan had killed Father Mirabal indicates a pattern of Indian resistance to Christianization. Another sign that many of these accused sorcerers were simply Native American leaders resisting conversion is the number of caciques, war captains, and other officials who were listed among the accused. At Taos there were Antonio, the war captain, and an unnamed Indian who was a brother to an *alguacil*; at Pojoaque, a cacique, and Juan Felipe, listed as the son of Poseyemu; at Tesuque, Anselmo was listed as cacique and teacher of sorcerers (probably a native leader who taught native dances and ceremonies to the youth); at Isleta was Antonio, El Cayguia (Kiowa), the son of the cacique; and at Picurís was Huelecoo, the alguacil. In all but four of the twelve pueblos listed (not including Abiquiu), an Indian official or his relatives were listed as accused sorcerers.[41]

A report from Alcalde Manuel García Parejas to Governor Vélez Cachupín three days after Toledo's report tended to confirm fray Juan José's version of the demonic possessions at Abiquiu and lent some credibility to Toledo's report.[42] García Parejas had recently been appointed alcalde mayor and in that capacity had enlisted Joaquinillo, El Descubridor, to help him "destroy and put an end to the Empire of the Devil" in Abiquiu.[43] As Carlos Fernández had done in June of 1763, García Parejas traveled with Father Toledo, the lieutenant alcalde, and a large group of witnesses, to exorcise and destroy an idol the Indians worshipped. Undoubtedly this was a ceremonial site held sacred by the Abiquiu Genízaros and nearby Pueblos. When they arrived at the site, Father Toledo found a stone, which he said had a contract with the Devil carved on it. Toledo, attired in his surplice and stole and carrying a cross and some holy water, abruptly threw down the stone, which broke into pieces. The priest then proceeded to exorcise the four elements and address Lucifer directly and censure him. Toledo concluded the ceremony by setting up a cross two varas high (almost six feet) next to the site. This entire procedure was the time-honored method that civil and religious authorities employed in the Southwest, Mesoamerica, and the Andes to attempt to eradicate indigenous religions. Those authorities found, however, as did Father Toledo and Alcalde García Parejas, that destruction or defacement of indigenous religious symbols served only to intensify native religious beliefs.[44]

After the exorcism of this religious site, Alcalde García Parejas visited Father Toledo's quarters as he was preparing to leave the pueblo and found the Franciscan drinking broth from a cup. One of the afflicted women was nearby, apparently undergoing intermittent exorcism. At the alcalde's approach, the woman flew into a rage, uttered a horrendous shout, and showed signs of superhuman strength. Speaking through her, the Devil possessing the woman said that he was sent to admonish Joaquinillo, Father Toledo, and García Parejas. The woman suddenly slapped Father Toledo in the face, telling him to desist from the exorcism. Then, the Devil addressed García Parejas directly, telling him that Satan would prove that his possession of the woman was authentic and not feigned by divulging some information known only to García Parejas. The Devil, speaking through the woman's body, said that "soon after being appointed alcalde mayor [García Parejas had] offered the cane [of authority] to the Blessed Virgin Mary and her most Holy Son [Jesus Christ]."[45] Astounded, García Parejas reported that this was indeed true, that his intention was secret, and that he had told no one about it. In addition, the Devil told García Parejas that his devotion to the rosary had kept evil spirits from entering his home, which was protected, so that these evil spirits could proceed only to the edges of his property. Then the Devil began to give García Parejas advice, more like an ally than an enemy. It told him about many personal things that had happened in his home with his wife that only he and his family knew. Almost like a modern day therapist, the Devil "advised him of what one of his daughters should do concerning her mother."[46] The Devil speaking through the unnamed woman proceeded to give García Parejas information about the location of specific indigenous shrines or idols that needed to be removed. It seems that García Parejas was chosen by the Devil to receive valuable information about the location of specific sites not pointed out by Joaquinillo.

The first "idol" the possessed woman identified for García Parejas was a figure of two lions that Father Toledo had already destroyed. The Devil said that the exorcism practiced at this site had ended its power and influence. The site referred to may be the present-day stone lions site within Bandelier National Park, a place still held sacred by members of Cochiti Pueblo. The power of these two stone lions, which today show evidence of defacement, is evident from offerings placed there by residents of nearby pueblos. Fray Juan José began the defacement of these shrines in the period from 1762 to 1764.[47]

Other sites the possessed women pointed out were "a powerful stone located in an ancient ruin of an Indian pueblo near the ranch that belonged to [Juan José] Lobato," and a stone in the form of a snake at Ojo Caliente.[48] The latter stone was held sacred by the Indians of San Juan Pueblo, who had covered it to hide it from the Spaniards. This was undoubtedly another Indian shrine similar to the stone lions, which some Pueblos revered as part of their religious belief system.

The information given to García Parejas is extraordinary in detail and accuracy. Even more striking is the fact that this information formed the core of a report to Governor Vélez Cachupín. It is unlikely that the governor ever received another report where the source of the information was the Devil possessing a woman and speaking through her to the alcalde. Still, Vélez Cachupín needed more information about "idols" that could be exorcised and destroyed and about suspected sorcerers who could be jailed or placed as servants in Spanish households. The report provided him with the names and locations of the "idols" he required. In contrast to the Salem witchcraft trials, where evidence from specters (spirits seen only by the afflicted) was eventually discounted and held not to be credible, Governor Vélez Cachupín accepted the information this evil spirit provided in the Abiquiu witchcraft proceedings as credible, and it became central to the case.[49]

In a second report of 1 February 1764, Alcalde García Parejas noted even more surprising information obtained from the unnamed possessed woman. Guided by that Devil, the woman took a group of people to a large tower twelve to fourteen varas (almost forty feet) high. The alcalde described the construction of the tower, part stone, part mud, as miraculous. García Parejas could still discern in the mud the handprints of the Indians who constructed the tower. In and around the tower were offerings of tobacco, herbs, and purple, yellow, and black maize. These ritual offerings indicate that this was a very sacred place to the nearby pueblos, but to the Spaniards it was simply a site of idolatry and witchcraft that had to be destroyed.[50]

The tower described is of particular interest because of the rock art painted or pecked into the rocks forming the tower or on separate rock outcroppings. García Parejas described "a pyramid-shaped rock with the figure of the Devil in the form of a snake with two heads... [and] above that figure, a pictograph [*pintada*] of a snake with horns looking eastward."[51] As the alcalde continued his description of the rock art it was even more impressive: there were a total of thirty-two figures and symbols, the most prominent of which was the lord of the world with [the earth] painted at his feet with his open hands forming an arch with sparks emanating from them. The moon was painted below his left shoulder, and above it were painted the stars."[52]

The horned snake or serpent is undoubtedly Awanyu, the water serpent, one of the most common images in southwestern rock art found among Pueblo and Jornada Mogollon petroglyphs. The water serpent is given different names in different pueblos and is depicted in a wide variety of ways, although the horns or crest are a common feature. The image of the water serpent was considered so powerful that one of Elsie Clews Parsons's informants refused to draw it because its potency made it "too dangerous to draw."[53] The water serpent was a guardian of springs and underground waters and could also "withhold water or cause floods as punishment for wrongdoing or neglect of ceremonies."[54] Awanyu had a fearsome destructive side and could cause earthquakes and landslides.[55] Connected to the horned water serpent was the two-headed snake image Alcalde García Parejas also described. These two images were often confused, but both were powerful deities associated with water that may have been connected to similar double or plural-headed serpents of the Aztec and Maya.[56]

What García Parejas saw and described was clearly a Puebloan religious site, not a place where witchcraft was practiced. Unfortunately, the Spaniards viewed it in the latter way, burning and destroying the offerings and as much of the site as they could. Then Father Toledo exorcised the site, as he had so many other religious shrines, with the community of Abiquiu Genízaros present.[57]

Meanwhile, Toledo continued to exorcise the group of afflicted girls and young women through late January and early February 1764. García Parejas's attendance at some of these exorcisms lent more credibility to their reports than if they were based solely on Father Toledo's testimony. While Governor Vélez Cachupín gave minimal credence to the possessions of the afflicted and the exorcisms Father Toledo performed, the evidence was accumulating that the witchcraft outbreak had not been stopped by jailing the most

Figure 18
Petroglyphs on the Abiquiu mesa near Abiquiu. *Photograph by Malcolm Ebright.*

powerful sorcerers. Governor Vélez Cachupín had to do something to end the Abiquiu witchcraft outbreak.

On 31 January 1764, the same day that he received the García Parejas report, Vélez Cachupín acted. The governor had been taken aback by the possessions and exorcisms described by Toledo and García Parejas, but he did not attempt to avoid responsibility for them since they were occurring in the Genízaro pueblo he had founded during his first term as governor. Instead, Vélez Cachupín minced no words, saying, "I take responsibility for the surprising nature of this matter, being of major gravity [concerning protecting] the faith and belief which must be given to the denunciations contained therein, made by the devils through the statements of the possessed women."[58]

Just as fray Juan José had taken responsibility for confronting the Devil in Abiquiu, Governor Vélez Cachupín took full responsibility for the witchcraft outbreak. In the first two phases, the conduct complained of had included both witchcraft and native resistance—sorcerers or native healers using their power to harm or heal others (including the priest) and Indian ceremonialism unconnected to witchcraft. Father Ordóñez was probably killed in an act of resistance to Christianization and in an attempt to protect the fragile religious structure of the Abiquiu Genízaros, just as native Andeans had bewitched Spanish officials seeking to extirpate Indian religion and its physical manifestations in Peru.[59] Governor Vélez Cachupín took charge of the second phase with the assistance of Alcalde Fernández, jailing confessed or suspected sorcerers; placing others in Spaniards' homes; and destroying, defacing, and exorcising Indian sacred sites. The governor treated the second phase as a criminal matter, just as witchcraft had usually been treated in New Mexico.

The Third Phase was a different matter. It involved not classic witchcraft, but demonic possession and exorcism. By themselves they did not constitute heresy. Possessed persons were thought to have been deprived of their will, so they were not considered responsible for their actions, and the priest exorcising the afflicted ones was performing a rite of the Church. Normally there was no reason for the Inquisition to be involved with possession and exorcism, but where there was the potential for serious damage to the Church, the Holy Office could take jurisdiction.[60] Vélez Cachupín was apparently aware of this situation, although he was reluctant to involve the Inquisition in the Abiquiu witchcraft outbreak. The governor had broken the power of the Franciscans when he forbade direct correspondence by the New Mexico Franciscans with Mexico City. The only exception was correspondence pertaining to the Inquisition. Vélez Cachupín outmaneuvered the Franciscans by staying clear of the Inquisition in the early 1750s, but narrowly escaped investigation by the Holy Office himself.

A decade and a half later, Governor Vélez Cachupín realized that Father Toledo was unable to quell the rash of demonic possessions that had broken out at Abiquiu in late 1763 and early 1764. Instead of dealing with the Devil directly, the priest faced legions of demons, some who were beginning to provide what appeared to be helpful information rather than simply causing pain. Toledo's exorcisms were not working as they had in mid-1763 at Ojo Caliente. Matters were getting out of hand, as Alcalde García Parejas, himself a believer in demonic possession, was picked by the devil possessing the unnamed woman to receive knowledge that could help end the witchcraft outbreak once and for all. The demonic possessions, once an opportunity to display the power of the Church and the faith of the priest, were becoming an embarrassment.[61] Governor Vélez Cachupín soon became aware that the criminal proceeding Alcalde Fernández was pursuing was insufficient to resolve the problem. Although most of the sorcerers had either been jailed in Santa Fe or placed in Spanish homes, witchcraft incidents were still occurring in Abiquiu, and they threatened the very foundation of the Church. Genízaros such as Atole Caliente were disrupting church services, challenging Father Toledo's authority, and mocking the sacred rite of the Mass.

In an attempt to finally end the witchcraft and demonic possessions at Abiquiu, Governor Vélez Cachupín ordered that a junta or commission of priests be formed to review the reports of diabolical possession by Toledo and García Parejas and to make recommendations on how to proceed. By moving the matter into the realm of the Church, Vélez Cachupín was trying to shift some responsibility from civil to religious authorities, since the demonic possessions were a threat to the authority of the Church. In the past, the intervention of the Inquisition had helped to stop several epidemics of demonic possessions; perhaps it would do so again. Governor Vélez Cachupín knew of the different forms of punishment the Inquisition had meted out and also probably knew of certain notorious cases in which the Holy Office had been consulted regarding demonic possession. Such cases often involved the formation of ecclesiastical councils. The junta he convened was similar in many ways to those earlier councils.[62]

On 31 January 1764, Vélez Cachupín appointed a commission of the top ecclesiastics of New Mexico: Vicar and Ecclesiastical Judge Santiago Roybal; fray Joaquín Rodríguez of San Ildefonso Pueblo; fray Francisco Campo Redondo of Santa Cruz de la Cañada; fray José García and fray José Burgos, both of Santa Fe; fray José Esparragoza y Adame of Nambe; and fray Juan José Toledo of Abiquiu. The priests were charged with the responsibility of examining the recent reports of possession and exorcism from Father Toledo and Alcalde García Parejas and making suggestions for dealing with these occurrences. Vélez Cachupín was in charge of the junta and presided at the first meeting held on 10 February 1764 in the headquarters of the priest who administered the parish of Santa Fe. Of the seven priests who comprised the junta, all but Father Toledo were present. It seems to have been understood by the rest of the commission that their deliberations would be more open and honest without Toledo's presence. The official excuse was that Father Toledo was burdened with work.[63]

It was just as well that fray Juan José was absent, for the debate over his reports, and those of García Parejas, was heated and extended. For two days the junta argued over whether evils spirits really possessed the women and girls. Finally the junta decided that they were in fact possessed and that the demons or evil spirits spoke through them with divine permission. The junta asked García Parejas to ratify the truth of his two reports, an indication of the skepticism with which Vélez Cachupín and the junta greeted the reports of an alcalde who held intimate conversations with the demons possessing the afflicted ones.[64]

In most matters, Tomás Vélez Cachupín was a man of action who preferred to be directly involved in the solution of problems he encountered as governor. He fought the Comanches at San Diego Pond at the head of his troops, went to Abiquiu to personally measure the land he granted to the Genízaros in the Abiquiu grant, and ordered Genízaros freed who had paid their debt to their masters and gave them land at Abiquiu. Still he had the good judgment to avoid, if possible, a direct confrontation with the Devil and his minions at Abiquiu, Santa Fe, or anywhere else.[65]

After extensive deliberations, the junta decided that those possessed by the Devil were evil sorcerers who should be denounced, although this was never carried out. The junta members also suggested that Governor Vélez Cachupín question Joaquinillo and then submit the matter, including the names of the sorcerers supplied by Father Toledo, to the Inquisition in Mexico

City. Special attention should be paid to the Spaniards on the list of sorcerers, but caution should be exercised regarding the witches of Chimayo. Finally the governor was to destroy any remaining idols.[66]

The governor concurred and ordered Alcalde García Parejas to proceed to "the well-known stones and places [which] are to be burned, rubbing out figures and characters and taking the Indian Joaquinillo along for this purpose."[67] In addition, he ordered that neither the Turtle Dance nor other dances about which there was a suspicion of idolatry, were to be permitted.[68] The Abiquiu Genízaros were prohibited from using the drum and performing their songs, "as well as all other vain observances and morning howls that are also practiced in other jurisdictions."[69] It is unclear why the Turtle Dance was singled out, especially since the junta did not mention it, but it was probably because of its association with the mythical figure of Poseyemu, who is said to have given the dance to the pueblos at the time of the Pueblo Revolt. The dance is associated with resistance and rebellion, good reasons in the mind of the governor to ban it. Nevertheless, Pueblos still dance the Turtle Dance.[70] Zuni, Hopi, Taos, Isleta, San Felipe, and San Juan have all performed the Turtle Dance in recent times.[71]

Governor Vélez Cachupín also ordered the alcalde "to destroy the stones and places referred to and burn whatever filthy idols and diabolic offerings they might find, erasing figures and characters as has been done... previously."[72] All missionaries were to perform the rite of exorcism at their pueblos "to uproot this wickedness of the Indians."[73] In spite of his rhetoric, Vélez Cachupín probably understood more about Pueblo and Genízaro religious observances than either of the two alcaldes or Father Toledo. The governor was also an astute observer of the Genízaros. Vélez Cachupín's letter to the viceroy showed him to be an advocate for the Genízaros, presenting a much more sympathetic yet realistic picture of the Genízaros than did either of the two alcaldes or Father Toledo.

On 14 February 1764 Governor Vélez Cachupín summoned Joaquinillo, who was then in jail, to the Governor's Palace for an interview. Alcalde Carlos Fernández had already examined Joaquinillo extensively and Vélez Cachupín had read those reports, but the governor wanted the opportunity to examine Joaquinillo personally as the junta had suggested. Vélez Cachupín reported that Joaquinillo was a Kiowa Indian who had been captured by the Comanches at a young age and then sold to a Spaniard at the Taos trade fair. Asked how he learned the arts of sorcery, Joaquinillo said that his father had taught him, but that he had forgotten most of it because it had been so long ago. Joaquinillo asked his brother, Juan Largo, a Genízaro raised at Santa Ana pueblo, to teach him again, and Juan Largo agreed. Joaquinillo explained that he wanted to learn sorcery to protect himself from the sorcerers at the Genízaro pueblo who were causing death and crippling people.[74]

When Governor Vélez Cachupín asked Joaquinillo how he was taught sorcery, Joaquinillo said he smeared his entire body with herbs and spittle and was then given some of the same herbs (possibly peyote) to chew. After singing a song and invoking a deity, whom Vélez Cachupín called the Devil, Joaquinillo filled an earthenware bowl with water and placed a white stone and what the governor called an idol on top of the water. Joaquinillo told Vélez Cachupín that he could see reflected in the water all the sorcerers from the pueblo of Abiquiu and beyond. Joaquinillo proceeded to name them, helping Governor Vélez Cachupín assemble a list of New Mexico sorcerers (both Indians and Spaniards), which he sent to the viceroy.[75] This was a much more condensed list than the one Joaquinillo had earlier given to Father Toledo.

Now that Governor Vélez Cachupín had the names he wanted, he interrogated Joaquinillo regarding the location of the sites Pueblos held sacred. Joaquinillo gave the governor some of what he wanted without revealing the totality of the Pueblo sacred world. He told the governor that there was a sacred site near San Felipe, which he described, and another near Taos.[76] Like the Stone Lions, these were undoubtedly Pueblo sacred places that may still be venerated today. Vélez Cachupín did not order the destruction or exorcism of these sites as he had the ones near Abiquiu. In his letter to the viceroy, Vélez Cachupín said he thought improvement in religious instruction of the Indians was more important than the destruction of Indian sites. The governor was simply following accepted protocol in asking Joaquinillo about the sites of Pueblo worship and ceremonial dances, but he was beginning to realize that destruction of those religious sites and repression of ceremonial dances did not bring about the Christianization of the Indians.[77]

Joaquinillo provided additional information on three dances performed at the Abiquiu Genízaro pueblo: the Kachina Dance, the Turtle Dance, and the Scalp Dance. He told Vélez Cachupín that the Kachina Dance was danced when Zuni Pueblo so ordered and that although he did not know what they did during the dance, he knew it was evil. Joaquinillo did not know very much about either the Kachina Dance or the Turtle Dance, but reported that the latter was performed on Christmas Eve, Holy Thursday, and Good Friday, intentionally competing with the Spanish Christian religious celebrations. Most startling was the information that during the Turtle Dance "the Devil becomes visible to them and orders what they are to do and predicts what is going to happen" during the coming year.[78] This seems to be a reference to the Tewa mythological figure Poseyemu, who was said to visit different Pueblo dances and rituals, ordering Kachina Dances to be held underground to hide them from the Spaniards, and counseling opposition to Catholicism.

Joaquinillo was most critical of the Scalp Dance as "the one in which all the laws of their heathenism come together." El Descubridor noted that during this dance "the women are shared," and if some Indian man or woman objects to this practice as being against God's law, "they insult him publicly, making a mockery of the law he follows." This probably did not shock Governor Vélez Cachupín, who was used to Pueblo and Plains Indian practices and accepted them, although he did not always agree with them. When he wrote to the viceroy in March, he agreed with the alcalde's recommendation that not all the dances should be banned, for doing so rigorously could cause revolt and incite abandonment of the Pueblo.[79]

Since much of Joaquinillo's declaration referred to his brother, Juan Largo [Trujillo] of Santa Ana Pueblo, Governor Vélez Cachupín decided to take his declaration as well, even though the ecclesiastical junta had not ordered him to do so. Juan Largo added little information regarding the sites where the Indians worshipped but confirmed that the primary site was a cave on San Felipe Mesa. He reported that the cacique of San Felipe had a site at the foot of Sandia Mountain and another one at the peak. At the base of the mountain was a white stone from which the cacique took pieces to his house where Indians from all the pueblos came to purchase them. Joaquinillo told Vélez Cachupín that the cacique asked twelve mantas and twelve knives as the price for a piece of the white stone. Juan Largo continued by saying that the stone at the peak of Sandia Mountain was also considered particularly sacred.[80]

Juan Largo told Governor Vélez Cachupín that sometimes the caciques from all the pueblos called a junta "to instruct the Indians in their law." Indian women were invited "to grind the flour necessary to feed the members of this Indian junta." These women do their work to the sound the musician plays, and when the work [of grinding the corn] is finished...the cacique orders his first official to give the musician one of those Indian women, regardless of her marital status, whom said musician receives as a public concubine." This promiscuity may have scandalized some Spaniards, but probably not Governor Vélez Cachupín or Father Toledo. Indeed, Toledo seems to have accepted native promiscuity when he was later quoted as saying that simple fornication (among the Indians) was not a sin.[81]

What did concern Governor Vélez Cachupín was not so much Indian promiscuity, but the failure of the missionary effort to convert the Indians to Christianity. Juan Largo's declaration explained some of the reasons for this failure. Since the Franciscan priests did not know the languages of the pueblos, their sermons were preached in Latin or Spanish and then interpreted to the Indian congregation by a native interpreter. Juan Largo revealed that most interpreters did not translate word-for-word everything the priest said. Instead, they gave their own interpretation of the substance of the priest's statements, deciding what to believe and what not to believe. After the sermon the Indians went to the interpreter's house and discussed the sermon, usually rejecting most of what the priest said. "They do not believe what the priest says; [they believe] that there is neither God nor Hell."[82] Juan Largo told his brother Joaquinillo that the religion of the Spaniards was not efficacious because "though he [Juan Largo] went to church and asked the saints for something, they never spoke to him nor gave him anything."[83] Belief in Catholicism for Juan Largo came down to the question of whether the Catholic saints were as effective in answering his prayers as were his own gods.

To Franciscan priests such as Father Toledo, Christianization of the Indians meant teaching them to pray and recite the catechism, which the Indians repeated by rote but did not fully understand. The priests taught the Indians the concepts of sin and confession, heaven and Hell, and God and the Devil. They sought to have the Indians participate in the sacraments of baptism, marriage, confession, and the Mass. The primary criticism of the Indian's religious practices was that they continued to believe in their own gods (which the priests called idolatry), often had multiple wives, and refused to participate in the sacraments of marriage or confession. Franciscans and civil authorities such as Governor Vélez Cachupín were split on the reasons for the failure; some believed the Indians' stubbornness in practicing their own religious ceremonies was to blame, others thought the priests' failure to explain Christian concepts in the Indian's own language was at fault. Father Toledo was of the former view, Vélez Cachupín the latter. Juan Largo's statement about the Indians not believing in Hell reflects the priest's use of fear and punishment as a primary tool for breaking Indian resistance. Governor Vélez Cachupín believed in the innate goodness of Pueblos and Genízaros who would embrace the positive side of the Christian religion if only the concepts were explained to them in their own language.[84]

Governor Vélez Cachupín then added a postscript to Juan Largo's declaration. Asked who had taught him the art of divination, the Genízaro responded that it was an unnamed Navajo, the same one that had taught the Indian called Janisco. Then Juan Largo sought to downplay the extent of his involvement with the Navajo by saying "the duties of serving his master did not give him the opportunity to frequent the school of his teacher."[85] Vélez Cachupín noted this down because he probably planned to find out who the unnamed Navajo was. The governor thought he could eradicate the witchcraft outbreak at Abiquiu by finding, jailing, and punishing the primary sorcerers and their teachers. Governor Vélez Cachupín did not count on the possibility that Juan Largo may have made up the Navajo teacher in order to tell the governor what he wanted to hear.

The second part of the governor's postscript showed that Vélez Cachupín might have been drawn into accepting the reality of demonic possession more than his skeptical report to the viceroy would indicate. Vélez Cachupín noted that Juan Largo felt throughout his statement "as though they were squeezing his throat and causing a dry cough that impedes his speaking. He attributes it to persecution by the Devil because he has repented."[86] The governor added the observation that Juan Largo had been coughing severely throughout his declaration, but when speaking of other matters he did not cough. It seems that Governor Vélez Cachupín was now seeing firsthand what it was like when the Devil had you by the throat.

Having completed everything the junta had ordered, Vélez Cachupín made copies of the declarations of Joaquinillo and Juan Largo, together with the reports from Alcalde García Parejas and Father Toledo and prepared to send the proceedings to the viceroy of New Spain, the Marqués de Ervillas, for his information and decision. Before dispatching these documents in March 1764, Governor Vélez Cachupín composed a long report of his own to accompany them, providing a masterful summary of the state of the Pueblos, the Genízaros, and the progress made in converting the Indians to

Christianity. The governor made recommendations for improving the religious instruction of the Pueblos and almost as an afterthought, discussed the strange matters contained in the reports and declarations of Toledo and García Parejas. Vélez Cachupín also appended the complete list of sorcerers—Indians and Spaniards—that Father Toledo sent with his February 1764 report (see Appendix A).[87]

Governor Vélez Cachupín admitted that, although he had taken steps to remedy the outbreak of witchcraft at Abiquiu, he had not fulfilled his duty to God and king. Rather than faulting Father Toledo and the other dedicated Franciscan priests who were trying to Christianize the Pueblos, Vélez Cachupín blamed the flawed system of religious instruction. As the governor succinctly and somewhat arrogantly put it, in the years since the reconquest of New Mexico "we have not gained the spiritual downfall of these wretched Indians."[88]

Spaniards never achieved the spiritual conquest of the Pueblos. In most pueblos today, native religious beliefs and practices still exist alongside an often superficial acceptance of Catholicism. In some cases ceremonial dances such as the Matachines Dance are performed in the Catholic Church. In other pueblos, the church building is considered to be owned by the pueblo, not by the Archdiocese of Santa Fe, just as some rituals of Catholicism have been adopted by the Pueblos and are considered to be more Indian than Hispanic.[89] At Abiquiu the situation was reversed. The Abiqueños still perform Genízaro-inspired dances (now more as a cultural expression than a religious one) at their late November feast day. Some of the names of the dances no one understands. On that one day their Genízaro Indian heritage is recognized, but during the rest of the year Abiquiu residents are Hispanos, indistinguishable from residents of other northern New Mexico villages.[90]

Governor Vélez Cachupín described for the viceroy the methods the priests used to Christianize the Indians and what he thought should be changed to help achieve true conversion to Catholicism. The missionaries "make all young Indians of both sexes attend religious training in the [Catholic] doctrine. On the feast day the entire pueblo prays in Spanish under the fiscal's guidance."[91] The biggest impediment to complete conversion was the failure of the Franciscan priests to learn Pueblo languages. Since all prayers, sermons, and religious instructions were rendered in Spanish or Latin, it was necessary to rely on an interpreter from the pueblo to translate and explain Catholic religious doctrines to the Indians. According to

Vélez Cachupín, the translator explained haphazardly and erroneously, so
that the doctrines he elucidated remained subject to his whim even if he was
not maliciously trying to manipulate the translation. This process was spelled
out in the testimony of Juan Largo.

Governor Vélez Cachupín had pointed out this problem on several occasions before and his criticisms finally inspired the viceregal decree of
November of 1764 ordering the replacement of priests who did not know
the native languages with those who spoke and understood or were willing
to learn them. Yet this decree did not produce fundamental changes in New
Mexico because there were few priests who knew even a smattering of Tewa,
Tiwa, Keresan, or any other Pueblo language.[92]

Another related problem the governor pointed out was the Indians' lack
of comprehension of Catholic doctrine. They were taught prayers, command-
ments, and articles of faith in Spanish, which they were compelled to mem-
orize from childhood. This often produced the effect that they parroted them
without any understanding of their meaning. Thus the governor gave the
Pueblos and especially the Genízaros the benefit of the doubt; they did not
follow Catholic doctrine because they did not understand it. They "only confess on the verge of death and by means of an interpreter who is incompe-
tent. For them to marry it becomes necessary that the justice catches them
living together, for they live in constant sin."[93]

In fact, Indians did not understand the Catholic concept of sin.
According to some anthropologists, teaching the Indians about sin, confession, and penance "played a critical supporting role in the colonization of
the native mind and...in the formation of a disciplined colonized will."[94]
Accordingly, for the Indians of Abiquiu, resistance to the Catholic concepts
of sin, confession, and penance signified resistance to the Spanish attempt
to achieve a spiritual conquest of the indigenous population. Much of the
"witchcraft" that the Genízaros were accused of can thus be seen as a form
of resistance to Christianization, a last protest to the attempted elimination
of their indigenous belief systems. Because the Genízaro's religious beliefs
were a composite of the beliefs of several different tribes, it may have been
easier for the missionaries to eradicate their religion than it was to eradicate that of the Pueblos.

In his report to the viceroy, Governor Vélez Cachupín went to some
lengths to describe the Genízaros and compare them with the Pueblos. As
did most Spanish observers, Vélez Cachupín admired the Pueblos because

they lived in compact, tight-knit communities that were more easily defended against Ute, Comanche, and Navajo raids than were the scattered Hispano settlements. In addition, the governor described the Pueblos as "humble, docile, and very capable of cultivating and working the fields, raising every kind of livestock, and being thrifty and respectable in their everyday dress."[95] Later New Mexico governors and many nineteenth-century Indian agents echoed this high opinion of Pueblos.[96] The Genízaros, according to the governor, were just the opposite of the Pueblos. Vélez Cachupín described them as "perverse, lazy, and with such serious vices, that they are most difficult to regulate and subdue, because they and their families love the life of the vagabond. They move from one place to another within these areas, causing much damage to the planted fields and livestock, living by theft without respect of justice. They are quarrelsome and stubborn in their ways, especially in their love of gambling to the greatest extent." After his glowing assessment of the Pueblos, the governor's view of the Genízaros seemed entirely negative.[97]

On the positive side, however, Vélez Cachupín reported that the Genízaros were the best fighters, serving as auxiliaries to Spanish troops assigned to protect Spanish settlements from attack. This was the reason Governor Vélez Cachupín established the Genízaro pueblo at Abiquiu in the first place, settling some sixty Genízaro families there in 1754 with the approval of the viceroy. Now Vélez Cachupín was seeking viceregal authorization to found another settlement of Genízaros in Gila Apache country on the banks of the Río del Oro in southern New Mexico. The governor could not be too critical of the Genízaros at Abiquiu, or the second settlement of Genízaros on the Río del Oro would not be approved.[98]

When Vélez Cachupín came to the question of whether the bad characteristics of the Genízaros were "an innate propensity" or the result of improper training by their masters, the governor chose the latter explanation. The Genízaros were not inherently bad, as some priests believed, but lacked proper training by their Spanish masters who assigned them work as "shepherds and wood-gatherers. Through this kind [of work] with [its] lack of responsibilities, they fall into vices through the coarse life of the country."[99] The governor considered the Genízaros to be Spaniards "because they were brought up since childhood by Spaniards who ransomed them from the *naciones bárbaras* [uncivilized nations] such as the Comanches, Utes, Navajos, and Apaches." Since the Genízaros were brought up in Spanish households from the time they were children, Vélez Cachupín believed they should be given responsibilities and raised like the other Spanish children in the family, not treated like servants and given the most menial tasks. But Genízaros were almost universally considered to be servants. They were purchased for that purpose, and their Spanish masters often did not take seriously their obligation to raise them as family members and teach them Christian doctrine. Thus, when they were given land, they were often unprepared to be farmers and support themselves with the crops they raised.[100]

The Genízaros that Vélez Cachupín settled at Abiquiu were more Indian than Spaniard. They preferred their old life based on hunting and their old religion, which supported the practices and rituals of hunting and other ceremonies focused on fertility and bringing the rain. Their sacred sites such as the Stone Lions were not pagan idols as Father Toledo and Governor Vélez Cachupín thought, but shrines venerated by Pueblos and the Genízaros alike. The Stone Lions shrine at Bandelier National Monument centers on a pair of mountain lions carved into the top of two side-by-side boulders near the ancient pueblo of Yapashe. The Stone Lions occupy the southwestern part of an enclosure of large boulders three to five feet high and are still considered a sacred shrine. In August 2003 the shrine was surrounded by an oval of interlocking antlers, another indication that the association of the mountain lion with its hunting prowess is the main reason for the veneration of the shrine.[101]

Governor Vélez Cachupín's vision for how the Genízaro settlement at Abiquiu could work for the benefit of the Indians as well as for the Spanish is succinctly expressed in the governor's plan "to bring together vagrant families of genizaros and settle them in places with ample [lands] capable of providing for their subsistence, with a priest, for their instruction and to administer the holy sacraments. It would serve as a foundation, drawing together all those of this nature that have been freed from their owners and are married."[102] The governor reminded Viceroy Ervillas that Vélez Cachupín had settled sixty families at Abiquiu "on good lands at an agreeable and comfortable place ... at the ancient Abiquiu pueblo which had been destroyed long ago by Plains Indians."[103] Echoing the language of the great book of laws applicable to the Americas, the *Recopilación de leyes de los reinos de las Indias*, Governor Vélez implied that the 1754 Genízaro pueblo was established in accordance with the *Recopilación*'s explicit provisions for the quantity and quality of land to be granted to Indians.[104]

Governor Vélez Cachupín told the viceroy that he had "removed and imprisoned six evil sorcerers who with their evil witchcraft have killed many people in that pueblo [of Abiquiu]," and that he had "destroyed various infernal hidden places of worship in those surrounding areas used for idolatry."[105] Vélez Cachupín's direct action against the persons and places connected with Abiquiu witchcraft, together with the list of sorcerers he provided, was all he could do to resolve the problem in his civil administration. The questions of demonic possession and exorcisms were religious matters that the governor hoped to pass off to the Inquisition.

Governor Vélez Cachupín also commented on the witchcraft allegations contained in the reports of Father Toledo and Alcalde García Parejas. Vélez Cachupín was quite skeptical of both reports: "These are very rare and unusual cases and demand further proof than the simple narrative of a single subject in order to be credible."[106] Perhaps the governor envisioned a proceeding before the Inquisition that would include testimony by Father Toledo and others who were witness to the possessions and exorcisms. Such a proceeding would take the question of their credibility out of the governor's jurisdiction. Then he could concentrate on the six sorcerers imprisoned in Santa Fe and devote his full energies to matters of frontier defense.

As much as he wanted to be rid of the issues of witchcraft, possessions, and exorcisms, Governor Vélez Cachupín could not resist making his own comments on the Toledo and García Parejas reports. He did not understand how possessed women could provide helpful information while the Devil possessed them. The unnamed woman's declaration named names and pointed out places of idolatrous worship. The governor wondered how the Devil and the lesser demons could possess this women and then point out manifestations of their own work in Abiquiu. What mystified Vélez Cachupín as he read the reports was that they did not conform to the traditional Christian concept of the Devil. Moreover, it seemed that the beginning of the end of the Abiquiu witch craze was coming from the Devil himself.[107] Apparently "God can compel the Devil to praise [God] and promote his honor and glory, and the good of all his souls, but it is very unusual that the Devil seeks to ease [the pain] of the holy souls in purgatory."[108] The governor was referring to statements made by the devil possessing the unknown woman who advised Alcalde García Parejas that the wife and children of the deceased former Alcalde Juan Esteban García (Noriega) should offer a novena of masses for the deceased, because his soul was in such grave danger for all the dealings that he had in this life with the *Orejones*, which is what the Genízaros called the priests. What was even more incredible was that some of the women possessed by the Devil urged the Abiquiu Genízaros to repent and disavow their indigenous religious practices for the good of their souls.

Neither the governor nor Father Toledo could disagree with this admonition to the Genízaros to give up their pagan practices, but by doing so they were agreeing with the Devil. The line between good and evil was becoming blurred. As Vélez Cachupín closed his report to the viceroy, it became clear that the governor did not know what to do in this ambiguous situation and was hoping that by submitting the case to the viceroy of New Spain and the Inquisition, the situation at Abiquiu would calm down and resolve itself. In fact, this is exactly what happened. Once Governor Vélez Cachupín expressed skepticism about the possessions and exorcisms, Father Toledo was no longer at center stage, and the possessions and exorcisms eventually died out. As the possessions began to subside in Abiquiu, Vélez Cachupín turned his attention to the criminal case Alcalde Fernández had been pursuing against the jailed sorcerers and the accused witches serving in Spanish households. The last document filed in the criminal proceeding was dated 16 August 1763, after which the trial was interrupted by the possession and exorcisms during the fall of 1763 and spring of 1764. The governor wanted to reopen the suspended criminal proceedings, but before filing the report regarding Father Toledo's afflictions, he decided to take matters in his own hands and try to find out the cause of Toledo's ailments and how to cure them.

Vélez Cachupín studied the accusations and confessions in the second phase of the witchcraft proceedings and came to the conclusion that María Trujillo, Vicente's wife, was the cause of Father Toledo's suffering. Paula, María's niece, had accused María and Vicente of trying to cause the priest's death by "putting herbs in his food and making a doll in his image which represents him."[109] María had refused to confess to this charge, although she admitted to some of the charges against her. Because of her partial confession, María was placed in the house of Miguel Tenorio and Corporal José Maldonado, and Vicente Trujillo was incarcerated in the Santa Fe jail. A further incident involving María and Father Toledo persuaded Governor Vélez Cachupín that he would have to use stronger methods to obtain her full confession.[110]

When Father Toledo came to Santa Fe to visit Tenorio and Maldonado, María Trujillo came out to see him, kissed his hand and hugged him, which he permitted because she was one of his parishioners. Several days later,

Toledo's pains came back with renewed force, similar to the pains he suffered before the sorcerers were imprisoned.[111] María had hexed Father Toledo again! Even after being placed in the Tenorio-Maldonado house as a servant, Trujillo had succeeded in furthering her attempt to kill Father Toledo. The brazen Trujillo had once again outwitted the Spanish authorities, continuing her attack on Father Toledo under the guise of a show of affection for her parish priest. Governor Vélez Cachupín could tolerate no more. Accustomed to dealing directly with problems confronting him, he made the following highly unusual order: Trujillo was to have her hands bound behind her and she was to be tied to the wheel of a gun carriage in an uncomfortable position, with the hope that this torture would induce her to confess her crime. Without any authorization from higher authorities, Governor Vélez Cachupín decided to administer a form of torture on María Trujillo. After eight hours of this ordeal, she called for Alcalde Fernández, telling him that if he would release her she would confess. Carlos Fernández untied María and brought her before Governor Vélez Cachupín. Exhausted by the torture, Trujillo made her confession.[112]

María admitted to Governor Vélez Cachupín that she had bewitched Father Toledo. It began, according to her testimony, when she was gathering *chimajá* (parsley), and wondering if she would meet "someone [who] should teach [her] to be a witch and to cast spells with some herbs that were around there." Suddenly a man appeared who was more dark skinned than light. When María told him what she wanted, the man (the Devil) told her "to gather an herb... called *Colorado*, properly speaking, Dragon's Blood, then dry it, grind it, and put it in the food or drink of the person she wanted to bewitch."[113]

Soon thereafter, Trujillo got the opportunity to try Dragon's Blood on Father Toledo. María put some of the herb in his food during the week when she was serving as the priest's cook. She put some Dragon's Blood in a plate of tamales with mutton that she served Toledo. María Trujillo was upset with Father Toledo for having punished a male servant, so when the Dragon's Blood herb worked and Toledo suffered stomach pains, María tried adding shelled piñones to Father Toledo's food with the intention that the piñones would make his stomach swell and a ball would form inside. When this happened, and Toledo had finally succeeded in expelling the first ball, María confessed that she gave Father Toledo another agent to make him ill, "a bit of cooked squash with the intention that his stomach pain would increase."[114]

This also worked, and María Trujillo finally confessed that this was why Father Toledo was suffering at the time.

It seems incredible that Father Toledo allowed María Trujillo to be his cook when he suspected her of witchcraft, especially after he began to suffer stomach pains. Of course Toledo did not have much choice when it came to a cook, since many of the Abiquiu Genízaras were also suspected of witchcraft. It should be remembered that for most of the first two phases of the witchcraft proceedings, Father Toledo did not suspect Trujillo of witchcraft but believed that either El Cojo or Agustín Tagle was responsible for his afflictions.

When asked whether she was responsible for the dizziness the priest was suffering, María denied it. As to other sorcerers, Trujillo said she did not know whether her husband, Vicente, was a sorcerer, but "he is reputed to be one [and]...he speaks badly [of people], swears, curses a lot, and is gone from the house at night a lot. At other times he returns at midnight."[115] Trujillo added that she overheard her husband in the presence of Juan Mascarenas of Chimayo say that he knew how to devour priests. Having confessed to the most important unsolved crime in Abiquiu, María Trujillo stated that she had not done harm to anyone other than fray Juan José.

Following Trujillo's confession, Vélez Cachupín took part in a most extraordinary proceeding involving the cure she had promised. Leaving nothing to chance, the governor confronted the confessed witch in Father Toledo's presence and asked her how she planned to cure the priest. "She answered that with the same red herb [Dragon's Blood] ground up and applied twice in this form to the stomach and surrounding area, as well as to the chest of the said reverend father." Governor Vélez Cachupín then supervised, in his typically direct and matter-of-fact manner, "both [the] grinding of the herb and applying the cure, without intervening ceremony of any kind."[116]

Governor Vélez Cachupín was careful to note that María Trujillo had not performed any ceremony, because the use of a ceremony in connection with an herbal cure—even a Christian ceremony—was considered heresy punishable by the Inquisition. Curanderos who were Indians were not subject to the Inquisition but were often punished by extirpators of idolatry under the ecclesiastical jurisdiction of bishops and archbishops. The supernatural origin of healing powers not associated with the Catholic Church irked Church authorities. Even when no ceremony was performed in connection with an herbal cure, Church officials often thought that mere knowledge of the curing properties of plants had to have a supernatural element—even a pact with the Devil—because such knowledge could not be obtained from books alone.[117]

After the application of the Dragon's Blood herb to Father Toledo, Vélez Cachupín reported that "the said reverend priest said . . . that he finds himself markedly relieved of his pains."[118] The cure had worked! The unorthodox procedure Governor Vélez Cachupín followed to obtain Trujillo's confession and induce her to cure Father Toledo had been so successful that Governor Vélez Cachupín was never criticized for using torture to obtain this positive result.

Having confessed and then cured Father Toledo, María Trujillo received a relatively light sentence and was apparently returned to the house of Tenorio and Maldonado to continue as a household servant. It is unknown whether the experience of being suspended on a gun carriage wheel for the better part of a day was enough to change her ways, but since no more is heard from her until her sentencing, it may well have been. The torture and confession of María Trujillo had a profound effect on the prisoners in the Santa Fe jail, however. A day after she cured Father Toledo, the imprisoned Genízaro Indians notified Governor Vélez Cachupín that they were ready to make new confessions.[119]

On 1 May 1764, Salvador Rivera, the royal guard in charge of the incarcerated sorcerers, notified Vélez Cachupín of the prisoners' willingness to confess. The governor again commissioned Alcalde Carlos Fernández to hear those confessions, "not just those who deny [witchcraft] but also those who confessed [already] in case they have anything new to add to their confessions."[120] It seems that the example of María Trujillo had persuaded the imprisoned sorcerers that confessions might be the way to obtain their freedom. They were learning that telling their Spanish prosecutors at least part of what they wanted to hear was a possible key to unlock the door of their prison.

The first accused sorcerer to make a new confession was Vicente Trujillo, María's husband, who was familiarly called Vicentillo by the Spanish authorities. Vicentillo denied that he had ever been a sorcerer, stating that he did not know the Devil and had never opposed God. When confronted with his wife's statement that "he knew how to devour priests," he denied ever having uttered those words.[121] What he did say was that since he had not done anything wrong, neither the priest nor anyone else should punish him.

Pedro Trujillo was the next accused sorcerer to confess, but he was more interested in pointing the finger at El Cojo and in defending himself against charges El Cojo made against him than he was in confessing wrongdoing on his own part. Pedro Trujillo noted that Miguel, El Cojo, had accused him of performing witchcraft by becoming a cat and asked that El Cojo be brought before him to repeat the allegation. This part of a criminal trial was called the *careo*, a face-to-face confrontation between parties to a criminal procedure. It was designed to get at the truth by requiring witnesses to repeat their allegations in front of the person they were accusing. In this instance, it seems there was a prearranged scheme whereby El Cojo was to change his testimony against Trujillo. The plan backfired, however, under the watchful eye of Alcalde Fernández who was taking down the "confessions."[122]

At first El Cojo told Alcalde Fernández that his accusation against Trujillo was coerced because "an Indian from Abiquiu named Francisco tied him up and whipped him cruelly."[123] When Fernández pointed out the inconsistency between this statement and El Cojo's first one, which failed to mention an Indian named Francisco, El Cojo reverted to his initial statement that Trujillo had performed witchcraft in the form of a cat. El Cojo said he heard this from María Francisca, an Indian woman from Abiquiu, who claimed that Trujillo, having assumed the shape an animal, was killing her.[124]

María Francisca said she knew Pedro Trujillo was a sorcerer because when he lived in Santa Ana Pueblo the priest there, Father Juan Elezaun, had written to Father Ordóñez in Abiquiu telling him not to admit Trujillo into Abiquiu because he had killed many people at Santa Ana with his witchcraft. While there Trujillo had been cohabiting with an unmarried Indian woman, and Father Elezaun told him either to get married or leave the pueblo. When Pedro tried to get married, the Santa Ana Indians would not let him, so Father Elezaun sent him to Santa Fe with a letter to Governor Marín del Valle. The governor ordered Trujillo to go live at Ojo Caliente, but before he could do that, Trujillo married María Francisca of Abiquiu Pueblo, the same one who charged him with attempting to kill her.[125] Trujillo admitted certain wrongdoing, such as cohabitation, but claimed to be innocent of witchcraft. Once again an accused sorcerer admitted some charges against him but denied the most serious charge of witchcraft.

Even though the remaining defendants also indicated they were ready to confess, most refused to admit they were involved in any activities connected with witchcraft. After Pedro Trujillo, several other accused sorcerers made so-called voluntary confessions, which Alcalde Fernández painstakingly recorded. Diego Tagle said that he took part in a hunting ceremony conducted by Antonio, El Chimayó, "when they went out to hunt with some feathers in order to catch many deer."[126] Tagle thus admitted to participating in a Native American hunting ritual, not a ceremony of witchcraft. He also denied being a sorcerer or having made a pact with the Devil.

Tagle added to his confession, but instead of admitting any conduct on his part he also accused El Cojo of being a sorcerer who had made a Devil's Pact. Tagle said that while they were all imprisoned, "there appeared Miguel, El Cojo, naked, laying on his back, [who] in a high voice began to sing [whereupon] there appeared in the skylight a swallow which he had not seen until Mauricio, one of the prisoners, praised the Holy Sacrament."[127] The introduction of the Christian symbol of the holy sacrament was a new element in Tagle's confessions and was another example of the Genízaros telling the Spaniards what they wanted to hear, though in this case the Spaniards were not convinced.

Pedro, El Paseño, confessed next. He admitted to being a curandero "when he lived in the Rio Abajo and [he] and Joaquinillo went about curing others."[128] He named El Cojo as the only sorcerer among the defendants, echoing what the other accused sorcerers and witches had said. El Paseño repeated the story of El Cojo summoning a swallow, adding that the swallow spoke to El Cojo through the skylight of the jail. He commented that he wondered what El Cojo could do as a free man if he could perform such sorcery while in prison. Everyone seemed to be attacking El Cojo as a way of establishing his or her own innocence.

The last prisoner questioned was the Genízaro Antonio Ulibarrí, who said he had nothing more to confess beyond what he had already stated.[129] Alcalde Fernández delivered these new confessions to Governor Vélez Cachupín with the request that the governor review them and do what he thought appropriate. The governor responded two weeks later by ordering Fernández to arrest and question Antonio Menchero and Janisco. If their answers were as evasive as were those of the other Genízaros, he was to imprison them until the governor sentenced all the defendants.[130]

Antonio Menchero proved as evasive as the other sorcerers and adept at providing bits of information that seemed helpful on the surface but usually led to a dead end. Menchero initially denied doing any harm by witchcraft but admitted having "illicit relations with a female Genízara Indian from [Abiquiu] Pueblo named María de la Luz." This statement followed the pattern of the declarations of the other Genízaros, strongly indicating that the defendants had discussed their so-called confessions, arriving at a similar story that was relatively consistent. One part of the agreed story was to deny being a sorcerer while admitting knowledge of something about the practice of witchcraft. Another part was to accuse someone else, particularly El Cojo, of being a sorcerer or having taught sorcery. Sometimes the sorcerer mentioned was from another pueblo or was conveniently dead.[131]

Menchero's declaration followed this pattern when he admitted that a deceased Indian named Patricio from San Felipe Pueblo had tried to teach him sorcery "by giving him some powders . . . [which he] ordered him to swallow [with] an arrow and that at the inception of swallowing the arrow, it began to hurt him and [he] then pulled it out of his mouth and returned it to the said Patricio along with the powders, telling him that he was no longer interested in learning."[132] Menchero's vivid account changed, however, when he was confronted with one of his accusers: Joaquinillo.

Aware of his right to be confronted by his accuser, Menchero asked that Joaquinillo be required to repeat the accusation he had made against him in Alcalde Fernández's presence. Once this was done, Menchero again admitted that he had started to learn sorcery from Patricio, but added an element of Christian belief to his story about being ordered to swallow the arrow. Menchero said that when ordered to swallow the arrow, he had shouted "Jesus and Mary," and though the arrow lodged in his throat, he was able to pull it out. To this Joaquinillo responded that when he and Menchero were at Sandia, Menchero had tried to bewitch and kill the priest there, Father Irigoyen, with an herb that was used both to bewitch and kill and as a love potion. Joaquinillo testified that Menchero had shown him the herb, which Menchero had "put in the water jar from which the priest drank."[133]

In a series of partial admissions and denials Menchero first acknowledged that he had once possessed an herb that he used as a love potion, but when Joaquinillo insisted that Menchero still had the herb and made use of it, Menchero denied it. Joaquinillo then accused Menchero of using the love potion to facilitate his illicit love affair with María de la Luz and of having killed her with a bewitched bone. Again Menchero denied the charge, admitting that he had given her a bone but denying that it was bewitched or that he had killed her. As a result of this extended form of questioning, which was similar to cross-examination, Joaquinillo was able to obtain a few admissions from Menchero but in the process implicated himself. Upon receiving this "confession" of Antonio Menchero, Governor Vélez Cachupín declared both Joaquinillo and Menchero to be liars.[134]

Besides Menchero, the other Genízaro Governor Vélez Cachupín ordered jailed and examined was Janisco. When Alcalde Fernández questioned him, Janisco admitted that "he knew how to cure bewitched people," and that he used herbs in his cures. When asked how he cured, Janisco responded that it was through God and the Holy Cross. Here again one of the most powerful sorcerers introduced Christian rituals and iconography into his confession with the hope that it would appease the Spaniards. Instead, Alcalde Fernández became so irritated with Janisco that he summarily increased his sentence when Janisco refused to answer any more questions by claiming he was deaf.[135]

Because of Janisco's reluctance to discuss fully the charges against him, Alcalde Fernández arranged a confrontation among Janisco, Joaquinillo, and Juan Largo. Joaquinillo stated that the Genízaros summoned Janisco to Abiquiu because "many suffered illnesses and deaths at that Bewitched Pueblo."[136] This was the first time that it was acknowledged—beyond what Father Toledo had reported—how widespread witchcraft had become at Abiquiu. When Janisco first arrived at the "bewitched pueblo," he performed a ceremony for the Genízaros gathered there and announced that the two main sorcerers at Abiquiu were Joaquinillo, who was an hechicero who cured and predicted the future, and El Cojo who killed people.[137] According to Joaquinillo, Janisco at that time was known throughout New Mexico as the main curandero and hechicero. Janisco responded that he knew how to cure with herbs and repeated that his method was through God and the Holy Cross and that he knew who the sorcerers were in Abiquiu. Alcalde Fernández noted that Janisco was probably not telling the truth.[138]

A few weeks later Juan Tagle made a declaration, which did not amount to a confession; rather, it was an accusation against Isabel, La Pastora. Tagle testified that La Pastora had cured an ill woman at the Abiquiu Genízaro pueblo by placing a toad that may have been alive or dead over part of the woman's body "leaving the rest of [her body] nude, and then she [Isabel, La Pastora] made horrible sounds as she sang and danced; and that was the cure which she made."[139] This accusation seems to have been based on an eyewitness account, and whether the cure was effective, it certainly smacked of witchcraft. What was unclear was why Tagle emphasized La Pastora's witchcraft, when no one else had mentioned her previously. Perhaps he was trying to deflect attention from his own activities.

The Spaniard Salvador García made the last of the declarations against Antonio Menchero. García stated that "it is publicly known in all of the Rio Abajo that the said Menchero is a sorcerer and that the Reverend Padre Irigoyen... told him that Menchero should be placed in the stocks, until he is dead for being a sorcerer."[140] Salvador García's contact with Menchero began when Menchero came to García's house needing some blacksmithing work done. Since García was away, his wife told Menchero to return another day when her husband was there. Nevertheless, Menchero stayed overnight, and according to García's wife, remained awake and tried to bewitch her. The next day García came home. After García completed the blacksmithing work, García's wife became ill, and it was thought that Menchero had bewitched her. At his wit's end, García obtained permission from fray Agustín Iniesta and Alcalde Antonio Baca to bring Menchero to his house and pay him to see if he could cure his wife.[141] García did not disclose how much he paid Menchero, but this desperate measure did not work. The cure performed was similar to the traditional Native American sweat lodge in which García's wife was given "steam from hot rocks and juniper branches."[142] When the patient did not improve, García went to San Felipe looking for an Indian called El Navajó, who Menchero said could cure her. While García was gone, Menchero again came to his house, unbidden, and attempted a second cure of García's wife. Menchero made a large pile of hot coals at the door of the house and walked barefoot on the live coals. He gathered them with his hands and placed them in his mouth, blowing on them and making horrible gestures and movements (this activity is similar to Mauricio's demonstration of power in Ojo Caliente in May 1763). Menchero approached the ill woman, surrounding her in smoke and sucking small stones and other items from her body. This second cure worked no better than the first, and a short time later, García's wife died.[143]

García was so enraged when he found out about the second attempted cure that he "called Menchero and told him to get away from his home and never return, because if he did he would shoot him dead."[144] It does not appear that García ever brought a lawsuit or made any claim against

Menchero, but he repeated the story to so many people that it soon became well known that Antonio Menchero was a sorcerer.

Governor Vélez Cachupín probably took this declaration with a grain of salt. He had already read the earlier declarations when Juan Largo and Joaquinillo had sucked objects out of the bodies of Agustín Tagle and Miguel Ontiveros (El Cojo), and he was probably unimpressed by these examples of shooting sorcery. García was in the same position Father Toledo had been earlier when he enlisted the Ute sorcerer to attempt a confrontation with El Cojo. That effort had also been a failure, but Father Toledo had gone to great pains to justify his use of one type of witchcraft against another.[145]

When Governor Vélez Cachupín received these so-called confessions, which Alcalde Fernández recorded from early May 1764 to early July 1764, he was unimpressed. The governor did not believe the testimony of Joaquinillo or his brother Juan Largo. Since Joaquinillo had been considered the most trustworthy Genízaro, Vélez Cachupín's loss of faith in him meant that there was no one left to believe. The governor's decree of 12 July 1764 reflected this skepticism, mixed with a degree of practicality. He ordered that the Genízaros who were in prison should remain there but be given more freedom of movement so that their labor could be harnessed for the benefit of the Spanish government. He ordered that for male prisoners, their shackles were to be removed and replaced by wooden fetters (*cormas de madera*) around the instep so that they could labor on public works projects on government buildings and the presidio but would not be able to escape from custody.[146]

Ever the pragmatist, Vélez Cachupín needed to keep the male sorcerers in jail because none of them had reformed, confessed, and become Christians; yet, he needed their labor. The governor could not return sorcerers to Abiquiu or relocate them to any other community lest they cause a new outbreak of witchcraft. The so-called confessions, in which most defendants named other defendants as sorcerers while denying their own guilt, made it clear to the governor that all were equally guilty. Since some defendants, such as El Cojo, practiced a form of witchcraft in jail, it was no less clear that many of them would revert to their old ways if released. Placing the wooden fetters on the feet of the male sorcerers meant that they could walk in a fashion but could not run away and escape. Thus the prisoners could work on the presidio and the Casas Reales, as those adobe structures were always in need of repair. Other governors had used the forced

labor of a defendant to repair the government buildings around the Santa
Fe Plaza, and Governor Vélez Cachupín was following this traditional punishment, but he was getting some free labor out of the sorcerers even before
they were sentenced.[147]

Governor Vélez Cachupín also gave some attention to the matter of the
women who had been accused of being witches and who had all been assigned
to various Spaniard's households as servants. One named Juana was ordered
freed so that she could return to her husband in Abiquiu because she was
found not guilty. Here, the governor exercised his authority as judge in the
witchcraft proceeding to release a defendant against whom there was insufficient evidence to proceed. As to other witches placed as servants in the
houses of leading Spanish citizens in Santa Fe, they were to be excluded from
the entertainment found in those houses. This was probably a provision
meant for the protection of the guests and residents of the households.[148]
As Governor Vélez Cachupín concluded his interim order in the witchcraft
proceedings, he remembered some wooden figurines that had been confiscated as part of the "rites of idolatry," which the Genízaros were said to have
performed. The governor ordered that "the wooden figurines...are to be
burnt in a bonfire along with the rest of the items such as feathers and glass
beads which are used in diabolic pacts."[149] Reminiscent of the burning of
the sacred books of the Maya Indians in the Yucatán by Bishop Diego de
Landa in the late sixteenth century, this theatrical exercise of a public burning of what must have been Native American sacred objects was meant to
inspire fear and a forced acceptance of Christian rituals.[150]

Finally Governor Vélez Cachupín, in a completely unforeseen move,
ordered Joaquinillo and Juan Largo released from jail and sent back to
Abiquiu under Father Toledo's care. This was a bit surprising in light of the
governor's skepticism about the veracity of these two Genízaros, but Vélez
Cachupín believed they had shown some repentance "with respect to the
magic that they confess to, while it is doubtful that they have used it in order
to injure anyone as witchcraft."[151]

The governor and Father Toledo had apparently discussed the question
of whether Joaquinillo and Juan Largo would be more useful in jail or back
at the pueblo. In the past, Joaquinillo had been an ally to Father Toledo, helping him root out sorcerers such as El Cojo, Vicente Trujillo, and his wife,
María. María and Vicente Trujillo, who had directed their sorcery at Father
Toledo himself, were either in jail or serving in Spanish households in Santa

Fe, although they turned up in Abiquiu two decades later. The threat to Father Toledo had been removed, and the priest had apparently recovered from his afflictions. The witchcraft outbreak in Abiquiu was coming to an end.

Having Joaquinillo and Juan Largo at the pueblo might help suppress any further outbreaks. In the confrontation between Joaquinillo, Juan Largo, and Janisco, Joaquinillo was described as a curandero, an hechicero who cured and predicted the future. Juan Largo stated that although "he [Joaquinillo] had the art of predicting and curing...he had...repented and could no longer use the art, and even if he could he would not do it, although he understood the superior power of the art."[152] Statements such as these may have persuaded Governor Vélez Cachupín that Joaquinillo and Juan Largo were primarily healers, and if they had engaged in harming people through witchcraft, they had repented and promised never to do it again. Most important, Joaquinillo and Juan Largo had learned more information from Janisco about how to identify any additional sorcerers who remained at the pueblo. This would be valuable to Father Toledo in keeping the lid on any further witchcraft outbreaks at Abiquiu, while allowing the healing by curanderos and the practice of native ceremonials, such as the Turtle Dance, to continue.

With this temporary order Governor Vélez Cachupín dealt with all aspects of the Abiquiu witchcraft outbreak except the possessions and exorcisms of December 1763 and January 1764. As to that inflammatory question he had gathered a council of clerics, which had referred that matter to the viceroy in Mexico City. The governor's move had pushed the demonic possession and exorcism situation off of center stage and calmed things down. The question of how the Inquisition would react to Father Toledo's marathon exorcisms and his confrontation with the Devil remained.

Figure 19
La Come Gallinas suffers public shame by being honeyed and feathered. *Drawing by Glen Strock.*

CHAPTER ELEVEN

The Witchcraft Proceedings

Phase Four: The Inquisition's Response and Punishment of the Genízaros

W hen the witchcraft file Governor Vélez Cachupín had assembled reached Mexico City, the viceroy's staff was somewhat baffled as to how to deal with it. In particular, the viceroy did not want anything to do with the charges of demonic possession, especially after the Querétaro debacle just over fifty years earlier. So the viceroy—as he usually did in cases such as this—asked Licenciado Felipe de Luna to summarize the documents and report with his recommendation. Rather than making his own review of this bulky file containing so much fantastical testimony, Luna simply summarized Vélez Cachupín's report, agreeing with the governor's points almost to the letter. Licenciado

Luna placed particular emphasis on the reports of Father Toledo and
Alcalde García Parejas.

Licenciado Luna thought that statements supposedly made by the Devil
speaking through a possessed person were not credible. According to Luna
the Devil was capable only of evil acts, and it was inappropriate for the Evil
One to counsel the Indians to seek atonement for their sins. Seeking forgiveness for their sins, including the sin of killing Father Ordóñez, was what
one would expect Father Toledo to counsel, not the Devil. Imputing the worthy act of seeking forgiveness and absolution for ones' sins to the Devil was
to turn the concept of the Devil on its head.

Franciscans, including Toledo, taught and preached that the primary
motivation for strict adherence to Christian doctrine (particularly the annual
confession of one's sins) was that failure to do so would mean eternal
damnation in a Hell presided over by the Devil. The depiction of Hell and
the Devil was one of absolute evil, where pain and torments of all imagi-
nable kinds awaited the sinner. This does not square with a Devil who
advised people to confess and seek atonement for their sins.[1] Also troubling
to Licenciado Luna was the notion that the Devil could penetrate the innermost core of one's being and learn one's private thoughts that had not been
communicated to any other living being. This, too, flew in the face of
accepted beliefs about the Devil. According to those beliefs, the Devil could
attack individuals from the outside, causing them to suffer disease and illness but could not penetrate the innermost core of a God-fearing Christian
who scrupulously followed the rituals of the Catholic Church. This is why
Licenciado Luna expressed skepticism about Alcalde García Parejas's
report that the Devil, speaking through the possessed woman, knew specific facts about the alcalde's personal life that no one else knew. As
Licenciado Luna put it, "It is the common opinion of [the learned authors]
that the Devil cannot penetrate one internally, although he can wound by
some external actions."[2]

Felipe de Luna thought many of García Parejas's reports strained
credulity. He said that the most incredulous parts were: when the Devil, speaking through María Vallejo, said he wanted to root out sorcerers so that the
evil in the land might be uncovered; when the Devil, speaking through one
of the possessed women, told Alcalde García Parejas things about his private life that only the alcalde knew; and when the Devil, speaking through
another possessed woman, counseled Abiquiu residents "that they should

ask forgiveness for their sins and for everything that happened with that father missionary [Father Félix Ordóñez]," who was said to have been bewitched and poisoned by one of the Genízaros.[3]

Faced with testimony from García Parejas and Father Toledo that challenged the traditional concept of the Devil, Luna raised doubts about *their* credibility, just as Governor Vélez Cachupín had done. These doubts were expressed in a subtle manner, because neither Luna nor Vélez Cachupín wanted to remove Toledo from the thankless job of parish priest at Santo Tomás Apóstol de Abiquiú. They simply wanted to rein in the out-of-control marathon exorcisms. The tactic of involving the authorities in Mexico City in a debate regarding the attributes of the Devil was similar to the approach inquisitors took in Querétaro where they found it easier "to blame the 'fantasies' and 'hypocrisies' of ignorant and sanctimonious women for whatever they found to be contrary to the traditional concept of the devil."[4] The difference between the Querétaro and Abiquiu cases was that Luna and Vélez Cachupín were willing to cast the net of skepticism over Toledo and García Parejas as well.

Felipe de Luna also flung a veil of doubt over other aspects of the reports from New Mexico. He found it incredible that Father Toledo would certify the truth of what appeared to be outlandish reports from Abiquiu. Luna also noted that it was amazing that the Devil, through the agency of the possessed ones, could provide a list of sorcerers and witches at Abiquiu and beyond (the short list) so that they could be eliminated for the good of the pueblo. In addition, it strained Luna's credulity to accept the report of what happened after proceedings at the *paraje* of El Torreón destroyed a so-called Indian temple. As witnessed by Joaquinillo, Father Toledo, and Alcalde García Parejas, the Devil speaking through one of the possessed women "rose up to impede the enterprise," warning the alcalde that "the people who went with him should receive the blessing and that on the road they should praise the Creator…and call on La Copetana (which is what they call the Most Holy Virgin)."[5] These were not the kinds of admonitions that the Devil was expected to utter.

As was often the case when authorities in Mexico City were asked to rule on legal and spiritual matters from New Mexico, Luna had no comprehension of what was happening on the ground in Abiquiu. Father Toledo, by contrast, understood it in his bones since the sorcerers had attacked him personally. Luna knew in his bureaucratic mind, however, that neither the viceroy

nor the Inquisition wanted to become mired in Father Toledo's struggle with
the Devil. For one thing, Toledo was losing the battle, and in addition, the
Devil who was speaking through the possessed women did not fit the traditional concept of Satan. All too often, the Devil's utterances seemed too
beneficent to be coming from the very embodiment of evil.

Vélez Cachupín had made a similar analysis, casting doubt on much that
Father Toledo and Alcalde García Parejas reported. Felipe de Luna essen-
tially adopted Vélez Cachupín's report, adding a few conclusions of his own.[6]
Licenciado Luna pointed out that it was not up to him or Governor Vélez
Cachupín to decide on the veracity of statements coming from the mouths
of the possessed. This was up to the judges who might finally decide the case.
So far as he was concerned, most of the statements the Devil made through
the possessed ones were incredible and not to be believed.[7]

Indians were not usually subject to the jurisdiction of the Inquisition
because they were not fully Christianized. Indians could not be guilty of
heresy (engaging in practices or holding beliefs contrary to Christian dogma)
because they had not fully learned the sacraments and beliefs of the Catholic
Church. This entirely reasonable position of the Inquisition broke down, however, when it came to the subject of witchcraft. Ecclesiastical judges under
the jurisdiction of the bishop of Durango did have jurisdiction over Indians
when it came to Indian witches and sorcerers, especially those that killed
with their magical incantations and malevolent intent. Luna pointed out that
when it came to witchcraft, "his Majesty's justices can proceed to the punishments of sorcerers and witches regardless of their class [or caste] in accordance with *Recopilación* book 6, title, 1, law 35 which orders royal justices to
proceed against Indian witches who kill with spells and evil intent."[8]

The *Recopilación* was clear on this point, but there was also an institution under the jurisdiction of the bishops with authority to punish *any*
religious offense by the Indians. It was called the Tribunal of the Faith of
Indians, or the Secular Inquisition, among other names. This little-known
court existed throughout New Spain alongside the Inquisition and held
numerous trials in most of the dioceses and archdioceses under the jurisdiction of the bishop or archbishop. In areas without bishops, missionary
priests had the authority to conduct such trials under a papal bull from
Pope Adrian VI dated 10 May 1522.[9] It was under this authority that the
trials Diego de Landa conducted in the Yucatán between 1561 and 1565 were
carried out, where there were more abuses than there were under the

Spanish Inquisition. Yet no action was taken against the sorcerers of Abiquiu under this authority.[10]

Another course open to the viceroy was to refer the cases of Spaniards accused of witchcraft directly to the Inquisition. Although there had been no extensive testimony against such Spaniards, the list of witches and sorcerers prepared by Father Toledo with the help of Joaquinillo (the long list) identified thirty-five Spanish sorcerers listed by where they lived, their physical characteristics, and sometimes their purported crimes.[11]

The accused sorcerers from Chimayo consisted of twenty Genízaros and thirty-five Spaniards. Most Spaniards were members of the Martín family, particularly Panchito Martín's family (two sons and two daughters), and the Genízaros were from the Cruz family. In some cases there were three generations of sorcerers, such as José Martín (the musician), a son of Panchito Martín, and José's son Manuel Ramos. Some Spanish sorcerers were listed only by first name, or by description, such as "son of Bernardino Trujillo, whose teeth overlapped." In many cases these descriptions would have provided little information for the Inquisition to go on, even if they wished to prosecute. That could be one reason there were no prosecutions of Spanish sorcerers. The Genízaros from Chimayo, particularly the members of the Cruz family, were mostly listed by their full names. Twelve out of the twenty Chimayo Genízaros were from the Cruz family, led by Sebastián, Andrés, Francisco, Joaquinillo, Salvador, and Domingo Cruz, none of whom were ever arrested or charged with witchcraft. The only accused sorcerer from Chimayo who was imprisoned was Cascabel, described as a Genízaro whose great powers came from a small black stone. Although Vélez Cachupín was quite concerned about the Chimayo witches and sorcerers, except for Cascabel, none were charged with witchcraft.[12]

After discussing the fine points of the jurisdiction of the Inquisition over Indians, Luna moved to the issue that Governor Vélez Cachupín thought was the primary source of all witchcraft and sorcery at Abiquiu and other pueblos: the failure of the missionaries to learn the language of the Indians. The priests in New Mexico gave their sermons and religious instruction in Spanish and Latin and relied on interpreters to explain their teaching and preaching, so Luna argued that the simple solution was for the Franciscans to learn the Indian languages. Given what is known about the apparent facility of Spanish-speakers in Abiquiu by the middle of the eighteenth century, it is unclear whether this was really a factor in the witchcraft outbreak, Vélez Cachupín's and Luna's opinion, notwithstanding.

Whether they understood Spanish perfectly, Abiquiu Genízaros, like their Pueblo neighbors, resisted confessing their sins to the Franciscans because to do so meant renouncing their identity as Indians. In a real sense, however, this is just what the Franciscans throughout the Americas wanted—to destroy the heathenness they believed was based on a Devil's Pact. To Licenciado Luna, and Governor Vélez Cachupín, the failure to fully Christianize the Indians and have them confess their sins on an annual basis led to the practice of witchcraft and the epidemic of possessions that afflicted Abiquiu Genízaro pueblo.[13]

Having identified to his satisfaction the cause of the failure to fully Christianize the Abiquiu Genízaros, and thus the cause of the witchcraft outbreak at Abiquiu, Luna proceeded to consider Governor Vélez Cachupín's proposal to establish another Genízaro pueblo on the Rio Grande in Gila Apache country. This second Genízaro pueblo would have had a similar mission as Abiquiu: to protect the interior settlements from hostile Indians, in this case the Gila Apaches. The proposal involved a grant of land to the Genízaros and "a missionary minister to instruct and teach them," an arrangement similar to the one at Abiquiu. Because of the precarious nature of Abiquiu Pueblo, Luna was dubious about the wisdom of establishing another such pueblo. Founding a new pueblo would require the royal expense of providing "cattle, oxen, and other livestock, tools and utensils that are accustomed to [be given to] new missions," so Luna recommended that the matter be referred to the Junta of War and the Treasury after hearing first from the fiscal.[14] Because Abiquiu was still problematical and because Governor Vélez Cachupín was nearing the end of his second term, nothing more was heard of the proposal to establish a second Genízaro pueblo in Gila Apache country.

Felipe de Luna opted not to decide the question of another Genízaro pueblo and wanted the fiscal's legal opinion on the matter of whether the problem of witchcraft and demonic possession at Abiquiu was under the civil jurisdiction, "or belonged exclusively to the cognizance of ecclesiastical jurisdiction."[15] He basically equivocated on these issues that Vélez Cachupín had placed before him. This was not unusual in matters dealing with New Mexico land, water, or witchcraft decided either in Mexico City or Guadalajara. Most bureaucrats in those capitols had never been to New Mexico. They were unfamiliar with the local situation and with matters other than witchcraft they tended to base their recommendations on the technicalities of laws from the *Recopilación* rather than on the realities of the Hispano-Indian land and water regime. Nevertheless, the decisions of the Audiencias of Mexico City and Guadalajara and of the Inquisition carried great weight in New Mexico. That is why the decision of the Inquisition, or some other body with jurisdiction over the Abiquiu witchcraft outbreak, was eagerly awaited in New Mexico.[16]

As he concluded his report to the viceroy, Felipe de Luna noted that no one was sure to what jurisdiction the province of New Mexico belonged. He had requested an opinion on the matter from the Royal Auditor and was told that New Mexico was part of the Captain Generalcy headquartered in Mexico City, but most experts and the custom and practice of New Mexico communities held that the province was legally subject to the Audiencia of Guadalajara.[17] Whatever the case, the report of Licenciado Luna, a lawyer with some expertise in matters of jurisdiction, made clear that New Mexico's position on the edge of the frontier was partially responsible for any confusion "because all that land is open war on the frontier to the four winds of barbarous enemies."[18] Even in the viceregal capital, New Mexico was known as a land of open warfare.

After making his report, Licenciado Luna referred the matter to the viceroy for final decision. Luna's skepticism about the veracity of the reports and his doubts about the jurisdiction to which this matter belonged must have eventually influenced both the viceroy and the Inquisition. On 17 February 1765, Viceroy Marqués de Cruillas sent Luna's report to the Inquisition with the offer to assist the Holy Office in any way required. It was a noncommittal cover letter, giving no hint of the viceroy's thinking except that he placed major emphasis on "some Spanish sorcerers."[19]

Another lawyer, identified only as Licenciado Vicente, drafted the response and opinion of the Inquisition. The first part of the opinion dealt solely with the Devil. Taking its cue from Luna, the Inquisition noted that the demonic possessions Father Toledo experienced were not credible for two, albeit contradictory, reasons. First the Holy Office did not believe the Devil was involved in the demonic possessions because it was contrary to their view of the Devil: "This goes against everything that he [the Devil] desires and commonly practices." Then the Holy Office reported that even if the demonic possessions were caused by the Devil, "they should not be believed because as productions of the Devil, it is all false and a lie."[20]

The second part of the Inquisition's opinion was equally contradictory. Although not wanting to be involved with demonic possessions and with the Devil, the Inquisition did consider asserting some jurisdiction over the Abiquiu witchcraft proceedings. The Inquisition suggested that someone be commissioned to go to New Mexico and examine everyone involved: Governor Vélez Cachupín, Alcalde Carlos Fernández, Father Juan José Toledo, Joaquinillo, and Juan Largo, among others. The Inquisition was particularly interested in the Spaniards accused of witchcraft, since its jurisdiction over the Indians was tenuous at best. Spaniards, however, were clearly subject to the jurisdiction of the Holy Office.[21]

The Inquisition opinion that ended the Abiquiu proceedings from Mexico City concluded with the words, "secret, 5 March 1765, Licenciado Vicente."[22] This was the last official communication from Mexico City regarding the Abiquiu witchcraft outbreak.

The secrecy of the Inquisition meant that its activities were not subject to review. They were also often unjust, as Henry Charles Lea wrote:

> [The inquisitors] were virtually a law unto themselves; no one dared to complain of them and the victims' mouths were closed by the oath of secrecy which bound them under severe penalties not to divulge their experiences...The world can never know the cruelties perpetrated under a system which relieved the tribunals from accountability.[23]

The Holy Office showed little enthusiasm for getting involved in the Abiquiu witchcraft outbreak and particularly in the demonic possessions that had been rampant in the Genízaro pueblo. The Inquisition had lost credibility when it tried unsuccessfully to sort out the demonic possessions at Querétaro a little more than a half century earlier and was not about to get burned again. Most important, the authorities in Mexico City saw the province of New Mexico as a war zone, a place where "all its Spanish citizens and Indian militia are always prepared with their weapons in hand waiting for the attacks that night and day the barbarous enemy nations that surround them are accustomed to carry out."[24] Another reason for the Inquisition's reluctance to take jurisdiction in the Abiquiu situation was that when José Gorráez first referred the question to them in December 1764, he noted that the pueblo had remained calm until June.[25] This is what Governor Vélez Cachupín had hoped would be the outcome of his plan to refer the demonic possession and exorcism part of the witchcraft outbreak to the Inquisition.

Vélez Cachupín did not want an investigation by the Inquisition that would open wounds that were beginning to heal. By the time the Inquisition's opinion was received in New Mexico, the witchcraft outbreak at Abiquiu was nearly over. Governor Vélez Cachupín had already dealt with the most important sorcerers and was not interested in opening new cases.

Once the possessions and exorcisms subsided, Governor Vélez Cachupín still had to sentence the sorcerers and witches remaining in the Santa Fe jail. He did this with his customary pragmatism, fashioning punishments that seemed relatively mild considering the offenses alleged to have been committed. The governor was mainly interested in ending the witchcraft outbreak at Abiquiu with as little disruption of the life of the Genízaro pueblo as possible, and he seems to have accomplished this goal, although the punishment meted out often fell more heavily on the female witches than on the male sorcerers.

This is similar to the Salem witchcraft trials and previous European witchcraft proceedings: accusations and convictions were primarily against women. Older women living alone often, in particular, had the reputation of being witches. During the sixteenth and seventeenth centuries in Europe about 80 percent of those accused of witchcraft were women, and the proportion of females convicted and executed was even higher. In New England between 1620 and 1725, 78 percent of the individuals accused of witchcraft were women. In the Salem communities the proportion of accused witches who were females was higher before and after the outbreak of accusations in 1692 (83 percent) than it was during the outbreak (76 percent). During the height of the Salem witch craze, suspicions and accusations extended beyond the accused, who were usually female, to their relatives, including husbands and associates who were more often male. This could help explain the increased numbers of men among the accused sorcerers at Abiquiu where, like Chimayo, the sorcerers and witches seem to have been

concentrated in specific families such as the Tagles and the Trujillos. After
succeeding in obtaining a confession from María Trujillo under torture by
having her hung by her arms on a cartwheel, Governor Vélez Cachupín
became frustrated with the other defendants and their quasi confessions and
decided to let them languish in the Santa Fe prison where they would at least
be incapable of engaging in any more witchcraft.[26] Still, Governor Vélez
Cachupín was nearing the end of his second term and needed to put the
Abiquiu witchcraft outbreak to rest. Father Toledo was cured, the possessions and exorcisms had stopped, and the frontier settlement of Abiquiu was
returning to normal. Only sentencing the remaining sorcerers still in jail in
Santa Fe was left to be done. Four of the defendants had died in prison and
thus were not part of the sentencing: Agustín Tagle; Antonio Ulibarrí;
Antonio, El Chimayó; and Diego Tagle.[27]

The marriage in Spain of the Prince of Asturias with his cousin, the
Princess of Parma, became the key event allowing the accused sorcerers to
receive a kind of amnesty from Governor Vélez Cachupín. On 16 September
1766, the remaining prisoners "requested the intercession of his highness the
honorable Prince of Asturias to terminate the case and free them from
prison."[28] It was traditional to grant relief such as a commuted prison sentence to criminals on the happy occasion of a state marriage of an heir to
the Spanish throne. The prisoners were apparently aware of this important
event in Spain, which they could use to their advantage, and Governor Vélez
Cachupín was quick to grant the prisoners' petition to achieve closure to
the decade-long witchcraft outbreak.

Vélez Cachupín took the opportunity to assess the prisoners' conduct
while incarcerated and mete out sentences accordingly. The governor noted
that although not all the prisoners confessed to committing witchcraft, "they
have been instructed in the Christian doctrine, confessed and received communion annually, singing praises to God and praying the most holy rosary
every night."[29] It is doubtful that all the prisoners had become quite so pious,
but Vélez Cachupín was apparently convinced that all but three of the defendants had mended their ways. The remaining prisoners received the following sentence: they were to be released from prison on condition that they
never return to their homes in Abiquiu, placed with masters whom they were
to serve for the customary time, and were to obey Christian doctrine and
not live as vagrants nor return to their former witchcraft. This group of sorcerers included Vicente Trujillo who had been accused of killing at least

twenty-two people. He was given the relatively light punishment that he should serve a Spanish master for the customary time. It is unclear what the customary time was, since it was usually computed as the time it would take to pay off the ransom paid for the Genízaro.[30]

Whether Vicente Trujillo actually served a Spanish master is unknown, but it is known that neither he nor his wife María observed their banishment from Abiquiu. By 1786 both were back in Abiquiu, and Vicente was again in trouble. Father Ramón Antonio González reported to Alcalde José Campo Redondo that Vicente had stolen a gold cross and a rosary from the statue of the Virgin Mary in the Abiquiu church and sold them. When the alcalde questioned Vicente, he admitted taking and selling the valuable church ornaments. Asked why he did it, Trujillo responded with what he had learned from his numerous dealings with both Church and civil authorities over a thirty-year period: "The Devil made me do it." When Governor Anza received the report of Alcalde Campo Redondo, he gave Trujillo a relatively light punishment. Instead of being banished from Abiquiu, Trujillo was ordered to sweep the church and the cemetery for three months under the supervision of Father González, who he was apparently assisting at the time of the theft. Trujillo received a less severe punishment than his codefendant José Domínguez because his crime did not reach the level of outrage and sacrilege as did the crime committed by Domínguez, who was banished from Abiquiu. In the case of Vicente Trujillo, instead of "singing praises to God and praying the most holy rosary every night," as Vélez Cachupín had said, Trujillo stole the rosary from the statue of the Virgin Mary and sold it, along with the gold cross, for whatever he could get.[31] Vicente Trujillo was no longer committing acts of sorcery and witchcraft, but he certainly had not reformed as much as Governor Vélez Cachupín thought.[32]

Three witches received the harshest sentences at the hands of the governor: María Trujillo; Isabel, La Pastora; and La Come Gallinas. Governor Vélez Cachupín had more confidence in the sorcerers he released for time served than he did in those three witches. The governor feared these women would try to escape from their masters and therefore provided prospective penalties in case that should happen. Vélez Cachupín notified María Trujillo that if she tried to escape from her master, the punishment would be fifty lashes and four years at the obraje at Encinillas. If Trujillo "should return once more to the practice of witchcraft, or being a curandera with herbs, or other superstitions [the punishment would be] two hundred lashes and perpetual incarceration at the [Encinillas] obraje."[33] Isabel, La Pastora, was assigned to the house of the teniente alcalde Tomás Madrid, who would have the responsibility of supervising her life and her activities, making her adhere to her Christian responsibilities. If she ran away from Tomás Madrid, she would be returned and kept there in chains.

The harshest punishment was reserved for La Come Gallinas, who had been accused, among other crimes, of killing certain Spaniards who were her enemies by inviting them to her house and giving them food containing the dust of a toad she had been drying in her chimney, an apparently lethal concoction. Governor Vélez Cachupín believed that the totality of Come Gallinas's offenses made her deserving of being made an example to others through a punishment known as *vergüenza*, or public shame. The punishment the governor selected was similar to a punishment imposed by the Inquisition in Mexico in 1664. So similar, in fact, that Vélez Cachupín must have been aware of it and modeled his punishment after that earlier case.

On 7 December 1664, in Mexico City, the Inquisition required a male defendant to strip to the waist whereupon he was smeared with honey and covered with feathers "in which guise he was made to stand in the sun for four hours on the staging."[34] Come Gallinas was subjected to public shame that was almost identical to the punishment inflicted on the unnamed defendant a century earlier.[35] In the case of La Come Gallinas, "to serve as a warning and example [to others]," she was to be "subjected to public shame, ['honeyed' and] feathered for four hours" and exhibited in the Santa Fe plaza.[36] Governor Vélez Cachupín also ordered that La Come Gallinas be "maintained *en depósito* [in the house of a Spaniard whom she must serve] until she dies."[37]

The end of the Abiquiu witchcraft proceedings was anticlimactic. After fray Juan José's marathon possessions and exorcisms, after the identification of more than thirty-five Spaniards accused of being witches and sorcerers, and after the exorcism and attempted obliteration of numerous Native American religious sites, no serious consequences were suffered as a result of the punishments administered by Governor Vélez Cachupín. To be sure, at least five sorcerers died in jail, and Come Gallinas was sentenced to public shame by being exhibited in the plaza, naked to the waist, covered with honey and feathers—not inconsequential outcomes.[38] Yet compared to Salem, where nineteen suspected witches were hanged and one was crushed to death, the punishment phase of the Abiquiu witchcraft proceedings was relatively benign.[39] No one was hanged as in Salem, no one was burned at the stake as happened during the European witch craze, and the repercussions of the Abiquiu witchcraft outbreak were comparatively mild. As a result of the Abiquiu witch craze Father Toledo was chastened for his overzealous desire to confront the Devil, Governor Vélez Cachupín was vindicated for his skillful handling of the whole affair, and the Genízaros themselves eventually became part of Spanish society, no longer marginalized, no longer set apart as neither Spanish nor Indian.[40]

Figure 20
The possessed women and girls accompanied by a flock of crows as they go to and from church.
Drawing by Glen Strock.

CHAPTER TWELVE

Conclusion

Abiquiu Witchcraft: Resistance, Revitalization, and a Clash of Beliefs

The witch craze that began in thirteenth- and fourteenth-century Europe did not end in Salem, Massachusetts, in 1692 as most everyone believes. The witchcraft outbreak that occurred in Abiquiu from 1756 until 1766 was the last major example of a phenomenon that began in Europe and was imported to the New World. Even though the Salem witchcraft trials are more well known, the Abiquiu trials are no less important. This outbreak of witchcraft identified a fairly large number of people who had been killed as the result of the activities of sorcerers and witches, revealed many indigenous ceremonial sites and practices that had nothing to do with witchcraft, and marked a turning point in the history of Indian-Hispano relations in New Mexico. Since the people the sorcerers killed were almost all Genízaros, the Abiquiu witchcraft proceedings were not taken as seriously as the activities of the Salem witches, where twenty people were executed and several of the accused were of the elite class. What set the Abiquiu witchcraft trials apart from previous witchcraft proceedings was the attack on the priest, Father Toledo, as an act of resistance to Christianization and the inclusion of many indigenous rock art and religious shrines as sites of "idolatry" where "Devil worship" was allegedly practiced.

The practices called witchcraft in the Abiquiu proceedings varied widely and often involved healing rather than harming people. Spaniards called all these practices hechicería, or witchcraft, and their practitioners, hechiceros, or sorcerers. They included curanderos who practiced healing, Native American religious leaders practicing the rituals and ceremonies of their native religions (including Pueblo, Plains, Navajo, and Ute religious practitioners or shamens), and diviners (*adivinadores*) who could predict the future, find lost objects, determine the cause of an illness, and find the real witches and sorcerers.[1] The distinction between native religious practitioners who were healers and those who were sorcerers and witches was understood throughout the Americas but was not always clearcut in practice, especially in Father Toledo's mind in mid-eighteenth-century Abiquiu. In seventeenth-century Peru the idolatry trials designed to extirpate all aspects of native religion made no distinction between curanderos and hechiceros. Both practitioners posed a challenge to the local Catholic priest's authority because they were making use of native religious practices instead of Christian ones. Governor Vélez Cachupín, however, made this very distinction between curanderos and witches. When he sent Joaquinillo and Juan Largo back to Abiquiu to be placed in Father Toledo's care, he stressed that neither was thought to have used their magical powers "in order to injure anyone with witchcraft." Instead they were considered healers.[2]

At the heart of the Abiquiu witchcraft trials is the problem of distinguishing among witchcraft practices that were malevolent, healing practices that were beneficent, and other techniques such as love magic that were somewhere in between. Both Spaniards and the Pueblos believed in witchcraft and these pueblo beliefs probably predated the arrival of the Spaniards. Belief in witchcraft was almost universal among many other southwestern Indian groups, including the Navajos, Hopis, Apaches, Zunis, and Plains Indians such as the Comanches. Indians from several of these groups formed the Abiquiu Genízaro community.[3]

The witchcraft outbreak at Abiquiu resulted mainly from a clash of religious belief systems and from the Spanish attempt to Christianize the Genízaros. Franciscans such as Father Toledo were taught a polarized worldview markedly different from the native religious view. In the Franciscan view most Indian practices and beliefs were considered hechicería. This polarized, fundamentalist worldview was often resisted but sometimes adopted by indigenous people. As Deward Walker pointed out, "Dramatic good/evil moral polarizations, with witchcraft and sorcery firmly assigned to the evil side of the universe, are particularly characteristic of recently Christianized and colonized native peoples of the Americas." The history of Indian colonization and conversion and the nature of both Christian and native belief systems is at the core of any attempt to understand what happened at Abiquiu in the mid-eighteenth century.[4]

When Spaniards initiated the process of converting the Indians in sixteenth-century Mexico, priests such as fray Bernardino de Sahagún learned Nahuatl and became the first ethnohistorians by studying and interviewing the Nahuas (or Aztecs).[5] They studied Nahua myths and religion and found many similarities between them and Christian practices. Nahua religion contained practices such as confession that were strikingly similar to Christian rituals. The Nahuas believed that confession of one's sins was a healing act that resulted in a restoration of internal balance and order. The Indians took to the Catholic rite of confession, attending frequently. The Nahua word for the indigenous confession rite translates to "straightening one's heart." The Indians meant this quite literally, believing that one's misdeeds caused physical disruptions that required a physical remedy such as the straightening of one's heart through confession. The Nahuas were thus eager to confess, often bringing "their sins written down or painted with hieroglyphs."[6] Catholic priests, such as the Dominican fray Diego Durán, however, had problems with the Indians' form of confession because they did not "always exhibit repentance and the intention to reform their behavior, elements irrelevant to the efficacy of indigenous confession."[7]

Other religious practices such as penance were also found in both Christian and Nahua religions. Until the mid-sixteenth century, missionaries made use of these similarities in their attempts at Christianization of the Indians. In Mexico City the missionaries established a college to train Nahua youths for the clergy based on pre-Hispanic Nahua *calmeac* schools that trained the Nahuas in their own religion. The first wave of missionaries led

by Motolinía believed that the apparent similarities between the two religions had facilitated an easy and complete conversion of the Nahuas. The
second wave of missionaries that arrived in New Spain, Sahagún among them,
realized as they learned Nahuatl that the "superficially similar concepts and
institutions could mean entirely different things in different cultures."[8]

Sahagún discovered, as his understanding of the Nahua psyche and religion increased, that the two cultures were worlds apart, and that the Nahuas
were using Motolinía and his fellow priests' gullibility to continue their old
practices under the guise of conversion to Christianity. This so frustrated
Sahagún that he denounced Motolinía to the Inquisition in 1572. The early
"nativization" of the mission program ended as Sahagún's view of the super-
ficiality of native conversion was gradually accepted. Programs for promot-
ing sermons in indigenous languages were canceled, and "suspecting the
survival of pagan rites, the ecclesiastical authorities attempted to implement
the careful regulation of indigenous displays of their Christian faith such
as the dancing, singing, and religious representations . . . held in honor of the
patron saints of villages."[9]

During the second wave of Franciscan evangelization the missionaries came
to believe "that satanic intervention was at the heart of Indian
cultures . . . [and] that the deities of the Indians were not merely false idols,
but 'lying and deceitful devils'" in the words of Sahagún.[10] Spanish priests
were taught that Christianization of the Indians required them to eliminate
all vestiges of the native belief system, even if those beliefs and practices were
harmless or beneficent. Thus all Indian rituals and ceremonies were characterized as idolatry, witchcraft, and Devil worship. Later, after harsh repression by Spanish authorities proved only partially successful, an
accommodation occurred throughout the Americas whereby the Church
became more tolerant of native beliefs and the Indians gradually accepted
a modified form of Christianity sometimes called Folk Catholicism.[11]

Father Toledo's tenure at Abiquiu overlapped these alternating tendencies of harshness and tolerance in the process of Christianization that had
been occurring since the arrival of Hernán Cortés in New Spain in 1521.

Cortés, like Vélez Cachupín two and a half centuries later, saw the Indians as normal human beings almost as civilized as the Spaniards, whose weaknesses were not the result of demonic intervention and were "susceptible to instruction and correction."[12] Toledo, as had Archbishop Juan de Zumárraga before him, displayed both tendencies at different times. Zumárraga began his career "as a Franciscan friar, who was also a humanist, conversant with the writing of Erasmus ... [who as inquisitor general] engaged in a ruthless and frantic persecution of unfaithful Indian apostates which culminated in the burning at the stake of a charismatic Indian leader."[13]

Like that of fray Diego de Landa in Peru, Zumárraga's shift to zealous persecution of the Indians grew out of the realization that the Indians, although nominally Christians, were still practicing their old religion by secretively worshipping their gods and engaging in bigamy and even human sacrifice. The shock of this realization caused a violent reaction among Franciscans such as Zumárraga and Landa because of their feeling of betrayal and extreme disappointment. Yet their excesses caused such a counterreaction that these priests were investigated and the laws changed to exempt Indians from the jurisdiction of the Inquisition.[14]

In a similar manner, Father Toledo began the witchcraft proceedings by seeking permission to torture El Cojo by literally holding his feet to the fire until he confessed. His early petitions contain numerous references to Toledo's application of physical punishment of Abiquiu Genízaros. For example, the priest placed El Cojo in the stocks and administered public whippings to force him to confess.[15] Father Toledo whipped the eight-year-old boy who revealed El Cojo's School of the Devil while talking in his sleep.[16] Toledo was so enraged by Atole Caliente's repeated disruption of his exorcisms and celebration of the mass that he publicly whipped her in front of the church. Eventually, however, Father Toledo mellowed as his ailments were cured, at least temporarily, with the help of a curandera.[17]

The activities of folk healers were just one of several practices condemned as witchcraft during the Abiquiu witch trials. All the following practices were characterized as hechicería and their practitioners called hechiceros in the Abiquiu witchcraft proceeding:

1. Native American, Hispanic, or Genízaro curanderos or medicine men, such as Joaquinillo and Juan Largo, healing through the use of medicinal plants.

2. Healers such as Janisco using herbs and medicinal plants in their cures, along with Christian rituals. Janisco testified that his cures were effected through the use of herbs and "through God and the Holy Cross."[18]

3. Those who used herbs and some form of magical practice to both heal and harm others. Often the same herb could heal or harm a person, depending on the concentration and application. An example was María Trujillo's use of the herb Dragon's Blood to cause Father Toledo's stomach problems and then to cure him when the same herb applied externally to his stomach.

4. The use of poison and malevolent magic to harm or kill someone, such as La Come Gallinas's use of ground toad dust to harm or kill those Spaniards she did not like by mixing it in their food.[19]

5. The use of shapeshifting to perform acts of witchcraft. The allegation that Miguel, El Cojo, performed witchcraft by turning himself into a cat fits into this category.

6. Native American ceremonial practices, such as the Turtle Dance, the Scalp Dance, or a hunting ritual that the Church viewed as witchcraft. The statement of Antonio, El Chimayó, that he took part in a hunting ritual and may have shapeshifted into the lead deer is an example of this activity.

7. Some practitioners used all or most of the above practices interchangeably. They were shamans who had acquired the power to heal and to harm. Using malevolent witchcraft to harm or kill another person was often induced by a feeling of being under attack by another sorcerer, in the atmosphere of fear, uncertainty, and conflict that existed at Abiquiu during the 1750s and 1760s.

Governor Vélez Cachupín's astute maneuvering finally contained the witchcraft outbreak at Abiquiu. By removing the most visible sorcerers from the community, he was able to bring back a level of normalcy to the Genízaro pueblo. By referring the demonic possession aspect of the witchcraft outbreak to the Inquisition, Vélez Cachupín calmed the situation in Abiquiu, especially the overzealous Father Juan José Toledo. Toledo's desire to battle the Devil seems to have brought forth Satan and his minions. Vélez Cachupín believed that Father Toledo was the priest best able to Christianize the Genízaro Indians at Abiquiu, but the governor was skeptical of the demonic possessions and of the exorcisms Toledo was performing. These demonic possessions were threatening to get out of control just when Vélez Cachupín had succeeded in imprisoning the main sorcerers from Abiquiu and in establishing the Genízaro pueblo as a permanent settlement.[20]

Governor Vélez Cachupín changed the relationship between Church and State in New Mexico by gaining the upper hand over the Franciscans so that he could implement his Indian policies without having to answer to the constant criticism from Church officials that plagued earlier civil administrations. Much of the earlier priestly criticism of New Mexico's Indian policy had been justified, but in Vélez Cachupín's case there was little basis for such fault-finding because his policy was eminently successful. Vélez Cachupín achieved peace with Comanches and Utes on the basis of his individual valor and successful policies. Yet the Indian peace the governor brokered so skillfully during his first term was shattered by the inept policies of the governors who succeeded him, particularly Governor Manuel del Portillo y Urrisola. When the Comanches and Utes went back to war with the Spanish settlers, Abiquiu and the surrounding settlements once again became a war zone.[21]

The uncertainty that resulted from not knowing whether the salutary peace policies of Governor Tomás Vélez Cachupín would be continued led to a climate of fear, both in the Abiquiu Genízaro pueblo and in the surrounding Spanish communities. In a similar way, the communities around Salem Village, Massachusetts, in 1692 were convinced that they were "in the Devil's snare" because of the Indian wars that so unsettled that region. Villagers and their priests linked the very real threat of attack by Wabanaki Indians to the witchcraft outbreak in Salem Village. Both the priests and the villagers equated the Indians with the Devil. In Abiquiu, the most virulent witchcraft outbreak came during Governor Vélez Cachupín's second term when he was trying to patch together the peace agreements between Indians and Spaniards he brokered in his first term. During this period, former residents living at Santa Cruz de la Cañada were reluctant to resettle grants at Abiquiu and Ojo Caliente that had been abandoned because of Ute/Comanche attacks. The situation at Abiquiu and its surrounding settlements was quite similar to Salem in 1692.[22]

Not only was the Abiquiu region a war zone, but it was also in the grips of major social change. The 1680 Pueblo Revolt had forever altered the relationship between Spaniard and Indian. The Spaniards, who had been forced to flee New Mexico for twelve years, returned in 1692 to a new system of land tenure. Spaniards no longer owned all the land and the right to Indian labor; they had to concede some land-ownership rights to Indians such as the Abiquiu Genízaros. Governor Vélez Cachupín was the first governor to grant property rights to Genízaros and the first to make true community land grants, often to Genízaros, mulattos, and marginalized mestizos who were willing to risk their lives on the frontier of the settled areas of New Mexico. In return the grantees received the promise of acquiring the status of full citizens through land ownership, the payment of tithes, and membership in a land grant community.

The new system of community land grants to Genízaros and mestizos that Vélez Cachupín implemented caused certain social stresses, however. These were set up by the continued practice of making large private grants and quasi-community grants adjacent to true community grants to elites who would acquire title to large tracts of land on which they might never settle.[23] Vélez Cachupín was walking the tightrope of maintaining the existing land grant system that favored elites who were often alcaldes, in return for their service in administering and defending the province, and the new system of community grants to Indians and mestizos who were often the ones marginalized and oppressed by the elites. With these very different types of grants and grantees living side by side, boundary disputes and issues of encroachment and trespass were not easily resolved in court, especially after Vélez Cachupín left office after his first and second terms.[24] While he was in office, Governor Vélez Cachupín was quite protective of the grants he made to Genízaros, such as the Abiquiu grant. When he granted the neighboring Polvadera grant to the west, Vélez Cachupín specified that it should not prejudice the Abiquiu grant. During the witchcraft proceedings the governor wrote supportive reports concerning the Abiquiu Genízaros, noting that their nomadic ways often meant they came into conflict with their neighbors.[25]

The Abiquiu Genízaros may also have resorted to witchcraft as a response to their change from a nomadic to a more sedentary lifestyle. It has been pointed out that among the few tribal societies free of witchcraft were the nomadic pastoral tribes of Africa. When social conflict arose among these tribes, their response was to move to a new environment "and if necessary to split into new groupings. As soon as they changed to a more sedentary existence, however, accusations of witchcraft started to proliferate among them, because their traditional methods for defusing conflict were no long available." This phenomenon was probably at work among the Abiquiu Genízaros as well. Recent studies of marginalized colonial populations from the archives of the Inquisition have revealed that resorting to witchcraft was a means of self-protection when dealing with elites in the communities around Mexico City. In a similar manner, Abiquiu Genízaros engaged in witchcraft as self-protection against elites such as Father Toledo and later priests who were attempting to change them spiritually.[26] New Mexico at midcentury was a place of conflict and accommodation, particularly as regards relations between Indians and Spaniards. Abiquiu was at the center of this conflict because many Genízaros settled at Abiquiu as Indians and later chose the designation "español," or Spaniard. As the Genízaros inter-married with Spaniards from nearby communities, they began to refer to themselves as españoles when the priest took down their casta or calidad in his books of births, baptisms, and marriages. As Lesley Poling-Kempes has noted, "Abiquiu may be the only community in the Southwest ever given the choice between legal designation as an Indian pueblo or a Hispanic village."[27]

The uncertainty regarding the residents of the pueblo of Abiquiu, and their calidad, was mirrored by the uncertainty regarding the stability of all New Mexico's frontier settlements in the face of continuous Ute and Comanche attacks. So long as Vélez Cachupín was governor, his policies for dealing with the nomads and with the Pueblo auxiliaries ameliorated this uncertainty. He posted Pueblo scouts at the locations Comanches traveled when entering the Rio Grande Valley and at the mountain passes near Mora where Comanches were accustomed to attack. He trained an elite group of

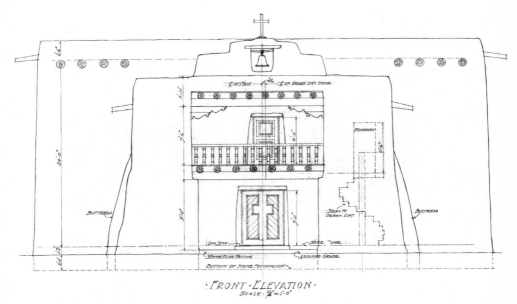

· FRONT · ELEVATION ·
SCALE · 1/6" = 1'-0"

Figure 21
Architect John Gaw Meem's front elevation for a new church of Santo Tomás de Abiquiú, 1935.
John Gaw Meem Collection, Center for Southwest Research, Zimmerman Library, University of
New Mexico, Albuquerque.

presidial soldiers to engage in a quick response to any attack. Such prepa-
rations and foresight were lacking at the time of the 1747 Comanche/Ute raid
on Abiquiu, which took everyone by surprise.

In addition to these precautions, Governor Vélez Cachupín realized
the importance of exchanging captives with the Comanches. He took
the first step by releasing the Comanche captives he had assigned to
Santa Fe to the chiefs with whom he was negotiating before receiving any
of the Hispanic captives they were holding. This gesture formed the basis
of the Comanche peace Vélez Cachupín achieved, particularly at the
beginning of his second term.[28]

Father Toledo was caught between opposing forces of major social
change in New Mexico at midcentury, just as the Genízaros were. Toledo
softened his stance regarding the Devil as he himself became the object
of repeated witchcraft attacks. The priest was forced to adjust his theological and theoretical concepts to realities on the ground when he became
ill from witchcraft attacks. Governor Vélez Cachupín's pragmatism aided

this adjustment. He determined the cause of the sufferings inflicted on Father Toledo and obtained a cure. The governor helped place Father Toledo in charge of Abiquiu and maintained his faith in the priest and the Genízaro pueblo.[29]

Father Toledo's dramatic desire to confront the Devil probably encouraged the number and severity of the demonic possessions. Historian Robert D. Martínez has argued that the beliefs of priests performing exorcisms affected the degree to which people in their community became possessed and in need of the rite of exorcism. Martínez based this notion on the work of Spanish historian Antonio Domínguez Ortiz who studied cases of exorcism in certain provinces of Galicia in northwestern Spain. Domínguez Ortiz found that in parishes where the priests believed in exorcism, groups of women periodically appeared claiming to be demon-possessed, while none appeared at other churches. The conduct of these possessed women in Spain that Domínguez Ortiz described who "made horrifying shrieks in the church when the priest lifted the host" seems remarkably similar to that of the possessed Abiquiu Genízaros.[30]

Father Toledo was motivated to meet the Devil face-to-face because of his lack of success in converting the Abiquiu Genízaros to Christianity and because of his inability to find a lasting cure for his own physical afflictions. He must have felt frustrated by his lack of control over the situation. Exorcising the Devil gave Toledo more power over the Christianization of the Genízaros because he could demonstrate his spiritual ability as a charismatic religious figure, and if successful he might also learn the cause and cure of his physical afflictions. Instead, the marathon exorcisms spun out of control, frustrating Father Toledo's hopes of achieving the spiritual conversion of the Indians and of learning the cause of his own physical ailments. It took Governor Vélez Cachupín to resolve both these issues in his own way.

The case was forwarded to the Inquisition and the viceroy at a time when the Inquisition was becoming skeptical about demonic possession and public exorcisms. Just as the views of individual priests who believed in demonic possession seemed to encourage the appearance of possessed women, the credibility of the Inquisition toward possession seemed also to result in more cases of possession and exorcism being referred to the Inquisition. Vélez Cachupín hoped for an outcome similar to what happened when the Querétaro case was submitted to the Inquisition in 1691. The Inquisition ordered the cessation of all exorcisms and all related public and private discussion. Eventually the excitement died away in Querétaro, and the possessed "left to themselves, for the most part, recovered their senses."[31]

The Abiquiu witchcraft outbreak is difficult to analyze because Spaniards wrote the documentary record. Even though the subjects were Indians and Genízaros, their voice is seldom heard directly; rather, it is always filtered through a Spaniard, such as Carlos Fernández, who took down the testimony in his own words. Therefore, it is necessary to read between the lines to find out whether what the Spaniards termed witchcraft was actually native ceremonialism, such as the Turtle Dance. In addition, interpreters were used in many cases to translate into Spanish from native languages (probably mostly Ute and Tewa), which the Genízaros spoke, but the interpreters did not always translate everything the witness said. Another filter obscuring a clear view of the Genízaros was Joaquinillo, the informer, who decided whom to accuse, whom to put on his list of sorcerers, and of what they would be accused. As an informer he was protected from witchcraft accusations and had a great deal of power in the process, since an accusation by Joaquinillo often assumed guilt.

Since there were no full-scale trials of the accused sorcerers, the complete story is still not known. There are only hints of the true situation. Witchcraft was closely connected with healing, and many curanderas were suspected of witchcraft. There was a fine line between sorcery and healing, especially since this was a time when medical knowledge was limited, and most people believed that witchcraft caused many illnesses. In fact, the idea that Satan was within one's heart until baptism banished him to make a home for Christ, was a common Christian idea taught by early Franciscans.[32] The causes of the Abiquiu witchcraft outbreak may never be fully understood but a major cause was Indian resistance to Christianization. Indigenous people used both active and passive forms of resistance to oppose the Spanish colonization effort to convert, civilize, and exploit them and place them under Spanish control.[33] Unwilling to forego their traditional beliefs, many native practitioners adopted a defiant stance toward priests such as Father Toledo, using witchcraft as a means of resistance.[34]

Indian resistance to colonization was present in New Mexico before and during the Pueblo Revolt, when many priests lost their lives. In the California missions a similar pattern was evident in the late 1700s and early 1800s. In 1812 Indians at the Santa Cruz mission killed Father Andrés Quintana by smothering him and cutting off one of his testicles. The Indians decided to act when the priest announced the introduction of the *cuarta de hierro*, a metal tipped whip that would cut the flesh of those Indians the priests were flogging.[35] In 1806 Father Pedro de la Cueva of Mission San José was wounded by an arrow in his eye when his party attempted to visit ill neophytes and was ambushed. A Spanish civilian was also killed, which led to a punitive expedition in California that killed eleven Indians and took twenty-five Indian women and children hostage.[36]

The tension between nominal and effective conversion—if effective conversion occurred at all—is observed in California, as in New Mexico, through the priestly concern over sin. Social and sexual practices of Indians proscribed as sinful were corrected by flogging, being hobbled with irons, and being placed in the stocks, among other punishments.[37] Harsh punitive measures imposed by the Franciscan clergy help explain the Indians' resistance to Franciscan control and religious conversion. Witchcraft and magic were used against the priests in California as they were in Abiquiu.

In Abiquiu as in California, the other side of the coin of witchcraft as resistance was witchcraft as a camouflaged revitalization movement, albeit a failed one. The list of sorcerers that Joaquinillo provided contains evidence that many of the accused witches were Indian civil and religious leaders, including a number of caciques, war captains, and other officials, as well as relatives of these officials. Father Toledo listed Anselmo of Tesuque as a cacique and teacher of sorcerers, meaning he was an Indian religious leader who taught young people dances and ceremonies, including initiation ceremonies. It is likely that Anselmo's influence extended beyond Tesuque to the surrounding pueblos. The list of sorcerers reveals a kind of network of religious leaders throughout the pueblos and beyond, evidence of a revitalization movement in New Mexico eighty-four years after the Pueblo Revolt.[38]

Further evidence of this network of Pueblo religious leaders in the list of accused sorcerers comes from an entry under Pojoaque where the cacique, Juan Felipe, is listed as the son of Poseyemu. Poseyemu, a Prometheus-like figure, was a culture hero who appears in myth and creation stories of virtually all the Pueblos. "He may be a god, a demigod, or a powerful mortal deified by tradition, but his distinguishing characteristic is that he brings mankind the arts of civilization by stealing fire from the gods, for example, or by instructing people."[39] At Pojoaque, Poseyemu may have been considered mortal, because Juan Felipe is listed as his son.

Poseyemu's role as a ritual leader takes three forms in Tewa mythology, all of which relate to the well-being of the Pueblos. In some of these myths when Poseyemu visits a pueblo, he "institutes dances and rituals [such as the Turtle Dance] during his stay in the village; in others he orders Kachina dances to be held underground for protection against the Spaniards; and in others he opposes the alien religious system in direct competition [with Pueblo religions]." In all cases Poseyemu acts as a "mediator between the Spanish and the native customs; he stands at the contact point between the Christian system and the native system."[40] The figure of Poseyemu himself represents Pueblo religious revitalization. He is continually exhorting the Pueblos to revive their rituals and protect them from Spanish interference. It is appropriate and ironic that he would be mentioned in the list of sorcerers, a list by its very nature that sought to demonize native religious leaders. Poseyemu's mediating role in the Pueblos is similar to the role of the Abiquiu Genízaro leaders. After a sermon by Father Toledo those Genízaro religious leaders gathered and decided what to believe and what not to believe. Then they discussed it with the entire pueblo. The Abiquiu Genízaros did not reject Christian teachings entirely, only those aspects of it that conflicted most strongly with their own religious beliefs.

Finally, the presence of a revitalization movement among the Pueblos is implied by the number of religious sites common to many Pueblos. Part of the mediating role that figures such as Poseyemu and even Joaquinillo exercised was one of telling the Spaniards a little of what they wanted to hear, such as the existence of common religious sites, but not with enough specificity to allow the Spaniards to find these sites. This was also a common tactic used by indigenous people in the extirpation of idolatry trials in seventeenth- and early eighteenth-century Peru.[41]

The Abiquiu witchcraft proceedings contain testimony about numerous fantastic events, many of which remain unexplained. This examination of the life and times of witchcraft in Abiquiu reveals multiply causes of the outbreak: native resistance to Christianization and revitalization, forced abandonment of traditional religious practices, misplaced attempts to destroy indigenous religious sites, prosecution of the beneficent healing practices of curanderas, nomads forced to adopt a sedentary existence, reaction to socioeconomic change, a climate of fear of devastating Comanche or Ute attacks, and a Franciscan predisposed to battle the Devil. Taken together, these factors contributed to the creation of the last major outbreak of witchcraft in North America.

Figure 22
Father Toledo and Alcalde Fernández exorcise the stone lion. *Drawing by Glen Strock.*

New Identities
at Abiquiu

A biquiu has been and is now a place full of mystery; its past as an Indian pueblo, a center for sorcery and witchcraft, as well as healing by curanderas. Abiquiu is not a federally recognized Indian pueblo, but most residents are aware of their Genízaro past.[1] Abiquiu is occasionally visited by delegations of Hopis who feel a connection with the community and tell Abiquiu residents that they are aware of a Hopi past at Abiquiu.[2]

While some of Abiquiu's past will remain unknowable—the stuff of legend and folk tale—it is possible to trace a transition from the Abiquiu Genízaro Indian pueblo of the witchcraft trials to the Abiquiu of today. The Abiquiu Genízaros gradually became Hispanized as full-fledged citizens of New Mexico and practicing Catholics as did most New Mexico Genízaros. The process can be documented more readily at Abiquiu because marriage and census records show the gradual decrease in population in the Genízaro pueblo and the increase in population in the surrounding plazas, as Genízaros acquired vecino status through marriage. For example, in 1777 an Isleta Indian named Juan Simón married an Abiquiu woman named Marta Martín. Marta's parents were officially considered "unknown," but the parish priest, who probably did know them, described her as a vecina. After the marriage both husband and wife were referred to as vecinos.[3]

Despite this early example of Indians or Genízaros passing into a higher casta, most Genízaros still considered themselves Indians well into the 1800s. Some even thought about going back to their original tribes when their relationship with the Spaniards became difficult. In 1780 a group of thirty-three Genízaros in Santa Fe who had purchased land, built houses, and become Catholics and were being ordered to establish a new settlement at the door of their enemies, the Comanches, told Governor Anza that if they were forced to move they might return to their own tribes.[4]

In Abiquiu during the period from 1815 to 1830, the pueblo and its common lands came under attack by the Hispanic elite and by fray Teodoro Alcina. The members of the Genízaro pueblo and its leaders had to organize themselves and determine a strategy to defend their lands. The tactic they employed centered on the assertion of the identity of Abiquiu as an Indian pueblo. Abiquiu continued to be treated as an Indian pueblo throughout this litigation, especially when former protector of Indians Ignacio María Sánchez Vergara got involved. He was appointed to present Abiquiu Pueblo's case against unauthorized land sales, arguing that Pueblo Indians could not sell their land without permission from a judge.

The Abiquiu Genízaros retained remarkable cohesion as they fought outside incursions on their land and water resources. The Genízaro pueblo received about the same amount of land as did the other New Mexico pueblos, whose pueblo leagues contained close to the 17,712 acres in four square leagues, though the measurement of the Abiquiu grant was conducted differently. In contrast to most other Indian pueblos, however, Abiquiu was able to hold onto much of its land. Abiquiu did this partly through its change of identity or shapeshifting from an Indian pueblo to a Hispanic land grant, and then to a livestock cooperative association.[5]

The Abiquiu Genízaros considered themselves Indians throughout most of the 1820s, although Father Alcina's famous curse when he damned the Genízaros in 1820 was a seminal event that started to turn Abiquiu from an

Indian pueblo into a Hispanic community, particularly from a religious standpoint. Yet a century passed before Abiquiu made the choice to be a Hispanic
village instead of an Indian pueblo. During the period from about 1820 to
1928 the Abiquiu land grant displayed a dual identity. When it came to fighting for its land, Abiquiu considered itself to be an Indian pueblo because
the laws seemed to protect Indian pueblos from sale of their land by individual Indians. Sánchez Vergara argued that Indian pueblos such as Abiquiu
could not sell their lands without governmental permission, knowing that
no such authority had been granted for any of the Abiquiu land sales.
Although Abiquiu pueblo had the law on its side, the political situation in
New Mexico under Governor Bartolomé Baca in the 1820s was such that
Spanish and Mexican laws were manipulated to prefer Hispanic citizens
attempting to acquire pueblo land over Indians and Genízaros attempting
to hold on to that land.

When Abiquiu approached the surveyor general and the Court of Private
Land Claims in the late 1800s, it was unclear whether it would be advan-
tageous to be an Indian pueblo or a Hispanic community. When Surveyor
General William Pelham submitted the first group of land grant claims to
Congress in 1846, he divided the Pueblo claims from the non-Indian claims
and recommended that all the pueblos be confirmed for the four square
leagues shown in the forged Cruzate grants most of them held. Abiquiu was
closer to being an Indian pueblo than a Hispanic land grant but was included
in neither category because the U.S. government was confused regarding
Abiquiu's classification. In the government's view it was not a pueblo because
all the eighteen pueblos in New Mexico had been submitted to Congress
and confirmed. Thus almost by default, Abiquiu was given the designation
"the Town of Abiquiu," a grant classification reserved for Hispanic community grants.[6]

In 1883 J. M. C. Chávez filed a grant claim on behalf of "the half-breed
Indians of Abiquiu" with Surveyor General Henry M. Atkinson, who took
no action on the claim. Later, when Surveyor General George Washington
Julian examined the Abiquiu grant in 1885, Abiquiu's genesis as an Indian
pueblo made all the difference in his analysis. Julian's thirty-page report followed his usual practice of reexamining the grant under a highly critical,
overly technical magnifying glass. In the first twenty-five pages of his report,
Julian sounded as if he was going to recommend rejection of the Abiquiu
grant. He listed the usual reasons, all fallacious under Spanish and Mexican

law: the original grant was not produced; the proper officials had not authenticated the copy of the grant that was produced; the grant was not approved by the king, the viceroy, or the audiencia; and the long-standing possession of the land by the Genízaros did not justify awarding them title under the doctrine of prescription. Just as it appeared that Surveyor General Julian was going to recommend rejection of the grant, he asked rhetorically whether these restrictive Spanish laws and decrees he had quoted applied to Indians. Amazingly, the surveyor general determined that they did not because "the Spanish government was very lenient towards the Indians," recognizing that they were entitled "to all the lands they have or have had in actual possession for cultivation, pasture, or habitation."[7] Accordingly, Julian recommended that Congress confirm the entire Abiquiu Genízaro land grant. The status of the Abiquiu grant as one made to Genízaro Indians, at least in Julian's eyes, saved the grant from a rejection recommendation. Even though by 1885 many residents of the Abiquiu grant considered themselves to be Hispanos, the fact that they were once Genízaros was of benefit to them according to Surveyor General Julian.

J. M. C. Chávez and Reyes Gonzales submitted the Abiquiu grant to the Court of Private Land Claims for confirmation in 1892. Chávez was the son of the famous general, José María Chávez, who served as a government official in the Spanish, Mexican, and American territorial periods. José María lived right on the plaza in Abiquiu in the house later made famous by Georgia O'Keeffe who bought it in 1945 and lived there most of the rest of her long life.[8] As his father had been, J. M. C. Chávez was a speculator who purchased interests in many land grants including the San Joaquín del Río de Chama grant, often in conjunction with Thomas B. Catron, the largest land speculator in Territorial New Mexico. When he filed a petition with the surveyor general for the confirmation of the Abiquiu grant, Chávez said the grant was made to the half-breed Indians and asked that it be confirmed to him and his associate owners on their behalf. It was probably a good choice to cast the Abiquiu grant into the mold of an Indian pueblo. Perhaps guided by Surveyor General Julian's positive recommendation, the Land Claims Court confirmed the Abiquiu grant to the half-breed Indians of Abiquiu in 1894.[9]

When Deputy Surveyor Sherrard Coleman surveyed the Abiquiu grant, it was found to contain a little more than 16,500 acres, about 1,000 acres short of four square leagues. The claimants protested the location of the northern boundary at the Chama River, arguing that the line should be established along the Chama River as it flowed in 1754. The Land Claims Court over-ruled the protest, and a patent was finally issued to the Abiquiu Board of Grant Commissioners on 11 November 1909.[10]

The Abiquiu grant is still managed by a board of commissioners and still contains about 16,500 acres, although some of this land has been privatized. The grant board conveyed about 150 acres into private hands, but the possibility that some individuals wanted to subdivide and sell their tracts to outsiders put a stop to the policy of providing private tracts to members of the Abiquiu land grant.[11]

After the patent for the Abiquiu grant was issued to the Abiquiu Grant Board of Commissioners in 1909, the common lands followed the rocky path of many land grants that were subject to taxes for the first time. Abiquiu became locked in a struggle between the speculators, represented by J. M. C. Chávez, and the land grant board that received the patent to the grant. According to oral history, Chávez began collecting taxes from land grant members in 1909 and then simply pocketed the taxes he collected from unsuspecting grant residents . Then around 1928, a historic vote took place among the members of the Abiquiu grant. The issue was simple: Did the members want to be an Indian pueblo or a Hispanic village?[12]

In the voting the majority favored becoming a Hispano village. Apparently many Abiquiu children had been sent to the Santa Fe Indian School but henceforth would be eligible to attend the Río Arriba public schools and the parochial schools of the Archdiocese of Santa Fe. Just as important as school attendance, however, was the payment of taxes on the common lands. The Abiquiu grant's commissioners were unable to pay the taxes on the common lands and could not collect those taxes from owners of private tracts of land within the grant. According to the current oral history, Chávez continued to collect and pocket the taxes.[13]

Before 1940 Abiquiu lost its common lands to the State of New Mexico for nonpayment of taxes. The Board of Grant Commissioners was devastated, but over the next ten years it came up with a solution: to form a corporation and recast itself as the Abiquiu Cooperative Livestock Association.

About eighty memberships were sold at $20.00 to persons acceptable to the board. With the help of U.S. Senator Dennis Chávez and the Farm Security Administration, the state tax authorities were talked into stalling the tax sale until the association was able to gather enough money to redeem their land. With the help of the Farm Security Administration, the members of the livestock cooperative bought the land in 1941.[14]

Since then, the Abiquiu land grant has been managed for the benefit of its members mainly for grazing their animals on the common lands. At the present time, the Abiquiu land grant is still used primarily for grazing since there is little irrigable land there. Of the approximately eighty members of the grant, from ten to fifteen members graze a total of 36 to 150 head of livestock on the grant. The fact that the Abiquiu grant still holds title to the approximately 16,500 acres it received in 1909 testifies to the Abiquiu Land Grant Board's good stewardship.[15]

While the political transformation of Abiquiu from Indian pueblo to Hispanic village took place around 1828, its religious transformation began more than a century earlier. By 1820 the Abiquiu Genízaros had become believers in their own expression of Christian doctrine. They knew that religion, the extended family, and the community were the three pillars upon which their unique lifestyle was built.[16] They knew that Father Alcina was not fulfilling his religious duties; rather he seemed intent on doing everything he could to destroy them. The Abiquiu Genízaros, along with their Hispanic neighbors, decided to take matters into their own hands and went in search of a priest. They found Father Bruno González at Picuris, who was willing to take the job, but Father Alcina's resistance and a lawsuit filed against him thwarted the transfer. During this period when Abiquiu was effectively without a priest, its religious identity was established.[17]

Starting around 1820, the Penitentes of Abiquiu began to carry on the religious tradition that Father Alcina's actions almost destroyed. They built two moradas in Abiquiu. The first one may date from as early as the 1820s and is known as the Morada del Alto, which is on the east side of the pueblo. The second, the Morada de Moqui, is on the south side of the pueblo.[18] It is likely that the beginning of the strong Penitente movement in Abiquiu coincided with Father Alcina's famous curse of the pueblo when he told the Genízaros in a public meeting that they were all damned.[19] Around this time, the religious component of Genízaro identity shifted dramatically and the Penitente movement began to grow and strengthen at Abiquiu.[20]

Figure 23
Virgil Trujillo, seventh-
generation Abiqueño and
Abiquiu Land Grant trustee,
examining petroglyphs on the
Abiquiu mesa. *Photograph by
Malcolm Ebright.*

Little is known for certain about the origins of the Penitentes, or La
Hermandad de Nuestro Padre Jesús Nazareno. Like the Genízaros themselves
and their origin, the answers are to be found in the documents rather than
in historical theories. Fray Angelico Chávez has considered and dismissed
both the Third Order of St. Francis and the penitential *cofradías* (lay religious associations) of Seville and other Spanish cities as the source of the
Penitentes in New Mexico, although Ahlborn believes that "some degree of
direct influence of the Third Order on 'penitentism' seems fairly certain."[21]
There are clues, however, that point to Abiquiu, along with Santa Cruz de
la Cañada, as points of local origin of the Penitentes.

Abiquiu was one of the first communities where Penitente-like
practices were observed in the 1770s, although there apparently was no
Penitente or religious organization there at that time. In his 1776 report
on the Abiquiu mission, Father Francisco Atanasio Domínguez noted that
fray Sebastián Fernández led an unusual service on Fridays during Lent.
After observing the devotion of the Way of the Cross, the priest scourged

himself after dark: "This discipline [being] attended by those who come voluntarily, because the father merely proposes it to them, and following his good example, there is a crowd of Indians and citizens [who do likewise]." Fray Angélico Chávez notes this reference in Domínguez's report, calling it "the closest thing to the idea of the Penitentes" that Domínguez saw. Chávez is quick to point out, however, that "there were no Penitente brotherhoods in all of New Mexico in 1776," a claim that Domínguez did not make. The first specific mention of the Penitentes that Chávez found is an 1833 decree by Bishop José Antonio Laureano de Zubiría, condemning and banning the Penitente brotherhood. Chávez himself gave different estimates for the origin of the Penitentes. On one occasion he stated that they arose about midway between Domínguez and Zubiría, "between 1790 and 1810."[22] On another occasion, Chávez indicated that the Penitente movement had come up from Mexico while Father Antonio José Martínez was a seminarian in Durango, which would mean between 1817 and 1821.[23] It is likely that Penitente activity in Abiquiu began in the early 1820s, about the same time as the lawsuit against Father Alcina by the citizens of Abiquiu and Ojo Caliente.

As Dennis Daily has demonstrated, the connection between the Penitentes and northern New Spain in general and Durango in particular is undeniable.[24] The brotherhood of Nuestro Padre Jesús Nazareno was well established in colonial Nueva Vizcaya in the seventeenth and eighteenth centuries. There were two such brotherhoods in Durango: one in the church of San Nicolás (which later became San Agustín), founded in 1673; the other in the church of Santa María de Tunal de Analco, founded in 1734.[25] There were also brotherhoods devoted to Jesús Nazareno in Cuencamé, Mapimí, and San Francisco del Malpaís. The rules governing these organizations and their practices are remarkably similar to those of New Mexico Penitentes. As further evidence, Daily notes that many of the traditional religious hymns, called *alabados*

> sung by the brothers in New Mexico are identical to those sung in and around Durango. The rhyme structure, meter, and themes of all the alabados show that they derive from the same source, although variation in melody indicate that the two streams diverged at sometime in the past.[26]

The Penitentes of New Mexico have been greatly misunderstood because writers have overemphasized their self-flagellation and underemphasized their community-building activities. "They cared for people in their human crises, especially those...[of] poverty, sickness, and death." These needs were even more acute as the quantity of Franciscans assigned to New Mexico's parishes dwindled during what Chávez referred to as the "Secular Period" (1790–1850), and the quality of some of those who remained also declined. Father Alcina is the best example of such a decline. When he refused to perform the last rites for the dying, to bury the dead, and to hear confessions, someone else had to perform these services. Although the Penitentes were not authorized to hear confessions, celebrate Mass, or perform the last rites, there were many services they could and did perform, such as providing comfort to the dying, making the coffin, digging the grave, and performing some sort of burial service. This they did without charge, in contrast to the exorbitant fees that Father Alcina collected. As the Penitentes filled the gap caused by the failure of Father Alcina and other priests to perform their duties, the brotherhood became one of the most important forces shaping the culture of Abiquiu.[27]

Among the complaints against Father Alcina was that even when he did celebrate Mass he did not do it properly. In their petition on behalf of the residents of the jurisdiction of Abiquiu, Mateo García, Manuel Montoya, and Mariano Martín stated that Father Alcina did not treat them kindly or honor his "obligation of preaching and teaching us the doctrine of the Holy Gospel as is ordered by the Council of Trent."[28] Since the petitioners trying to have Father Alcina replaced included both Genízaros and their Hispanic neighbors, it seems that by 1820 the Genízaros were no longer practicing their old native religions; they had been replaced by a modified form of Catholicism some have called folk Catholicism. Unlike the neighboring Indian pueblos where Pueblo religion and Catholicism coexisted, at Abiquiu Catholicism almost completely replaced the former religious practices of the Genízaros.[29]

A process of religious acculturation took place in Abiquiu during a sixty-year period from the end of the witchcraft outbreak to the petition to oust Father Alcina in 1820. The process was slow and subtle, and it began with the preaching of Father Juan José Toledo in the 1750s and 1760s. At that time the Genízaros were required to attend the services Father Toledo held in the Abiquiu church, but they could not understand much of what he said. Toledo preached the sermon or homily in Spanish, celebrated the Mass in Latin, and probably employed some Ute or other indigenous language the Genízaros were familiar with as well.[30] A translator provided the Indians a loose rendering, but everything was filtered through the translator's belief system. Thus much of what Toledo said in his sermon was lost in translation. After church the Genízaros would go to the translator's house and discuss the sermon. He would tell the Genízaros what to believe and what not to believe. This was the beginning of a homegrown Catholicism that replaced the Genízaros' traditional religious beliefs, which, along with their customs, were fading away. As Genízaros such as Vicente Trujillo drifted back to the pueblo, they became part of the emerging religious structure of Abiquiu, performing tasks for the new priests who followed Father Toledo. This is how Vicente Trujillo obtained access to the golden cross that was part of the "valuables of Our Lady" that Father Domínguez inventoried in 1776.[31] By 1786 Trujillo was becoming a Catholic, but not a particularly good one. He was no longer practicing witchcraft; instead, he was helping Father Ramón Antonio González take care of the church valuables. He was also stealing and selling some of these valuables such as the gold cross belonging to the Virgin Mary.[32]

Thirty-five years later, by 1820 most Genízaros had reformed and become fairly good Catholics, and it was their putative spiritual leader, Father Alcina, who was breaking Church law and abandoning his duties. By then only about 10 percent of the members of the Abiquiu communities referred to themselves as Indians, although Abiquiu proper was still referred to as an Indian pueblo. On the outside Abiquiu was still seen as a pueblo, but on the inside it had become more Christianized and Hispanicized, closer to the Abiquiu of today.[33]

Residents of Abiquiu still retain the Hispano-Indian duality that is their strength. Old-timers, or *ancianos*, interviewed about the history of the Abiquiu grant tell stories that demonstrate that the Abiquiu of the 1820s when Father Alcina cursed the pueblo has changed. Nevertheless, witchcraft stories still circulate in Abiquiu. These stories are reminiscent of the witchcraft proceedings that are the central focus of this book. They include stories of the tecolote who perches outside someone's house, uttering sounds almost like human speech. When a frustrated neighbor shoots the owl, he finds his mother-in-law has a severe wound the next morning, in the same place the owl was shot. Abiquiu "villagers still tell stories of seeing balls of fire traveling through the skies at night . . . or recall legends that *brujas* or *la muerte* (death) would appear at dances as handsomely dressed individuals with enchanting eyes. Suddenly without warning they would disappear; often

Figure 24
Current church at Abiquiu with the cross erected by the village in 1888 in response to the continuing witchcraft outbreak at Abiquiu. *Photograph by Isabel Trujillo.*

times, a black dog was seen running from the plaza. It is said that the dancer was often the devil or death carrying out their nefarious work."[34]

Abiquiu's identity as an Indian pueblo or a Hispanic community remains undecided. Some would like to revert to an Indian pueblo.[35] Abiquiu residents are proud of their unique past and are taking control of their future. Witchcraft stories are still heard and witches sometimes seen. La Llorona, the mythical figure who is said to weep as she searches for her dead children, has been recently heard wandering along the Chama River. All are part of the legend and history of Abiquiu, one of the strongest communities in northern New Mexico. Governor Tomás Vélez Cachupín and fray Juan José Toledo would doubtless be proud that Abiquiu pueblo has survived and is thriving to this day.[36]

APPENDIX A

List of Accused Sorcerers

NAME	CLASS	DESCRIPTION
***Pueblo of Abiquiu* (5)**		
Atole Caliente	Indian female	
Jacinta	Indian	daughter of Atole Caliente
Miguel, El Cojo	Indian	invoked Devil while in prison
La Pastora	Indian female	
Pedro [Trujillo]	Indian	from Santa Ana, invoked the Devil while in prison
***Pueblo of San Juan* (5)**		
	Indian male	small eyes, tall, thin
El Temba	Indian	
Largo, Juan	Indian	
Palma	Indian female	
Pichulo	Indian	thick-lipped, very swarthy
Quiteria	Indian female	head cook who took the life of Father Mirabal
***Pueblo of Taos* (24)**		
	female	wife of José Romero, musician
	female	wife of El Gavilán

NAME	CLASS	DESCRIPTION
	Indian	brother of José Romero, who is an alguacil
	Indian boy	small, fat, round-faced, and flat-nosed
	Indian male	old and blind, round face, gray hair, and good nose
	Indian female	old, has one clouded eye, and is flat-nosed
Agustín	Indian	son of an Indian named Burro
Ana María	female	flat-nosed and married
Antonia	Indian female	swarthy and married
Antonia	female	fat, married to an Indian with pockmarks, thin, and swarthy
Antonio	Indian	war captain
Antonio	Indian	wanted to be a lieutenant
Antonio	male	black, ugly, and lives in the Callejón that faces north
Burro	Indian	father of Agustín
Damacia	female	daughter of Gaspar
Encarnación	Indian female	pretty face and single
Felachi, Julián		
Gaspara		
Getona	Indian female	wrinkled face, sometimes wears a snake skin for a belt.
Gregorio	male	wide-faced, narrow forehead, swarthy, whose house and doorway face north
Isabel	Indian female	resembles Atole Caliente and in one night goes to and returns from Mexico City
Juanillo	Indian	musician
Michaela	Indian female	small and missing a tooth
Romero, José	Indian	musician

Pueblo of Picurís (5)

NAME	CLASS	DESCRIPTION
	Indian male	tall, thin, pockmarked, swarthy, and missing a tooth
Huelecoo	Indian male	Indian alguacil
Luisa	female	swarthy, wide nose, and grimaces

NAME	CLASS	DESCRIPTION
Manuel	male	round-faced and swarthy
Pascual		

Pueblo of San Ildefonso (5)

	Indian male	old with a wide nose
	male	chief fiscal
Guadalupe	Indian female	long straight hair
Luis	Indian male	small, thick lips, swarthy, and flat-nosed
Margarita	Indian female	old, flat-nosed, curly hair

Pueblo of Nambe (5)

Antonia	female	from San Juan and has a daughter by Miguel, the governor of Nambe
Antonio	Indian male	captain of Tesuque
Eusebio	mixed-blood male	swarthy
Griego, Juan Pancho	male	
Juan Antonio	Indian male	captain of Nambe
Mateo	Indian	from San Juan
Vicentillo		the Devil said through one of the possessed females that he wanted to set free from jail the sorcerers who call on him [the Devil]
	Indian male	small, thin, swarthy, good-looking, cacique, and teacher of sorcerers

Pueblo of Pojoaque (4)

	Indian male	cacique
	female	wife of Juan Felipe of Pojoaque
Francisco	male	husband of the coyota Gertrudis
Juan Felipe	Indian male	son of Poseyemu

Pueblo of Tesuque (4)

	Indian male	fat-faced, pockmarked, with a pockmark on his chin
	Indian male	swarthy, crooked nose, pockmarked, and thin
Anselmo	Indian male	tall, swarthy, thick lips, cacique, and teacher of sorcerers

NAME	CLASS	DESCRIPTION
Petrona	Indian female	long face, high nose, white

Pueblo of Galisteo (1)

María Jémez	female	

Pueblo of Isleta (15)

Antonio	Indian male	son of Bárbara Canosa, also a sorcerer
Antonio, El Cayguia (Kiowa)	Indian male	
Caiguia	Indian male	son of the cacique
Canosa, Bárbara	Indian female	curved nose and rosy cheeks
Cosas	Indian	
Gregoria	Indian female	
Jiron	Indian male	
Juana	Indian female	young, pretty, large eyes, and good hair
Martín	Indian male	crippled
Pachura, Manuela	Indian female	
Ramos	Indian male	
Reyes	Indian female	
Roque	Indian male	
Siusa	Indian female	mother of Roque
Toribio	Indian male	son of Manuela

Pueblo of Sandia (7) *not including Antonio and Bárbara Canosa listed at Isleta*

Antonio	Indian/mixed blood	thin
Antonio	Indian male	son of Bárbara Canosa, also a sorcerer (also listed at Isleta)
Canosa, Bárbara	Indian female	curved nose, rosy cheeks
Catarina	Indian female	fat, double chin, and sores on neck
Cabellada, Juan Francisco	Indian male	small stature, swarthy, with whiskers
De la Luz, María	Indian female	white, small, chubby-faced, has a blanket made of Britanny
Leonardo	Indian male	fat, tall, ugly looking
Manuela	Indian female	turned-down eyes, flat nosed
Salvador	Indian male	bear bite scar on left side of face, small stature, black and gray hair

NAME	CLASS	DESCRIPTION

Pueblo of Laguna (1)

| El Conejo | Hopi Indian male | |

Genízaros of the Pueblo of Belen (3)

Janisco and his wife	male/female	
Matías	male	married
Petrona	female	

Chimayo (20)

Genízaros

Agustín	male	son-in-law of Córdoba
Antonio Bárbara	Indian	of [from] Casilla
Antonio, El Quino	male	son-in-law of Salvador Cruz
Brother of Juan	male	
Cascabel	Genízaro	imprisoned, has his art in a small black stone and is very powerful
Cayetano	Indian male	Indian of Marcial Martín
Cruz, Andrés	male	
Cruz, Andrés (wife of)	female	
Cruz, Domingo		
Cruz, Francisco	male	
Cruz, Joaquinillo	male	
Cruz, Salvador	male	
Cruz, Sebastián	male	
Cruz, Teresa de Francisco	female	
Domingo	male	son-in-law of Salvador Cruz
Juan	male/coyote	coyote of Luis López, deceased
María, wife of Luis Cruz	female	
Quiteria	female	daughter of Pronco Cruz
Rosa	female	servant of Martín Fernández
Talee	coyote	evil-named, servant of the deceased Ignacio Pacheco

Spaniards (gente de razón) from the jurisdiction of Chimayo

Francisca, La Carrilla	female	with her mother
Martín, Ana	female	
Martín, Josefa	female	
Martín, Nicolás	male	

NAME	CLASS	DESCRIPTION
Martín, María Antonia	female	daughter of Nicolás
Martín, Justo	male	son of Nicolás
Martín, Lorenza	female	daughter of Nicolás
Martín, Javier	male	
Martín, Panchito	male	
Martín, Juan María	male	son of Panchito Martín
Martín, Dolores Ascensio	female	daughter of Panchito Martín
Martín, José, El Músico	male	son of Panchito Martín
Martín, La Reyes	female	daughter of Panchito Martín
Martín, Encarnación	female	daughter of Javier Martín
Juan Domingo	male	
Gertrudis	female	daughter of Chalo
Juan Antonio	male	son of Chalo
Sangil, María	female	her daughter recently married to Lorenzo Montoya
Medina, Isidro	male	
Montaño, Josefa	female	
Montaño, Ana María	female	daughter of Josefa Montaño
George	male	child of Anna
Ramos, Manuel	male	son of José, the musician
Montaño, Salvador	male	
Sangil, Juan Antonio	male	son of Marcial Sangil
Domingo	male	son-in-law of Pancho Regil
Cruz, Domingo	male	
(no name)	male	son of Bernardino Trujillo (whose teeth are piggy-backed over each other)
Sangil, Santiago	male	
Juan Antonio	male	fugitive, lives in the Rio Abajo
López, José	male	alias Barranco de Chimayó, married
Juan	male	brother of Apolinar, nephew of Gregorio López, a tailor from [Santa Cruz] de la Cañada
Martín, Julián	male	son of Manuela Varas [who is] a son of Jerónimo Martín, wife of Martín Fernández
Martín, Luis	male	brother of Agustín
Martín	male	son-in-law of Antonio Córdoba

NAME	CLASS	DESCRIPTION

Accused Sorcerers from Different Places

NAME	CLASS	DESCRIPTION
Martín, Cristóbal	male Indian	from Truchas
Juan Alonzo	old man	from [Santa Cruz] de la Cañada
Rosa	female	called La Pesena de Albuquerque, wife of Francisco Perea
Peralta, Antonio	male	from Tome
Tafoya, Rosalía	female/Spaniard	wife of Simón Martín of Abiquiu
A son of Jerónimo López	male	from the villa of Santa Fe, light-complexioned and with a pretty face
López, José José Montaño	male mulatto	from Pueblo Quemado, student of
Tafoya, Antonio	male	son of Cristóbal Tafoya of [Santa Cruz] de la Cañada
La Contreras	female	woman from Rio Abajo

Presidio of Sonora

NAME	CLASS	DESCRIPTION
Luz	female/Spaniard	has a pretty *terrenate*, face, and body; married to Juan Andrés González
No name	male	lives in Rio Arriba, missing two white teeth
Marcella	female/Spaniard	vecina of Oaxaca, *mosa y galana*; learned her art from someone from León
Archuleta, Juan	male	vecino of [Santa Cruz] de la Cañada
Coyote, Juan	male	dark complexioned, rosy skinned, son of Antonio Peralta of Tome
Crisóstomo, Juana	female/Spaniard	from Oaxaca, stout with light skin, black eyes, black eyebrows; very evil
Gallegos, Santiago	male/coyote	short, fat, and dark-complexioned, from Tome
Manuela, La Poseña	Female	vecina of the Rio Abajo, *tercera*
Rodríguez, Catarina	Female	vecina of Mexico City; killed her husband
Candelaria, Bárbara	female/Spaniard	from El Paso
Candelaria, Quiteria	female/Spaniard	from El Paso
Candelaria, Rita	female/Spaniard	from El Paso
Candelaria, Rosalía	female/Spaniard	from El Paso
Candelaria, Victoria	female/Spaniard	from El Paso

APPENDIX B

Abiquiu Genízaro Land Grant, 1754

En la villa de Santa Fe a diez días del mes de mayo de mil setecientos cincuenta y cuatro años, don Tomás Vélez Cachupín, gobernador de este reino de Nuevo México en virtud de lo mandado por el excelentísimo señor virrey capitán general de esta Nueva España Conde de Revillagigedo en testimonio remitido por su excelencia con los dictámenes del señor fiscal de su majestad y señor auditor general en la guerra sobre los puntos de los autos de visita y en aprobación de ella y por lo perteneciente a la congregación de los indios Genízaros que en el antiguo pue[blo de] Abiquiú con la providencia de haberse nombrado por su excelencia el señor virrey religioso doctrinero para su administración en su formal radicación y establecimiento y sobre que se

In the villa of Santa Fe on 10 May 1754, don Tomás Vélez Cachupín, governor of this kingdom of New Mexico, by virtue of what was ordered by the most excellent viceroy captain general of this New Spain, the Conde de Revillagigedo, in the certified copy sent by his excellency with the opinions of his majesty's fiscal and the auditor general of war about the points from the proceedings of the inspection and in approval of it and with regard to the congregation of the Genízaro Indians in the old pueblo of Abiquiu, his excellency the viceroy having taken the measure of having named a teacher of Christian doctrine for its administration in its formal settlement and establishment and regarding the said Genízaro Indians being given sufficient

les diese a dichos indios Genízaros las tierras suficientes de pan llevar como pide el señor fiscal arreglado a la ley octava título tres libro sexto de la Recopilación de estos reinos de las Indias en que manda su majestad que en los {sitios} en que se hayan de formar pueblos y reducciones tengan comodidad de aguas, tierras, montes, entradas y salidas y labranzas y una legua de ejido de largo para que puedan tener los ganados sin mezclar con los españoles A cuyo cumplimiento pasé yo, dicho gobernador al {dicho pueblo de A}[biquiú...] doctrinero que nuevamente vino de México para la administración espiritual de dicho pueblo fray Félix José de Ordóñez y Machado del orden de nuestro padre San Francisco y de esta feligresía de su jurisdicción; y previéndolo su posesión de ella habiéndola tomado en consorcio de su prelado el vice custodio de esta santa custodia fray Tomás Maríano de la Cruz procedí al reconocimiento de todas las tierras, labores, montes, pastos y aguas para el efecto de señalar al dicho pueblo de indios Genízaros nuevamente congregados lo mandado por la citada ley y viendo todo con correspondiente comodidad de pingües tierras de bella calidad abundancia de aguas pastos y [...] se midió al referido pueblo de Santo Tomás Apóstol de Abiquiú, por sur desde el centro del referido pueblo cinco mil varas castellanas por las orillas de un arroyo permanente que desciende por dicho

irrigable land as the fiscal requests in accord with law 8, title 3, book 6 of the *Recopilación* of these kingdoms of the Indies in which his majesty orders that in the places in which pueblos and reductions are to be formed, they are to have the convenience of water, land, woods, ingresses, egresses, farmland, and an ejido one league in length so that they can have cattle without mixing with the Spaniards in fulfillment of which I, the said governor, went to the said pueblo of A[biquiu...] {with} the minister of Christian doctrine newly arrived from Mexico City for the spiritual administration of said pueblo, fray Félix José de Ordóñez y Machado of the order of Our Father St. Francis and of this parish of its jurisdiction, giving him possession of it. Having taken it in conjunction with his prelate, the vice custodian of this holy custody, fray Tomás Mariano de la Cruz, I proceeded to the examination of all the land, fields, woods, pastures, and water with the aim of designating for the said pueblo of newly congregated Genízaro Indians, what was ordered by the cited law. Seeing everything with the appropriate conveniences of abundant land of good quality, abundance of water, pastures, and [...] measured for pueblo of Santo Tomás Apóstol de Abiquiú, on the south from the center of the aforesaid pueblo five thousand Castilian varas along the banks of a permanent arroyo that descends in said direction along the edges of the pueblo

rumbo por las orillas del pueblo con disposición de regar todas las tierras del referido rumbo. Por el norte midiendo también esde el centro se le señaló dos mil y cuatrocientos varas por haberse encontrado con el río caudaloso que llaman de Chama que corre de poniente a oriente y sin vado por esta parte el que sirve de lindero por el referido rumbo. Por el oriente cogiendo asimismo el centro se los midió dos mil quinientas cincuenta varas dichas castellanas habiéndose comprendido en dicha medida la casa y tierras de un vecino nombrado Juan Trujillo y los herederos de Miguel Martín. Por el poniente igualmente medidas desde el centro del referido pueblo se les señaló otras dos mil quinientas y cincuenta varas comprendidas en dicha medida parte de las tierras del rancho de Jerónimo Martín. Y todas las dichas tierras así medidas y señaladas con asistencia del justicia mayor de aquella jurisdicción y villa de La Cañada Juan José Lobato son de pan llevar de buena cualidad y todas debajo de riego con comodidad de muchas aguas de montes y bosques. Por el rumbo del sur se les señaló y midió la legua de ejido siendo sus linderos al norte las medidas de las tierras del pueblo. Por el sur el Camino Real que va a Navajó. Por el oriente el nacimiento del arroyo que desciende a orilla del dicho pueblo. Y por el poniente el alto del Río de los Frijoles con pastos superabundantes de bella calidad por ser grama y otros de la

with the capacity to irrigate all the land in that direction; on the north, also measuring from the center 2,400 varas were designated because it met the plentiful river called the Chama that flows from west to east and without a ford at this point, which serves as the boundary in the aforesaid direction; on the east, likewise beginning from the center, 2,550 of those said Castilian varas were measured for them, having included within said measurement the house and land of a vecino named Juan Trujillo and the heirs of Miguel Martín; on the west also measured from the center of the aforesaid pueblo another 2,550 varas were designated including in said measurement some of the land of the rancho of Jerónimo Martín. All the said land [was] thus measured and designated with the assistance of the justicia mayor of that jurisdiction and the villa of La Cañada, Juan José Lobato. It is irrigable land of good quality and all under irrigation with the convenience of much water and woods. On the south the league of ejido was designated and measured, its boundaries being on the north the measurements of the land of the pueblo, on the south by the Camino Real that goes to Navajo, on the east the beginning of the arroyo that descends along the edge of the said pueblo, and on the west the high ground of the Río de los Frijoles with superabundant pastures of beautiful quality because they are of grama and other {grasses} of the same quality

misma con muchas aguas. Y para que
así conste todo lo referido y practicado
arreglado a lo mandado por el excelentísimo señor virrey y pedido por el
señor fiscal de su majestad con
arreglamento a sus reales leyes y
cons[entimiento d]el dicho pueblo de
Santo Tomás Apóstol de Abiquiú de la
nación de los Genízaros nuevamente
congregados para su fijo estableci-
imiento en el en forma de república la
puse por diligencia que firmé con dicho
justicia mayor y los testigos de mi asistencia con quienes actúo a falta de
escribanos que de ninguna clase los hay
en este reino. Doy fe.

> Tomás Vélez Cachupín
> Juan José Lobato
> Manuel Sáenz de Garvizu
> Tomás de Albear y Collado

Concuerda con su original que queda
en este archivo de gobierno de donde a
petición de los principales del pueblo
de Santo Tomás de Abiquiu yo, don
Pedro Fermín de Mindinueta, caballero
del Orden de Santiago, coronel de
infantería de los reales ejércitos, gobernador y capitán general de este reino de
Nuevo México, lo hice sacar. Va fiel-
mente sacado, corregido y concertado y
a lo ver sacar, corregir y concertar
fueron testigos los de mi asistencia con
quienes actúo a falta de escribanos que
de ninguna clase los hay en esta gober-
nación. En testimonio de verdad hago
mi firma.

> Pedro Fermín de Mindinueta

with much water. So that everything
mentioned, carried out, and arranged
according to what the most excellent
viceroy ordered and requested by his
majesty's fiscal in accord with his royal
laws may be of record and with the
consent of the said pueblo of Santo
Tomás Apóstol de Abiquiú of the nation
of the Genízaros newly congregated for
their fixed establishment therein in the
form of a body politic. I set this down
as a proceeding that I signed with said
justicia mayor and my attending witnesses with whom I acted in the absence
of scribes of which there are none of
any kind in this kingdom. I so attest.

> Tomás Vélez Cachupín
> Juan José Lobato
> Manuel Sáenz de Garvizu
> Tomás de Albear y Collado

This agrees with the original that
remains in this government archive from
which, at the request of the leaders of the
pueblo de Santo Tomás de Abiquiú, I,
don Pedro Fermín de Mindinueta,
knight of the Order of Santiago, colonel
of infantry of the royal armies, governor
and captain general of this kingdom of
New Mexico, had it copied. It is faithfully
copied, corrected, and reconciled. The
witnesses who [saw] it copied, corrected,
and reconciled were my attending witnesses with whom I acted in the absence
of scribes of which there are none of any
kind in this administration. In testimony
of the truth I make my signature.

> Pedro Fermín de Mindinueta

NOTES

ARCHIVAL MATERIAL
Archives of the Archdiocese of Santa Fe (AASF)
Archivo General de Indias (AGI)
    Audiencia of Guadalajara
Archivo General de la Nación, Mexico City (AGN)
    Inquisición
    Provincias Internas
Archivos Históricos del Arzobispado de Durango, New Mexico State (AHAD) University
    Library, Microfilm, Archives and Special Collections Department, Las Cruces,
    New Mexico
Archivo Histórico de Hidalgo del Parral, New Mexico State University Library, Microfilm,
    Las Cruces, New Mexico
Beinecke Library, Yale University
New Mexico State Archives and Records Center, Santa Fe, New Mexico
    Mexican Archives of New Mexico (MANM)
    Records of the Court of Private Land Claims (PLC)
    Records of the Office of the Surveyor General (SG)
    Spanish Archives of New Mexico (SANM)
Pinart Collection, Bancroft Library, University of California, Berkeley
Ritch Collection of Papers Pertaining to New Mexico, Huntington Library, San Maríno, California
Uribe Collection, Ms. 352, Box 1, Folder 3, C. L. Sonnichsen Collection, University of Texas at
    El Paso Library.

INTRODUCTION

1.   Teófilo F. Ruiz, "The Terror of History: Mystics, Heretics, and Witches in the Western
    Tradition," Lecture 23, The Witches of Essex and Salem. Audiotaped lecture, course no.
    892 (Chantily, Va.: The Teaching Company, 2002).

2.   Very little has been published about New Mexico in the eighteenth century, a period
    Bancroft described in 1889 in the following, ethnocentric way: "From 1700 New
    Mexico settled down into that monotonously uneventful career of inert and non-pro-
    gressive existence which sooner or later is to be noted in the history of every Hispano-
    American province." Hubert Howe Bancroft, *History of Arizona and New Mexico,*
    1530–1888 (Albuquerque: Horn and Wallace, 1962), 225.

3.   Frank C. Hibben, "Excavation of the Riana Ruin and Chama Valley Survey," *University*
    of New Mexico Anthropological Bulletin 2:1 (Albuquerque: University of New Mexico
    Press, 1937), 10. The ruins of one of Abiquiu's prehistoric pueblos lie beneath the
    Abiquiu Genízaro Pueblo. Lesley Poling-Kempes, *Valley of Shining Stone: The Story of*

Abiquiú (Tucson: University of Arizona Press, 1997), 12–15. Ancient Abiquiu's sister pueblo, Po-shu-ouinge, was excavated in 1919 by Jeançon, his assistant, and four Santa Clara Pueblo men. J. A. Jeançon, "Excavations in the Chama Valley, New Mexico," *Smithsonian Institution Bureau of American Ethnology Bulletin 81* (Washington, D.C.: Government Printing Office, 1923).

4.   Jack D. Forbes, *Apache, Navaho, and Spaniard* (Norman: University of Oklahoma Press, 1960), 120.

5.   A similar dislocation of Indian identity took place in the extirpation of idolatry trials in sixteenth- and seventeenth-century Peru. There, shamans were forced to play a double game of outward acquiescence with Christianity while continuing to patronize native religious practices. Nicholas Griffiths, *The Cross and the Serpent: Religious Repression and Resurgence in Colonial Peru* (Norman: University of Oklahoma Press, 1996), 158–59.

6.   Examples of a narrow definition of Genízaros are Fray Angélico Chávez, "Genízaros," in *Southwest*, ed., Alfonso Ortiz, vol. 9 of *Handbook of North American Indians*, ed. William C. Sturtevant (Washington, D.C.: Smithsonian Institution, 1979), 198–200. Morfi defined Genízaros as "the children of the captives of different [Indian] nations who have married in the province." Fray Agustín Morfi, "Geographical Description of New Mexico," translated in Alfred Barnaby Thomas, *Forgotten Frontiers: A Study of the Spanish Indian Policy of Don Juan Bautista de Anza, Governor of New Mexico, 1777–1787* (Norman: University of Oklahoma Press, 1932), 91–92. A broad definition of Genízaros is in Richard L. Norstrand, *The Hispano Homeland* (Norman: University of Oklahoma Press, 1992), 44. For a good discussion of the different definitions of Genízaros, see Oakah L. Jones Jr., "Rescue and Ransom of Spanish Captives from the indios bárbaros on the Northern Frontier of New Spain," *Colonial Latin American Historical Review* 4 (spring 1995): 131–32.

7.   Horvath argues for a broader definition of Genízaros to include Pueblo Indians no longer living in their pueblos, non-Indians who lived in the Genízaro plaza, and freed Indian servants no matter how they were acquired in "The Genízaro of Eighteenth Century New Mexico: A Reexamination," *Discovery* (1977): 25–40.

8.   Certainly baptism alone was not enough to establish Christianization of an Indian. Most Genízaros, and especially those at Abiquiu, were closer to their native belief systems than they were to Christianity. Petition of Los Genízaros, April 1733, SANM I: 1208.

9.   For a Vélez Cachupín decision regarding Genízaro land rights based on land usage, see Governor Tomás Vélez Cachupín, Order, Santa Fe, *José Marcelo Gallegos v. Pedro Iturbieta*, Santa Fe, 1765, SANM I: 362. This was not a final decision but did uphold the possessory rights of José Marcelo Gallegos until a full hearing could be held. The case is discussed in Malcolm Ebright, "Frontier Land Litigation: A Determinant of Spanish Custom and Law," *Western Legal History* 8 (summer–fall 1995): 211–14.

10. The land grants made by Governor Vélez were: (1) Las Trampas (1751); (2) Francisco Montes Vigil (1754); (3) Truchas (1754); (4) Abiquiu (1754); (5) Bernabé Montaño or Nuestra Señora de la Luz y San Fernando y San Blas (1752); (6) Carnuel (1763); (7) San Gabriel de las Nutrias; (8) Cañada de Santa Clara (1763); (9) Juan Gabaldón (1752); (10) Miguel and Santiago Montoya (1766); (11) San Marcos (1754); (12) Santa Ana, Jemez, and Zia (1766); (13) Antonio Baca (1762); (14) Piedra Lumbre (1766); (15) Polvadera (1766); (16) Cochiti Pueblo pasture grant; and (17) Sabinal (1765).

CHAPTER ONE: ABIQUIU, THE MIDDLE GROUND

1.   Edward P. Dozier, *Hano: A Tewa Indian Community in Arizona* (New York: Holt, Rinehart and Winston, 1966), 1; Michael B. Stanislawski, "Hopi-Tewa," in *Southwest*, ed., Alfonso Ortiz, vol. 9 of *Handbook of North American Indians*, ed. William C. Sturtevant (Washington, D.C.: Smithsonian Institution, 1979), 587–602; Poling-Kempes, *Valley of Shining Stone*, 15; and Hibben, *Excavation of the Riana Ruin*; contains

a map showing the location of the Chama Valley prehistoric pueblo sites. For a chart showing the period of occupation of these pueblos, see Henry Dobyns, "Puebloan Historic Demographic Trends," *Ethnohistory* 49 (winter 2002): 171. Some of these sites are discussed in Charles M. Carrillo, "Oral History-Ethnohistory of the Abiquiú Reservoir Area," in "History and Ethnohistory Along the Rio Chama," U.S. Army Corps of Engineers, Albuquerque, 1992. See also, J. A. Jeançon, *Excavations in the Chama Valley, New Mexico*, Smithsonian Institution, *Bureau of American Ethnology Bulletin* 81 (Washington, D.C.: Government Printing Office, 1923), 75–76.

2.   Polly Schaafsma, "War Imagery and Magic: Petroglyphs at Comanche Gap, Galisteo Basin, New Mexico" (paper presented at the symposium, Social Implication of Symbolic Expression in the Prehistoric American Southwest, 55th Annual Meeting of the Society for American Archaeology, Las Vegas, Nevada, 1990).

3.   Hibben, *Excavation of the Riana Ruin*, 49.

4.   Ibid., [61], Plate 13(a).

5.   *New Mexico Magazine*, August 1933, cited in Dennis Slifer, *Signs of Life: Rock Art of the Upper Rio Grande* (Santa Fe: Ancient City Press, 1998), 87. Renaud described the destruction of the Comanche petroglyph north of Abiquiú as follows: "One of the most significant petroglyphs of New Mexico is gone forever entirely destroyed by the inexorable march of progress!" E. B. Renaud, "Pictographs and Petroglyphs of the Western High Plains," *Archeological Survey Series, 8th Report* (Denver: University of Denver Press, 1936), 18.

6.   Scott Thybony, *Rock Art of the American Southwest* (Portland, Ore.: Graphic Arts Center Publishing, 2002), 119. Around Abiquiu, overlapped images are not frequent. In the Abiquiu area, however, there are other examples of the multiple use of boulders, which are often power places themselves. Richard I. Ford, personal communication, Santa Fe, 22 August 2003.

7.   Jean Clottes and David Lewis-Williams, *The Shamans of Prehistory: Trance and Magic in the Painted Caves* (New York: Harry N. Abrams, Inc., 1998), 85–86.

8.   The term *adoratorio* referred to the name given to temples of idols in New Spain. *Diccionario de autoridades* (1726–37; reprint, Madrid: Gredos, 1979), 1:91.

9.   *The Santa Fe New Mexican*, 28 August 2003, C1–C2; and Ford, personal communication. Ford, who is the former director of the Museum of Anthropology and Ethnobotanical Laboratory at the University of Michigan, has also been documenting rock art at Mesa Prieta near Alcalde, southeast of Abiquiu.

10. Alcalde Carlos Fernández, Report, Abiquiu, 3 June 1763, Pinart Collection, PE 52: 5, Bancroft Library, University of California, Berkeley (hereinafter Pinart Collection).

11. The León Fuerte (strong lion) site is similar to the Stone Lions Shrine connected with the prehistoric Yapashe Pueblo, both of which are part of Bandelier National Monument. Cochiti Pueblo, whose ancestors lived at Yapashe Pueblo, still consider the Stone Lions a sacred shrine and leave offerings, such as antlers and pottery sherds there. Arthur H. Rohn, William Ferguson, and Lisa Ferguson, *Rock Art of Bandelier National Monument* (Albuquerque: University of New Mexico Press, 1989), 17, 39, 117–18, 121–24, 132.

12. Schaafsma, "War Imagery," 18.

13. Forbes, *Apache, Navaho, and Spaniard*, 83. Regarding prehistoric Pueblo agriculture and irrigation, see R. G. Matson, *The Origins of Southwestern Agriculture* (Tucson: University of Arizona Press, 1991); and Jonathan E. Damp, Stephen Hall, and Susan Smith, "Early Irrigation on the Colorado Plateau near Zuni Pueblo, New Mexico," *American Antiquity* 67 (Oct. 2002): 665–76.

14. Schaafsma, "War Imagery," 16; and Polly Schaafsma, *Warrior, Shield, and Star: Imagery and Ideology of Pueblo Warfare* (Santa Fe: Western Edge Press, 2000), 3–7. For a contrary view of the pueblos as "peaceful and civilized" as compared to nomadic *indios bárbaros*, see Joe S. Sando, "The Pueblo Revolt," in *Southwest*, ed. Alfonso Ortiz,

vol. 9 of *Handbook of North American Indians*, ed. William C. Sturtevant (Washington, D.C.: Smithsonian Institution, 1979), 194.

15. Rohn, Ferguson, and Ferguson, *Rock Art*, 48, 106, 115, 127, 130–31. Slifer, *Signs of Life*, 74, 78, 104, 106. Figure 48 on page 78 shows a ceremonial figure with the tail and head of a bird carrying a shield and knife pecked into a rock at Black Mesa in Rio Arriba County. See also Poling-Kempes, *Valley of Shining Stone*, 19, 22.

16. Here we are using the notion of a middle ground to describe a community originally established as a defensive buffer between hostile nomadic Indians raiding from the plains and the more heavily settled areas of New Mexico. Although at times this zone was embroiled in active warfare, more frequently it was an area where cultural contact was facilitated. White applied the concept of a middle ground between the Indians and the European invaders where a mutually beneficial accommodation is achieved, at least temporarily, to the Great Lakes region. Richard White, *The Middle Ground: Indians, Empires, and Republics in the Great Lakes Region, 1650–1815* (Cambridge: Cambridge University Press, 1991).

17. Curtis Schaafsma, *Apaches de Navajo: Seventeenth Century Navajos in the Chama Valley of New Mexico* (Salt Lake City: University of Utah Press, 2002), 303–17.

18. Forbes, *Apache, Navaho, and Spaniard*, 121.

19. Ibid., 119–21.

20. This slave trade is discussed in Rick Hendricks and Gerald Mandell, "The Apache Slave Trade in Parral, 1637–1679," *The Journal of Big Bend Studies* 16 (2004): 59–81.

21. Picuris was probably the most active New Mexico pueblo in the Apache slave trade. Rick Hendricks and Gerald J. Mandell, "Juan Manso, Frontier Entrepreneur," *New Mexico Historical Review* 75 (July 2000): 345.

22. France V. Scholes, "Church and State in New Mexico," *New Mexico Historical Review* 11 (1936): 300–301.

23. Among the early grants in the Abiquiu area were the Cristóbal Torres grant in 1724 (SANM I: 943) and the 1734 grant to Bartolomé Trujillo and nine others (SANM I: 954).

24. Elsie Clews Parsons, "Witchcraft among the Pueblos: Indian or Spanish," *MAN* 27 (June 1927): 106.

25. France V. Scholes, "The First Decade of the Inquisition in New Mexico," *New Mexico Historical Review* 10 (July 1935): 205, 233–34.

26. David J. Weber, ed., *What Caused the Pueblo Revolt of 1680?* (Boston: St. Martín's Press, 1999), 10–11.

27. John Kessell, "Spaniards and Pueblos: From Crusading Intolerance to Pragmatic Accommodation," in *Archaeological and Historical Perspectives on the Spanish Borderlands West*, vol. 1 of *Columbian Consequences,* ed. David Hurst Thomas (Washington, D.C.: Smithsonian Institution Press, 1989), 127–38.

28. Hibben, *Excavation of the Riana Ruin*, 49.

29. Fray Juan Sanz de Lezaun reported that one of the captives from the raid "was brought back at the end of seven years by the Comanches, they having been the ones responsible for the misdeed, while the . . . Yutahs paid for it." Father Sanz de Lezaun assumed that since Comanches had one of the captives from the raid, they must have been responsible for it. It is more probable, however, that Utes were responsible and were attacked by Comanches who took one or more of the captives. See SANM I: 494, a report by Ventura, a Kiowa Indian, who while with a group of Navajos, intercepted the Utes and another tribe who said they were responsible for the raid. Fray Juan de Sanz Lezaun, "Account of lamentable happenings in New Mexico," in Charles W. Hackett, ed., *Historical Documents Relating to New Mexico, Nueva Vizcaya and Approaches Thereto to 1773* (Washington, D.C.: Carnegie Institution, 1937), 3:476–77.

30. Governor Tomás Vélez Cachupín, to Viceroy Revillagigedo, Report, Santa Fe, 27 November 1751, Alfred Barnaby Thomas, *The Plains Indians and New Mexico, 1751–1778* (Albuquerque: University of New Mexico Press, 1940), 73, 130–31; Albert Schroeder,

"Brief History of the Southern Utes," *Southwestern Lore* 30 (1965): 59; and Bancroft, *History of Arizona and New Mexico*, 249.

31. Petition of Juan de Abeyta, Santa Fe, 28 March 1748; and Governor Joaquín Codallos y Rabal, Decree, Santa Fe, 30 March 1748, SANM I: 28.

32. *Ídolos, adoratorios y aras de los falsos dioses.* Viceroy Marqués de Cruillas, Edict prohibiting idolatry, Mexico City, 13 November 1764, Pinart Collection, PE 52: 18.

33. Vélez Cachupín's Instructions and Recommendations to his successor, Francisco Antonio Marín del Valle, in Thomas, *Plains Indians* 134–35.

34. Ibid., 137.

35. For an excellent recent treatment of Governor Anza and his Indian policy, see Carlos R. Herrera, "The King's Governor: Juan Bautista de Anza and Bourbon New Mexico in the Era of Imperial Reform, 1778–1788" (Ph.D. diss., University of New Mexico, 2000), 21–79. New Mexico population figures begin to show a rapid increase after the 1786 Comanche peace treaty was signed by Governor Anza. Some scholars have attributed this solely to Anza's policies without recognizing the earlier contribution of Governor Vélez Cachupín's Indian policy. Ross Frank, *From Settler to Citizen: New Mexico Economic Development and the Creation of Vecino Society, 1750–1820* (Berkeley: University of California Press, 2000), 30–44. Frank gives Anza major credit for ending New Mexico's defensive crisis without recognizing Vélez Cachupín's contribution. Vélez achieved peace and a resumption of trade with the Utes, Comanches, and Navajos. Flawed policies of succeeding governors brought an end to these friendly relations.

36. *Se hallaba intimidado y atemorizado de la mencionada nación, y que eran infinitos los clamores de aquellos indios y vecindario de él.* Viceroy Revillagigedo, Mexico City, Communiqué to Governor Codallos y Rabal, Pinart Collection, PE 49: 3.

37. *Ser numerosos dichos comanches y tan disiplinados en las armas que han triunfado."* Ibid.

38. *Hubiesen reportado el correspondiente . . . terror . . . para la reputación de nuestras armas.* Ibid.

39. The underlying purpose of the *requerimiento* was to provide legal cover and justify the Spanish right of conquest and lay responsibility for damages incurred squarely on the Indians. Lewis Hanke, "The Requerimiento and Its Interpreters," *Revista de Historia de América* 1 (Mar. 1938): 25–34. Charles Gibson, ed., *The Spanish Tradition in America* (Columbia: University of South Carolina Press, 1968), 58–60.

40. The Auditor General of War cited *Recopilación* laws 19 and 21 of title 4, book 3 of the *Recopilación de leyes de los reinos de las Indias* for the requirements of waging a just war against the Comanches. *Recopilación de leyes de los reinos de las Indias* (Madrid: Cultura Hispánica, 1973).

41. James Axtell, *The European and the Indian: Essays in the Ethnohistory of Colonial North America* (Oxford: Oxford University Press, 1981), see particularly ch. 2, "The Unkindest Cut, or Who Invented Scalping?: A Case Study," and ch. 8, "Scalping: The Ethnohistory of a Moral Question."

42. Stanley Noyes, *Los Comanches* (Albuquerque: University of New Mexico Press, 1993), 37–38.

43. *Ocupados de un temor pánico han concebido los comanches debiendo las acciones pasadas tenidas con dicha nación.* Governor Pedro Fermín de Mendinueta, Decree, Santa Fe, 31 March 1769, SANM I: 656.

44. *La mucha hostilidad de enemigos que ha combatido en el Ojo Caliente, logrando el haber muerto algunos cuya lástima no olvida el corazón ni enjuga las lágrimas del alma.* Statement of nineteen settlers regarding resettlement of Ojo Caliente, n.d., ibid.

45. *Haber visto por sus ojos haberle por primera matádole catorce reses los comanches y llevádoles las pocas bestias que tiene . . . y por segunda el haberle muerto un mozo y su descabellerádole otro y hacerle a su familia gran dificultad el subir a dicho repuelo . . . no quieren ver sus mujeres cautivas.* Gregorio Sandoval et al., Statement, 14 May 1769, ibid.

46. Criminal cause against the Indian Pedro de la Cruz for intending to flee to the Comanche nation, Santa Fe, 1747. SANM II: 477.

47.   The governors who served between the two terms of Vélez Cachupín were Francisco
       Antonio Marín del Valle (1754–60), Mateo Antonio de Mendoza (1760), and Manuel
       del Portillo y Urrisola (1760–62).
48.   See, for example, James F. Brooks, *Captives & Cousins: Slavery, Kinship, and
       Community in the Southwest Borerlands* (Chapel Hill: University of North Carolina
       Press, 2002), 304–6.
49.   Mary Beth Norton, *In the Devil's Snare* (New York: Alfred A. Knopf, 2002), 59, 343–44, n.
       33–35. Norton points out that the Salem witchcraft crisis was not confined to Salem Village
       and Salem Town but was spread throughout Essex County. See her map on page 9.

CHAPTER TWO: THE GENÍZAROS

1.   In his 1776 census of Santa Fe, Father Domínguez counted 164 Genízaros and 1167
       Spaniards. Eleanor B. Adams and Fray Angélico Chávez, trans. and annots., *The
       Missions of New Mexico, 1776: A Description by Fray Francisco Atanasio Domínguez with
       Other Contemporary Documents* (Albuquerque: University of New Mexico Press), 42.
       For Ojo Caliente, see SANM I: 650, 655, 656; and E. Boyd "Troubles at Ojo Caliente, A
       Frontier Post," *El Palacio* (Nov.–Dec. 1957): 347–60. For the Belen, Sabinal, and San
       Gabriel de las Nutrias grants, see Malcolm Ebright, "Breaking New Ground: A
       Reappraisal of Governors Vélez Cachupín and Mendinueta and their Land Grant
       Policies," *Colonial Latin American Historical Review* 5 (spring 1996): 195–230.
2.   Adams and Chávez, *Missions of New Mexico*, 42; Carroll Riley, *Kachina and Cross: Indians
       and Spaniards in the Early Southwest* (Provo: University of Utah Press, 1999), 130; and
       Marc Simmons, "Tlascalans on the Spanish Borderlands," *New Mexico Historical Review*
       39 (Apr. 1964): 101–10. Scholars differ as to whether the pre-Revolt settlement of Analco
       was comprised primarily of Tlascalan Indians. Simmons believes that it was, citing in
       particular the 1693 statement of fray Salvador de San Antonio that "the chapel of San
       Miguel ... served as the parish church of the Tlascalan Indians." Ibid., 110.
3.   The first Brito grant was made to Juan de León Brito by Governor Bustamante in 1728.
       Brito told the governor in his petition that the grant had been made to his father by
       Governor Vargas, but he had lost the grant papers and asked that the grant be revali-
       dated. The grant was bounded on two sides by acequias. In 1742 Brito requested a sec-
       ond grant from Governor Mendoza possibly on the theory that the first grant was his
       father's, so Brito, the son, was entitled to a grant in his own name. Normally grantees
       were entitled to only one grant because of the scarcity of farmland, especially in Santa
       Fe. Juan de León Brito grants, SANM I: 85. Juan de León Brito, the son of Juan Brito
       and Antonia Úrsula Durán, was a member of the Conquistadora Confraternity. In 1710
       he and Diego Brito helped make adobes for the reconstruction of the San Miguel
       Chapel in Santa Fe. Fray Angélico Chávez, *Origins of New Mexico Families in the
       Spanish Colonial Period* (Santa Fe: William Gannon, 1954), 149–50.
4.   Jones, *Pueblo Warriors*, 36, 173.
5.   Some scholars have defined Genízaros as those Indian servants who had completed
       their term of service and thus had been freed. Up to that point they would be desig-
       nated as servants (*criados*). This was not a uniform designation. Russell M. Magnaghi,
       "The Genízaro Experience in Spanish New Mexico," in Ralph Vigil, Frances Kaye, and
       John Wunder, eds., *Spain and the Plains: Myths and Realities of Spanish Exploration
       and Settlement on the Great Plains* (Niwot: University Press of Colorado, 1994), 118.
6.   L. R. Bailey, *Indian Slave Trade in the Southwest* (Los Angeles: Westernlore Press, 1996),
       141–44. For a chronology of laws dealing with Indian slavery in New Spain, Mexico,
       and the United States, beginning with the 1452 decree of Pope Nicholas V allowing
       Portugal to "sell into slavery all heathens and 'foes of Christ,'" see Sondra Jones, *The
       Trial of Don Pedro León Luján: The Attack Against Indian Slavery and Mexican Traders
       in Utah* (Salt Lake City: University of Utah Press, 2000), 132–33.
7.   The characterization of Cruzat y Góngora as strict and conservative is based on several

instances where he reacted negatively to petitions for other land grants or revoked grants made by his subordinates. In 1734 Santa Ana Pueblo attempted to purchase lands from Baltasar Romero that the Indians claimed as their traditional lands. Even though the pueblo was willing to pay for the lands, Governor Cruzat y Góngora nullified the sale as being "against the dispositions of the royal laws of his majesty." The governor apparently acted on his own and without a specific law prohibiting the sale. Governor Gervasio Cruzat y Góngora, Order, Santa Fe, March 1, 1734, SANM I: 1345; and Laura Boyer with Floyd Montoya and the Pueblo of Santa Ana, *Santa Ana: The People, the Pueblo, and the History of Tamaya* (Albuquerque: University of New Mexico Press, 1994), 77–79. In addition, his rulings and participation in the Antonio Casados and Pedro de la Cruz trials discussed later in this chapter reveal a distinct anti-Genízaro bias. SANM I: 183; and SANM II: 477.

8.　Governor Gervasio Cruzat y Góngora, Order, Santa Fe, 21 April 1733, SANM I: 1208.

9.　Later censuses at Belen and Abiquiu would provide more information. Steven M. Horvath Jr., "The Genízaro of Eighteenth-Century New Mexico: A Reexamination," *Discovery: School of American Research* (1977): 25–40.

10.　A Pawnee custom that differentiated them from other Plains Indians was the sacrifice of a captive girl to the god of the morning star (Venus), a practice with strong similarities to Nahua ritual sacrifice. The practice was discontinued by 1838. Colin F. Taylor, *The Plains Indians: A Cultural and Historical View of the North American Plains Tribes of the Pre-Reservation Period* (London: Salamander Books, Ltd., 1994), 67–75; and Douglas R. Parks, "Pawnees," in *Plains*, ed. Raymond J. DeMallie, vol. 13, part 1, of *Handbook of North American Indians* (Washington, D.C.: Smithsonian Institution, 2001), 515–47, 537.

11.　Nancy Parrott Hickerson, *The Jumanos: Hunters and Traders of the South Plains* (Austin: University of Texas Press, 1994); and Carroll L. Riley, *Río del Norte: People of the Upper Rio Grande From Earliest Times to the Pueblo Revolt* (Salt Lake City: University of Utah Press, 1995), 190–93.

12.　Morris W. Forster and Martha McCollough, "Plains Apache," in *Plains*, ed. Raymond J. DeMallie, vol. 13, part 1, of *Handbook of North American Indians* (Washington, D.C.: Smithsonian Institution, 2001), 926–40.

13.　Jerrold E. Levy, "Kiowa," ibid., 907–25.

14.　Marc Simmons, "The Mysterious A Tribe of the Southern Plains," in *The Changing Ways of Southwestern Indians: A Historic Perspective*, ed. Albert H. Schroeder (Glorieta, N. Mex.: Rio Grande Press, 1973), 73–89.

15.　Donald Calloway, Joel Janetsky, and Omer C. Stewart, "Ute," in *Great Basin*, ed. Warren L. D'Azevedo, vol. 11 of *Handbook of North American Indians* (Washington, D.C.: Smithsonian Institution, 2001), 336–67.

16.　The presence of a few Pueblos in the group who were acculturated into Hispanic culture was not unusual.

17.　Los Genízaros, Response, April 1733, SANM I: 1208.

18.　Governor Gervasio Cruzat y Góngora, Order, Santa Fe, 23 April 1733, SANM I: 1208.

19.　Los Genízaros, Petition, April 1733, SANM I: 1208.

20.　The 1750 census of Belen lists Antonio Gurulé, Cristóbal Luján, and Antonio Padilla. Virginia Langham Olmsted, *Spanish and Mexican Censuses of New Mexico, 1750 to 1830* (Albuquerque: New Mexico Genealogical Society, 1981), 96.

21.　The Las Trampas settlers were an extended family group closely related by blood who were probably neighbors in Analco. They were of mixed Spanish, Indian, and African ancestry and included Melchor Rodríguez, son of Sebastián Rodríguez, the African drummer and herald for Diego de Vargas. Myra Ellen Jenkins, "Documentation Concerning San José de Gracia del Río de las Trampas" (unpublished manuscript in authors' possession).

22.　There has been renewed interest among scholars about Genízaros. Scholars who identify themselves as Genízaro are Gilbert Benito Córdova, Charles Carrillo, and Moises Gonzales. A session on Genízaros at the April 2000 Historical Society of New Mexico's annual meeting in Valencia included papers by Robert Tórrez, "Genizaros and Captives through the 20th Century"; Moises Gonzales, "Genizaros and Their Role in Frontier Communities"; and Andrew S. Hernández III, "Contested State Control of the Indian Slave Trade, 1694–1848."

23. For a discussion of Genízaro property rights on the Belen grant, see Malcolm Ebright, "Frontier Land Litigation," 199–226, 211–13; and PLC 52, r. 38, frames 884 et seq.

24. Ibid., 116–17.

25. Alfred B. Thomas, *After Coronado: Spanish Exploration Northeast of New Mexico, 1696–1727* (Norman: University of Oklahoma Press, 1935), 13–14.

26. Governor Gervasio Cruzat y Góngora, Edict prohibiting sale of Apache captives to Pueblos, Santa Fe, 6 December 1732, SANM II: 378.

27. Carlos Fernández and Nicolás Ortiz, Report, Santa Fe, 22 May 1766; and Governor Tomás Vélez Cachupín, Decree, Santa Fe, 24 May 1766, Pinart Collection, PE 52: 28.

28. Report of fray Pedro Serrano, cited in Hackett, *Historical Documents*, 3:486; and Magnaghi, "Genízaro Experience," 118–19.

29. Francisca Salas and José Salas were classified as español and española by Alcalde Lucero, and as mestizo and mestiza by Vélez Cachupín. Juan Domingo Jaramillo was classified as español by Lucero and as mestizo by Vélez Cachupín. Juan Antonio Baca was classified as español by Lucero and as mestizo by Vélez Cachupín. Alcalde Miguel Lucero, Census, Fonclara, 14 February 1764, SANM I: 780; Governor Vélez Cachupín, Census, San Gabriel de las Nutrias, 28 November 1765, SANM I: 780; and Ebright, "Breaking New Ground," 231–33.

30. *Todas estas catorce familias están reputadas y conocidas por blancas.* Ebright, "Breaking New Ground," 232.

31. SANM I: 494; and Steven M. Horvath Jr., "Indian Slaves for Spanish Horses," *The Museum of the Fur Trade Quarterly* 14 (winter 1978): 5.

32. Estevan Rael-Galvez, "Identifying and Capturing Identity: Narratives of American Indian Servitude, Colorado and New Mexico, 1750–1930" (Ph.D. diss., University of Michigan, 2002).

33. Jones, *Trial of Don Pedro*, 38–39, 109.

34. "Once Indian servants had paid their debts, they were free to leave the Spanish household and became known as Genízaros." Magnaghi, "Genízaro Experience," 118.

35. Alcalde Antonio José Ortiz, Investigation and report, Ojo Caliente, 11 June 1769, SANM I: 656; and Herbert E. Bolton, *Pageant in the Wilderness* (Salt Lake City: Spanish Historical Society, 1950), 142, 156, 159.

36. Donald Cutter, "An Anonymous Statistical Report On New Mexico In 1765," *New Mexico Historical Review* 50 (1975): 349–51.

37. Antonio Casados, plaintiff in the lawsuit about the Genízaros who claimed to have established a pueblo at Belén, was a Kiowa, purchased by a Genízaro named Miguelillo, a servant of Sebastián Martín. Malcolm Ebright, "Advocates for the Oppressed: Indians, Genízaros and their Spanish Advocates in New Mexico, 1700–1786," *New Mexico Historical Review* 71 (Oct. 1996): 318.

38. For the Abiquiu Genízaro plaza, see 1790 census for Abiquiu, Pinart Collection, PE 55: 3; for Belen, see, Steven Michael Horvath, "The Social and Political Organization of the Genízaros of Plaza de Nuestra Señora de Belén, New Mexico" (Ph.D. diss., Brown University, 1979), 130–33.

39. John R. Van Ness, *Hispanos in Northern New Mexico: The Development of Corporate Community and Multi-Community* (New York: AMS Press, 1991), 150–51.

40. David Snow, "A Note on Encomienda Economics in Seventeenth Century New Mexico," in *Hispanic Arts and Ethnohistory in the Southwest*, ed. Marta Weigle with Claudia Larcombe and Samuel Larcombe. (Santa Fe: Ancient City Press, 1983), 325.

41. James F. Brooks, "This Evil Extends Especially... to the Feminine Sex: Negotiating
     Captivity in the New Mexico Borderlands," *Feminist Studies* 22 (summer 1996):
     279–309; and J. Manuel Espinosa, trans. and ed., *The First Expedition of Vargas into
     New Mexico, 1692* (Albuquerque: University of New Mexico Press, 1940), 237.
42. Rancho de Galván grant, NMLG, PLC 282, r. 54, f. 1095 et seq. For a discussion of this
     grant and Juana Galván, see Frances Swadesh [Quintana], "They Settled by Little
     Bubbling Springs," *El Palacio* 84 (fall 1978): 19–20, 42–49.
43. SANM II: 345. For a further analysis of Juana Hurtado Galván's position in society and
     special negotiating skills she acquired through her experience as a captive woman, see
     Brooks, "This Evil Extends," 279–309.
44. The property listed in Juana Galván's estate shows that she had ties to both Pueblo and
     Hispanic culture. One of her three houses was located within the land of Zia Pueblo,
     and she was considered to be a native of that place. Estate proceedings for the coyota,
     Juana Galván, SANM I: 193. For a sketch of four other eighteenth-century women of
     property, see Jenkins, "Some Eighteenth-Century Women of Property," in *Hispanic
     Arts and Ethnohistory*, eds. Marta Weigle and Claudia and Samuel Larcombe (Santa Fe:
     Ancient City Press, 1983), 335–45.
45. Estate proceedings for the coyota, Juana Galván, SANM I: 193.
46. Pedro León Luján was a Genízaro from Abiquiu who traded with Utes and acquired
     property and prestige in mid-nineteenth-century Abiquiu. He was referred to in mili-
     tary and census records as don Pedro León. His father was an Indian from Abiquiu,
     and his mother was a vecina. Jones, *Trial of Don Pedro*, 53–59.
47. Another Casados, Francisco Casados who is listed in the Santa Fe church records as a
     Christian Apache, may also have been a Genízaro. Marriage of Francisco Casados and
     María Antonia Joséfa (Christian Apaches), 5 April 1739. New Mexico marriages, Santa Fe,
     St. Francis Parish and Military Chapel of Our Lady of Light (La Castrense), Archives of
     the Archdiocese of Santa Fe, r. 31, f. 31, State Records Center and Archives, Santa Fe.
48. For a brief discussion of the Belen grant, see Ebright, "Frontier Land Litigation," 212–14.
49. Antonio Casados to the Viceroy, the Conde de Fuenclara, Petition, n.p., n.d., SANM I: 183.
50. *Molestias y vejaciones que les hubieren causado y causaren los españoles que expresan.*
     Viceroy Revillagigedo, Decree, Mexico City, 20 October 1745, SANM I: 183.
51. SANM I: 183.
52. Governor Joaquín Codallos y Rabal, Inventory of cases turned over to Governor
     Tomás Vélez Cachupín, Santa Fe, 3 April 1749, SANM I: 1258.
53. Teniente Alcalde Pedro Martín, Report, Ojo Caliente, 22 February 1747; Lucas Miguel
     de Moya as attorney for Pedro de la Cruz, Petition, Santa Fe, 5 May 1747; and Criminal
     cause against the Indian Pedro de la Cruz, for intending to flee to the Comanche
     nation, Santa Fe, 1747, SANM II: 477.
54. Charles R. Cutter, *The Legal Culture of Northern New Spain, 1700–1800* (Albuquerque:
     University of New Mexico Press, 1995), 109.
55. Manuel Jorge, Jerónimo Martín, María de la Luz, and Magdalena, Declarations; Ojo
     Caliente, 22 February 1747; Lucas Miguel de Moya, Petition as attorney for Pedro de la
     Cruz, Santa Fe, 5 May 1747; and Criminal cause against the Indian Pedro de la Cruz for
     intending to flee to the Comanche nation, Santa Fe, 1747, SANM II: 477.
56. Lucas Miguel de Moya as attorney for Pedro de la Cruz; and Criminal cause against
     the Indian Pedro de la Cruz, ibid.
57. *Que es autor de todo.* Lucas Miguel de Moya as attorney for Pedro de la Cruz, ibid.
58. *Con plena prueba de testigos.* Judicial decree, Santa Fe, 25 June 1747; and Criminal cause
     against the Indian Pedro de la Cruz, ibid.
59. Antonio Tiburcio de Ortega was the son of Tiburcio de Ortega and Margarita de Otón
     who were large landowners in the El Paso area. Tiburcio de Ortega began the practice
     of adding his first name as part of the last name of his children to honor himself and
     the early Christian martyr, St. Tiburtius. Antonio Tiburcio purchased several *sitios* of

land south of El Paso in 1724, which became known as the Rancho of Nuestra Señora de la Soledad de los Tiburcios or Los Tiburcios for short. In 1787 Los Tiburcios was ordered abandoned because of frequent Apache raids. It became the site of the presidio of San Elizario, which was moved in 1789. Rick Hendricks and W. H. Timmons, *San Elizario: Spanish Presidio to Texas County Seat* (El Paso: Texas Western Press, 1998), 9–15.

60. Criminal cause against the Indian Pedro de la Cruz. SANM II: 477.

61. A full discussion of this raid is at page 19 and 277 n. 42 above.

62. John L. Kessell, *Kiva, Cross, and Crown: The Pecos Indians and New Mexico, 1540–1840* (Washington, D.C.: National Park Service, U.S. Dept. of the Interior, 1979), 378; Charles R. Cutter, *The Protector de Indios in Colonial New Mexico 1659–1821* (Albuquerque: University of New Mexico Press, 1986), 57; Alfred Barnaby Thomas, "Governor Mendinueta's Proposals for the Defense of New Mexico, 1772–1778," *New Mexico Historical Review* 6 (1931): 21; and Thomas, *Plains Indians*, 63.

63. Criminal proceedings against Bernabé and Baltasar Baca, Aug.–Sept. 1752. SANM II: 523.

64. *A donde sean instruidas de la doctrina y cristianas costumbres y sean alimentadas y vestidas por su servicio casero y propio del sexo.* Criminal proceedings brought by two Albuquerque Genízaras against their masters, 12–15 October 1763, SANM II: 574.

65. Proceedings concerning complaint of Gertrudes Cuellar and José María Montaño against Juan Bautista Montaño, Santa Fe, May 1766, Pinart Collection, PE 52: 28.

66. Gertrudes de Cuellar and José María Montaño, Petition, [Santa Fe] [June] 1766, ibid.

67. *En lugar de darnos doctrina nos tiene en un infierno.* Ibid.

68. Juan Cristóbal Sánchez, alcalde mayor and war captain of the villa of Alburquerque and Fonclara, Report, Puesto of Belen, 14 May 1766. Ibid. Sánchez took the testimony of Domingo Baca who had sold José María Montaño (he would not have been named Montaño then) to Juan Bautista Montaño for sheep valued at eighty pesos nine years earlier.

69. *Según la práctica y costumbre de este país; declaro por libre del el servicio a que le quiere compelar Juan Bautista Montaño.* Governor Tomás Vélez Cachupín, Decree, Santa Fe, 24 May 1766, ibid.

70. *Pase a dicho pueblo con su mujer en donde se le señalarán tierras de labor y solar de casa para que con su trabajo o industria se alimenten y que sea empadronado con los demás individuos de aquel pueblo.* Ibid.

71. *Totalmente libres y vagos por no tener possesiones ni domicilio propio.* Ibid.

72. Magnaghi, "Genízaro Experience," 118–19. The practice of selling Genízaros as servants in Hispanic households continued well into the Territorial Period. See 1870 Tierra Amarilla census listing fifteen of the eighty-one households as having Indian servants. See also Lafayette Head, "Statement of Mr. Head of Abiquiú in Regard of the Buying and Selling of Payutahs, 30 April 1852," Doc. no. 2150, Ritch Collection of Papers Pertaining to New Mexico, Huntington Library, San Maríno, California.

73. Joseph P. Sánchez, *Explorers, Traders, and Slavers: Forging the Old Spanish Trail, 1678–1850* (Salt Lake City: University of Utah Press, 1997), 99–100; and Frances León Swadesh, *Los Primeros Pobladores: Hispanic Americans on the Ute Frontier* (Notre Dame: University of Notre Dame Press, 1974), 43.

74. Thomas, *Plains Indians*, 152. Vélez Cachupín's decree temporarily prohibiting the sale of Comanche Genízaros was referred to in *Juan Antonio Rodríguez v. Sebastián Salas*, Santa Fe, 12 July 1762, SANM II: 555.

75. Bolton, *Pageant in the Wilderness*, 142, 156, 159; and Swadesh, *Primeros*, 42–43. The Muñiz brothers apparently arranged for other Genízaros or coyotes from the Abiquiú area, including Juan Domingo and Felipe, to join the party for the purpose of trading with Utes.

76. Fray Angélico Chávez, trans., and Ted J. Warner, ed., *The Domínguez-Escalante Journal: Their Expeditions Through Colorado, Utah, Arizona, and New Mexico in 1776* (Provo, Utah: Brigham Young University, 1976), entry for 1 September 1776, English translation, 33; Spanish transcription, 150; and Bolton, *Pageant in the Wilderness*, 157–59.

77. Luján's first wife was María Manuela García (married 1826), though census records show Luján living with doña Juana Jaramillo in 1845, and an Anamaría in 1850–70. Jones, *Trial of Don Pedro*, 53–59.

78. Ibid.; Mexican Archives of New Mexico (MANM), r. 22, f. 809:25, State Archives and Record Center, Santa Fe; and MANM, r. 26, f. 516–19; Report on militia strength, f. 515.

79. Bailey, *Indian Slave Trade*, xv–xvi, 84–86, 100, 105, 114, 177–78; and David M. Brugge, *Navajos in the Catholic Church Records of New Mexico, 1694–1875* (Window Rock, Ariz.: Research Section, Parks and Recreation Dept., Navajo Tribe, 1968), 35, 73–75, 86–88, 135.

80. Jones, *Trial of Don Pedro*, 150.

81. Governor Pedro Fermín de Mendinueta, Order, Santa Fe, 10 May 1769, SANM I: 656.

82. Alcalde Antonio José Ortiz, Inspection, Ojo Caliente, 11 June 1769, SANM I: 656.

83. S. A. Russell to Commissioner of Indian Affairs, Tierra Amarilla, 15 March 1876, National Archives Records, r. 547, Letters Received by the Office of Indian Affairs, 1824–1881, New Mexico Superintendency, 1854–1855, New Mexico State Records Center and Archives.

84. Governor Tomás Vélez Cachupín to Viceroy Marqués de Ervillas, AGN, Inquisición, 1001:12.

85. Van Ness, *Hispanos in Northern New Mexico*, 137–38.

86. Swadesh, *Primeros Pobladores*, 38.

87. Poling-Kempes, *Valley of Shining Stone*, 69–70. These Genízaros were as young as eighteen months, as old as twenty-six years, with the majority between four and seven years old. Poling-Kempes made this determination by examining the compilations of Abiquiu baptisms (1754–1870), Santa Cruz de la Cañada baptisms (1710–1860), and San Juan de los Caballeros baptisms (1726–1870) prepared by Thomas Martinez.

88. Hano is one of the three villages on the Hopi First Mesa. All the other villages on First, Second, and Third Mesas are Hopi-speaking with Hopi customs. Dozier, *Hano*, 1–2; and Poling-Kempes, *Valley of Shining Stone*, 12–13.

89. Córdova, "The Genízaro" (unpublished manuscript in the authors' possession).

90. Córdova, "The Genízaro," 1–3. Abiquiu has two feast days, one for Santa Rosa de Lima in late August, and the other for Santo Tomás the last week in November. The latter one is when Indian and Genízaro rites are performed.

91. Miguel Gandert, Enrique Lamadrid, Ramón Gutiérrez, Lucy Lippard, and Chris Wilson, *Nuevo México Profundo: Rituals of an Indo-Hispanic Homeland* (Santa Fe: Museum of New Mexico Press; Albuquerque: National Hispanic Cultural Center of New Mexico, 2000), 58.

92. Ibid.

CHAPTER THREE: THE PRIEST

1. Manuel Toledo and Paula Mejía, Amonestaciones, 3 June 1714, LDS, Amonestaciones de españoles, 0035256.

2. Baptism of Juan José Felipe de Toledo, 31 May 1715, LDS, Sagrario Metropolitano, Baptisms, 0035178.

3. Lázaro Iriarte de Aspurz, O.F.M. Cap., *Franciscan History: The Three Orders of St. Francis of Assisi*, trans. Patricia Ross (Chicago: Franciscan Herald Press, 1982), 258–59. The term "ascesis" comes from the Greek *askesis* and means exercise, effort, or exploit. For the Franciscans the term referred to the inner struggle required for the spiritual to attain control of the material. http://www.tuirgin.com/files/texts/orthodoxy accessed on 16 December 2004.

4. Iriarte, *Franciscan History*, 259.

5. Francisco Morales, *Inventario del Fondo Francisco del Museo de Antropología e Historia de México* (Washington, D.C.: Academy of American Franciscan History, 1978), 1:308.

6. Dr. Alonso de la Peña Montenegro, Bishop of Quito, first published this work in 1663.

Anuario Histórico Jurídico Ecuatoriano, 9, *Itinerario para párrocos de indios, en que se tratan las materias más particulares tocantes a ellos para su buena administración* (1771; reprint, Quito: Ediciones Corporación de Estudios y Publicaciones, 1985).

7. Excellent examples of Toledo's use of these works are found in his letters in Pinart Collection, PE 52: 5.

8. Bachiller Francisco Pedro Romano, who served in El Paso, owned a copy of the *Itinerario* that was listed among his property after his death in May 1746. Rick Hendricks, "Material Culture of Diocesan Clergy in Eighteenth-Century El Paso" (paper presented at the Historical Society of New Mexico Annual Conference, Valencia County, 2000); and Eleanor B. Adams, "Two Colonial New Mexico Libraries, 1704, 1776," *New Mexico Historical Review* 19 (Apr. 1944): 158.

9. Copies of all these works were in the Franciscan library in Santo Domingo in 1776. Adams, "Two Colonial Libraries," 152–63.

10. See especially fray Juan José Toledo, Letter, Abiquiu, 15 May 1763, PE 52: 5.

11. Jim Norris, *After "The Year Eighty": The Demise of Franciscan Power in Spanish New Mexico* (Albuquerque: University of New Mexico Press, 2000), 21.

12. Ibid.

13. Sombrerete native, fray Antonio de Miranda served in New Mexico missions for thirty years before withdrawing to the Franciscan missionary college in Tlatelolco. While there fray Antonio dedicated himself to writing a primer or catechism in Keres. Although, according to Norris, Father Miranda was at Tlatelolco for only one year, he remained active in New Spain through the late 1740s. According to Father Varo, fray Antonio did not have his grammar and catechism printed because of the great difficulty he encountered in explaining the exact significance of many words of Christian doctrine and catechism and therefore of the divine mysteries. Fray Andrés Varo, Response to the charges of Governor Tomás Vélez Cachupín and Inspector Juan Ornedal, 5 February 1751, Beinecke Library, Yale University (another copy is in BNM 9, 53); Adams and Chaves, *Missions*, 336; and Norris, *After "The Year Eighty,"* 98, 171.

14. Rick Hendricks, "The Exile and Return of Fray Isidro Cadelo, 1793–1810," *New Mexico Historical Review* 70 (Apr. 1995): 132.

15. Inga Clendinnen, "Disciplining the Indians: Franciscan Ideology and Missionary Violence in Sixteenth-Century Yucatan," *Past and Present* 94 (Feb. 1982): 42–43.

16. De la Peña Montenegro, *Itinerario*, 138.

17. Franciscans traveling to New Mexico accompanied governors-elect in 1617, 1659, 1677. Kessell, *Kiva, Cross, and Crown*, 109, 174, 223.

18. This analysis is based on the sketches of New Mexico friars in Norris, *After "The Year Eighty,"* 165–74.

19. Joaquín Codallos y Rabal to Nicolás de Echiñique, Durango, 20 September 1743, Archivos Históricos del Arzobispado de Durango (AHAD), New Mexico State University Library, Archives and Special Collections Department, r. 47, f. 138–41.

20. Bishop Benito Crespo, Report on the missions of New Mexico, Durango, 28 April 1731, AHAD-39, f. 176–81; and Viceroy Marqués de Casafuerte, Title of curate, Mexico City, 16 February 1731, AHDP-39, 182–84.

21. Bachiller José Pérez de Bustamante, a relative of Governor Bustamante, served as vicar and ecclesiastical judge when Roybal was at Santa María de las Caldas. Norris mistakenly refers to this individual as Perea de Bustamante. Chávez and Norris indicate that he disappears from the records in 1736. In fact, the following year he traveled to Durango bearing mail from El Paso to authorities at the diocesan see. José de la Sierra to Dr. Baltasar Colomo and Lic. Diego Jáquez Gutiérrez, El Paso, AHAD-107, f. 345–46; Chávez, *Origins*, 151; Norris, *After "The Year Eighty,"* 79; and Bishop Bentio Crespo, Order, Durango, 2 August 1734, AHAD-43, f. 624–27.

22. Adams and Chávez, *Missions of New Mexico*, 339.

23. Fray Angélico Chávez, O.F.M., *Archives of the Archdiocese of Santa Fe, 1678–1900* (Washington, D.C.: Academy of American Franciscan History, 1957), 195.

24. Frank D. Reeve, "The Navaho-Spanish Peace, 1720s-1770s," *New Mexico Historical Review* 34 (Jan. 1959): 12–13.

25. Ibid.

26. Chávez, *Archives*, 219.

27. The expeditions of Fathers Delgado and Menchero are briefly recounted in Father Andrés Varo's defense of the Franciscans in New Mexico. Fray Juan José merited mention in each of the summaries of the events in Navajo and Hopi country. Fray Andrés Varo, Response to the charges of Governor Tomás Vélez Cachupín and Inspector Juan Ornedal, 5 February 1751, Beinecke Library, Yale University.

28. Adams and Chávez, *Missions*, 339.

29. It is customary to count only five Hopi pueblos. Henry W. Kelly, "Franciscan Missions of New Mexico, 1740–1760," *New Mexico Historical Review* 16 (Jan. 1941): 46.

30. Ibid.; and Fray Carlos Delgado to Commissary General fray Juan Fogueras, Isleta, 15 November 1745, translated in Hackett, *Historical Documents*, 3:414–15.

31. Chávez, *Archives*, 257.

32. Archives of the Archdiocese of Santa Fe, B-17 (Box 19).

33. Ibid., 223.

34. *Diccionario de la Real Academia Española*, http://buscon.rae.es/drael, accessed on 10 December 2004.

35. Ibid.

36. Henry W. Kelley, "Franciscan Missions of New Mexico, 1740–1760," *New Mexico Historical Review* 15 (Oct. 1940): 346.

37. Reeve, "Navaho-Spanish Peace," 20–23.

38. Norris, *After "The Year Eighty,"* 119.

39. Fray Andrés Varo, Response to the charges of Governor Tomás Vélez Cachupín and Inspector Juan Ornedal, 5 February 1751, Beinecke Library, Yale University.

40. http://www.geocities.com/pentagon.

41. Fray Juan Sanz de Lezaun, Report on an expedition to Hopi, 30 June 1749, BNM 8:63.

42. Alonso Victores Rubín de Celis, Inspection of the Presidio of El Paso, El Paso, 13–16 July 1749, AHP, r. 1749, f. 3–15.

43. Chávez, *Archives*, 257.

44. BNM 9: 53.

45. Jim Norris, "The Franciscans of New Mexico, 1692–1754: Toward a New Assessment," *The Americas* 51 (Oct. 1994): 166.

46. Kessell, *Kiva, Cross, and Crown*, 330.

47. De la Peña Montenegro, *Itinerario*, 115.

48. Kessell, *Kiva, Cross, and Crown*, 389.

49. Ibid., 389–90.

50. Fray Andrés Varo, Response to the charges of Governor Tomás Vélez Cachupín and Inspector Juan Ornedal, 5 February 1751, Beinecke Library, Yale University.

51. Ibid.

52. Frederic J. Athearn, *A Forgotten Kingdom: The Spanish Frontier in Colorado and New Mexico, 1540–1821* (Denver: Colorado State Office, Bureau of Land Management, 1992), 120.

53. Kelly, "Franciscan Missions," *New Mexico Historical Review* 16 (Oct. 1940): 368.

54. Varo charged that eight or ten Indians go every week from each pueblo in its turn as shepherds to take care of the cattle and sheep at the ranch called that of the governor. This charge did not apply to Vélez Cachupín for he did not have such a ranch. Report of fray Pedro Serrano to the viceroy, the Marquis of Cruillas, 1761, translated in Hackett, *Historical Documents*, 3:485; and Jim Norris, "Franciscans Eclipsed: Church and State in Spanish New Mexico, 1750–1780," *New Mexico Historical Review* 76 (Apr. 2001): 166.

55.   For a similar conflict with Governor Juan Bautists de Anza (177–87), see Rick
        Hendricks, "Church-State Relations in Anza's New Mexico, 1777–1787," *Catholic
        Southwest* 9 (1998): 31–33.
56.   The Vélez Cachupín's decree requiring his approval of outgoing Franciscan mail is
        found at BNM, leg. 8, part 3, no. 76.
57.   One of the first charges made against Vélez Cachupín was that he moved or attempted
        to move priests from one mission to another without the authority to do so. Hackett,
        Historical Documents, 3:442–43. Whether Vélez Cachupín had that power during his
        first, ad interim term is not clear, but by 1764 he received a viceregal decree that clari-
        fied his authority under the Patronato Real. Viceroy Marqués de Cruellas to Governor
        Tomás Vélez Cachupín, Mexico City, 13 November 1764, Pinart Collection, PE 52: 18.
        See also Hendricks, "Church-State Relations," 33.
58.   Chávez, *Archives*, 257.
59.   See page 143 below.
60.   A notation in the marriage book that Father Toledo received at Abiquiu upon
        taking up the post at that mission indicated that it was written in Tewa language
        by fray Manuel Sopeña, although everything is written in Spanish. Archives of
        the Archdiocese of Santa Fe, Loose Documents, Mission, 1756: 3; Chávez,
        Archives, 36; and Eleanor B. Adams, ed., "Bishop Tamarón's Visitation of New
        Mexico, 1760," *Publications in History* 15 (Albuquerque: Historical Society of New
        Mexico, 1954), 64.
61.   Journal of the ecclesiastical visitation of Bishop Pedro Tamerón y Romeral, 14 June
        1760, Santa Cruz de la Cañada, Archives of the Catedral of Durango, University of
        Texas at El Paso, microfilm, r., 10, f. 704.
62.   Implicit in the criticism of the Franciscans for their inability or unwillingness to learn
        indigenous languages is that someone else or some other method would have pro-
        duced better results. The Franciscans would have relished being privy to the examina-
        tion of a petition by the ecclesiastical cabildo of the Cathedral of Durango in 1735. The
        request came from a diocesan priest, none other than Father Santiago Roybal, who
        sought to be relieved from his duties at Santa María de las Caldas for, among other
        reasons, his inability to learn the language of the Indians. Here was Bishop Crespo's
        handpicked man admitting that he could not master the Suma language. Acts of the
        Cabildo of the Cathedral of Durango, 2 September 1735, Archive of the Cathedral of
        Durango, University of Texas at El Paso, microfilm, r. 1, f. 449.
63.   Tracy Brown, "Ideologies of Indianness in New Mexico, 1692–1820: Personhood and
        Identity in the Colonial Encounter" (Ph.D. diss., Duke University, 2000), 38–39.
64.   Adams and Chávez, *Missions*, 339.
65.   Archives of the Archdiocese of Santa Fe, Loose Documents, Mission, 1756: 3.
66.   Adams and Chávez, *Missions*, 339; and Nómina, Mexico City, n.d., Museo Nacional,
        Asuntos (Center for Southwest Studies, University of New Mexico Library).
67.   Chávez, *Archives*, 257.
68.   BNM 10: 4, cited in Norris, *After "The Year Eighty,"* 145.
69.   Charges against Father Juan José Toledo, Santa Fe and Mexico City, 1771–76, AGN,
        Inquisición 769.
70.   BNM 10: 4, cited in Norris, *After "The Year Eighty,"* 145.
71.   Charges against Father Juan José Toledo, Santa Fe and Mexico City, 1771–76, AGN,
        Inquisición 769.

CHAPTER FOUR: THE GOVERNOR

1.   Alcalde Juan José Lobato to Governor Vélez Cachupín, Santa Cruz de la Cañada, 28 August
        1752, translated in Thomas, *Plains Indians*, 115. Alcalde Lobato was taking a statement from

a woman who had been purchased by Antonio Martín from a Ute who had captured her from the Comanches. Alcalde Lobato deemed the woman's testimony reliable.

2.   Governor Vélez Cachupín was the first governor to make true community land grants in New Mexico. Many of these communities were built around defensive plazas. For comparison of Vélez Cachupín's land grant policies with those of Governor Mendinueta, see Ebright, "Breaking New Ground," 195.

3.   For a discussion of Vélez Cachupín's land-related legal decisions, see Ebright, "Frontier Land Litigation," 199–226.

4.   Governor Anza has been championed by Donald T. Garate, "Anza: A Basque Legacy on New Spain's Northern Frontier," in *Basque Portraits in the New World*, ed. Richard Etulain and Jerónima Echeverría (Reno: University of Nevada Press, 1999); and Herrera, "The King's Governor." Governor Anza served two consecutive full terms. Governor Vargas has received devoted attention by J. Manuel Espinoza and most notably by the Vargas Project.

5.   Bancroft, *History of Arizona and New Mexico*, 256–58.

6.   This criticism may be somewhat wide of the mark. Vélez Cachupín was one of the most successful governors in dealing with Plains Indian's raids, making peace with the Comanches and most other nomadic tribes by demonstrating firmness in punishing Indian depredations, while exercising leniency in dealing with peaceful Plains Indian tribes. Kessell, *Kiva, Cross, and Crown*, 378–79.

7.   Cutter cites a case in which Vélez Cachupín defied an official appointed by the viceroy to protect the Pueblos, warning him not to exercise the powers of his office or he would consider him an enemy. Cutter, *Protector de Indios*, 56–57.

8.   Frank argues that the 1780s were a turning point in New Mexico when the economy improved and the Hispanic population began to increase largely due to Governor Anza's achievement of peace with the Comanches. Frank ignores Vélez Cachupín's even greater comprehensive peace with Utes, Comanches, and Navajos during the 1750s and 1760s. Frank, *Settler to Citizen*, 1–3, 30–34.

9.   Thomas, *Plains Indians*, 57–58.

10.   There were several types of mayorazgos. As a rule, a regular mayorazgo passed to the first-born son, although the founder could make other stipulations. Other mayorazgos provided for different inheritance schemes, whereby other heirs were designated under specified circumstances. Joaquín Escriche. *Diccionario razonado de legislación y jurisprudencia*, ed. Juan B. Guim (Bogotá: Temis, 1977), 4:30–43; and Guillermo Cabanellas de las Cuevas and Eleanor C. Hoague, *Diccionario Jurídico Español-Inglés Butterworths* (Austin: Butterworth Legal Publishers, 1991), 396.

11.   Malcolm Ebright, Teresa Escudero, and Rick Hendricks. "Tomás Vélez Cachupín's Last Will and Testament, His Career in New Mexico, and His Sword with a Golden Hilt," *New Mexico Historical Review* 78 (summer 2003): 285–321. Coauthor Escudero has spent her summers in the Casa Palacio del General Benito Zarauz, one of the Casas Cachupinas, since she was a little girl.

12.   In his will, Vélez Cachupín set up an annuity (*censo*) with the 700,000 reales he had earned as governor of New Mexico and provided that it go to the Casas Cachupinas estate that he had been cut out of, but instead of going to the first son, Vélez Cachupín stipulated that the inheritance would go to the second son. Tomás Vélez Cachupín, Last Will and Testament, Document P18796, Archivo Histórico de Protocolos de Madrid, Madrid, Spain, published in Ebright, Escudero, and Hendricks, "Tomás Vélez Cachupín's Last Will and Testament," 285–321.

13.   Ibid.

14.   *Aunque el mío es de los Cachopines de Laredo . . . no le osaré yo poner con el del Toboso de la Mancha, puesto que, para decir verdad, semejante apellido hasta ahora no ha llegado a mis oídos.* Miguel de Cervantes Saavedra, *El Ingenioso Hildalgo Don Quijote de la Mancha*, ed. Luis Andrés Murillo (Madrid: Clásicos Castalis, 1978), 177.

15. Tomás Vélez Cachupín, petition [Madrid, 1761] AGI, Audiencia of Guadalajara, 300, Bancroft Library, Berkeley; Adams, *Bishop Tamarón's Visitation*, 24; and *Instrucciones y memorias de les virreyes novohispanos* (Mexico City: Editorial Porrúa, 1991), 795.

16. Tomás Vélez Cachupín, Act of possession, Santa Fe, 6 April 1749, SANM II: 503.

17. José Ignacio Gallegos C., *Historia de la iglesia en Durango* (Mexico City, Editorial Jus, 1969), 233.

18. Tomás Vélez Cachupín to Juan Manuel Díaz Tagle, Santa Fe, 30 June 1749, AHAD-108, f. 300–32.

19. Norris states that fray Francisco González de la Concepción was a native of Burgos as were his parents. It is clear from Vélez Capuchín's letter that he was a trusted, fellow montañés. The confusion arrises from the fact that Santander was historically in the Archbishopric of Burgos, and residents of the region tended to describe themselves as being from the "*montañas de Burgos*," or mountains of [the Archbishopric of] Burgos, hence they were montañeses. Norris, *After "The Year Eighty*," 167.

20. González Calderón was the financial agent for another notable montañés active on the northern frontier, Alonso Victores Rubín de Celis, longtime captain of the El Paso Presidio. Alonso Victores Rubín de Celis to Lic. Francisco Javier de Gamboa, Santiago Sáenz, and Diego Sánchez Barrero, Parral, 9 February 1764, Archivo Histórico de Hidalgo del Parral, New Mexico State University Library, microfilm, r. 1765, f. 308b-10b.

21. Francisco Tagle Bustamante was a native of Puente San Miguel in the province of Santander. Inventory of the possessions of Francisco Tagle Bustamante, 4 June 1752–24 January 1753, Uribe Collection, Ms. 352, Box 1, Folder 3, C. L. Sonnichsen Collection, University of Texas at El Paso Library.

22. Kessell, *Kiva, Cross, and Crown*, 378–80, 383.

23. Thomas, *Plains Indians*, 74, 117–18.

24. Ibid., 67–76.

25. Kessell is the most balanced in his treatment of Vélez Cachupín, but his assessment that Vélez was "in the habit of exaggerating his own merits and the faults of others" is unfair. Vélez Cachupín's reports to the viceroy were accurate and not found to contain exaggeration. Kessell, *Kiva, Cross, and Crown*, 378–82.

26. Beck's work is dated and should be used with caution as it contains many errors. It also contains a bias evident in his description of Franciscan missions in the pueblos: "These friars were forced to live alone among the savages." His characterization of effective frontier defense as starting with Anza has been followed by more recent historians. Warren A. Beck, *New Mexico: A History of Four Centuries* (Norman: University of Oklahoma Press, 1962), 91. Frank attributes the Comanche peace and the resulting economic growth in New Mexico to the Bourbon reforms begun by José de Gálvez in 1765 and implemented in the 1770s by Teodoro de Croix and others. Croix appointed Anza to replace Governor Mendinueta in 1778 because of Anza's proven skill and experience as an Indian fighter. Frank barely mentions Vélez Cachupín, whose victory against the Comanches at San Diego Pond is even more impressive when one compares the support Anza had for his expedition with the forces Vélez Cachupín had during his November 1759 campaign against the Comanches. Vélez Cachupín's force totaled 164 including soldiers, civilian militia, and Indian auxiliaries. Anza's command comprised 85 soldiers, 203 civilian militia, 259 Indian auxiliaries, and 200 friendly Utes and Apaches who agreed to join the expedition if the spoils were divided equally except for captives taken by individuals. Frank, *From Settler to Citizen*, 65–75.

27. For a map of Pueblo languages, see Kessell, *Kiva, Cross, and Crown*, 66.

28. Robert Ryal Miller, "New Mexico in Mid-Eighteenth Century: A Report Based on Governor Vélez Cachupín's Inspection," *Southwestern Historical Quarterly* 79 (1975–76): 174.

29. According to fray Francisco Antonio de la Rosa Figueroa, Father Varo's 1751 report was deemed too frank to submit to the viceroy, who was still the Conde de Revillagigedo.

Varo's open condemnation of the viceroy's handpicked governor, who was a relative and former member of his household could not have been calculated to produce the desired effect. When Serrano drafted his own report, he copied verbatim
much of what Varo had included in his report. Fray Andrés Varo, Response to the
charges of Governor Tomás Vélez Cachupín and Inspector Juan Ornedal, 5
February 1751, Beinecke Library, Yale University; and Father Provincial Pedro
Serrano to the Viceroy Marqués Cruillas, 1761, translated in Hackett, *Historical
Documents*, 3:493–94.

30.   Viceroy Marqués de Cruellas to Vélez Cachupín, Mexico City, 13 November 1764,
       Pinart Collection, PE 52: 18.
31.   The issue of exercise of what was referred to as vice-patron authority under the
       Patronato Real was a bone of contention in New Mexico between governors and
       Franciscans through much of the colonial period. The main issue regarded who con-
       trolled the assignment of priests to particular missions. An early example of a thor-
       ough airing of the issues took place during the administration of Governor José
       Chacón Medina Salazar y Villaseñor (1707–12). Governor Anza was involved in a very
       similar dispute. Hendricks, "Church-State Relations," 33; and Norris, *After "The Year
       Eighty,"* 61–61.
32.   Richard E. Greenleaf, "The Inquisition in Eighteenth Century New Mexico," *New
       Mexico Historical Review* 60 (Jan. 1985): 423–23; and Norris, "Franciscans Eclipsed," 167.
33.   Instructions which Vélez Cachupín left to his successor Francsico Marín del Valle on
       the order of the viceroy, Count Revillagigedo, 1754 AGN, Provincias Internas, 102,
       translated in Thomas, *Plains Indians*, 133–34.
34.   Thomas, *Plains Indians*, 69, 74.
35.   Ibid., 72.
36.   Tomás Vélez Cachupín, Report to Viceroy Revillagigedo, Santa Fe, 27 November 1751,
       AGN, Provincias Internas, 102, translated in Thomas, *Plains Indians*, 69–72.
37.   Alcalde Juan José Lobato to Tomás Vélez Cachupín, Villa Nueva de Santa Cruz, 28
       August 1752, translated in Thomas, *Plains Indians*, 114–17. For a discussion of Vélez
       Cachupín's policy toward Comanches and other Plains Indians and the defects in the
       diplomacy of interim Governors Marín del Valle and Portillo y Urrisola that led to
       increased Comanche raids, see Kessell, *Kiva, Cross, and Crown*, 393; and Noyes,
       Comanches, 49–59.
38.   Vélez Cachupín was the first governor to use a combination of prowess in battle with
       diplomacy to achieve peace with the Comanches, yet some historians have accepted
       the Franciscan charge that he exaggerated his accomplishments or even created them
       out of whole cloth. A thorough examination of all the documents in connection with
       the 11 November 1751 Battle of San Diego Pond reveals a substantial amount of inter-
       nal evidence that the events described actually took place as narrated.
39.   Kessell, *Kiva, Cross, and Crown*, 383.
40.   Report of Vélez Cachupín to Viceroy Revillagigedo, Thomas, *Plains Indians*, 73, 78.
41.   Ibid., 74.
42.   Alcalde Juan José Lobato to Vélez Cachupín, Villa of Santa Cruz, 28 August 1752, trans-
       lated in Thomas, *Plains Indians*, 116.
43.   Ibid.
44.   Ibid., 114–17.
45.   Ibid.
46.   Jones, "Rescue and Ransom," 147–48.
47.   Fray Sanz de Lezaun, Account of the lamentable happenings in New Mexico, 1760,
       translated in Hackett, *Historical Documents*, 3:477.
48.   Governor Tomás Vélez Cachupín to Viceroy Revillagigedo, 29 September 1752, trans-
       lated in Thomas, *Plains Indians*, 122.
49.   In a bit of hyberbole characteristic of his report, Father Serrano referred to Father

Varo's lament about "how ancient is the persecution of the missionaries by the governors and captains, of whom, doubtless Hell had made use in order to destory Christianity in that kingdom from its beginnings and to prevent the progress of the propagation of the holy gospel, the said father has lamented the sorrowful distresses sufered by the evangelical laborers in the years 1617, 1624, 1644, and 1699." Father Pedro Serrano to translated in Hackett, *Historical Documents*, 3:494–95.

50.   Father Pedro Serrano to Viceroy Marqués de Cruillas, 1761, translated in Hackett, *Historical Documents*, 3:482–501.

51.   Ibid.

52.   Ibid.

53.   Ibid.

54.   Father Pedro Serrano to Viceroy Marqués de Cruillas, 1761, translated in Hackett, *Historical Documents*, 3:490–92.

55.   Viceroy Revillagigedo to Governor Joaquín Codallos y Rabal (with note of compliance by Codallos y Rabal), Mexico City, 26 October 1746, Pinart Collection, PE 49: 3.

56.   In his report of the November 1751 Comanche campaign, Viceroy Revillagigedo said of Vélez Cachupín after the Galisteo attack, "As soon as he received news of the event, he was ready. *With the people he had prepared*, he set out in search of the Indians with unusual diligence." Revillagigedo to the Marqués de la Ensenada, Mexico City, 26 June 1753, translated in Thomas, *Plains Indians*, 112 (emphasis added).

57.   Governor Tomás Vélez Cachupín to Viceroy Revillagigedo, Santa Fe, 29 September 1752, translated in Thomas, *Plains Indians*, 123.

58.   Ibid.

59.   Ibid.

60.   Governor Tomás Vélez Cachupín to Viceroy Revillagigedo, Santa Fe, 29 September 1752, translated in Thomas, *Plains Indians*, 122–23.

61.   Juan José Lobato to Governor Tomás Vélez Cachupín, San Juan, 17 August 1752, translated in Thomas, *Plains Indians*, 117–18.

62.   Ibid.

63.   Governor Tomás Vélez Cachupín to Viceroy Revillagigedo, 29 September 1752, translated in Thomas, *Plains Indians*, 123–24.

64.   Viceroy Revillagigedo to the Marqués de Ensenada, Mexico City, 28 June 1753, translated in Thomas, *Plains Indians*, 112.

65.   The Marqués de Ensenada to Viceroy Revillagigedo, Madrid, 16 December 1753, translated in Thomas, *Plains Indians*, 145.

66.   Instructions from Governor Tomás Vélez Cachupín to his successor [Francisco Marín del Valle] at the order of Viceroy Revillagigedo, 12 August 1754, translated in Thomas, *Plains Indians*, 133.

67.   Ibid.

68.   Ibid.

69.   Kessell, *Kiva, Cross, and Crown*, 392; and Jack B. Tykal, "Taos to St. Louis: The Journey of María Rosa Villalpando," *New Mexico Historical Review* 65 (Apr. 1990): 168–69.

70.   These figures differ from those of Bishop Tamarón who reported fifty-six women and children taken captive and forty-nine dead Comanches. Adams, *Bishop Tamarón's Visitation*, 58–59; and Adams and Chávez, *Missions of New Mexico*, 2–4.

71.   Manuel Portillo Urrisola to Bishop Pedro Tamarón, Santa Fe, 24 February 1762, translated in Adams, *Bishop Tamarón's Visitation*, 59–60.

72.   Ibid., 60–62.

73.   In his instructions to his successor, Vélez Cachupín stated, "If this tribe [the Comanches] should change its idea and declare war, your grace may fear the complete ruin of this government. The armed forces of this government . . . would not be able to resist, in continuous action, their great numbers and ferocious attacks, supported by their allies, the Pawnees and Jumanos, all warlike and equipped with guns."

Instructions from Governor Tomás Vélez Cachupín to his successor [Francisco Antonio Marín del Valle] at the order of Viceroy Revillagigedo, 12 August 1754, translated in Thomas, *Plains Indians*, 133.

74. Governor Tomás Vélez Cachupín to Viceroy Marqués de Cruillas, concerning the reestablishment of peace with the Comanches, Santa Fe, 27 June 1762, translated in Thomas, *Plains Indians*, 148.

75. Ibid.

76. Ibid., 149–50; emphasis added.

77. Ibid., 149–51.

78. Ibid.

79. Ibid.

80. Ibid., 151–52.

81. Ibid., 152.

82. Vélez Cachupín's decree temporarily prohibiting the sale of Comanche Genízaros was referred to in *Juan Antonio Rodríguez v. Sebastián Salas*, Santa Fe, 12 July 1762, SANM II: 555.

83. Jones, *Pueblo Warriors*, 132–33; and Thomas, *Plains Indians*, 152–53.

84. Ibid., 36–38.

85. Manuel Portillo Urrisola to Bishop Pedro Tamarón, Santa Fe, 24 February 1762, translated in Adams, ed., *Bishop Tamarón's Visitation*, 62.

86. Ibid.

87. Governor Tomás Vélez Cachupín to Viceroy Marqués de Cruillas, concerning the reestablishment of peace with the Comanches, Santa Fe, 27 June 1762, translated in Thomas, *Plains Indians*, 152–54.

88. Governor Tomás Vélez Cachupín to Viceroy Marqués de Cruillas, concerning the reestablishment of peace with the Comanches, Santa Fe, 27 June 1762, translated in Thomas, *Plains Indians*, 152–53.

89. Ibid.

90. Jones, *Pueblo Warriors*, 129–38.

91. Instructions from Governor Tomás Vélez Cachupín to his successor [Francisco Marín del Valle] at the order of Viceroy Revillagigedo, 12 August 1754, translated in Thomas, *Plains Indians*, 137.

92. Jones, *Pueblo Warriors*, 128.

93. Ibid., 128–29; and Governor Tomás Vélez Cachupín to Viceroy Revillagigedo, translated in Thomas, *Plains Indians*, 68.

94. Jones, *Pueblo Wariors*, 137–39.

95. Vélez Cachupín to the King, Cadiz, 12 August 1768. Thomas, "Governor Mendinueta's Proposals," 35. By 1772 the Navajos had forced the abandonment of all Spanish settlements along the Río Puerco, and by mid-1774 New Mexico was the focus of an all-out Comanche attack on virtually every settlement in the province. Marc Simmons, ed. and trans., *Indios and Mission Affairs in New Mexico, 1773. Pedro Femín de Mendinueta* (Santa Fe: Stagecoach Press, 1965), 10. The 1770s was a period of almost continuous nomadic Indian raiding in central and northern New Mexico. Dan Scurlock, *From the Rio to the Sierra: An Environmental History of the Middle Rio Grande Basin* (Fort Collins, Colo.: U. S. Department of Agriculture, Forest Service, Rocky Mountain Research Station, 1998), 40–41.

96. Vélez Cachupín to the King, Cadiz, 12 August 1768.

97. Ebright, Hendricks, and Escudero, "Tomás Vélez Cachupín's Last Will and Testament", 311.

98. Ibid.

99. Ibid.

100. Ibid., 299, 319 n. 46.

CHAPTER FIVE: THE ABIQUIU GENÍZARO LAND GRANT

1. The Belen grant, which Diego Torres settled with twenty Genízaros in 1746, is an

example of a grant to Genízaros. Ebright, "Frontier Land Litigation," 212–13, n. 44, 45.

2.   The alcalde of Santa Cruz de la Cañada, Juan Páez Hurtado, placed the grantees of the Bartolomé Trujillo grant in possession on 31 August and 1 September 1734, at which time it became clear that some of the grantees, including Bartolomé Trujillo and Antonio de Salazar were already in possession of the land. J. Richard Salazar, "Santa Rosa de Lima de Abiquiú," *New Mexico Architecture* 18 (Sept.–Oct. 1976): 15–17.

3.   Van Ness, *Hispanos in Northern New Mexico*, 120.

4.   Ibid., 120; and SANM I: 36. Initially Governor Codallos y Rabal ignored Father Pérez Mirabal's first report, but after a second report and under pressure from "an aroused public opinion," the soldiers chased the fleeing Ute/Comanche raiders but never caught them because they had a four-day lead. Salazar, "Santa Rosa de Lima," 16–17.

5.   Van Ness, *Hispanos in Northern New Mexico*, 121; and Salazar, "Santa Rosa de Lima," 16–17.

6.   Salazar, "Santa Rosa de Lima," 17; Van Ness, *Hispanos in Northern New Mexico*, 121; and Baxter, "Irrigation in the Chama Valley" (a study prepared for the U.S. District Court in connection with Water Rights Adjudication of the Rio Chama, 31 March 1994).

7.   Van Ness, *Hispanos in Northern New Mexico*, 120–21.

8.   *Recopilación*, book 6, title 3, law 8.

9.   In 1750 Viceroy Revillagigedo ordered the resettlement of Abiquiu. SANM I: 1129. The 1754 Genízaro grant is at SG 140, r. 26, frames 281 et seq.

10.   Vélez Cachupín's statement that he settled sixty Genízaro families at Abiquiu appears in his report to the viceroy about the witchcraft outbreak at the Abiquiu Genízaro pueblo, Governor Vélez Cachupín to Viceroy Marqués de Ervillas, Santa Fe, 28 March 1764, AGN, Inquisición, 1000: 12, Mexico City. For Father Domínguez's visitation and census, see Adams and Chávez, *Missions of New Mexico*, 120–26.

11.   Governor Pedro Fermín de Mendinueta, Decree Ordering the Resettlement of Abiquiu, Santa Fe, 6 November 1770, SANM I: 36.

12.   Ibid.

13.   Abiquiu grant, SG 140, r. 26, f. 281–82.

14.   For a comparison of the land grant policies of Governors Mendinueta and Vélez Cachupín, particularly as they relate to Indians, see Ebright, "Breaking New Ground," 195–233.

15.   Governor Pedro Fermín de Mendinueta, Decree, Santa Fe, 31 March 1769, SANM I: 656.

16.   For Genízaros staying at Ojo Caliente, see Alcalde Antonio José Ortiz, Inspection, Ojo Caliente, 11 June 1769, SANM I: 656.

17.   Adams, *Bishop Tamarón's Visitation*, 64.

18.   Adams and Chávez, *Missions of New Mexico*, 126.

19.   Ibid.

20.   *Obligación de predicarnos punta de la doctrina o el Evangelio como lo ordena el Santo Concilio de Trento.* Constitucional Alcalde Santiago Salazar, Petition on behalf of the vecinos of the jurisdiction of Abiquiu, Abiquiu, 8 October 1820, AASF, 1820:15.

21.   The Council of Trent (1545–63) was a series of councils held by the Catholic Church at Trent, Italy. One of the reforms enacted was the adoption of the Catechism of the Council of Trent, which described in a clear and lucid fashion the doctrinal beliefs of Roman Catholics. Hubert Jedin, *The Council of Trent*, trans. Ernest Graf (St. Louis, Mo.: B. Herder Book Co., 1957), 2:99–100.

22.   *Entró sin ser llamado el Ministro Reverendo Padre y sin ningún motivo vimos todos los congregados que con voz alterada amenazó diciendo que los conjuraría con maldiciones censuras hasta sumergirlos en la tierra.* Constitucional Alcalde Santiago Salazar, Petition on behalf of the vecinos of the jurisdiction of Abiquiu, Abiquiu, 8 October 1820, AASF, 1820:15.

23.   *Profirió por tres veces estas expresiones maldito sea el partido.* Manuel Martín[ez], Testimony, Abiquiu, 21 October 1820, AASF, 1820:15.

24. *La venta nula, y devuelva la tierra a la comunidad.* MANM, r. 42, f. 11–12.

25. *Genízaros of Abiquiu v. Father Alcina,* Abiquiu, 18 May 1824, SANM I: 208.

26. Mateo García, Manuel Montoya, and Maríano Martín to Alcalde Santiago Salazar, Abiquiu, 18 September 1820, and testimony of Manuel Martín before Juez Comisario Francisco de Hozio, [Abiquiu], 21 October 1820. Archives of the Archdiocese of Santa Fe, 15, State Records Center and Archives, Santa Fe.

27. *Nadie puede vender tierras del pueblo, y si alguna se ha vendido, es compra nula y de ningún valor.* Governor Alberto Máynez, Decree, Santa Fe, 22 May 1815, SANM I: 208.

28. Malcolm Ebright and Rick Hendricks, "The Pueblo League and Pueblo Indian Land in New Mexico, 1692–1846," in *Ysleta del Sur Pueblo Archives* (El Paso, Tex.: Book Publishers of El Paso, 2001), 4:114–22, 141–52; G. Emlen Hall and David J. Weber, "Mexican Liberals and the Pueblo Indians, 1821–1829," *New Mexico Historical Review* 59 (Jan. 1984): 5; Hall, "Juan Estevan Pino, 'Se Los Coma': New Mexico Land Speculation in the 1820s," *New Mexico Historical Review* 59 (Jan. 1982): 27–42; and Ebright, "Advocates for the Oppressed," 305–39.

29. García de la Mora to Governor Vizcarra, Santa Fe, 3 March 1823; and Governor Vizcarra, Decree, Santa Fe, 13 April 1823, SANM I: 208.

30. García de la Mora to Governor Vizcarra, [Santa Fe], [13] April 1823, SANM I: 208; and García de la Mora to the commandant general.

31. Ibid.

32. *Miro ya a este pueblo no como a tal, y si como a una plaza de vecinos sujetos a diezmos, primicias y demas obvenciones y de consiguente...debe seguirse el reparto de tierras en iguales partes...los vecinos pobres que no tengan [tierras].* Ibid.

33. Jesús María Mena, Opinion, Chihuahua, 20 June 1823, adopted by Commandante General Gaspar de Ochoa, Chihuahua, 21 June 1823, SANM I: 208. For a discussion of the commandency general during the Spanish period, see Marc Simmons, *Spanish Government in New Mexico* (Albuquerque: University of New Mexico Press, 1968), 9–24.

34. Francisco Jaramillo, Decree, Abiquiu, 20 April 1824, SANM I: 208.

35. Governor Baca ruled that "the said land must be farmed by the legitimate owners, [and]...until title...has been cleared no obstruction shall be placed against the present owners." Governor Bartolomé Baca, Decree, Santa Cruz de la Cañada, 4 May 1824.

36. Francisco Márquez, Francisco Trujillo, and Miguel Antonio García on behalf of Abiquiu pueblo, Petition to Governor Baca, Santa Fe, 13 May 1824, SANM I: 208.

37. Ignacío María Sánchez Vergara, Petition, Abiquiu, 24 May 1824, SANM I: 208.

38. Petition of the Genízaros of Abiquiu, signed by Francisco Trujillo, Abiquiu, [20 April 1824], SANM I: 208.

39. Richard E. Ahlborn, *The Penitente Moradas of Abiquiú* (Washington, D.C.: Smithsonian Institution Press, 1968), 128.

40. Governor Alberto Máynez, Decree, Santa Fe, 22 May 1815, SANM I: 208; and Francisco Trujillo, Order, Abiquiu, 18 May 1824, SANM I: 208. Governor Chávez's decree is quoted in one of Francisco Trujillo's petitions. It reads in part, "I provide that at once you demand the return to the pueblo of Abiquiu of the lands belonging to their grant, and without delay, immediately, and without any excuse." Alcalde Francisco Trujillo, Report, Abiquiu, 8 April 1824, SANM I: 208.

41. In his petition to Governor Bartolomé Baca in 1825, Santiago Salazar said that he had purchased land from fourteen Abiquiu Pueblo members. SANM I: 1066. In 1824 María Manuela Perea told Governor Baca that she had purchased land from natives of the pueblo, but Alcalde José García de la Mora had refused to deliver possession to her. SANM I: 709.

42. Swadesh, *Primeros Pobladores,* 49.

43. Ebright, "Advocates for the Oppressed," 308, 323–30.

44. *Donde los indios puedan tener sus ganados, sin que se revuelan con otros de españoles.* *Recopilación,* book 6, title, 3, law 8.

45.   *No ser en perjuicio de los indios del pueblo de Abiquiú; de sus sementeras y ejidos.*
       Governor Tomás Vélez Cachupín, Grant, Santa Fe, 12 February 1766, Polvadera grant,
       SG 131, r. 25, f. 447 et seq.

46.   By treating the irrigated fields the same as the ejidos Vélez Cachupín was protecting
       the Abiquiu ejido as Indian land. This was equitable because the Polvadera grant was
       made only to one person, Juan Pablo Martín and his family, and was of sufficient size
       to provide adequate grazing for Martín's livestock. The Polvadera grant was confirmed
       by the Court of Private Land Claims in August 1893 and was surveyed at more than
       thirty-five thousand acres, five thousand acres of which conflicted with the Abiquiu
       and Juan José Lobato grants. The survey was approved and a patent was issued in
       September 1900. J. J. Bowden, "Private Land Claims in the Southwest" (M.A. thesis,
       Southern Methodist University, 1969), 1083–89.

47.   Hall and Weber, "Mexican Liberals," 5–32.

48.   Abiquiu grant, Bowden, "Private Land Claims," 4: 1101–2.

49.   *Del centro del pueblo se le midan al sur cinco mil varas de tierra lindando al frente del
       referido pueblo el camino real de los teguas que va para Navajo.*

50.   The lawsuit between the Abiquiu grant and the Vallecitos grant is discussed in
       Swadesh, *Primeros Pobladores*, 54–57.

51.   *No es fácil encontrar en un archivo como tan antiguo este, documentos viejos y más
       cuando no se expresa la fecha de ellos.* Governor José Antonio Chávez to the regidor in
       charge of the administration of justice at Abiquiu. Santa Fe, 17 August 1831. Abiquiu
       grant, PLC 52, r. 38, f. 899. Swadesh, *Primeros Pobladores*, 56.

52.   *Dos hombres los más ancianos de la jurisdicción que se han criado desde tiernos en el
       Vallecito de pastores para que me señalaran el camino de los teguas que va para Navajo.*
       Alcalde José Francisco Vigil to Governor Chávez, Abiquiu, 10 October 1831, Abiquiu
       grant, PLC 52, r. 38, f. 899.

53.   Ibid.

54.   Ibid.

55.   *Quince ciuidadanos principales de la jurisdicción que asistieron conmigo a la entrega de
       dicha tierras.* Alcalde José Francisco Vigil, Report, Abiquiu, 21 September 1832, Abiquiu
       grant, SG 52, r. 38, f. 306.

56.   *Con tumulto de todo el pueblo de viejos, mancebos, y mujeres queriendo quitarme de las
       manos los documentos sacudiendo con la mano la rienda del freno de mi caballo después
       de varios oprobios y razones insolentes con que me insultaron.* Ibid.

57.   *Lo sobrante hasta encontrarme con el camino de los teguas que va para Navajo.* Ibid.

58.   *El camino de los teguas que va a Navajo y una mojonera antigua.* Ibid.

59.   Chief Justice Joseph R. Reid, Opinion, Abiquiu grant, SG 140, r. 26, f. 441–42.

60.   Bowden, "Private Land Claims," 4: 1106–7.

CHAPTER SIX : WITCHCRAFT TRIALS

1.   Don Carlos of Texcoco was an Indian leader who counseled his people to resist
       Christianization, allegedly telling them "that Christian doctrine was nothing, [and] that
       the pronouncements of the friars, viceroy, and bishop were of no consequence." He was
       denounced before the Inquisition on 22 June 1539, and on 4 July he was ordered
       arrested. A search of his house turned up "idols" (some embedded in the walls) repre-
       senting the gods Quetzalcoatl, Xipe, Tlaloc, and Coatlicue. After an investigation, don
       Carlos was adjudged a heretic and executed in the Zócalo of Mexico City before Viceroy
       Mendoza, Archbishop Zumárraga, the audiencia, and the citizens of Mexico City and
       Texcoco. Richard E. Greenleaf, *Zumárraga and the Mexican Inquisition, 1536–1543*
       (Washington, D.C.: Academy of American Franciscan History, 1961), 68–74.

2.   Riley, *Kachina and Cross*, 91–92.

3.   *Holy Office v. Luis de Rivera*, AGN, Inquisición, 366.

4. *Holy Office v. Juan de la Cruz* [and his wife], AGN, Inquisición, 304.

5. Declaration of fray Nicolás de Villar, Isleta, 23 March 1668. Hackett, *Historical Documents,* 3: 275.

6. The case of Bernardo Gruber is found in AGN, Inquisición, 666 and is summarized by Joseph P. Sanchez, "Bernardo Gruber and the New Mexico Inquisition," in *The Rio Abajo Frontier, 1540–1692: A History of Early Colonial New Mexico* (Albuquerque: Albuquerque Museum, 1987), 120–28.

7. Francisco del Castillo Betancur to Juan de Ortega, Parral, 1 September 1670, AGN Inquisición, 666, fr. 402, cited in Sanchez, *Rio Abajo Frontier,* 128.

8. Sánchez, *Rio Abajo Frontier,* 128.

9. For a summary of the career of Juan Páez Hurtado, and the numerous charges made against him, especially in connection with his 1695 expedition to recruit colonists in the Zacatecas area, see John B. Colligan, *The Juan Paez Hurtado Expedition of 1695: Fraud in Recruiting Colonists for New Mexico* (Albuquerque: University of New Mexico Press, 1995), 3–11.

10. *Si quería ser rico que ella la hacía y que le sobra todo. Antonia Luján v. Francisca Caza,* 2 July 1715, SANM II: 225.

11. *Te sobrara todo y no faltarán los grandes de tu casa.* Ibid.

12. Ibid.

13. Ibid.

14. Kenneth Mills, *Idolatry and its Enemies, Colonial Andean Religion and its Extirpation, 1640–1750* (Princeton, N.J.: Princeton University Press, 1997), 102. The idolatry/superstition dichotomy discussed by Mills is based on De la Peña Montenegro.

15. *Antonia Luján v. Francisca Caza,* 2 July 1715, SANM II: 225.

16. The twenty-third question in the fifteenth chapter of Pablo José de Arriaga's manual for the extirpation of idolatry contains the question: "If the witness had spoken with the Devil and in what form the latter had appeared." Pablo José de Arriaga, "La Extirpación de la Idolatría del Perú," in *Crónicas peruanas de interés indígena,* ed. Francisco Esteve Barba, Biblioteca de Autores Españoles (Madrid: Atlas, 1968), 209; cited in Griffiths, *Cross and the Serpent,* 87.

17. In a 1708 witchcraft case, two curanderos when asked whom they had cured named Agustina Romero, the wife of Miguel Tenorio [de Alba], and María Luján, the wife of Sebastián Martín. They stated that they had accomplished these cures with beneficial herbs and not "with any spell or diabolic art." Case against Caterina Luján, Caterina Rosa, and Angelina Pumazho. Ralph Emerson Twitchell, *The Spanish Archives of New Mexico* (Glendale, Calif.: The Arthur H. Clark Co., 1914), 2:142–64, esp. 160.

18. Noemi Quesada, "The Inquisition's Repression of Curanderos," in *Cultural Encounters: The Impact of the Inquisition in Spain and the New World,* ed. Mary Elizabeth Perry and Anne J. Cruz (Berkeley: University of California Press, 1991), 37–57.

19. *Presumiendo la tenía hecho mal con maleficio.* Alcalde Juan Paez Hurtado, Witchcraft investigation, Santa Fe, 2 July 1715, SANM II: 225.

20. Governor Vélez Cachupín, Report. 28 April 1764, Pinart Collection, PE 52:50.

21. Scholes, "First Decade of the Inquisition," 223–24.

22. Leonor Domínguez, Criminal complaint, Santa Fe, 13 May 1708, SANM II: 137b. Translation in Twitchell, *Spanish Archives of New Mexico,* 2:142–64.

23. Juan García de las Rivas, Proceeding and compliance, 13 May 1708, SANM II: 137b.

24. Ibid.

25. Governor José Chacon, Order, Santa Fe, 13 May 1708; and Alcalde Juan García de las Rivas, Writ and arrest San Juan de los Caballeros, 15 May 1708, SANM II: 137b.

26. Alcalde Juan García de las Rivas, Prosecution of writs Santa Fe, 16 May 1708, SANM II: 137b.

27. Angelina Puma-zho, and Caterina Rosa, wife of Zhiconqueto, Declarations, Santa Fe, 16 May 1708, SANM II: 137b.

28. Governor José Chacon, Order, Santa Fe, 18 May 1708, SANM II: 137b.
29. Casilda Contreras, Soledad; María, wife of Pedro de Avila, and Miguel Martín, husband of Leonor Domínguez, Declarations, 22 May 1708. Ibid.
30. Leonor Domínguez, New declaration, Santa Fe, 22 May 1708. Ibid.
31. For a discussion of love magic in sixteenth-, seventeenth-, and eighteenth-century Spain with an emphasis on love spells and conjurations, see María Helena Sánchez Ortega," Sorcery and Eroticism in Love Magic," in *Cultural Encounters: The Impact of the Inquisition in Spain and the New World,* ed. Mary Elizabeth Perry and Anne J. Cruz (Berkeley: University of California Press, 1991), 58–92. Sánchez Ortega defines a *hechizar* as "a type of incantation which controls the bewitched person in such a way that his judgement is distorted and he desires what would normally repel him." Ibid., 87–88, n. 2.
32. Leonor Domínguez, New declaration, Santa Fe, 22 May 1708, SANM II: 137b.
33. Juanchillo and wife, Declarations, San Juan, 25 May 1708, SANM II: 137b.
34. Catarina Rosa, wife of Zhiconqueto, and Juan de Ulibarrí, Declarations, Santa Fe, 27 May 1708, SANM II: 1376.
35. Juan de Ulibarrí to Governor José Chacón, Transmittal decree, Santa Fe, 27 May 1708; and Governor José Chacón, Decree, Santa Fe, 31 May 1708, SANM II: 225.
36. In colonial New England, the stereotype of the deceitful Indian meant that Indian testimony was "usually suspect in most courts of law." The same stereotypes existed in colonial New Mexico. Elaine G. Breslaw, *Tituba, Reluctant Witch of Salem: Devilish Indians and Puritan Fantasies* (New York: New York University Press, 1996), 157.
37. *Holy Office v. Micaela de Contreras,* El Paso, 1745, AGN, Inquisición, 892.
38. *Holy Office v. Beatriz de Cabrera,* El Paso, 1745, AGN, Inquisición, 913.
39. *Holy Office v. María Domínguez,* Santa Fe, 1734, AGN, Inquisición, 849.
40. *Holy Office v. Getrudis Sánchez,* Isleta, 1743, AGN, Inquisición, 914.
41. *Holy Office v. Magdalena Sánchez,* Santa Cruz de la Cañada, 1748, AGN, Inquisición, 901.
42. *Holy Office v. Juana María Apodaca or Venegas,* San Elizario, 1800, AGN, Inquisición, 1468: 29.
43. Lara Semboloni, "Cacería de brujas en Coahuila, 1748–1751," *Historia Mexicana* 214 (Oct. 2004): 325.
44. Ibid., 235–26, 340–42.
45. Ibid., 346–47.
46. Ibid., 348–49.
47. Ibid., 338.
48. Ibid., 361–62.
49. Ibid., 339.

CHAPTER SEVEN: PHASE ONE, EL COJO

1. For an anecdotal discussion of Pueblo and Spanish witchcraft, see L. S. M. Curtin, "Spanish and Indian Witchcraft in New Mexico," *The Masterkey* 45 (July–Sept. 1971): 89.
2. Kessell, "Spaniards and Pueblos," 127–38. Kessell emphasizes the connection between the Pueblos' role as auxiliaries to Spanish troops and the extent of Spanish oppression of the Pueblos. When the Spaniards felt secure from Plains Indian raiding, suppression of Pueblo religion increased; when the need for Pueblo allies increased, oppression eased. For another balanced look at Pueblo-Spanish relations through Pueblo and Spanish eyes, see David J. Weber, "The Spanish-Mexican Rim," in *The Oxford History of the American West,* ed. Clyde A. Milner II, Carol A. O'Connor, and Martha A. Sandweiss (New York: Oxford University Press, 1994).
3. For a translation of this report, see Thomas, *Plains Indians,* 29–43, cited in Jones, *Pueblo Warriors,* 127; and Kessell, "Spaniards and Pueblos."

4. *Los que viven lo experimentan los que vienen al lugar a diligencia o paseo lo confirman según lo que observan.* Fray Juan José Toledo to Governor Francisco Antonio Marín del Valle, Abiquiu, 26 July 1760, Pinart Collection, PE 52: 5.

5. *Que decir mucho en poco es concedido a pocos.* Ibid.

6. *Se quejó todo este pueblo al teniente Juan Trujillo de un indio nombrado Miguel El Cojo.* Ibid.

7. Gilberto Benito Córdova, "Missionization and Hispanicization of Santo Thomás Apóstol de Abiquiú, 1750–1770" (Ph.D. diss., University of New Mexico, 1979).

8. Hunting in strictly controlled groups was more typical of Northern Plains Indians than Comanches. Miguel, El Cojo, testified that he was Pawnee. When the principal game was bison, Comanches tended to hunt alone or in small groups because they could easily succeed among the great herds. In contrast, "on the northern Plains where there were more people and fewer buffalo, buffalo hunts were tightly controlled by hunt leaders and closely supervised by warriors acting as hunt police." Willard H. Rollings, *The Comanche* (New York: Chelsea House Publishers, 1989), 35. When accused of witchcraft, El Cojo said he practiced only the arts of healing he had learned from the Pawnees. Córdova, "Missionization and Hispanicization."

9. Simmons, *Witchcraft in the Southwest*, 16–35; and Scholes, "First Decade of the Inquisition," 208–26.

10. *No se puede detener el cuerpo para enterrarlo.* Fray Juan José Toledo to Governor Francisco Antonio Marín del Valle, Abiquiu, 26 July 1760, Pinart Collection, PE 52: 5.

11. José Garduño is referred to in particular as a soldier who witnessed ill people who vomited flint stones, threads, and worms. Fray Juan José Toledo to Governor Francisco Antonio Marín del Valle, Abiquiu, 26 July 1760, Pinart Collection, PE 52: 5.

12. *Gozar con más libertad de la manceba.* Ibid.

13. *Acábase de darle muerte.* Ibid.

14. *Puso a la mujer en paz con el marido.* Ibid.

15. Cordova, "Missionization and Hispanicization." It was not uncommon in eighteenth-century Chihuahua for a parish priest to persuade a battered wife to reconcile with an abusive husband. See 1718 case of *Catalina Cos Madrid v. Pedro Pérez Carrasco,* cited in Cheryl English Martín, *Governance and Society in Colonial Mexico: Chihuahua in the Eighteenth Century* (Stanford, Calif.: Stanford University Press, 1996), 154–55.

16. *Se me afirmó que era verdad dicho pacto.* Fray Juan José Toledo to Governor Francisco Antonio Marín del Valle, Abiquiu, 26 July 1760, Pinart Collection, PE 52: 5.

17. Irene Silverblatt, *Moon, Sun, and Witches: Gender Ideologies and Class in Inca and Colonial Peru* (Princeton, N.J.: Princeton University Press, 1987), 162–66; and Irene Silverblatt, "The Evolution of Witchcraft and the Meaning of Healing in Colonial Andean Society," *Culture, Medicine and Psychiatry* 7 (1983): 415–17.

18. Ramón A. Gutiérrez, "Franciscans and the Pueblo Revolt," in Weber, *What Caused the Pueblo Revolt of 1680?,* 49–50.

19. A famous history of the late middle ages sums up what it must have been like to stand in Father Toledo's shoes alone in an alien culture where he had to learn as well as teach and be changed in the process: "All events had much sharper outlines than now... every experience had that degree of directness and absoluteness that joy and sadness still have in the mind of a child." Johan Huizinga, *The Autumn of the Middle Ages,* trans. Rodney Payton and Ulrich Mammitzsch (Chicago: University of Chicago Press, 1996), 1.

20. Some saw the Devil's Pact as a parody of the individual's covenant with God that regulated all aspects of life. Breslaw, *Tituba,* 123.

21. Fernando Cervantes, *The Devil in the New World: The Impact of Diabolism in New Spain* (New Haven, Conn.: Yale University Press, 1994), 40–41; Simmons, *Witchcraft in*

the *Southwest*, 14; and Keith Thomas, *Religion and the Decline of Magic: Studies in Popular Beliefs in Sixteenth- and Seventeenth-Century England* (London: Weidenfeld and Nicolson, 1971), 443–45. Simmons notes that "Indians, {be} they the Aztecs of Mexico or the Pueblos, . . . viewed evil as a shadowy negative force present to some degree in every man and God." Simmons, *Witchcraft in the Southwest*, 14.

22. Cervantes, *Devil in the New World*, 40–41; Thomas, *Religion and the Decline of Magic*, 443–45.

23. Howard L. Harrod, *The Animals Came Dancing: Native American Sacred Ecology and Animal Kinship* (Tucson: University of Arizona Press, 2000), 102–3.

24. Breslaw, *Tituba*, 135; and Griffiths, *Cross and the Serpent*, 6–7.

25. *Ser mentira que lo estaba enseñando a danar gente su tío El Cojo*. Fray Juan José Toledo to Governor Francisco Antonio Marín del Valle, Abiquiu, 26 July 1760, Pinart Collection, PE 52: 5.

26. De la Peña Montenegro also recommended withdrawal of communion and other rites of the Church. De la Peña Montenegro, *Itinerario*, section VI (5).

27. For examples of battles between priests and local shamans in Colonial Peru over spiritual authority, see Griffiths, *Cross and the Serpent*, 151–52, 160–61.

28. *Se tocan advierten, se miran y admira en este pueblo . . . quebrarle la cabeza cuando no la hay para explicarlo*. Fray Juan José Toledo to Governor Francisco Antonio Marín del Valle, Abiquiu, 26 July 1760, Pinart Collection, PE 52: 5.

29. Horvath, "Indian Slaves," 65–66; see also David Weber, *The Taos Trappers* (Norman: University of Oklahoma Press, 1968), 27–28.

30. *Miro dicho Cojo a la yuta con ojos bien airados . . . Salió la Yuta del pueblo para su ranchito . . . (corsando sangre por boca y narices) cayó muerta*. Fray Juan José Toledo to Governor Francisco Antonio Marín del Valle, Abiquiu, 26 July 1760, Pinart Collection, PE 52: 5. For more on the Evil Eye or the sickness thought to be caused by it (el mal de ojo), see Alan Dundes, ed., *The Evil Eye: A Casebook* (Madison: University of Wisconsin Press, 1992), 173–75 and passim.

31. *Ser demonio de mayor jerarquía el del dicho Cojo . . . haber obrando el demonio mejor en el gentil muriendo en su pecado*. Toledo to Marín del Valle. 26 July 1760, Pinart Collection, PE 52:5.

32. De la Peña Montenegro, *Itinerario*.

33. Ibid., V:188–89.

34. Ibid., V:(2) and (3) on countering witchcraft, 189.

35. Ibid.

36. Ibid.

37. Sticking thorns into an image was one of the sorcerer's devices taught by El Cojo in his School for the Devil. The use of the confession had not been an effective method with the defiant Cojo, though it was later used by Governor Vélez Cachupín along with a form of torture on another accused witch. Fray Juan José Toledo to Governor Francisco Antonio Marín del Valle, Abiquiu, 26 July 1760, Pinart Collection, PE 52: 5.

38. De la Peña Montenegro, *Itinerario*, V:188–89.

39. Fray Juan José Toledo to Governor Francisco Antonio Marín del Valle, Abiquiu, 26 July 1760, Pinart Collection, PE 52: 5.

40. Toledo's ambivalence here is the beginning of a process that will ultimately lead to his siding with the superstition of a curandera if she can heal him of his own afflictions.

41. *Tenía El Cojo una víbora oculta y viva*. Fray Juan José Toledo to Governor Francisco Antonio Marín del Valle, Abiquiu, 26 July 1760, Pinart Collection, PE 52:5.

42. *Ni que este dicho Cojo sea el solo malechor que tengan los hechiceros*. Ibid.

43. *Que tardó de morir*. Ibid.

44.   Presumably this was either fray Joaquín Maríano Rodríguez de Jerez or fray Maríano
      Rodríguez de la Torre, both of whom coincided in New Mexico with Toledo. Chávez,
      Archives of the Archdiocese of Santa Fe, 155.

45.   *Dichos animales dan las respuestas de lo que le piden al Demonio.* Fray Juan José Toledo
      to Governor Francisco Antonio Marín del Valle, Abiquiu, 26 July 1760, Pinart
      Collection, PE 52:5.

46.   *La prudencia con que he procedido en dicha materia es observar movimientos y no
      obstante conocer y confesar todos los indios ser cosa mala la dicha víbora.* Ibid.

47.   *The Holy Bible* (King James Version), Genesis 3:14; M. Jack Suggs, Katharine Sakenfeld,
      and James Mueller, *Oxford Study Bible* (New York: Oxford University Press, 1992), 13–14.

48.   Griffiths, *Cross and the Serpent*, 3–6.

49.   Dennis Slifer, *The Serpent and the Sacred Fire: Fertility Images in Southwest Rock Art*
      (Santa Fe: Museum of New Mexico, 2000), 43–143; and Carol Patterson-Rudolph,
      Petroglyphs and Pueblo Myths of the Rio Grande (Albuquerque: Avanyu Publishing,
      1993), 68.

50.   Harry C. James, *Pages from Hopi History* (Tucson: University of Arizona Press, 1996),
      219–20; Jesse Walter Fewkes, *Hopi Snake Ceremonies* (Albuquerque: Avanyu Publishing,
      1986), 305–11; and John G. Bourke, *The Snake-Dance of the Moquis of Arizona* (Tucson:
      University of Arizona Press, 1984), xii–xvi.

51.   Polly Schaafsma, *Indian Rock Art of the Southwest* (Santa Fe: School of American
      Research, 1980), 233–39, esp. 204, fig. 157 (rattlesnake) and 235, fig. 196; and Enrique
      Florescano, *The Myth of Quetzalcoatl* (Baltimore, Md.: John Hopkins University Press,
      1999), 1–5.

52.   Snakes are mentioned in the second phase when the Genízara Paula is brought to the
      cave where Vicente Trujillo and his wife practiced their art and told to remove her
      cross and kiss the snakes and toads inhabiting the cave.

53.   Fray Juan José Toledo to Governor Francisco Antonio Marín del Valle, Abiquiu, 26 July
      1760, Pinart Collection, PE 52: 5. The ambivalence of the Church toward torture
      stemmed primarily from the concern that torture was an unreliable means of arriving
      at the truth. Especially if it was excessive, most people would confess to anything sug-
      gested by their interrogator with the application of torture. For this reason, the
      Church prohibited judicial torture until the middle of the thirteenth century. Brian P.
      Levack, *The Witch-Hunt in Early Modern Europe* (New York: Addison Wesley
      Longman, 1995), 77–78.

54.   Fray Juan José Toledo to Governor Francisco Antonio Marín del Valle, Abiquiu, 26 July
      1760, Pinart Collection, PE 52: 5.

55.   Montenegro, *Itinerario.* "Witchcraft is . . . the classical resort of vulnerable subordinate
      groups, who have little or no safe, open opportunity to challenge a form of domina-
      tion that angers them." James C. Scott, *Domination and the Arts of Resistance: Hidden
      Transcripts* (New Haven, Conn.: Yale University Press, 1990), 144.

CHAPTER EIGHT: PHASE TWO, JOAQUINILLO

1.   The similarities between the Abiquiu witchcraft trials and those of Salem,
      Massachusetts, in 1692 are particularly apparent in light of a new treatment of the
      Salem witchcraft crisis. Norton connects the mind-set of Salem to the broader context
      of the Indian wars on the Maine frontier. Norton, *Devil's Snare*, 4–5, 11–12.

2.   Alcalde Carlos Fernández to Alcalde Juan Pablo Martín, Nuestra Señora de la Soledad
      del Río Arriba, 6 April 1763, Pinart Collection, PE 52: 5.

3.   Alcalde Juan Pablo Martín, Report, Abiquiu, 9 April 1763, Pinart Collection, PE 52: 5.

4.   "When used sparingly to attract the opposite sex or win friends [love magic] is not
      negatively sanctioned and among older Apaches is considered a definite asset." Keith
      H. Basso, "Southwest: Apache," in *Witchcraft and Sorcery of the American Native
      Peoples,* ed. Deward E. Walker Jr. (Moscow: University of Idaho Press, 1989), 175.

5. France Scholes, in discussing the Inquisition's case against Beatriz de los Angeles and Juana de la Cruz for killing enemies (including a spurned lover) through witchcraft, states, "To the glory of Perea, he had a sense of proportion and a healthy scepticism... concerning conditions that did not endanger the essential rights of the Church... or the honor of its ministers." Scholes, "First Decade of the Inquisition," 226. For a discussion of cases of love magic prosecuted by the Spanish Inquisition, see Sánchez Ortega, "Sorcery and Eroticism in Love Magic," 58–92.

6. Alcalde Juan Pablo Martín to Governor Tomás Vélez Cachupín, Abiquiu, 9 April 1763, Pinart Collection, PE 52: 5. Keith H. Basso, *Western Apache Witchcraft* (Tucson: University of Arizona Press, 1969), 36; and Clyde Kluckhohn, *Navajo Witchcraft* (Boston: Beacon Press, 1944), 34–35, 154–57; Parsons, "Witchcraft among the Pueblos," 206–7.

7. The possibility that knowledge of witchcraft activities would brand the informant as a witch was also a major concern during the 1692 Salem witch craze. Norton, *Devil's Snare*, 117–18.

8. Alcalde Carlos Fernández, Report, Soledad, 7 April 1763, Pinart Collection, PE 52: 5.

9. Silfer discusses these images and translates parts of the June 1763 document describing them. Slifer, *Signs of Life*, 85–86.

10. Timothy J. Knab, *A War of Witches: A Journey into the Underworld of the Contemporary Aztecs* (New York: Harper San Francisco, 1993), 60–63.

11. When Governor Vélez Cachupín sentenced María, the wife of Vicente, he specified that her punishment would increase if she returned to the practice of witchcraft, or being a curandera with herbs.

12. See Appendix A, List of Accused Sorcerers. At the 6 April 1763 hearing before Alcalde Pedro Martín, Joaquinillo agreed to name the *hechicerios maléficos* in Abiquiu and beyond, along with his brother, Juan Largo, who was raised at Santa Ana. Juan Largo, however, was never as cooperative as was Joaquinillo. From the beginning Joaquinilo was the sole informer, although Juan Largo may have been assisting him behind the scenes. Alcalde Juan Pablo Martín to Governor Tomás Vélez Cachupín, Abiquiu, 9 April 1763, Pinart Collection, PE 52: 5.

13. Vicente Trujillo, Miguel, El Cojo, Pedro Trujillo, and Agustín Tagle, having been identified as witches, were sent to Santa Fe and jailed by Governor Vélez Cachupín. Alcalde Carlos Fernández, Report, Soledad, 7 April 1763, Pinart Collection, PE 52: 5.

14. Alcalde Carlos Fernández, Abiquiu, Report, 30 April 1763, Pinart Collection, PE 52: 5.

15. Gustav Henningsen, *The Witches Advocate: Basque Witchcraft and the Spanish Inquisition, 1609–1614* (Reno: University of Nevada Press, 1980), 58, 78–79. Henningsen was concerned with the question of whether the witchcraft activities described in this and other trials actually took place. On the question of whether it was possible to fly, he cites Carlos Casteñeda's use of a flying ointment made from the root of the datura plant in Casteñeda, *The Teachings of Don Juan: A Yaqui Way of Knowledge* (Berkeley: University of California Press, 1968), 91–94.

16. Susana Eger Valadez, "Wolf Power and Interspecies Communication in Huichol Shamanism," in *People of the Peyote: Huichol Indian History, Religion, and Survival*, ed. Stacy Schaeffer and Peter Furst (Albuquerque: University of New Mexico Press, 1996), 267–305.

17. Alcalde Carlos Fernández, Report, Abiquiu, 30 April 1763, Pinart Collection, PE 52: 5.

18. Owls were also thought to be harbingers of death. Anita U. Baca, Interview, 1 August 1989, in Nasario García, *Brujas, Bultos, y Brasas: Tales of Witchcraft and the Supernatural in the Pecos Valley* (Santa Fe: Western Edge Press, 1999), 28–31. According to Navajo belief, witches could roam about at night in the form of a wolf, coyote, bear, fox, crow, or owl. Kluckhohn, *Navajo Witchcraft*, 26.

19. Father Ordóñez was at Abiquiu from May 1754 to February 1756 and was then assigned to Laguna where he served during April 1756. Chávez, *Archives of the Archdiocese of Santa Fe*, 252.

20. Report of Alcalde Carlos Fernández, Abiquiu, 30 April 1763, Pinart Collection, PE 52: 5.
21. Ibid.
22. Ibid.
23. Ibid.; Julio Caro Baroja, *Las brujas y su mundo* (Madrid: Alianza Editorial, 1969), 37.
24. Ibid.; and Ruth Behar, "Sexual Witchcraft, Colonialism and Women's Powers: Views from the Mexican Inquisition," in *Sexuality and Marriage in Colonial Latin America*, ed. Asunción Lavrin (Lincoln: University of Nebraska Press, 1989), 178–81.
25. Ibid.
26. Scholes, "First Decade of the Inquisition," 215–18.
27. Ibid., 218–19.
28. Sánchez Ortega, "Love Magic," 58–62.
29. Cervantes, *Devil in the New World*, 135–41.
30. *Haviendo muerto de enfermedad durante el tiempo de su carcelería.* Report of Alcalde Carlos Fernández, Abiquiu, 30 April 1763, Pinart Collection, PE 52: 5.
31. Kluckhohn, *Navajo Witchcraft*, 34–35, 193–95. Among Apaches the practice of shooting sorcery was also fairly common, especially between 1920–25, when a nativistic movement swept the Fort Apache and San Carlos reservations. Basso, *Western Apache Witchcraft*, 36.
32. Prudencia Trujillo, Declaration, Carlos Fernández, Report, Abiquiu, 30 April 1763, Pinart Collection, PE 52: 5.
33. In 1628 Bartolomé Romero, the younger, testified before Father Benavides that his wife had failed to recover completely from a illness because of a spell cast on her by the wife of Juan Griego. Chávez, *Origins,* 97.
34. Fray Juan José Toledo to Governor Francisco Antonio Marín del Valle, Abiquiu, 26 July 1760. Document 1, Pinart Collection, PE 52: 5.
35. Alcalde Carlos Fernández to Fray Juan José Toledo, Abiquiu, [n.d.], Pinart Collection, PE 52: 5.
36. Fray Juan José Toledo, Report, Abiquiu, 6 May 1763, Pinart Collection, PE 52: 5.
37. Cervantes, *Devil in the New World*, 18–19.
38. The Book of Job, *Oxford Study Bible*, 510–50.
39. Father Juan José Toledo, Reports, Abiquiu, 6 May 1763 and 15 May 1763, Pinart Collection, PE 52: 5.
40. *Si no que con sus artificios hace que parezcan animales domésticos; las más veces los hace parecer gatos.* Fray Juan José Toledo, Report, Abiquiu, 6 May 1763, Pinart Collection, PE 52: 5.
41. *Lo quemó y amaneció en el bosque de San Juan cierto indio muerto y chamuscado.* Ibid.
42. *Que a fuerza de subidos con las manos en el pecho y espalda me alienten para llegar.* Ibid.
43. *Atrevimiento tan osado fue este que la prudencia y canas del reverendo padre Sopeña no pudo responder.* Ibid.
44. *Cayó muerto tan repentino que al levantarle yo la cabeza del suelo ya era difunto.* Ibid.
45. Between 1776 and 1782 California Indians set the mission at San Luis Obispo on fire by shooting burning arrows into the reed roofs. Franciscans were also rumored to have been poisoned at the missions at San Miguel and San Diego. James A. Sandos, *Converting California: Indians and Franciscans in the Missions* (New Haven, Conn.: Yale University Press, 2004), 162–63.
46. *Muy curioso adornado de muchas plumas de águilas, gavilán, gernicalo, urraca, y de otros pájaros no conocidos; en que daba la adoración y se la hacia dar a otros; cuando iba con ellos a cazar.* Fray Juan José Toledo, Report, Abiquiu, 6 May 1763, Pinart Collection, PE 52: 5.
47. *Tenía el aviso donde habia dichos venados.* Ibid.
48. *No le tirasen al que venía de guia en la punta.* Ibid.
49. *Discurrió le pondria el demonio en dicha figura porque no puede transformar este dicho*

[*Antonio, el Chimayó*]. Ibid. For a case where an accused curandera named Juana
Agustina admitted that her healing practices were the work of the Devil, thus
accept[ing] the terminology of her accusers, see Griffiths, *Cross and the Serpent*,
134–36.

50.   Catherine S. Fowler, "Subsistence," in *Great Basin*, ed. Warren L. D'Azevedo, vol. 11 of
       Handbook of North American Indians (Washington, D.C.: Smithsonian Institution
       Press, 2001), 79.

51.   David Hurst Thomas, Lorann S. A. Pendleton, and Stephen C. Cappannari, "Western
       Shoshone," in *Great Basin*, ed. D'Azevedo, 267.

52.   Warren L. D'Azevedo, "Washoe," in *Great Basin*, ed. D'Azevedo, 477–78.

53.   Harrod, *Animals Came Dancing*, 15–16.

54.   Polly Schaafsma, "Rock Art," in *Great Basin*, ed. D'Azevedo, 220–21.

55.   Fray Juan José Toledo, Report, Abiquiu, 6 May 1763, Pinart Collection, PE 52: 5.

56.   El Cojo's full name was Miguel Ontiveros and despite Father Toledo's statement that
       El Cojo had been deprived of the Church's rites, three of his children were baptized: a
       son, Pablo de la Cruz, baptized 30 December 1754, with María Martín listed as the
       mother; a son, Francisco Esteban, baptized 6 April 1760, with María García listed as the
       mother; and a daughter, María, baptized 3 August 1762, with María García, also listed
       as the mother. Father Toledo baptized the latter two children. The *padrino* for
       Francisco Esteban Ontiveros was Juan Antonio, El Paseño, who was later charged with
       witchcraft in these proceedings. Tomas Martinez, *Abiquiú Baptisms, 1754–1870* (San
       José, Calif.: n.p., 1993), 276.

57.   *Arrancarla luego, desahogando para que crezca el trigo más sano.* Fray Juan José Toledo,
       Report, Abiquiu, 15 May 1763, Pinart Collection, PE 52: 5.

58.   *Pues señor con vuestra licencia y con vuestro gusto, vamos a arrancarle dijieron los siervos
       del Divino Padre de familias.* Fray Juan José Toledo, Report, Abiquiu, 15 May 1763,
       Pinart Collection, PE 52: 5. In this section of his report, Toledo quoted Father Antonio
       Ruiz's *La conquista espiritual del Paraguay.*

59.   For a vivid and masterful discussion of the Yucatán idolatry proceedings, see Inga
       Clendinnen, *Ambivalent Conquests: Maya and Spaniard in Yucatán, 1517–1570*
       (Cambridge: Cambridge University Press, 1987), 45–111; for the Andean idolatry trials,
       see Griffiths, *Cross and the Serpent*, 29–64 and passim.

60.   David J. Weber, "Pueblos, Spaniards, and History," in Weber, *What Caused the Pueblo
       Revolt of 1680?*, 8.

61.   Fray Juan José Toledo, Report, Abiquiu, 15 May 1763, Pinart Collection, PE 52: 5.

62.   Clendinnen, *Ambivalent Conquests*, 114.

63.   Report of Governor Tomás Vélez Cachupín, Thomas, *Plains Indians*, 74. Alcalde Juan
       José Lobato to Governor Tomás Vélez Cachupín, Villa of Santa Cruz, 28 August 1752,
       translated in Thomas, *Plains Indians*, 116.

64.   Fray Juan José Toledo, Report, Abiquiu, 15 May 1763, Pinart Collection, PE 52: 5.

65.   *Se me apareció una mujer vestida de española acostada al lado de mi cama ocultándome
       el rostro.* Ibid.

66.   *Estafiate (Artemisia Mexicana)* was used by the Maya and Aztecs, who called the plant
       yztauhiatl in Nahuatl. Given as a tea or a poultice, it is still used to cure coughs, excess
       phlegm, and to rid one of intestinal obstructions. L. S. M. Curtin, *Healing Herbs of the
       Upper Rio Grande* (Los Angeles: Southwest Museum, 1965), 82–83. Estafiate, the
       Spanish name for wormwood, is a classic stomach tonic used for indigestion and
       stomach acidity. Michael Moore, *Medicinal Plants of the Mountain West* (Santa Fe:
       Museum of New Mexico Press, 1979), 162.

67.   Fray Juan José Toledo to Governor Francisco Antonio Marín del Valle, 26 July 1760,
       Pinart Collection, PE 52: 5.

68.   Clendinnen, *Ambivalent Conquests*, 45–46.

69.   *Que tuve abultado el vientre tanto tiempo con mucho desgane.* Fray Juan José Toledo to

Governor Francisco Antonio Marín del Valle, 26 July 1760, Pinart Collection, PE 52: 5.

70. *Asmodeo, príncipe de la injuria y tercero de Lucifer para bajo.* Fray Juan José Toledo, Report, Abiquiu, 15 May 1763, Pinart Collection, PE 52: 5. Tobit 3:8, Suggs, Sakenfeld, and Mueller, *Oxford Study Bible*, 1060.

71. Clendinnen, *Ambivalent Conquests*, 114.

72. De la Peña Montenegro, *Itinerario*, 188–89. For a recent article about descriptions of the Devil and the Devil's Pact from testimony before the Inquisition, see Nora Reyes Costilla and Martín González de la Vara, "El demonio entre los marginales: Población negra y el pacto con el demonio en el norte de Nueva España, siglos xvii," *Colonial Latin American Historical Review* 10 (spring 2001): 199–221.

73. *Llegó un remolino chico [y] peleó con muchas fuerza manotadas y mordidas con lo que tenía debajo ... en la silla afianzado con las manos de las clinas de en medio de las [do]s orejas.* Fray Juan José Toledo, Report, Abiquiu, 15 May 1763, Pinart Collection, PE 52: 5.

74. Ibid.

75. Father Toledo's meandering style was commented on by Governor Vélez Cachupín in February 1764 when a commission of priests called together to deal with Toledo's exorcism report argued for two days over the wanderings of Toledo. Governor Vélez Cachupín, Report of the junta of priests, Santa Fe, 10 February 1764. AGN, Inquisición, 1001.

76. Fray Juan José Toledo, Report, Abiquiu, 15 May 1763, Pinart Collection, PE 52: 5. The connection between ants and witchcraft is not limited to anthill pebbles. In New Mexico, red ants were used as a cure for someone who is bewitched. The ants are washed, toasted in the oven, and ground into powder, which is ingested after a pinch of powder is placed on a strip of paper. Added to the powder are a teaspoon of sugar and a teaspoon of Wizzard Oil. Curtin, *Healing Herbs of the Upper Rio Grande*, 101–2.

77. *Los jueces al brazo con el Demonio partido para quitar de sus sangrientas garras tantas almas y privarle del culto antiguo que le dan muchos y estos maléficos ... que tengan ardor en el pecho y en las ocasiones sepan convertirse en volcán encendido. La resolución, el temor de Dios, la rectitud, fidelidad, prudencia, desinterés, ciencia y sabiduría son las armas para tan ardua empresa.* Fray Juan José Toledo, Report, Abiquiu, 15 May 1763, Pinart Collection, PE 52: 5.

78. For a discussion of how the confessional in Central Mexico had the effect of stripping Indians of their identity, see J. Jorge Klor de Alva, "Sin and Confession among the Colonial Nahuas: The Confessional as a Tool for Domination," in *La ciudad y el campo en la historia de México*, ed. Ricardo A. Sánchez Flores et al. (Mexico: Instituto de Investigaciones Históricas, Universidad Nacional Autónoma de México, 1992), 1:91–101; and J. Jorge Klor de Alva, "'Telling Lives': Confessional Autobiograhy and the Reconstruction of the Nahua Self," in *Spiritual Encounters: Interactions between Christianity and Native Religions in Colonial America*, ed. Nicholas Griffiths and Fernando Cervantes (Lincoln: University of Nebraska Press, 1999).

CHAPTER NINE: THE DEVIL

1. *Yo no hallo que decir ni como corren la pluma para comenzar a declarar la que a mí se me ofrece, pues es la lid y contienda con el Demonio, a que como ministro de Dios no puedo excusarme por ser dentro de mi jurisdicción y en mi casa.* Fray Juan José Toledo Toledo to Governor Tomás Vélez Cachupín, Abiquiu, 22 January 1764, Mexico, Inquisición, 1001:12.

2. Elaine Pagels, *The Origin of Satan* (New York: Random House, 1995), xxii, xxiii.

3. Cervantes, *Devil in the New World*, 17–21.

4. Heinrich Kramer and James Sprenger, *Malleus Maleficarum,* trans. Montague Summers (New York: Dover Publications, 1971), 1–88.

5. Montague Summers, Introduction to the 1928 edition of *Malleus Maleficarum*, viii.
    While we believe the Summers's translation to be accurate, there is much in his intro-
    duction that is not based on good scholarship and with which we do not agree, such as
    a statement that "the *Malleus Maleficarum* is among the most important, wisest, and
    weightiest books in the world," viii. Summers's notes and commentary should be used
    with extreme caution. Cervantes, *Devil in the New World*, discusses the *Malleus* and
    cites the Summers translation in his bibliography.
6. Ibid.
7. Ibid.
8. The best treatment of the Las Casas-Sepúlveda debate is Lewis Hanke, *The Spanish
    Struggle for Justice in the Conquest of the America* (Boston: Little, Brown, and
    Company, 1965); and Lewis Hanke, *Aristotle and the American Indians: A Study of Race
    Prejudice in the Modern World* (Bloomington: Indiana University Press, 1959). The lat-
    ter work focuses on how both Sepúlveda and Las Casas accepted Aristotle's theory that
    some men are born to be slaves. See also Ebright, "Advocates for the Oppressed,"
    305–6, 333, n.
9. José de Acosta, *Historia natural y moral de las Indias*, ed. Edmundo O'Gorman
    (Mexico: Fondo de Cultura Económica, 1962), 217, 231, 235, 255, 278; quoted in
    Griffiths, *Cross and the Serpent*, 51.
10. Griffiths, *Cross and the Serpent*, 85.
11. Ibid., 85–93.
12. Ibid., 92–93. Visionary experiences by the pre-Hispanic Incas were of great interest
    to Spanish theologians though they were discredited as superstition. During a water
    shortage in the ancient city of Cuzco, the Inca Roca prayed for a vision of a place
    where an irrigation canal could be constructed. While praying he heard a thunder-
    chap, put his ear to the ground, and heard water running underground. The Inca
    ordered an irrigation canal built on the spot, which eventually brought a plentiful
    supply of water to Cuzco. Since Andean religion was defined as devoid of value, such
    an event was seen as superstition, although Catholic Christianty is replete with mir-
    acles that are given credence. Sabine MacCormack, *Religion in the Andes: Vision and
    Imagination in Early Colonial Peru* (Princeton, N.J.: Princeton University Press,
    1991), 285–86, 386.
13. The early Christian theologians, such as Augustine, held that evil did not exist in itself
    but was subordinate to the will of God. In the thirteenth century Thomas Aquinas
    expanded on the idea that nothing was by nature evil, so that a principle of evil inde-
    pendent of God was an absurdity. About the same time Aquinas was writing, the idea
    that evil did exist independent of God began to take hold, led by a new emphasis on the
    Ten Commandments, instead of the seven deadly sins, as the basis of the traditional
    Christian moral system. The Devil, as the embodiment of evil, became the antitype of
    God, the embodiment of good and love. Cervantes, *Devil in the New World*, 18–20.
14. Arriaga, "La extirpación de la idolatría del Peru"; cited in Griffiths, *Cross and the
    Serpent*, 87–88, n. 60.
15. The term Nahua for the Nahuatl-speaking inhabitants of central Mexico is currently
    preferred over Aztec by anthropologists and historians of Mesoamerica. James
    Lockhart, *The Nahuas After the Conquest: A Social and Cultural History of the Indians
    of Central Mexico, Sixteenth through Eighteenth Centuries* (Stanford, Calif.: Stanford
    University Press, 1992), 1.
16. Louise M. Burkhart, *The Slippery Earth: Nahua-Christian Moral Dialogue in Sixteenth
    Century Mexico* (Tucson: University of Arizona Press, 1989), 26, 38–57.
17. Silverblatt, *Moon, Sun, and Witches*, 162–66; and Silverblatt, "Evolution of Witchcraft,"
    415–17.
18. Quoted in Burkhart, *Slippery Earth*, 55.
19. Ibid., 53–55.

20. Cervantes, *Devil in the New World*, 56–57.
21. Burkhart, *Slippery Earth*, 47–48.
22. Ibid., 47, 58–59.
23. Sarah L. Cline, "Native Peoples of Colonial Central Mexico," in *Mesoamerica*, ed. Richard E. W. Adams and Murdo J. MacLeod, vol. 2 of *The Cambridge History of the Native Peoples of the Americas* (Cambridge: Cambridge University Press, 2000), 199.
24. Burkhart, *Slippery Earth*, 38–39.
25. Florescano, *Myth of Quetzalcoatl*, 1.
26. Ibid., 38–45.
27. Griffiths, *Cross and the Seprent*, 3–7.
28. MacCormack, *Religion in the Andes*, 56–57.
29. Alcalde Carlos Fernández, Report, Abiquiu, 30 April 1763, Pinart Collection, PE 52: 5; for a drawing of a petroglyph near Abiquiu that contained added Christian crosses designed to eradicate the evil magic of the images, see Slifer, *Signs of Life*, 84–86.
30. In Peru the Spaniards went to great lengths to destroy all vestiges of stone deities such as grinding down the stone remains and throwing them in fast-flowing rivers. Even this extreme measure was not successful for the natives insisted that the site of the stone deity remained sacred. Griffiths, *Cross and the Serpent*, chap. 5, "Stones that Are Gods: The Response to Extirpation," 185–217, 197–98.
31. Riley suggests the likelihood that southwestern turquoise was traded to Mesoamericans for parrots and their feathers, and possibly peyote. Carroll L. Riley, "Mesoamerican Indians in the Early Southwest," *Ethnohistory* 21 (winter 1974): 33.
32. Riley estimates as many as two hundred Mexican Indians could have defected. Riley traces the similarities in religion and ceremonialism and material culture between Mesoamerican Indians and the New Mexico pueblos, as well as Zuni and Hopi. Riley, *Río del Norte*, 213–20.
33. Alfonso Ortiz, "Ritual Drama and the Pueblo World View," in *New Perspectives on the Pueblos*, ed. Alfonso Ortiz (Albuquerque: University of New Mexico Press, 1972), 140–45.
34. Griffiths, *Cross and the Serpent*, 67, 74–77.
35. In the Abiquiu witchcraft proceedings most of those who confessed to causing harm through witchcraft were sentenced to serving in the household of a Spaniard. In only one case did a sentence involve the possibility of banishment from New Mexico to serve in an obraje.
36. *Pleito criminal a Luis de Rivera, por tener pacto con el demonio y haberle ofrecido el alma en un adula que hizo con su sangre.* 1629–30. AGN, Inquisición, 366; cited and discussed in Scholes, "First Decade of the Inquisition," 208–14.
37. Ibid., 208–10; and Riley, *Kachina and the Cross*, 108–9.
38. Scholes, "First Decade of the Inquisition," 208–10.
39. Ibid., 208, 210–11.
40. Ibid., 212–13. The use of torture became accepted in both secular and ecclesiastic courts in medieval witchcraft trials. Torture was used as a last resort by the Spanish and Mexican Inquisitors and only in a minority of cases. Henry Kamen, *The Spanish Inquisition: A Historical Revision* (London: Weidenfeld and Nicolson, 1997), 188; Greenleaf, *Zumárraga*, 23; Levack, *Witch-Hunt*, 69–70.
41. Ibid., 211–13. For more on the use of herbs in New Mexico and the Inquisition, see Noemí Quesada, "The Inquisition's Repression of Curanderos," in *Cultural Encounters: The Impact of the Inquisition in Spain and the New World*, ed. Mary Elizabeth Perry and Anne J. Cruz (Berkeley: University of California Press, 1991), 37–57.
42. Scholes, "First Decade of the Inquisition," 210–13.
43. Michael Taussig, *The Devil and Commodity Fetishism in South America* (Chapel Hill: University of North Carolina Press, 1980), xi–xii, 13–14, 94–96.
44. Cervantes, *Devil in the New World*, 113–24.
45. Ibid., 116.

46. Case of Francisca Mejía, August 1691. Ibid., 116–17.
47. Fray Pablo Sarmiento to the Inquisition, Querétaro, 2 January 1692. Cervantes, *Devil in the New World*, 117–19.
48. Ibid., 121–24.
49. Ibid., 119.
50. Ibid., 130.
51. Ibid., 135–36.
52. Ibid., 129–32.
53. Ibid., 134–38.
54. AGN, Inquisición, 727.18, fols. 503 r.; cited in ibid., 137.
55. AGN, Inquisición, 760.22, fols. 241 v–261v; 760.23, fols. 265n–269v; cited in ibid., 137.
56. AGN, Inquisición, 803.54, fols. 510n, 511v, 519n; 817.30 fols 520r–525r; cited in ibid., 137.
57. Cervantes, *Devil in the New World*, 139.
58. Ibid., 139–40. The basic approach to medicine from the time of Hippocrates, who invented it, through the Renaissance was the theory of the four humours, the balance of which was the goal of medical practitioners. The humours were blood, phlegm, black bile, and yellow bile. A person whose constitution was dominated by the humour of phlegm, for instance, was phlegmatic. James Longrigg, "Medicine in the Classical World," in *Western Medicine: An Illustrated History*, ed. Irvine London (Oxford: Oxford University Press, 1997), 31–32.
59. Cervantes, *Devil in the New World*, 138–41.
60. Reyes Costilla and González de la Vara, "El pacto con el demonio," 199–207.
61. Ibid., 208, n. 22–24.
62. Ibid.
63. Ibid. 212, n. 38.
64. Ibid., 214, n. 43–45. Stacy Schaefer, "The Crossing of the Souls: Peyote Perception and Meaning Among the Huichol Indians," in *People of the Peyote*, ed. Schaefer and Furst, 138–68.
65. Reyes Costilla and González de la Vara, "El pacto con el demonio," 216–17, n. 49.
66. Ibid., 218, n. 52, 53.
67. Griffiths described nepantlism as one of four kinds of incomplete conversion to Christianity. The other three are compartmentalization, external syncretism, and internal syncretism. Griffiths, *Cross and the Serpent*, 14–15.
68. Ibid.
69. Robin Briggs, *Witches and Neighbors: The Social and Cultural Context of European Witchcraft* (New York: Viking, 1996), 3–4.

CHAPTER TEN: THE EXORCISMS

1. *Que consta de mucho tiempo estar maleficiado y ser buen indio; con la condición de que Joaquín no tentase ni sobase al enfermo ni menos lo sacase cosa alguna al enfermo.* Father Toledo to Alcalde Carlos Fernández, Abiquiu, 31 May 1763, Pinart Collection, PE 52: 19.
2. *Le sacó echó en la lumbre, y después de lo dicho se sentó en las brazas ardiendo en cueros, sin quemarse, subiéndole las llamas por todas partes, y que después como tomó unas brazas y se las metió en la boca y comenzó a expedir por boca y ojos chispas y llamas.* Ibid.
3. Ibid.
4. *Le arrimaba al dicho marido un diablo para que aborreciese a su mujer porque ésta no quería condescender en el acto.* Ibid.
5. *El maléfico Cascabel no consiguió su gusto.* Ibid.
6. Robert D. Martínez, "Fray Juan José Toledo and the Devil in Spanish New Mexico" (M.A. thesis, University of New Mexico, 1997), 57. Martínez's thesis contains a complete translation of the 22 January 1764 communication between Father Toledo and Alcalde Fernández, 56–73.
7. *De volver comenzó a hacerse pedazos con fuerzas más que naturales.* Father Toledo to

Alcalde Carlos Fernández, Abiquiu, 22 January 1764, AGN, Inquisición, 1001: 12.

8. *Tuvo cierta moción en el cuerpo con grande temor y espanto sin conocer de donde le provenía.* Ibid.

9. *Comenzó a dar furiosos espantosos gritos a que acudió la gente; respondió lo dicho admirada la trajeron a esta misión.* Ibid.

10. *A mi presencia luego que llegó y me vido fueron inponderables los gritos que dio y el extruendo de los miembros de su cuerpo y movimiento de los ojos: le daba necesitaba fatigarse la gente que la tenía para que no se le saliese . . . de las manos que era lo que procuraba poniéndose muy renegrida la fuerza de salirse soltando moquetes procurando morder y agarrar do los cabellos.* Ibid.

11. *Tan vivamente remedaba a los cochinos, vacas, burros, tecolotes y otros animales.* Ibid.

12. *Al instante tomo el libro de los exorcismos; chivato, coletudo, mulato.* Ibid.

13. *Haciendo el cuerpo un arco ya para arriba y ya para un lado y en el instante de dicho descaecimiento un pie se descalzaba con tal violencia que era incapaz excusarlo.* Ibid.

14. *Hasta la madrugada que el descanso que se le arbitró fue tirada en el suelo dando de rato en rato un alarido con voz muy alta como el que acostumbran dar los indios de la tierra.* Ibid.

15. *La india que por mal nombre le llaman la Atole Caliente.* Ibid.

16. Peter Charles Hoffer, *The Devil's Disciples: Makers of Salem Witchcraft Trials* (Baltimore, Md.: John Hopkins University Press, 1996), 58.

17. *Todas a una par cayeron en el suelo empezándose a exasperar y hacerse pedazos a que acudió gente a tenerlas y conociéndose presas comenzaron con grande alboroto a dar fuertes alaridos de indio cantos de guerra del que acostumbran los indios cuando muelan maíz y haciendo demostraciones con las manos de dicho exercicio y cuando paraban de alguna manía cantaban como tecolote, zora, cochino, vaca, etcétera.* Father Toledo to Alcalde Carlos Fernández, Abiquiu, 22 January 1764, AGN, Inquisición, 1001: 12; the Introit is the first of three parts of the Mass, the other two being the canon and communion. It included a psalm on humanity's sinfulness, followed by a general confession and absolution, the singing of the Gloria, and the recitation of the epistles, gospel, and Nicene Creed. Ramón Gutiérrez, *When Jesus Came, the Corn Mothers Went Away* (Stanford, Calif.: Stanford University Press, 1991), 61.

18. *En su desvergüenzas y gritos mayores cuando estaba sentado en la silla a la Gloria que fue menester mandarla echar de la iglesia.* Ibid.

19. *Sintió mucho el Demonio como se conoció en el cuerpo de dichas enfermas.* Ibid.

20. *Pasé por en medio a echar a la referida india cuyo atrevimiento me causó grande indisposición.* Ibid.

21. *A la vista de tanto concurso así.* Ibid.

22. In one sense, the girls' fits and spasms were similar to those suffered by the afflicted at Salem. Children, women, and men possessed or attacked by evil spirits often had fits. Well-known New England ministers such as Increase and Cotton Mather wrote books and gave sermons about these episodes, and, as John Hale noted, the accounts were widely read. Hoffer, *Devil's Disciples*, 58.

23. *Acuden andar los cuervos encima de sus cabezas delante o atrás de sus cuerpos en todos los viajes.* Father Toledo to Alcalde Carlos Fernández, Abiquiu, 22 January 1764, AGN, Inquisición, 1001: 12.

24. *Estuvieron sosegadas hasta en tanto que empecé a cantar las primeras cláusulas del Evangelio que se fueron soltando unas tras otras con sus visages extremecimientos temblores desmayos fuerzas y otras diferencias con muchas rizadas jácara ecétera.* Ibid.

25. *Con más fuerte maleficio que rinde a cuatro o seis hombres se la desató su lengua en su mal y comenzó a hablar.* Ibid.

26. Norton, *Devil's Snare*, 7, 120–22.

27. Malachi Martín, *Hostage to the Devil: The Possession and Exorcism of Five Contemporary Americans* (New York: Quality Paperback Book Club, 1976), append. 1: "The Roman Ritual of Exorcism," 465.

28.   *Todas en dicho día en lo que respondían se conocía entendían el latin que es la señal a más cierta en las palabras de los mayores misterios se reían daban alaridos haciendo jacara a lo decir in nomine Patri etcétera hacían con la cabeza la demostración de que no era trino . . . así de esta manera Francisca Varela preguntándola en latín que porque lastimaban dicha criatura respondió que venía de lo alto.* Father Toledo to Alcalde Carlos Fernández, Abiquiu, 22 January 1764, AGN, Inquisición, 1001: 12.

29.   A good discussion of the ways in which native belief systems in the Andes existed along side Catholicism, each influencing the other, is found in Griffiths, *Cross and the Serpent*, 13–21.

30.   *En Chimayó por maltratar y acabar con la ciudad.* Father Toledo to Alcalde Carlos Fernández, Abiquiu, 22 January 1764, AGN, Inquisición, 1001: 12.

31.   *Al demonio encolerizada y fuera de sí el que no se hizo sordo a venir trayiendo por señas extremeserse la casa como lo declaran los que se hallaban.* Ibid.

32.   *Teniéndola echó por la boca un diente de caballo con tanto trabajo que fue menester darle repetidas veces con la estola en la espalda.* Ibid. A stole was a long narrow band worn by a priest as one of his vestments; it sits around the neck and falls from the shoulders.

33.   Burkhart, *Slippery Earth*, 55.

34.   *Limpiar de tanta inmundicia la tierra . . . era voluntad del criador se acábase tanta adoración al Demonio.* Father Toledo to Alcalde Carlos Fernández, Abiquiu, 22 January 1764, AGN, Inquisición, 1001: 12.

35.   Joaquinillo, El Descubridor, provided another list of suspected sorcerers in response to a question from Governor Vélez Cachupín. See Appendix A for the names and descriptions of these accused sorcerers.

36.   Appendix A, List of Accused Sorcerers.

37.   Father Toledo to Alcalde Carlos Fernández, Abiquiu, 22 January 1764, AGN, Inquisición, 1001: 12.

38.   Appendix A, List of Accused Sorcerers.

39.   Ibid.

40.   Ibid.

41.   Ibid.

42.   Manuel García Parejas to Governor Tomás Vélez Cachupín, Abiquiu, 25 February 1764. AGN, Inquisición, 1001: 12.

43.   *Acabar de destruir y aniquilar el imperio del Demonio.* Ibid.

44.   During the extirpation of idolatry trials in colonial Peru, the Indians would often gather the pieces of sacred stones the Spaniards destroyed and continue to worship them at the old site. This led the Spaniards to resort to such extreme measures as grinding down stone remains and disposing them in fast-flowing rivers. Even when the stones, or *huacas*, were completely destroyed, the natives continued to bring offerings to the site because the soul of the huaca was thought to inhabit the spot where the huaca stood. Griffiths, *Cross and the Serpent*, 196–98.

45.   *Que luego que recibir el empleo de alcalde mayor haya ofrecido el bastón a María Santísima y a su Santísimo Hijo.* Manuel García Parejas to Governor Tomás Vélez Cachupín, Abiquiu, 25 February 1764, AGN, Inquisición, 1001: 12.

46.   *Me avizó de lo que debía hacer con su madre una hija mía.* Ibid.

47.   Martínez, "Fray Juan José Toledo," 85–86; and Rohn, Ferguson, and Ferguson, *Rock Art*, 117–18, 121–24.

48.   *Una piedra fuerte que estaba en la ruina antigua de un pueblo de gentiles cerca del rancho que era de Lobato.* Manuel García Parejas to Governor Tomás Vélez Cachupín, Abiquiu, 25 February 1764. AGN, Inquisición, 1001: 12.

49.   Norton, *Devil's Snare*, 213–17, 281–82, 287–88, 291; and Martínez, "Fray Juan José Toledo," 86.

50.   Martínez, "Fray Juan José Toledo," 89.

51.   *Un peñasco piramidal la figura del Demonio en forma de sierpe con dos cabezas . . . arriba*

de dicha figura una víbora pintada con cuernos mirando al oriente. Manuel García Parejas to Governor Tomás Vélez Cachupín, Abiquiu, 25 February 1764. AGN, Inquisición, 1001: 12.

52.   *Por todas figuras caracteres son treinta y dos mostrando una de ellas que era la mayor ser señor de mundo por tenerlo pintado a los pies y estar con las manos abiertas en forma de arce despidiendo centellas de cada mano bajo del brazo isquierdo tenía la luna y arriba tenía pintados las estrellas.* Ibid.

53.   Elsie Clews Parsons, *Pueblo Indian Religion* (Lincoln: University of Nebraska Press, 1996), 1:184–86, 186, n. *.

54.   Ibid.; Slifer, *Signs of Life*, 16–17.

55.   Parsons, *Pueblo Indian Religion*, 1:184–86.

56.   Ibid., 1:185, n. *.

57.   Martínez, "Fray Juan José Toledo and the Devil," 89.

58.   *Me cargo de su contexto con admiración del asunto, siendo de la mayor gravedad y difícil de la fe, y creencia que debe darse a las denuncias quese contienen hechas por los mismos Demonios por articulación de las mujeres energumeras.* Governor Tomás Vélez Cachupín, Decree, Santa Fe, 31 January 1764, AGN, Inquisición, 1001: 12.

59.   Vicente Trujillo, who had been governor of the Genízaro pueblo, was probably responsible for Father Ordoñéz's death. Simmons, *Witchcraft in the Southwest*, 32; and Griffiths, *Cross and the Serpent*, 195–96.

60.   Henry Charles Lea, *A History of the Inquisition of Spain* (New York: AMS Press, 1966), 4:348–49.

61.   Lyndal Roper, *Oedipus and the Devil: Witchcraft, Sexuality and Religion in Early Modern Europe* (London: Routledge, 1994), 174–75. In sixteenth-century Europe the spectacle of extended public exorcisms became so sensational that they were banned in 1568 and again in 1618.

62.   The most famous such case took place in Spain, beginning in the early decades of the seventeenth century and lasting to midcentury. It centered around Jerónimo de Villanueva, the Marqués de Villaba. The case is discussed at length in Lea, *History of the Inquisition*, 2:33–59.

63.   Governor Tomás Vélez Cachupín, Decree, Santa Fe, 31 January 1764, AGN, Inquisición, 1001: 12.

64.   Junta, Report, Santa Fe, 10 February 1764, AGN, Inquisición, 1001: 12.

65.   Governor Tomás Vélez Cachupín, Report, AGN, Provincias Internas, 102, translated in Thomas, *Plains Indians*, 69–72.

66.   Junta, Report, Santa Fe, 10 February 1764, AGN, Inquisición, 1001: 12.

67.   *Las piedras y lugares consabidos sean destruidos y reconocido se quemen cuantos ídolos se encontraren borrando figuras y caracteres llevando en su compañia al indio Joaquinillo para el efecto.* Governor Tomás Vélez Cachupín, Order, Santa Fe, 11 February 1764, AGN, Inquisición, 1001: 12.

68.   Ibid.

69.   *Y todas las vanas observancias y alaridos de la mañana lo que asi mismo se practicara en todas las demás jurisdicciones.* Ibid.

70.   Parsons, *Pueblo Indian Religion*, 438, 499, and 533; and Richard Parmentier, "The Mythological Triangle: Poseyemu, Montezuma, and Jesus in the Pueblos," in *Southwest*, ed. Alfonso Ortiz, vol. 9 of *Handbook of North American Indians*, ed. William C. Sturtevant (Washington, D.C.: Smithsonian Institution Press, 1979), 612. To the Pueblos, Poseyemu was more than a mythical figure. He was real as evidenced from Toledo's list of sorcerers (see Appendix A). Juan Felipe from Pojoaque was listed as the son of Poseyemu.

71.   Zuni gets its turtle shells from "the Zuni sacred lake on the summer solstice pilgrimage." Parsons, *Pueblo Indian Religion*, 141, 384–85, 438, 499, 533, 546.

72.   *A destruir las piedras parajes y lugares que se referían y quemar cuanto se*

encontrase de inmundos ídolos y diabólicas ofrendas borrando figuras y caracteres como se había hecho y mandado por mi antes. Junta, Report, Santa Fe, 10 February 1764, AGN, Inquisición, 1001: 12.

73. *A desterrar esta malicia de los indios.* Ibid.

74. Joaquinillo, Declaration, Santa Fe, 14 February 1764, AGN, Inquisición, 1001: 12.

75. The sorcerers that Joaquinillo said he could see reflected on the surface of the water were "Janisco, the Genízaro; Temba, San Juan Indian; Vicente, Nambe Indian (comes and goes by his art and spreads the news he brings from the people of Chimayo); Agustín, son of Cristóbal, interpreter from Santa Ana; Martín, Isleta Indian; El Cojo; an Indian from Sandia; Joaquín, the Suma; Mauricio, coyote from Ojo Caliente; Petrona, Come Gallinas, Genízara who is a prisoner in Santa Fe; Miguel Arias, Genízaro from Santa Fe; Petrona, Genízara; and José Manuel, son of the Genízaro Antonio, cacique from Belen." Joaquinillo, Declaration, Santa Fe, 14 February 1764, AGN, Inquisición, 1001: 12.

76. Ibid.

77. Vélez Cachupín took his characteristic pragmatic approach during this religious conflict dealing with the Genízaros. While he believed whole-heartedly in the goal of Chrisitianzing the Genízaros, he did not want to be so repressive that they would abandon the pueblo. Ibid.

78. *Se les manifiesta visible el Demonio y les manda lo que han de hacer y pronostica lo que ha de suceder.* Ibid.; and Parmentier, "Mythological Triangle," 612.

79. *En el que concurren todos las leyes de su gentilidad pues en el se le dan gracias a sus ídolos y éstos; las mujeres son comunes; los injurian públicamente haciendo irrición de la ley que sigue.* Juan Largo, Declaration, Santa Fe, 15 February 1764; and Governor Tomás Vélez Cachupín to Marqués de Ervillas, Viceroy of New Spain, Santa Fe, 28 March 1764, AGN, Inquisición, 1001: 12.

80. Juan Largo, Declaration, Santa Fe, 15 February 1764, ibid.

81. *Para instruir a los indios en su ley; para moler la harina que considera necesaria para dar de comer a los de la junta y estas hacen su trabajo . . . el casique a su primer oficial entregue a su músico una de aquellas indias sin exceptuar estado la que recibe dicho músico por manceba pública.* Ibid.

82. *Determinado que no crean lo que el padre dice que no hay Dios ni infierno.* Ibid.

83. *Pues aunque fuese a la Iglesia y pidiese algo a los santos nunca le hablarían ni le darían nada.* Joaquinillo, Declaration, Santa Fe, 14 February 1764, AGN, Inquisición, 1001: 12.

84. The nature of the Indians in the Americas had been debated since the famous debate between Juan Ginés de Sepúlveda and fray Bartolomé de las Casas. Hanke, *Spanish Struggle*; and Ebright, "Advocates for the Oppressed," 305, 333, n. 1.

85. *Las ocupaciones de servir a su amo no le daban tanto lugar de frecuentar la escuela de su maestro.* Juan Largo, Declaration, Santa Fe, 15 February 1764, AGN, Inquisición, 1001: 12.

86. *Siente que le aprietan la garganta y ocacionar una tos seca que le impide a hablar y lo atribuye a persecución del Demonio por hallarse arrepentido.* AGN, Inquisición, 1001: 12.

87. Governor Tomás Vélez Cachupín to Viceroy Marqués de Ervillas, Santa Fe, 28 March 1764. AGN, Inquisición, 1001: 12.

88. *La ruina espiritual de estos desdichados naturales no faltándoles.* Ibid.

89. Sylvia Rodríguez, *The Matachines Dance: Ritual Symbolism and Interethnic Relations in the Upper Rio Grande Valley* (Albuquerque: University of New Mexico Press, 1996), 65–91; and Leslie White, "The Pueblo of Santa Ana, New Mexico," *American Anthropologist* 44 (Oct.–Dec. 1942); reprint, New York: Kraus Reprint Co., 1969, 60–65.

90. Miguel Gandert, Enrique Lamadrid, Ramón Gutiérrez, Lucy Lippard, and Chris Wilson, *Nuevo México Profundo: Rituals of an Indo-Hispano Homeland* (Santa Fe and Albuquerque: Museum of New Mexico Press and National Hispanic Cultural Center of New Mexico, 2000), 56–59; and Gilbert Benito Cordova, "The Genízaro," manuscript in authors' possession.

91.   *Hacen asistir a todos los indios pequeños de ambos sexos a la doctrina hasta la edad en que se sacan y el día de fiesta al tiempo de la misa la resa todo el pueblo en lengua castellana guiados del fiscal.* Governor Tomás Vélez Cachupín to Viceroy Marqués de Ervillas, Santa Fe, 28 March 1764, AGN, Inquisición, 1001: 12.

92.   Viceroy Marqués de Cruillas to Governor Tomás Vélez Cachupín, Mexico City, Pinart Collection, PE 52: 18.

93.   *Sólo se confiesa en el artículo de muerte y por intérprete bien se arguye su incapacidad para que se casen y se hace preciso que las más veces los coja la justicia amancebados y hasta tanto viven en continua incontinencia.* Governor Tomás Vélez Cachupín to Viceroy Marqués de Ervillas, Santa Fe, 28 March 1764, AGN, Inquisición, 1001: 12.

94.   Klor de Alva, "Sin and Confession," 1:91–101; and Klor de Alva, "Sahagún and the Birth of Modern Ethnography: Representing, Confessing, and Inscribing the Native Other," in *The Work of Bernardino de Sahagun: Pioneer Ethnographer of Sixteenth-Century Aztec Mexico*, ed. J. Jorge Klor de Alva, H. B. Nicholson, and Eloise Quiñones Keber (Albany: Institute for Mesoamerican Studies, State University of New York, 1988), 31–52; Griffiths, *Cross and the Seprent*, 195–96.

95.   *Dóciles humildes y muy aplicados al cultivo y labor del campo cría de toda especie de ganados económicos y decentes en su vestuario.* Governor Vélez Cachupín to Viceroy Marqués de Ervillas, Santa Fe, 28 March 1764, AGN, Inquisición, 1001: 12.

96.   In his 1883 inspection of New Mexico Pueblos, Inspector C. H. Howard described the Pueblos as "peaceful, self-governing, self-supporting, and [of] well-disposed character."

97.   *Perversos y ociosos y con tales vicios que son ya muy gravosos en el país dificilísimos de sujetar y arreglarlos amantes de vivir vagos con sus familias de unos lugares a otros dispersos entre estas vecindades causando muchos perjuicios en laboras y ganados manteniéndose de lo que roban sin respecto de justicia cavilosos e incorregibles en sus excesos poseyendo el del juego en sumo grado.* Governor Vélez Cachupín to Viceroy Marqués de Ervillas, Santa Fe, 28 March 1764, AGN, Inquisición, 1001: 12.

98.   Governor Vélez Cachupín to Viceroy Marqués de Ervillas, Santa Fe, 28 March 1764, AGN, Inquisición, 1001: 12.

99.   *Los emplean en pastores y leñadores ejemplaresándolos en vicios de que abundan por lo escaso de sus obligaciones y rústica crianza de campo.* Governor Vélez Cachupín to Viceroy Marqués de Ervillas, Santa Fe, 28 March 1764, AGN, Inquisición, 1001:12.

100.   Jones, *Don Pedro León Luján*, 25–26.

101.   Rohn, Ferguson, and Ferguson, *Rock Art of Bandelier National Monument*, 117–18, 121–24.

102.   *Recoger estas vagas familias de genízaros y poblarlos en sitios cómodos a su subsistencia con doctrinero que los instruyese y administrase los santos sacramentos y que fuese fundación donde se recogiesen todos los que fuesen de esta naturaleza que en lo sucesivo saliesen del poder de sus amos ya casados.* Governor Vélez Cachupín to Viceroy Marqués de Ervillas, Santa Fe, 28 March 1764, AGN, Inquisición, 1001: 12.

103.   *En tierras útiles y competentes en el paraje más ameno y cómodo...Abiquiú Pueblo arruinado de los antiguos gentiles.* Governor Vélez Cachupín to Viceroy Marqués de Ervillas, Santa Fe, 28 March 1764, AGN, Inquisición, 1001:12.

104.   *Recopilación* book 6, title 3, law 8.

105.   *Ha sacado y puesto en prisiones seis malévolos indios que con sus maléficas hechicerías han dado muerte a mucha gente en aquel pueblo; ha destruido en aquellos contornos varios infernales parajes adoratorios ocultos de su idolatría.* Governor Tomás Vélez Cachupín to Viceroy Marqués de Ervillas, Santa Fe, 28 March 1764, AGN, Inquisición, 1001: 12.

106.   *Son casos muy raros y peregrinos, y nesecitan de más prueba que la simple narrativa de un solo sujeto para creerse.* Ibid.

107.   Ibid.

108. *Es muy irregular que el Demonio solicite el alivio de las almas santas del purgatorio.* Ibid.

109. *Hechándole hierbas en la comida y formando muñeca que lo representaba.* Governor Tomás Vélez Cachupín, Order reopening criminal proceedings and report, Santa Fe, 28 April 1764, Pinart Collection, PE 52: 5.

110. Miguel Tenorio seems to be the individual Chávez refers to as Miguel Tenorio II, who first married Bárbara Tafoya and then married in 1758 Teodora Fernández de la Pedrera, widow of Nicolás Baca of La Cienega. Chávez, *Origins,* 293.

111. Governor Tomás Vélez Cachupín, Order reopening criminal proceedings, Santa Fe, 28 April 1764, Pinart Collection, PE 52: 5.

112. The torture of hanging María from a cart's wheel was similar to, but less severe than, the torture imposed in the Yucatán idolatry proceedings where the priests administered a form of torture known as the *garrucha,* or hoist. "The friars proceeded to string up many of the Indians, having tied their wrists together with cord, and thus hoisted them from the ground, telling them that they must confess all the idols they had, and where they were. The Indians continued saying they had no more . . . and so the friars ordered great stones attached to their feet, and so they were left to hang for a space, and if they still did not admit to a greater quantity of idols they were flogged as they hung there, and had burning wax splashed on their bodies." Clendennin, *Ambivalent Conquest,* 74. Governor Tomás Vélez Cachupín, Report, Santa Fe, 28 April 1764, Pinart Collection, PE 52: 5.

113. *Que si hallara quién la enseñara a hechizar para hacer mal con alguna de las hierbas que por allí había.* María Trujillo, Confession, Santa Fe, 28 April 1764, Pinart Collection, PE 52: 5. Curtin lists Dragon's Blood as Sangre de Venado, literally deer's blood, "but it is in fact the Dragon's Blood of commerce, obtained particularly from the red resin of the Malayan rattan palm, Calamus draco." Curtin, *Healing Herbs of the Upper Rio Grande,* 179–80.

114. *Pedro Trujillo de que maleficiaba hecho gato; Pedro Trujillo la estaba matando hecho animal. Una poca de calabaza cocida con la intención de que se le aumentase el dolor de barriga.* Ibid.

115. *Tiene fama de serlo; pero que le consta que es muy negado, jurador, y maldiciente y que falta muchas noches de su casa y otras viene a media noche.* Ibid.

116. *Respondió que con la misma hierba colorado frotando con este polvo, el vientre, estómago, y pulmón de dicho reverendo padre; así el moler la hierba como la cura, sin intervenir ceremonia alguna.* Governor Tomás Vélez Cachupín, Report, Santa Fe, 30 April 1764; and María Trujillo, Confession, Santa Fe, 28 April 1764, Pinart Collection, PE 52: 5.

117. Indians in the Americas were formally removed from the jurisdiction of the Inquisition in 1571 by the Spanish crown. Osvaldo Pardo, "Contesting the Power to Heal: Angels, Demons, and Plants in Colonial Mexico," in *Spiritual Encounters: Interactions between Christianity and Native Religions in Colonial America,* ed. Nicholas Griffiths and Fernando Cervantes (Lincoln: University of Nebraska Press, 1999), 163–84. Quezada studied the cases of seventy-one curanderas prosecuted and sentenced by the Inquisition. She found that the curanderas were repressed for the magical part of their treatment, which frequently contained hallucinogens, but were tolerated if their curing procedures did not contain this element of superstition. Given the scarcity of doctors, curanderas offered a solution to the health problems of most of the population of colonial Mexico. Quezada, "Inquisition's Repression," 37–57.

118. *Dicho reverendo padre se halla notablemente aliviado de sus dolencias.* Governor Tomás Vélez Cachupín, Report, Santa Fe, 28 April 1764, Pinart Collection, PE 52: 5. Usually the Inquisition required a vote of the inquisitors that torture was necessary before it was applied in order to prevent the abuse and overuse of this severe procedure. Nevertheless, torture was commonly used by most courts in Europe from ancient times. Levack, *Witch-hunt,* 76–84; and David Pickering, *Dictionary of Witchcraft* (London: Cassell, 1996), 262–66.

119. Governor Tomás Vélez Cachupín, Decree, Santa Fe, 1 May 1764; and María Trujillo, Confession, Santa Fe, 28 April 1764, Pinart Collection, PE 52: 5.

120. *No sólo a los que están negativos, sino también a los confesos por si tuvieren que añadir a lo ya confesado.* Governor Tomás Vélez Cachupín, Decree, Santa Fe, 1 May 1764, Pinart Collection, PE 52: 5.

121. *Ni conoce al Diablo ni ha sido en nada contra Dios. Sabía comer padres.* Vicente Trujillo, Confession, Santa Fe, 4 May 1764, Pinart Collection, PE 52: 5.

122. For a discussion of the careo and examples of its use, see Cutter, *Legal Culture*, 128.

123. *Un indio de Abiquiú llamado Francisco que lo amarró y azotó cruelmente.* Pedro Trujillo and Miguel, El Cojo, Voluntary confessions, Santa Fe, 4 May 1764, Pinart Collection, PE 52: 5.

124. *Pedro Trujillo de que maleficiaba hecho gato; Pedro Trujillo la estaba matando hecho animal.* Ibid.

125. Governor Tomás Vélz Cachupín, Final Decree, Santa Fe, 16 September 1766, Pinart Collection, PE 52: 5.

126. *Cuando iban a cazar con unas plumas para cojer muchos venados.* Diego Tagle, Voluntary confesion, Santa Fe, 4 May 1764, Pinart Collection, PE 52: 5.

127. *Estando ya presos un día se puso Miguel, El Cojo, desnudo acostado boca arriba a contar y que llegó a la lumbreza una golondrina la que no había visto hasta que Mauricio una de los presos alabó al santísimo sacramento.* Ibid.

128. *Cuando . . . vivía en el Río Abajo, y el dicho Joaquín andaba curando.* Pedro, El Pasano, Voluntary confession, Santa Fe, 5 May 1764, Pinart Collection, PE 52: 5.

129. Antonio Ulibarrí, Voluntary confession, Santa Fe, 5 May 1764, Pinart Collection, PE 52: 5.

130. Alcalde Carlos Fernández, Report, Santa Fe, 5 May 1764, Pinart Collection, PE 52: 5.

131. *Ilícita amistad con una india genízara de dicho pueblo que se llamaba María de la Luz.* Antonio Menchero, Declaration, Santa Fe, 22 May 1764, and Governor Vélez Cachupín, Order, Santa Fe, 22 May 1764, Pinart Collection, PE 52: 5.

132. *Para ello le dio unos polvos, y le mando tragar una flecha y que al comenzar a tragarla le lastimó y la volvió a sacar de la boca y se la volvió al dicho Patricio junta con los polvos diciéndole que ya no quería aprender.* Ibid.

133. *Echándola en la tinaja de agua de que bebía dicho padre.* Antonio Menchero and Joaquinillo, Confrontation (careo) Santa Fe, 25 June 1764, Pinart Collection, PE 52: 5. Much of what was occurring at Abiquiu can be attributed to simple poisoning with or without associated witchcraft practices. The use of such poisons was widespread in Peru and Mexico before the Spanish conquest. Jan G. R. Elferink, "The Use of Poison and Malevolent Magic in Criminal Practices among the Incas in Pre-Columbian Peru," *Colonial Latin American Historical Review* 8 (summer 1999): 339–49; and Jan G. R. Elferink, José Antonio Flores, and Charles D. Kaplan, "The Use of Plants and Other Natural Products for Malevolent Practices Among the Aztecs and Their Successors," *Estudios de Cultura Nahuatl* 24 (1994): 27–47.

134. Antonio Menchero and Joaquinillo, Confrontation (careo) Santa Fe, 25 June 1764, Pinart Collection, PE 52: 5.

135. *Sabe curar hechizos.* Janisco, Declaration, Santa Fe, 22 May 1764, Pinart Collection, PE 52: 5. Nicholas Griffiths, "Andean Curanderos and their Repressors: The Persecution of Native Healing in Late Seventeenth- and Early Eighteenth-Century Peru," in *Spiritual Encounters: Interactions between Christianity and Native Religions in Colonial America*, ed. Nicholas Griffiths and Fernando Cervantes (Lincoln: University of Nebraska Press, 1999), 185–97.

136. *Muchos que padecían enfermedades y morían en aquel Pueblo Maleficiado.* Janisco, Joaquinillo and Juan Largo, Confrontation (careo), Santa Fe, 25 June 1764, Pinart Collection, PE 52: 5. To this day Abiquiu has an association with the reality and mythology of witchcraft. Father Stanley [Francis Louis Crocchiola], *The Abiquiú Story* (N.p.: n.d.), 1.

137.   *Joaquinillo era hechicero para curar y adivinar, y El Cojo mataba gente.* Janisco, Joaquinillo and Juan Largo, Confrontation (careo), Santa Fe, 25 June 1764 Pinart Collection, PE 52: 5.

138.   *Por dios, y con la Santa Cruz.* Ibid.

139.   *Dejando todo lo demás del cuerpo desnudo y de este modo haciendo horribles visages cantaba y bailaba y que esta era la cura que hacía.* Juan Tagle, Declaration, Santa Fe, 8 July 1764, Pinart Collection, PE 52: 5.

140.   *Es pública voz en todo el Río Abajo que el dicho Menchero es hechicero, y que el reverendo Padre Irigoyen . . . le dijo a el que declara que en un cepo habia de poner al mencionado Menchero hasta que muriese por hechicero.* Salvador García (Spaniard), Declaration, Santa Fe, 8 July 1764, Pinart Collection, PE 52: 5.

141.   *A dormir en ella, y aquella noche observó la mujer del declarante que Menchero no dormía sino que estaba despierto y como que la hechizaba; ya mencionado Menchero a su casa para ver si con alhajas y paga curaba a su mujer.* Ibid.

142.   *Un vapor con piedras calientes y ramas de sabina.* Ibid.

143.   Ibid.

144.   *Llamó a Menchero y le dijo: que se fuese de su casa y no volviese más a ella porque si lo hacía lo había de matar de un balazo.* Ibid.

145.   Joaquinillo El Descubridor, and Juan Largo, Declarations, Pinart Collection, PE 52: 5.

146.   *Quitados los grillos y puestos unas cormas de madera en la garganta de la pierna para que así estén aptos a salir a trabajar en las obras que se ofrezcan en estas casas del rey y presidio.* Governor Tomás Vélez Cachupín, Order, Santa Fe, 12 July 1764; and Salvador García (Spaniard), Declaration, Santa Fe, 8 July 1764, Pinart Collection, PE 52: 5.

147.   An example of a similar punishment was the one administered in the case against Tomás Méndez for his assault of Cristóbal Maese. In addition to paying Maese's medical expenses, Méndez was also required to make five hundred adobes to repair buildings in the Villa of Santa Fe. Cutter, *Legal Culture*, 137, citing SANM II: 105, Santa Fe, 28 December 1704.

148.   Governor Tomás Vélez Cachupín, Order, Santa Fe, 12 July 1764; and Salvador García (Spaniard), Declaration, Santa Fe, 8 July 1764, Pinart Collection, PE 52: 5.

149.   *Los muñecos figuras de madera . . . vuelta se quemen en una hoguera como los demás instrumentos de plumas y cuentas de vidrio que suponer pacto diabólico.* Ibid.

150.   Cervantes, *Devil in the New World*, 15–16.

151.   *Para que respecto a la magia en que están confesos, no obstante que se debe dudar cierta, y que no usado de ella para dañar con maleficio.* Governor Tomás Vélez Cachupín. Order, Santa Fe, 12 July 1764, Pinart Collection, PE 52: 5.

152.   *Había tenido el arte de adivinar y curar . . . ya le . . . estaba arrepentido, y así no podía usar del arte, y que aunque pudiera no lo hiciera, pues reconocía en el superiordad en dicho arte.* Ibid.

CHAPTER ELEVEN : PUNISHMENT

1.   The scepticism of Licenciado Felipe de Luna was similar to that exhibited by the Mexican Inquisition when confronted by the demoniacs of Querétaro, who threatened to turn the traditional concept of the Devil into an incredible and ridiculous idea. Cervantes, *Devil in the New World*, 136.

2.   *Es común sentir de los autores que el Demonio no puede penetrar interiores bien que puede inferirlos por algunas acciones externas.* Licenciado Felipe de Luna to the Viceroy, Mexico City, 29 June 1764, AGN, Inquisición, 1001:12.

3.   *Pidiese perdón de los agravios y todo lo que aconteció con dicho padre misionero.* Licenciado Felipe de Luna to the Viceroy, Mexico City, 29 June 1764, AGN, Inquisición, 1001: 12.

4.   Cervantes, *Devil in the New World*, 136.

5.   *Tiraba a impedir la empresa... la gente que iba con el tomáse la benedición y en el camino se fuese alabando al criador... y llamando a la Copetona que así nombra a la Santísima Virgen.* Licenciado Felipe de Luna to the Viceroy, Mexico City, 29 June 1764, AGN, Inquisición, 1001: 12.

6.   Ibid.

7.   Ibid.

8.   *Las justicias de su magestad al castigo de los hechiceros y maléficos son de la calidad que se fuesen y por la ley treinta y cinco, título primero, libro sexto de la Recopilación de Indias está mandado que contra los indios hechiceros que matan son hechizos y usan otros maleficios.* Ibid.

9.   Richard E. Greenleaf, *The Mexican Inquisition of the Sixteenth Century* (Albuquerque: University of New Mexico Press, 1969), 7–8.

10.   *Recopilación*, book 1, title 19, law 17. The tribunal of the Faith of Indians was also called the Office of Provisor of Natives, the Vicarage of the Indians, and Native's Court. Robert Moreno de los Arcos, "New Spain's Inquisition for Indians from the Sixteenth to the Nineteenth Century," in *Cultural Encounters: The Impact of the Inquisition in Spain and the New World*, ed. Mary Elizabeth Perry and Anne J. Cruz (Berkeley: University of California Press, 1991), 23–36, 23. See also the books and articles of Richard E. Greenleaf: *Zumáraga;* "The Mexican Inquisition and the Indians: Sources for the Ethnohistorian," *The Americas* 34 (Jan. 1978): 315–44; and "Persistence of Native Values: The Inquisition and the Indians of Colonial Mexico," *The Americas* 50 (Jan. 1994): 351–76.

11.   List of Accused Sorcerers (Appendix A), AGN, Inquisición, 1001:12; Martínez, "Fray Juan José Toledo," 131–36.

12.   List of Accused Sorcerers (Appendix A), AGN, Inquisición, 1001:12.

13.   Ibid.

14.   *Rejas, bueyes y otros ganados herramientas y utencilios que acostumbran darse a las nuevas misiones.* Licenciado Felipe de Luna to the Viceroy, Mexico City, 29 June 1764, AGN, Inquisición, 1001: 12.

15.   *O es precisamente de la jurisdicción eclesiástica.* Ibid.

16.   For a controversy regarding land rights and boundaries of Santa Ana Pueblo that was decided in a similar way by the Audiencia of Guadalajara, see Malcolm Ebright and Rick Hendricks, "Making the Best of Both Worlds: Santa Ana Pueblo's Land Acquisitions, 1700–1850" (unpublished manuscript), 40–43. New Mexico was under the jurisdiction of the Audiencia of Guadalajara throughout the Spanish colonial period. Cutter, *Legal Culture*, 53.

17.   Licenciado Felipe de Luna to the Viceroy, Mexico City, 29 June 1764, AGN, Inquisición, 1001: 12.

18.   *Por ser todo aquel terreno de guerra viva fronterizo por todos cuatro vientos de naciones bárbaras enemigas,* Ibid.

19.   Viceroy Marqués de Cruillas to the Holy Tribunal of the Inquisition, Mexico City, 17 February 1765, AGN, Inquisición, 1001: 12.

20.   Licenciado Vicente on behalf of the Holy Tribunal of the Inquisition, Mexico City, 5 March 1765, AGN, Inquisición, 1001: 12.

21.   Ibid.

22.   Ibid.

23.   Lea, *History of the Inquisition of Spain*, 2: 181.

24.   *Todos sus vecinos españoles e indios milicianos que siempre están prevenidos con las armas en la mano esperando las irrupciones que de la noche a la mañana suelen hacer las enemigas bábaras naciones.* Licenciado Felipe de Luna to the Viceroy, Mexico City, 29 June 1764, AGN, Inquisición, 1001: 12.

25.   Ibid.

26.   Pedro Trujillo and Miguel, El Cojo, Voluntary confessions, Santa Fe, 4 May 1764, Pinart Collection, PE 52: 5.

27. Governor Tomás Vélez Cachupín, Final decree, Santa Fe, 16 September 1766, Pinart Collection, PE 52: 5.
28. *Han suplicado poniendo por intercesor a nuestro señor, Príncipe de Asturias, la terminación de su causa y libertad de prision.* Ibid.
29. *Se le ha hecho instruir en la doctrina cristiania confesado y comulgado anulmente cantanda alabanzas a Dios y rezando todas las noches el Santísimo Rosario.* Ibid.
30. Ibid.
31. *Cantanda alabanzas a Dios y rezando todas las noches el Santísimo Rosario.* Ibid.
32. Vicente Trujillo's codefendant, José Domínguez, admitted to having sexual intercourse with Polonia Mestas, after she had received the last rites and was about to die. José Domínguez "convinced her that copulation was what she required to get well" [*Pretendió para tener cópulo con el pretexto de medicinarla en esta forma*]. Besides banishment from Abiquiu, Domínguez was tied to the whipping post (*picota*), where he was to be given twenty lashes for three consecutive days in front of the entire population of the pueblo of Abiquiu. After receiving the whipping he was to remain tied to the picota (without his wounds being treated) for an hour as a warning and lesson to the rest of the pueblo. Case against José Domínguez, Abiquiu, 1782, AASF, Loose Documents, 1782: 5.
33. *Si volvieren a incurir en la culpa de hechiceros maleficios o curanderos por ensalmos supersticiosos la de docientos azotes y perpetua cárcel en el dicho obraje.* Vélez Cachupín, Final decree. 16 September 1766.
34. Lea, *History of the Inquisition*, 3:133–34.
35. Another well-known example of public shame inflicted on a female defendant was the case of Ana María Romero, who was sentenced to being paraded through the Santa Fe plaza on a horse, stripped naked to the waist, and banished to Albuquerque. Case against Ana María Romero for slander, Santa Fe, 20 January 1716, SANM II: 267.
36. *Que sirva de escarmiento y ejemplar;" "sea puesta a la vergüenza pública, emplumada por quatro horas.* Vélez Cachupín, Final decree. 16 September 1766.
37. *Se mantega en perpetuo deposito hasta su muerto.* Ibid.
38. The five sorcerers who died in the Santa Fe jail were Agustín Tagle, Antonio Ulibarrí, Antonio Chimayó, Diego Tagle, and Juan Tagle. Governor Tomás Vélez Cachupín, Final decree, Santa Fe, 16 September 1766, Pinart Collection, PE 52: 5.
39. At Salem, four of the accused witches and sorcerers died in prison. Giles Corey was pressed to death for refusing to take part in the proceedings, and nineteen of the accused were executed between June 10 and September 22, 1692. For a complete listing of confessions, executions, and other outcomes of the Salem witchcraft trials, see Breslaw, *Tituba*, 183–86.
40. In Europe in the three centuries from 1450 to 1750 it has been estimated that 110,000 individuals were tried for the crime of witchcraft and 60,000 were executed. Levack, *Witch-hunt in Early Modern Europe*, 24–25.

CHAPTER TWELVE: RESISTANCE AND REVITALIZATION

1. For a discussion of the types of native shamanic practitioners in colonial Peru, see Griffiths, *Cross and the Serpent*, 99, 151–52.
2. *Para dañar con maleficio.* Vélez Cachupín, Final decree. 16 September 1766. Griffiths, *Cross and the Serpent*, 99, 151–52.
3. Riley, *Kachina and Cross*, 107–8; Kluckhohn, *Navajo Witchcraft*, 8; Keith H. Basso, *Western Apache Witchcraft* (Tucson: University of Arizona Press, 1969), 29–39; and Jerrold E. Levy, Raymond Neutra, and Dennis Parker, *Hand Trembling, Frenzy Witchcraft, and Moth Madness: A Study of Navajo Seizure Disorders* (Tucson: University of Arizona Press, 1987), 19–38; and Walker, *Witchcraft and Sorcery*, 1–3.
4. Walker, *Witchcraft and Sorcery*, 4.
5. Fray Bernardino de Sahagún was born about 1499 in Sahagún, Spain (near León),

came to New Spain in 1529 and died in 1590. Burkhart, *Slippery Earth*, 199–202; Walden Browne, *Sahagún and the Transition to Modernity* (Norman: University of Oklahoma Press, 2000), 186–87 takes a somewhat contrary view regarding many of the accepted notions regarding Sahagún. According to Brown, Sahagún "was not convinced that everything about Nahua culture was demonic. He was, in fact, interested in the good qualities of the pre-Hispanic Nahuas as he was in what he saw as the bad qualities."

6. Burkhart, *Slippery Earth*, 181–82.

7. Ibid.

8. Motolinía was a Nahuatl name adopted by fray Toribio de Benavente, "who was one of the so-called 'First Twelve' missionaries to arrive in New Spain in 1524." Walden Browne, "When Worlds Collide: Crisis in Sahagún's *Historia universal de las cosas de la Nueva España*," *Colonial Latin American Historical Review* (spring 1996): 103–10; and Robert Ricard, *The Spiritual Conquest of Mexico: An Essay on the Apostolate and the Evangelizing Methods of the Mendicant Orders in New Spain, 1523–1572*, trans. Lesley Byrd Simpson (Berkeley: University of California Press, 1966), 117–20.

9. Browne, "When Worlds Collide," 110–11; Ricard, *Spiritual Conquest*, 57, 186–87, 230; and Riley, *Kachina and the Cross*, 125.

10. Cervantes, *Devil in the New World*, 15.

11. Mills, *Idolatry*, 13–14.

12. Cervantes, *Devil in the New World*, 11.

13. Ibid., 13. See also Richard E. Greenleaf, *Zumárraga and the Mexican Inquisition, 1536–1543* (Washington, D.C.: Academy of American Franciscan History, 1961), 37–75 and passim.

14. Greenleaf, "Mexican Inquisition and the Indians," 323–25; and Greenleaf, "Persistence of Native Values," 351–54, 372–74.

15. Fray Juan José Toledo to Governor Francisco Antonio Marín del Valle, Abiquiu, 26 July 1760, Pinart Collection, PE 52: 5.

16. Ibid.

17. Father Toledo to Alcalde Carlos Fernández, Abiquiu, 22 January 1764, AGN, Inquisición, 1001: 12.

18. Declaration of Janisco, Santa Fe, 22 May 1764, Pinart Collection, PE 52: 5.

19. Elferink, *Use of Poison*, 339–60.

20. Martínez, "Fray Juan José Toledo," 101–3.

21. Kessell, *Kiva, Cross, and Crown*, 383–85, 392–93.

22. Norton, *Devil's Snare*, 297–98.

23. Examples of these early community grants made by Governor Vélez Cachupín are the Las Tampas grant, Malcolm Ebright, *Land Grants and Lawsuits in Northern New Mexico* (Albuquerque: University of New Mexico Press, 1994), 145–68; and the 1764 San Gabriel de las Nutrias grant. Ebright, "Breaking New Ground," 203–10.

24. For example, west of the Abiquiu grant was the Polvadera grant made to Juan Pablo Martín Serrano by Governor Vélez Cachupín.

25. Governor Tomás Vélez Cachupín, Report, Santa Fe. 28 March 1764, AGN, Inquisicion, 1001:12.

26. Briggs, *Witches and Neighbors*, 3; and Laura A. Lewis, *Hall of Mirrors: Power, Witchcraft and Caste in Colonial Mexico* (Durham, N.C.: Duke University Press, 2003), 232–33, n. 5.

27. Poling-Kempes, *Valley of Shining Stone*, xviii. The Abiquiu commuity still believes that it could be either a pueblo or a Hispano community.

28. Portillo y Urrisola had attacked the Comanches who came to Taos to negotiate the release of Hispanic prisoners taken in the Villalpando Raid. The Comanches were willing to release these captives, three women and four boys, in return for the right to trade at Taos. Manuel Portillo Urrisola to Bishop Tamarón, Santa Fe, 24 February 1762, translated in Adams, *Bishop Tamarón's Visitation*, 59–62.

29. Governor Tomás Vélez Cachupín, Report. Santa Fe, 28 April 1764. Pinart Collection, PE 52:5.

30.   Antonio Domínguez Ortiz, "Iglesia institucional y religiosidad popular en la España barroca," in *La fiesta, la ceremonia, el rito* (Granada, Spain: Casa de Velásquez, 1990), 19. Martínez, "Fray Juan José Toledo," 101–102.

31.   Lea, *History of the Inquisition in Spain*, 4:350–51; see also, Cervantes, *Devil in the New World*, 113–24.

32.   Burkhart, *Slippery Earth*, 173–74.

33.   Sandos, *Converting California: Indians*, 156; citing Bolton, "The Mission as a Frontier Institution in the Spanish American Colonies," 44–45.

34.   "Witchcraft is... the classical resort of vulnerable subordinate groups, who have little or no safe, open opportunity to challenge a form of domination that angers them." Scott, *Domination and the Arts of Resistance*, 144.

35.   Sandos, *Converting California: Indians*, 158–59.

36.   Ibid., 162–63.

37.   Ibid., 164.

38.   List of Accused Sorcerers, Appendix A.

39.   Ibid.; Parmentier, "Mythological Triangle," 609, 612–13.

40.   Parmentier, "Mythological Triangle," 612–13.

41.   Griffiths, *Cross and the Serpent*, 158–59, 189.

EPILOGUE: NEW IDENTITIES

1.   The possibility of having Abiquiu declared a Genízaro pueblo is buttressed by the fact that the patent is to the half-breed Indians of Abiquiu. Isabel Trujillo, Interview, Abiquiu, 8 October 2004; and Floyd Trujillo, Inverview, Abiquiu, 8 January 2005.

2.   In 2003 a delegation of twenty-five Hopis visited Abiquiu. Virgil Trujillo, Interview, Abiquiu, 10 October 2004.

3.   Swadesh, *Primeros Pobladores*, 46.

4.   Protest by Ventura Bustamante, teniente de los indios Genízaros, on behalf of thirty-three companions against being removed from Santa Fe to the Comanche frontier, SANM II: 1138.

5.   The southern boundary of the Abiquiu pueblo grant was established by measuring 10,700 varas from the Abiquiu pueblo. Since the pueblo with its plaza, church, and community buildings is on the far northern side of the grant, measuring from this point approximately 10,000 varas to the south was similar to measuring 5,000 varas in each direction from the center of the pueblo. Survey and field notes for the Abiquiu grant, BLM, Santa Fe. Ebright and Hendricks, "Pueblo League," 4:91–178.

6.   For more on the Cruzate grants, see Sandra K. Mathews-Lamb, "'Designing and Mischievous Individuals': The Cruzate Grants and the Office of the Surveyor General," *New Mexico Historical Review* 71 (Oct. 1996): 341–59; and Town of Abiquiu grant, SG 140, roll (r.) 26, frame (f). 279, PLC 52, r. 38, f. 884, et seq.

7.   Surveyor General Julian, Report, Santa Fe, 28 October 1885. Abiquiu grant, SG 140, r. 26, f. 409–40, esp. f. 434–35.

8.   Lesley Poling-Kempes, "A Call to Place," in *Georgia O'Keeffe and New Mexico* (Princeton, N.J.: Princeton University Press; and Santa Fe: Georgia O'Keeffe Museum, 2004), 87. Georgia O'Keeffe lived from 1887 to 1986, but her predecessor in the house on the Abiquiu plaza, José María Chávez, lived to 101 years, most of the nineteenth century.

9.   Abiquiu grant, PlC 52, r. 38, f. 884, et seq. For a discussion of the machinations of General José María Chávez, Thomas B. Catron, and Ramón Salazar to acquire control of the Piedra Lumbre grant northwest of the Abiquiu grant, see Poling-Kempes, *Valley of Shining Stone*, 108–11.

10.   Bowden, "Private Land Clams," 4:1107.

11.   Virgil Trujillo, Interview, 8 January 2005.

12.   Floyd Trujillo and Virgil Trujillo, Interview, Abiquiu, 8 January 2005. Virgil Trujillo

interviewed his grandfather, Benjamín Archuleta, in 1984–89 who recounted the story of Abiquiu's vote to become a hispanic village instead of an Indian Pueblo. An unannotated version of this story is in Poling-Kempes, *Valley of Shining Stone*, 143–44.

13.   Poling-Kempes, *Valley of Shining Stone*, 143–44. Until recent years, children from Abiquiu have been considered eligible for and have attended the Indian School in Santa Fe. Floyd Trujillo, Interview, Abiquiu, 8 January 2005.

14.   Suzanne Forrest, *The Preservation of the Village: New Mexico's Hispanics and the New Deal* (Albuquerque: University of New Mexico Press, 1989), 146–47; Poling-Kempes, *Valley of Shining Stone*, 143–44; and Virgil Trujillo, Interview, Abiquiu, 9 October 2004.

15.   Virgil Trujillo, Interview, Abiquiu, 8 January 2005.

16.   Steele and Rivera, *Penitente Self-Government*, 11, n. 16.

17.   *Abiquiu citizens v. fray Teodoro Alcina*, ibid.; AASF, Loose Documents 1820:15 and fray Bruno González to fray Teodoro Alcina, ibid.: 26.

18.   Ahlborn, *Penitente Moradas*, 130, 136; Poling-Kempes, *Valley of Shining Stone*, 90.

19.   Petition to the ayuntamiento complaining of Father Alcina's neglect of duty and asking for changes in saying Mass and in the amount of fees. Ojo Caliente, 1 October 1820, SANM II: 2934, and *Abiquiu citizens v. fray Teodoro Alcina*, AASF, Loose Documents, 1820: 15.

20.   Fray Angélico Chávez, "The Penitentes of New Mexico," *New Mexico Historical Review* 29 (1954): 108–11; and Ahlborn, *Penitente Moradas*, 128–29.

21.   Ahlborn notes that in 1888 Archbishop Jean Bapiste Salpointe pleaded for the penitentes "to return" to the Third Order. Ahlborn, *Penitente Moradas*, 126.

22.   Chávez, "Penitentes of New Mexico," 108–11; Ahlborn, *Penitente Moradas*, 128–29; Adams and Chávez, *Missions of New Mexico*, 124.

23.   Fray Angélico Chávez, *But Time and Chance: The Story of Padre Martínez of Taos, 1793–1867* (Santa Fe: Sunstone Press, 1981), 21, 45.

24.   Dennis Daily, "Tropas de Jesús: Brotherhood Ties on New Spain's Northern Frontier" (manuscript in authors' possession, May 2004), 16.

25.   Information about the number of cofradías and brotherhoods in the districts and pueblos of the province of Durango, 1789, AHAD-4, f. 534–86; cited in Daily, "Tropas de Jesús."

26.   Ibid., 17.

27.   One of the charges against Father Alcina was that he tried to charge José Manuel Montoya a fee to bury his sister-in-law. The fee was a male mule (*macho*), about fifty pesos. José Manuel Montoya, Testimony, Abiquiu, 21 October 1820, AASF, 1820: 15.

28.   *Obligación de predicarnos punta de la doctrina o el Evangelio como lo ordena el Santo Concilio de Trento*. Constitucional Alcalde Santiago Salazar, Petition on behalf of the vecinos of the jurisdiction of Abiquiu, Abiquiu, 8 October 1820, AASF, 1820:15.

29.   According to Dozier, Pueblo religious practices "are free of Catholic elements," and the observance of Catholic ritual "is separate and distinct from that accorded their own native practices." Edward P. Dozier, response to Edward H. Spicer, "Spanish-Indian Acculturation in the Southwest," *American Anthropologist* 56 (1954): 681. Genízaro religious practices are still celebrated at the Santo Tomás feast day in November when the Nanillé dance is performed. Gandert, et al., *Nuevo México Profundo*, 57–58.

30.   John Kessell, Personal communication, 7 June 2005.

31.   Domínguez lists all the "valuables of Our Lady," and then states, "The saint's adornment is changed, and what she is not wearing is kept in a small chest." Adams and Chávez, *Missions of New Mexico*, 123. It was in that chest that Vicente Trujillo found the gold cross that he took from the chest and sold.

32.   *Fray Ramón Antonio González v. José Domínguez and Vicente Trujillo*, AASF, Loose Documents, 1782: includes a May–June 1786 case against Domínguez and Vicente Trujillo.

33.   Ahlborn, *Penitente Moradas*, 126–29.

34.   Frank J. Wozniak, Meade F. Kemrer, and Charles M. Carrillo, *History and Ethnohistory*

Along the Rio Chama (Albuquerque: U.S. Army Corps of Engineers, 1992), 127, citing "Juanita Córdova, personal communication, 1982." Isabel Trujillo, Interview, Abiquiu, 8 October 2004; and Floyd Trujillo, Inverview, Abiquiu, 8 January 2005.

35.   According to one story, the Abiquiu villagers decided to become a Hispanic village because the pueblo communities were treated so badly by the U.S. government that it would behoove the community to become a village, not an official Indian pueblo. Poling-Kempes, *Valley of Shining Stone*, 144.

36.   Dede Happe, Interview, Abiquiu, 8 January 2005.

GLOSSARY

Alabado	Penitente hymn
Alcalde	Local official with civil and judicial functions
Alguacil	An Indian or Hispanic official who performs the function of a bailiff or constable (similar to a policeman); a disciplinarian within a pueblo
Audiencia	The highest court of appeal in New Spain
Cacique	The title of a native religious leader
Calidad	Class
Careo	A stage in a criminal proceeding involving a face-to-face confrontation between parties
Casas reales	Government buildings
Casta	Lineage, caste
Cepos	Stocks used for punishment; similar to the wooden stocks the Puritan's used in Salem
Cofradía	A lay religious association for devotional and charitable purposes
Cormas de madera	Wooden fetters tied to the instep of a prisoner's foot so he could not run away
Cruzate grant	Land grants to most New Mexico pueblos supposedly issued by Governor Domingo Jironza Petrís de Cruzate in 1689 but later determined to be forgeries
Curandera	Traditional healer who often uses herbs to heal
Custos	Franciscan prelate, head of a jurisdiction called a "custodia," ranking below that of a province
Demonio	A demon or the Devil
Fiscal	A warden of a church who is often in charge of discipline
Grilletes	Smaller version of the *grillo*, used only for the wrist (like handcuffs)

Grillos	Shackles or leg irons
Hechicería	Sorcery, witchcraft
Hechicero/a	Sorcerer/witch, medicine man, shaman
Hechizo	A spell or bewitchment
Heresy	Beliefs that contradict the dogma or orthodox belief of one's own belief system
Hermitage	Small chapel or place of refuge and meditation; not a mission
League	A land measurement used in Spanish colonial New Mexico and elsewhere equivalent to 5,000 varas or 2.63 miles; the distance a horseback rider could cover in one hour over level terrain at a normal gait
Licenciado	A university graduate, lawyer, or priest
Macana	An obsidian-edged wooden club
Nepantla	A Nahuatl word meaning "in the middle," used by priests such as Diego Durán to describe the religious status of native populations such as the Nahua in Mexico
Patronato real	An agreement between the Catholic monarchs and the pope whereby in return for assistance in maintaining the Church, the monarchs and their delegates enjoyed certain patronage rights involving appointments, offices, and finances
Picota	Pillory; a vertical stake to which a person was tied, often while they were whipped
Poseyemu	A culture hero in Pueblo creation stories, a god or powerful mortal who brings mankind the arts of civilization by stealing fire from the gods, for example
Reo	Prisoner, defendant, accused
Sapo	Toad
Sacristan	A pueblo official in charge of maintaining the cleanliness and order in the sacristy of the church
Sortílego	Diviner, soothsayer
Sumaria	A fact-finding inquiry by a magistrate commissioned to investigate the circumstances surrounding the commission of a crime
Surplice	An outer vestment of white linen worn by a priest over his cassock
Vara	A Castilian yard, about 33 inches or 84 centimeters
Vecino	Land-owning Spanish citizen; a householder in a census
Yerba	Herb, medicinal plant

WORKS CITED

PUBLISHED WORKS

Acosta, José de. *Historia natural y moral de las Indias.* Edited by Edmundo O'Gorman. Mexico: Fondo de Cultura Económica, 1962.

Adams, Eleanor B., ed. *Bishop Tamarón's Visitation of New Mexico, 1760.* Albuquerque: Historical Society of New Mexico, 1954.

———. "Two Colonial New Mexico Libraries, 1704, 1776." *New Mexico Historical Review* 19 (Apr. 1944): 135–67.

Adams, Eleanor B., and Fray Angélico Chávez, translators and annotators. *The Missions of New Mexico, 1776: A Description by Fray Francisco Atanasio Domínguez, with other Contemporary Documents.* Albuquerque: University of New Mexico Press, 1956.

Ahlborn, Richard E. *The Penitente Moradas of Abiquiú.* Washington, D.C.: Smithsonian Institution Press, 1968.

Arriaga, Pablo José de. "La extirpación de la idolatría del Perú." In *Crónicas peruanas de interés indígena.* Biblioteca de Autores Españoles, 209. Edited by Francisco Esteve Barba. Madrid: Atlas, 1968.

Athearn, Frederic J. *A Forgotten Kingdom: The Spanish Frontier in Colorado and New Mexico, 1540–1821.* Denver: Colorado State Office, Bureau of Land Management, 1992.

Axtell, James. *The European and the Indian: Essays in the Ethnohistory of Colonial North America.* Oxford: Oxford University Press, 1981.

Bailey, L. R. *Indian Slave Trade in the Southwest.* Los Angeles: Westernlore Press, 1966.

Bancroft, Hubert Howe. *History of Arizona and New Mexico, 1530–1888.* Albuquerque: Horn and Wallace, 1962.

Basso, Keith H. "Southwest: Apache." In *Witchcraft and Sorcery of the American Native Peoples.* Edited by Deward E. Walker Jr. Moscow: University of Idaho Press, 1989.

———. *Western Apache Witchcraft.* Tucson: University of Arizona Press, 1969.

Beck, Warren A. *New Mexico: A History of Four Centuries.* Norman: University of Oklahoma Press, 1962.

Behar, Ruth. "Sexual Witchcraft, Colonialism, and Women's Powers: Views from the Mexican Inquisition." In *Sexuality and Marriage in Colonial Latin America.* Edited by Asunción Lavrin. Lincoln: University of Nebraska Press, 1989.

Bolton, Herbert E. *Pageant in the Wilderness.* Salt Lake City: Spanish Historical Society, 1950.

Bourke, John G. *The Snake-Dance of the Moquis of Arizona.* Tucson: University of Arizona Press, 1984.

Bowden, J. J. "Private Land Claims in the Southwest." M.A. thesis. Southern Methodist University, 1969.

Boyd, E. "Troubles at Ojo Caliente: A Frontier Post." *El Palacio* (Nov. –Dec. 1957): 347–60.

Boyer, Laura, with Floyd Montoya, and the Pueblo of Santa Ana. *Santa Ana: The People, the Pueblo, and the History of Tamaya.* Albuquerque: University of New Mexico Press, 1994.

Breslaw, Elaine G. *Tituba, Reluctant Witch of Salem: Devilish Indians and Puritan Fantasies.* New York: New York University Press, 1996.

Briggs, Robin. *Witches and Neighbors: The Social and Cultural Context of European Witchcraft.* New York: Viking Press, 1996.

Brooks, James F. *Captives & Cousins: Slavery, Kinship, and Community in the Southwest Borderlands.* Chapel Hill: University of North Carolina Press, 2002.

———. "This Evil Extends Especially to the Feminine Sex: Negotiating Captivity in the New Mexico Borderlands." *Feminist Studies* 22 (summer 1996): 279–309.

Brown, Tracy. "Ideologies of Indianness in New Mexico, 1692–1820: Personhood and Identity in the Colonial Encounter." Ph.D. diss. Duke University, 2000.

Browne, Walden. *Sahagún and the Transition to Modernity.* Norman: University of Oklahoma Press, 2000.

———. "When Worlds Collide: Crisis in Sahagún's *Historia universal de las cosas de la Nueva España.*" *Colonial Latin American Historical Review* (spring 1996): 101–49.

Brugge, David M. *Navajos in the Catholic Church Records of New Mexico, 1694–1875.* Window Rock, Ariz.: Research Section, Parks and Recreation Dept., Navajo Tribe, 1968.

Burkhart, Louise M. *The Slippery Earth: Nahua-Christian Moral Dialogue in Sixteenth Century Mexico.* Tucson: University of Arizona Press, 1989.

Cabanellas de las Cuevas, Guillermo, and Eleanor C. Hoague. *Diccionario Jurídico Español-Inglés Butterworths.* Austin: Butterworth Legal Publishers, 1991.

Calloway, Donald, Joel Janetsky, and Omer C. Stewart. "Ute." In *Great Basin.* Edited by Warren L. D'Azevedo. Vol. 11 of *Handbook of North American Indians.* Washington, D.C.: Smithsonian Institution, 2001.

Caro Baroja, Julio. *Las brujas y su mundo.* Madrid: Editorial Alianza, 1969.

Carrillo, Charles M. "Oral History-Ethnohistory of the Abiquiú Reservoir Area." In *History and Ethnohistory Along the Rio Chama.* Albuquerque: U.S. Army Corps of Engineers, 1992.

Castañeda, Carlos. *The Teachings of Don Juan: A Yaqui Way of Knowledge.* Berkeley: University of California Press, 1968.

Cervantes, Fernando. *The Devil in the New World: The Impact of Diabolism in New Spain.* New Haven, Conn.: Yale University Press, 1994.

Cervantes Saavedra, Miguel. *El ingenioso hidalgo don Quijote de la Mancha.* Ed. Luis Andrés Murillo. Madrid: Clásicos Castalis, 1978.

Chávez, Fray Angélico Chávez, O.F.M. *Archives of the Archdiocese of Santa Fe, 1678.* Washington, D.C.: Academy of American Franciscan History, 1957.

———. *But Time and Chance: The Story of Padre Martínez of Taos, 1793–1867.* Santa Fe: Sunstone Press, 1981.

———. "Genízaros." In *Southwest.* Edited by Alfonso Ortiz. Vol. 9 of *Handbook of North American Indians.* Washington, D.C.: Smithsonian Institution, 1979.

———. *Origins of New Mexico Families in the Spanish Colonial Period.* Santa Fe: William Gannon, 1954.

———. "The Penitentes of New Mexico." *New Mexico Historical Review* 29 (1954): 97–123.

Chávez, Fray Angélico, trans., and Ted J. Warner, ed. *The Domínguez-Escalante Journal: Their Expedition through Colorado, Utah, Arizona, and New Mexico in 1776.* Provo, Utah: Brigham Young University Press, 1976.

Clendinnen, Inga. *Ambivalent Conquests: Maya and Spaniard in Yucatan, 1517–1570.* 2d ed. Cambridge: Cambridge University Press, 2003.

———. "Disciplining the Indians: Franciscan Ideology and Missionary Violence in Sixteenth-Century Yucatan." *Past and Present* 94 (Feb. 1982): 27–48.

Cline, Sarah L. "Native Peoples of Colonial Central Mexico." In *Mesoamerica.* Edited by Richard E. W. Adams and Murdo J. MacLeod. Vol. 2 of *The Cambridge History of the*

Native Peoples of the Americas. Cambridge: Cambridge University Press, 2000.

Clottes, Jean, and David Lewis-Williams. *The Shamans of Prehistory: Trance and Magic in the Painted Caves.* New York: Harry N. Abrams, Inc., 1998.

Colligan, John B. *The Juan Paez Hurtado Expedition of 1695: Fraud in Recruiting Colonists for New Mexico.* Albuquerque: University of New Mexico Press, 1995.

Córdova, Gilberto Benito. "The Genízaro." Unpublished manuscript in authors' possession.

———. "Missionization and Hispanicization of Santo Thomas de Abiquiú, 1750–1770." Ph.D. diss., University of New Mexico, 1979.

Cortez, Constance. "The New Aztlan: Nepantla (and other Sites of Transmogrification)." In *The Road to Aztlan: Art from a Mythic Homeland.* Edited by Virginia M. Fields and Victor Zamudio-Taylor. Los Angeles: Los Angeles County Museum of Art, 2001.

[Crocchiola], Father Stanley [Francis Louis]. *The Abiquiú Story.* N.p.: n.d.

Curtin, L. S. M. *Healing Herbs of the Upper Rio Grande.* Los Angeles: Southwest Museum, 1965.

———. Spanish and Indian Witchcraft in New Mexico." *The Masterkey* 45 (July–Sept. 1971): 89–101.

Cutter, Charles. *The Legal Culture of Northern New Spain, 1700–1810.* Albuquerque: University of New Mexico Press, 1995.

———. *The Protector de Indios in Colonial New Mexico 1659–1821.* Albuquerque: University of New Mexico Press, 1986.

Cutter, Donald. "An Anonymous Statistical Report on New Mexico in 1765." *New Mexico Historical Review* 50 (1975): 349–51.

Daily, Dennis. "Tropas de Jesús: Brotherhood Ties on New Spain's Northern Frontier." May 2004. Unpublished manuscript in authors' possession.

Damp, Jonathan E., Stephen Hall, and Susan Smith. "Early Irrigation on the Colorado Plateau near Zuni Pueblo, New Mexico." *American Antiquity* 67 (Oct. 2002): 665–76.

D'Azevedo, Warren L. "Washoe." In *Great Basin.* Edited by Warren L. D'Azevedo. Vol. 11 of *Handbook of North American Indians.* Washington, D.C.: Smithsonian Institution, 2001.

De la Peña Montenegro, Alonso. *Anuario Histórico Jurídico Ecuatoriano, 9. Itinerario para párrocos de indios, en que se tratan las materias más particulares tocantes a ellos para su buena administración.* 1771. Reprint, Quito, Ecuador: Ediciones Corporación de Estudios y Publicaciones, 1985.

Dobyns, Henry. "Puebloan Historic Demographic Trends." *Ethnohistory* 49 (winter 2002): 171–218.

Domínguez Ortiz, Antonio. "Iglesia institucional y religiosidad popular en la España barroca." In *La Fiesta, la ceremonia, el rito.* Granada: Casa de Velásquez, 1990.

Dozier, Edward P. *Hano: A Tewa Indian Community in Arizona.* New York: Holt, Rinehart and Winston, 1966.

———. Response to Edward H. Spicer. "Spanish-Indian Acculturation in the Southwest." *American Anthropologist* 56 (1954): 681.

Ebright, Malcolm. "Advocates for the Oppressed: Indians, Genízaros and their Spanish Advocates in New Mexico, 1700–1786." *New Mexico Historical Review* 71 (Oct. 1996): 305–39.

———. "Breaking New Ground: A Reappraisal of Governors Vélez Cachupín and Mendinueta and Their Land Grant Policies." *Colonial Latin American Historical Review* (spring 1996): 195–233.

———. "Frontier Land Litigation in Colonial New Mexico: A Determination of Spanish Custom and Law." *Western Legal History* 8 (summer–fall 1995): 199–226.

———. *Land Grants and Lawsuits in Northern New Mexico.* Albuquerque: University of New Mexico Press, 1994.

Ebright, Malcolm, Teresa Escudero, and Rick Hendricks. "Tomás Vélez Cachupín's Last Will and Testament, His Career in New Mexico, and His Sword with a Golden Hilt." *New Mexico Historical Review* (summer 2003): 285–321.

Ebright, Malcolm, and Rick Hendricks. "Making the Best of Both Worlds: Santa Ana Pueblo's Land Acquisitions, 1700–1850." Unpublished manuscript in authors' possession.

————. "The Pueblo League and Pueblo Indian Land in New Mexico, 1692–1846." In *Ysleta del Sur Pueblo Archives*. El Paso, Tex.: Book Publishers of El Paso, 2001.

Elferink, Jan G. R. "The Use of Poison and Malevolent Magic in Criminal Practices among the Incas in Pre-Columbian Peru." *Colonial Latin American Historical Review* 8 (summer 1999): 339–60.

Elferink, Jan G. R., José Antonio Flores, and Charles D. Kaplan. "The Use of Plants and Other Natural Products for Malevolent Practices Among the Aztecs and Their Successors." *Estudios de Cultura Nahuatl* 24 (1994): 27–47.

Ellis, Florence Hawley. *San Gabriel del Yunque as Seen by an Archaeologist*. Santa Fe: Sunstone Press in conjunction with the Florence Hawley Ellis Museum of Anthropology at Ghost Ranch, Abiquiú, New Mexico, 1989.

Escriche, Joaquin. *Diccionario razonado de legislación y jurisprudencia*. Edited by Juan B. Guim. Bogotá, Colombia: Temis, 1977.

Espinosa, Manuel J., ed. and trans. *The First Expedition of Vargas into New Mexico, 1692*. Albuquerque: University of New Mexico Press, 1940.

Fewkes, Jesse Walter. *Hopi Snake Ceremonies*. Albuquerque: Avanyu Publishing, 1986.

Florescano, Enrique. *The Myth of Quetzalcoatl*. Baltimore, Md.: John Hopkins University Press, 1999.

Forbes, Jack D. *Apache, Navaho, and Spaniard*. Norman: University of Oklahoma Press, 1960.

Forrest, Suzanne. *The Preservation of the Village: New Mexico's Hispanics and the New Deal*. Albuquerque: University of New Mexico Press, 1989.

Forster, Morris W., and Martha McCollough. "Plains Apache." In *Plains*. Edited by Raymond J. DeMallie. Vol. 13, Part 1 of *Handbook of North American Indians*. Washington, D.C.: Smithsonian Institution, 2001.

Fowler, Catherine S. "Subsistence." In *Great Basin*. Edited by Warren L. D'Azevedo. Vol. 11 of *Handbook of North American Indians*. Washington, D.C.: Smithsonian Institution, 2001.

Frank, Ross. *From Settler to Citizen: New Mexican Economic Development and the Creation of Vecino Society, 1750–1820*. Berkeley: University of California Press, 2000.

Gallegos C., José Ignacio. *Historia de la Iglesia en Durango*. Mexico City: Editorial Jus, 1969.

Gandert, Miguel, Enrique Lamadrid, Ramón Gutiérrez, Lucy Lippard, and Chris Wilson. *Nuevo México Profundo: Rituals of an Indo-Hispano Homeland*. Santa Fe and Albuquerque: Museum of New Mexico Press and National Hispanic Cultural Center of New Mexico, 2000.

Garate, Donald T. "Anza: A Basque Legacy on New Spain's Northern Frontier." In *Basque Portraits in the New World*. Edited by Richard Etulain and Jerónima Echeverría. Reno: University of Nevada Press, 1999.

García, Nasario. *Bultos, y Brasas: Tales of Witchcraft and the Supernatural in the Pecos Valley*. Santa Fe: Western Edge Press, 1999.

Gibson, Charles, ed. *The Spanish Tradition in America*. Columbia: University of South Carolina Press, 1968.

Greenleaf, Richard E. "The Inquisition in Eighteenth Century New Mexico." *New Mexico Historical Review* 60 (Jan. 1985): 29–60.

————. "The Mexican Inquisition and the Indians: Sources for the Ethnohistorian." *The Americas* 34 (Jan. 1978): 315–44.

————. *The Mexican Inquisition of the Sixteenth Century*. Albuquerque: University of New Mexico Press, 1969.

————. "Persistence of Native Values: The Inquisition and the Indians of Colonial Mexico." *The Americas* 50 (Jan. 1994): 351–76.

————. *Zumárraga and the Mexican Inquisition, 1536–1543*. Washington, D.C.: Academy of American Franciscan History, 1962.

Griffiths, Nicholas. "Andean *Curanderos* and their Repressors: The Persecution of Native Healing in Late Seventeenth- and Early Eighteenth-Century Peru." In *Spiritual Encounters: Interactions between Christianity and Native Religions in Colonial America*.

Lincoln: University of Nebraska Press, 1999.

———. *The Cross and the Serpent: Religious Repression and Resurgence in Colonial Peru.* Norman: University of Oklahoma Press, 1996.

Griffiths, Nicholas, and Fernando Cervantes, eds. *Spiritual Encounters: Interactions between Christianity and Native Religions in Colonial America.* Lincoln: University of Nebraska Press, 1999.

Gutiérrez, Ramón A. "Franciscans and the Pueblo Revolt." In *What Caused the Pueblo Revolt of 1680?* Edited by David J. Weber. Boston: St. Martin's Press, 1999.

———. *When Jesus Came, the Corn Mothers Went Away.* Stanford, Calif.: Stanford University Press, 1991.

Hackett, Charles W., ed. *Historical Documents Relating to New Mexico, Nueva Vizcaya and Approaches Thereto to 1773.* 3 vols. Washington, D.C.: Carnegie Institution, 1937.

Hall, G. Emlen. "Juan Estevan Pino, 'Se Los Coma': New Mexico Land Speculation in the 1820s." *New Mexico Historical Review* 57 (Jan. 1982): 27–42

Hall, G. Emlen, and David J. Weber. "Mexican Liberals and the Pueblo Indians, 1821–1829." *New Mexico Historical Review* 59 (Jan. 1984): 5–32.

Hanke, Lewis. *Aristotle and the American Indians: A Study of Race Prejudice in the Modern World.* Bloomington: Indiana University Press, 1959.

———. "The Requerimiento and Its Interpreters." *Revista de Historia de América* 1 (Mar. 1938): 25–34.

———. *The Spanish Struggle for Justice in the Conquest of the Americas.* Boston: Little, Brown and Company, 1965.

Harrod, Howard L. *The Animals Came Dancing: Native American Sacred Ecology and Animal Kinship.* Tucson: University of Arizona Press, 2000.

Hendricks, Rick. "Church-State Relations in Anza's New Mexico, 1777–1787." *Catholic Southwest: A Journal of History and Culture* 9 (1998): 25–42.

———. "The Exile and Return of Fray Isidro Cadelo, 1793–1810." *New Mexico Historical Review* 70 (Apr. 1995): 129–57.

———. "Material Culture of Diocesan Clergy in Eighteenth-Century El Paso." Paper presented at the Historical Society of New Mexico Annual Conference, Valencia County, 2000.

Hendricks, Rick, and Gerald Mandell. "The Apache Slave Trade in Parral, 1637–1679." *The Journal of Big Bend Studies* 16 (2004): 59–81.

———. "Juan Manso, Frontier Entrepreneur." *New Mexico Historical Review* 75 (July 2000): 339–65.

Hendricks, Rick, and W. H. Timmons. *San Elizario: Spanish Presidio to Texas County Seat.* El Paso: University of Texas Press, 1998.

Henningsen, Gustav. *The Witches' Advocate: Basque Witchcraft and The Spanish Inquisition.* Reno: University of Nevada Press, 1980.

Herrera, Carlos R. "The King's Governor: Juan Bautista de Anza and Bourbon New Mexico in the Era of Imperial Reform, 1778–1788." Ph.D. diss., University of New Mexico, 2000.

Hibben, Frank C. "Excavation of the Riana Ruin and Chama Valley Survey." *University of New Mexico Anthropological Bulletin* 2, no. 1. Reprint, Albuquerque: University of New Mexico Press, 1937.

Hickerson, Nancy Parrott. *The Jumanos: Hunters and Traders of the South Plains.* Austin: University of Texas Press, 1994.

Hoffer, Peter Charles. *The Devil's Disciples: Makers of Salem Witchcraft Trials.* Baltimore, Md.: Johns Hopkins University Press, 1996.

Horvath, Steven Michael, Jr. "The Genízaros of Eighteenth-Century New Mexico: A Reexamination." *Discovery: School of American Research* (1977): 25–40.

———. "Indian Slaves for Spanish Horses." *The Museum of the Fur Trade Quarterly* 14 (winter 1978).

Huizinga, Johan. *The Autumn of the Middle Ages.* Translated by Rodney Payton and Ulrich Mammitzsch. Chicago: University of Chicago Press, 1996.

Instrucciones y memorias de les virreyes novohispanos. Biblioteca Porrúa, 102. Estudio preliminar de Ernesto de la Torre Villar. Mexico City: Editorial Porrúa, 1991.

Iriarte de Aspurz, O.F.M. Cap. Lázaro. *Franciscan History: The Three Orders of St. Francis of*

Assisi. Translated by Patricia Ross. Chicago: Franciscan Herald Press, 1982.

James, Harry C. *Pages from Hopi History.* Tucson: University of Arizona Press, 1996.

Jeançon, J. A., *Excavations in the Chama Valley, New Mexico,* Smithsonian Institution, Bureau of American Ethnology Bulletin 81. Washington, D.C.: Government Printing Office, 1923.

Jedin, Hubert. *The Council of Trent.* Translated by Ernest Graf. 2 vols. St. Louis, Mo.: B. Herder Book Co., 1957.

Jenkins, Myra Ellen. "Documentation Concerning San José de Gracía del Rio de Las Trampas." Unpublished manuscript in author's possession.

———. "Some Eighteenth-Century New Mexico Women of Property." In *Hispanic Arts and Ethnohistory in the Southwest.* Edited by Marta Weigle and Claudia and Samuel Larcombe. Santa Fe: Ancient City Press, 1983.

Jones, Oakah L., Jr. *Pueblo Warriors and Spanish Conquest.* Norman: University of Oklahoma Press, 1966.

———. "Rescue and Ransom of Spanish Captives from the *indios bárbaros* on the Northern Frontier of New Spain." *Colonial Latin American Historical Review* 4 (spring 1995): 131–33.

Jones, Sondra. *The Trial of Don Pedro León Luján: The Attack Against Indian Slavery and Mexican Traders in Utah.* Salt Lake City: University of Utah Press, 2000.

Kamen, Henry. *The Spanish Inquisition: A Historical Revision.* London: Weidenfeld and Nicolson, 1997.

Kelley, Henry W. "Franciscan Missions of New Mexico, 1740–1760." *New Mexico Historical Review* 15 (Oct. 1940): 345–68.

Kessell, John L. *Kiva, Cross and Crown.* Washington, D.C.: National Park Service, U.S. Department of the Interior, 1979.

———. "Spaniards and Pueblos: From Crusading Intolerance to Pragmatic Accomodation." In *Archaeological Perspectives on the Spanish Borderlands West.* Vol. 1 of *Colombian Consequences.* Edited by David Hurst Thomas. Washington, D.C.: Smithsonian Institution, 1989.

Klor de Alva, J. Jorge. "Sahagún and the Birth of Modern Ethnography: Representing Confessing and Inscribing the Native Other." In *The Work of Bernardino de Sahagún: Pioneer Ethnographer of Sixteenth-Century Aztec Mexico.* Edited by J. Jorge Klor de Alva, H. B. Nicholson, and Eloise Quiñones Keber. Albany: Institute for Mesoamerican Studies, State University of New York, 1988.

———. "Sin and Confession among the Colonial Nahuas: The Confessional as a Tool for Domination." In *La ciudad y el campo en la historia de México.* Edited by Ricardo A. Sánchez Flores et al. Mexico City: Instituto de Investigaciones Históricas, Universidad Nacional Autónoma de México, 1992.

———. "'Telling Lives': Confessional Autobiography and the Reconstruction of the Nahua Self." In *Spiritual Encounters: Interactions between Christianity and Native Religions in Colonial America.* Edited by Nicholas Griffiths and Fernando Cervantes. Lincoln: University of Nebraska Press, 1999.

Kluckhohn, Clyde. *Navajo Witchcraft.* Boston: Beacon Press, 1944.

Knab, Timothy J. *The War of the Witches: A Journey into the Underworld of the Contemporary Aztecs.* San Francisco: Harper, 1995.

Lea, Henry Charles. *A History of the Inquisition of Spain.* 4 vols. New York: AMS Press, 1966.

Levack, Brian P. *The Witch-Hunt in Early Modern Europe.* London: Longman Group, Ltd., 1995.

Levy, Jerrold, E. "Kiowa." In *Plains.* Edited by Raymond J. DeMallie. Vol. 13, Part 2 of *Handbook of North American Indians.* Washington, D.C.: Smithsonian Institution, 2001.

Levy, Jerrold E., Raymond Neutra, and Dennis Parker. *Hand Trembling, Frenzy Witchcraft, and Moth Madness: A Study of Navajo Seizure Disorders.* Tucson: University of Arizona Press, 1987.

Lewis, Laura A. *Hall of Mirrors: Power, Witchcraft and Caste in Colonial Mexico.* Durham, N.C.: Duke University Press, 2003.

Lockhart, James. *The Nahuas After the Conquest: A Social and Cultural History of the Indians of Central Mexico, Sixteenth through Eighteenth Centuries*. Stanford, Calif.: Stanford University Press, 1992.

Longrigg, James. "Medicine in the Classical World." In *Western Medicine: An Illustrated History*. Edited by Irvine London. Oxford: Oxford University Press, 1997.

MacCormack, Sabine. *Religion in the Andes: Vision and Imagination in Early Colonial Peru*. Princeton, N.J.: Princeton University Press, 1991.

Magnaghi, Russell M. "The Genízaro Experience in Spanish New Mexico." In *Spain and the Plains: Myths and Realities of Spanish Exploration and Settlement on the Great Plains*. Edited by Ralph Vigil, Frances Kaye, and John Wunder. Niwot: University Press of Colorado, 1994.

Martin, Cheryl English. *Governance and Society in Colonial Mexico: Chihuahua in the Eighteenth Century*. Stanford, Calif.: Stanford University Press, 1996.

Martin, Malachi. *Hostage to the Devil: The Possession and Exorcism of Five Contemporary Americans*. New York: Quality Paperback Book Club, 1976.

Martínez, Robert D. "Fray Juan José Toledo and the Devil in Spanish New Mexico: A Story of Witchcraft and Cultural Conflict in Eighteenth-century Abiquiú." M.A. thesis, University of New Mexico, 1997.

Martinez, Thomas. *Abiquiú Baptisms, 1754–1870*. San José, Calif.: Self-published, 1993.

Matthews-Lamb, Sandra K. "'Designing and Mischievous Individuals': The Cruzate Grants and the Office of the Surveyor General." *New Mexico Historical Review* 71 (Oct. 1996): 341–59.

Matson, R. G. *The Origins of Southwestern Agriculture*. Tucson: University of Arizona Press, 1991.

Miller, Robert Ryal. "New Mexico in Mid-Eighteenth Century: A Report Based on Governor Vélez Cachupín's Inspection." *Southwestern Historical Quarterly* 79 (Oct. 1975): 166–81.

Mills, Kenneth. *Idolatry and Its Enemies: Colonial Andean Religion and Extirpation, 1640–1750*. Princeton, N.J.: Princeton University Press, 1997.

Moore, Michael. *Medicinal Plants of the Mountain West*. Santa Fe: Museum of New Mexico Press, 1979.

Morales, Francisco. *Inventario del Fondo Francisco del Museo de Antropología e Historia de México*. Washington, D.C.: Academy of American Franciscan History, 1978.

Moreno de los Arcos, Robert. "New Spain's Inquisition for Indians from the Sixteenth to the Nineteenth Century." In *Cultural Encounters: The Impact of the Inquisition in Spain and the New World*. Edited by Mary Elizabeth Perry and Anne J. Cruz. Berkeley: University of California Press, 1991.

Norris, Jim. *After "The Year Eighty": The Demise of Franciscan Power in Spanish New Mexico*. Albuquerque: University of New Mexico Press, 2000.

———. "Franciscans Eclipsed: Church and State in Spanish New Mexico, 1750–1780." *New Mexico Historical Review* 76 (Apr. 2001): 161–74.

———. "The Franciscans of New Mexico, 1692–1754: Toward a New Assessment." *The Americas* 51 (Oct. 1994): 151–71.

Norstrand, Richard L. *The Hispano Homeland*. Norman: University of Oklahoma Press, 1992.

Norton, Mary Beth. *In the Devil's Snare: The Salem Witchcraft Crisis of 1692*. New York: Alfred A. Knopf, 2002.

Noyes, Stanley. *Los Comanches*. Albuquerque: University of New Mexico Press, 1993.

Olmsted, Virginia Langham. *Spanish and Mexican Censuses of New Mexico, 1750 to 1830*. Albuquerque: New Mexico Genealogical Society, 1981.

Ortiz, Alfonso, ed. *Southwest*. Vol. 9 of *Handbook of North American Indians*. Washington, D.C.: Smithsonian Institution, 1979.

———. "Ritual Drama and the Pueblo World View." In *New Perspectives on the Pueblos*. Edited by Alfonso Ortiz. Albuquerque: University of New Mexico Press, 1972.

Pagels, Elaine. *The Origin of Satan*. New York: Random House, 1995.

Pardo, Osvaldo. "Contesting the Power to Heal: Angels, Demons, and Plants in Colonial Mexico." In *Spiritual Encounters: Interactions between Christianity and Native Religions in Colonial America*. Edited by Nicholas Griffiths and Fernando Cervantes. Lincoln: University of Nebraska Press, 1999.

Parks, Douglas, R. "Pawnees." In *Plains*. Edited by Raymond J. DeMallie. Vol. 13, Part 1 of *Handbook of North American Indians*. Washington, D.C.: Smithsonian Institution, 2001.

Parmentier, Richard. "The Mythological Triangle: Poseymu, Montezuma, and Jesus in the Pueblos." In *Southwest*. Edited by Alfonso Ortiz. Vol. 9 of *Handbook of North American Indians*. Washington, D.C.: Smithsonian Institution, 1979.

Parsons, Elsie Clews. *Pueblo Indian Religion*. Lincoln: University of Nebraska Press, 1996.

————. "Witchcraft among the Pueblos: Indian or Spanish?" *MAN* 27 (June 1927): 106–12, 125–28.

Patterson-Rudolph, Carol. *Petroglyphs and Pueblo Myths of the Rio Grande*. Albuquerque: Avanyu Publishing, 1993.

Pickering, David. *Dictionary of Witchcraft*. London: Cassell, 1996.

Poling-Kempes, Lesley. "A Call to Place." In *Georgia O'Keeffe and New Mexico*. Edited by Barbara Buhler Lynes, Lesley Poling-Kempes, and Frederick W. Turner. Princeton, N.J.: Princeton University Press; and Santa Fe: Georgia O'Keeffe Museum, 2004.

————. *Valley of Shining Stone: The Story of Abiquiú*. Tucson: University of Arizona Press, 1997.

Quezada, Noemí. "The Inquisition's Repression of Curanderos." In *Cultural Encounters: The Impact of the Inquisition in Spain and the New World*. Edited by Mary Elizabeth Perry and Anne J. Cruz. Berkeley: University of California Press, 1991.

Rael-Galvez, Estevan. "Identifying and Capturing Identity: Narratives of American Indian Servitude, Colorado and New Mexico, 1750–1930." Ph.D. diss. University of Michigan, 2002.

Recopilación de leyes de los reinos de las Indias. 4 vols. 1681. Facs. ed. Foreword by Ramón Menéndez y Pidal, a preliminary study by Juan Manzano Manzano. Madrid: Cultura Hispánica, 1973.

Reeve, Frank D. "The Navaho-Spanish Peace, 1720s-1770s." *New Mexico Historical Review* 34 (Jan. 1959): 9–40.

Renaud, E. B. "Pictographs and Petroglyphs of the Western High Plains." *Archeological Survey Series, 8th Report*. Denver, Colo.: University of Denver Press, 1936.

Reyes Costilla, Nora, and Martín González de la Vara. "El Demonio entre los marginales: la población negra y el pacto con el demonio en el norte de Nueva España, siglos xvii y xviii." *Colonial Latin American Historical Review* 10 (spring 2001): 199–221.

Ricard, Robert. *The Spiritual Conquest of Mexico: An Essay on the Apostolate and the Evangelizing Methods of the Mendicant Orders in New Spain, 1523–1572*. Trans. by Lesley Byrd Simpson. Berkeley: University of California Press, 1966.

Riley, Carroll L. *Kachina and Cross: Indians and Spaniards in the Early Southwest*. Provo: University of Utah Press, 1999.

————. "Mesoamerican Indians in the Early Southwest." *Ethnohistory* 21 (winter 1974): 25–36.

————. *Rio del Norte: People of the Upper Rio Grande From Earliest Times to the Pueblo Revolt*. Salt Lake City: University of Utah Press, 1995.

Rodríquez, Sylvia. *The Matachines Dance: Ritual Symbolism and Interethnic Relations in the Upper Rio Grande Valley*. Albuquerque: University of New Mexico Press, 1996.

Rohn, Arthur, William Ferguson, and Lisa Ferguson. *Rock Art of Bandelier National Monument*. Albuquerque: University of New Mexico Press, 1989.

Rollings, Willard H. *The Comanche*. New York: Chelsea House Publishers, 1989.

Roper, Lyndal. *Oedipus and the Devil: Witchcraft, Sexuality and Religion in Early Modern Europe*. London: Routledge, 1994.

Roth, Cecil. *The Spanish Inquisition*. New York: W. W. Norton and Company, 1964.

Salazar, Richard. "Santa Rosa de Lima de Abiquiú." *New Mexico Architecture* 18 (Sept.–Oct. 1976): 13–19.

Sánchez, Joseph, P. *Explorers, Traders, and Slavers: Forging the Old Spanish Trail, 1678–1850*. Salt Lake City: University of Utah Press, 1997.

———. *The Rio Abajo Frontier, 1540–1692: A History of Early Colonial New Mexico*. Albuquerque: Albuquerque Museum, 1987.

Sánchez Ortega, María Helena. "Sorcery and Eroticism in Love Magic." In *Cultural Encounters: The Impact of the Inquisition in Spain and the New World*. Edited by Mary Elizabeth Perry and Anne J. Cruz. Berkeley: University of California Press, 1991.

Sandos, James A. *Converting California: Indians and Franciscans in the Missions*. New Haven, Conn.: Yale University Press, 2004.

Schaafsma, Curtis. *Apaches de Navajo: Seventeenth Century Navajos in the Chama Valley of New Mexico*. Salt Lake City: University of Utah Press, 2002.

Schaafsma, Polly. *Indian Rock Art of the Southwest*. Santa Fe School of American Research; Albuquerque: University of New Mexico Press, 1980.

———. "Rock Art." In *Great Basin*. Edited by Warren L. D'Azevedo. Vol. 11 of *Handbook of North American Indians*. Washington, D.C.: Smithsonian Institution, 2001.

———. "War Imagery and Magic: Petroglyphs at Comanche Gap, Galisteo Basin, New Mexico." Paper presented at the symposium "Social Implication of Symbolic Expression in the Prehistoric American Southwest," 55th Annual Meeting of the Society for American Archaeology, Las Vegas, Nevada, 1990.

———. *Warrior, Shield, and Star: Imagery and Ideology of Pueblo Warfare*. Santa Fe: Western Edge Press, 2000.

Schaefer, Stacy. "The Crossing of the Souls: Peyote Perception and Meaning Among the Huichol Indians." In *People of the Peyote: Huichol Indian History, Religion, and Survival*. Edited by Stacy Schaefer and Peter T. Furst. Albuquerque: University of New Mexico Press, 1996.

Scholes, France. "Church and State in New Mexico." *New Mexico Historical Review* 11 (Jan. 1936): 9–76; (Apr. 1936): 145–78; (July 1936): 283–94; (Oct. 1936): 297–349.

———. "The First Decade of the Inquisition in New Mexico." *New Mexico Historical Review* 10 (July 1935): 195–241.

Schroeder, Albert. "Brief History of the Southern Utes." *Southwestern Lore* 30 (1965): 53–78.

———, ed. *The Changing Ways of Southwestern Indians: A Historic Perspective*. Glorieta, Tex.: Rio Grande Press, 1973.

Scott, James C. *Domination and the Arts of Resistance: Hidden Transcripts*. New Haven, Conn.: Yale University Press, 1990.

Semboloni, Lara. "Cacería de brujas en Coahuila, 1748–1751." *Historia Mexicana* 214 (Oct. 2004): 325–64.

Silverblatt, Irene. "The Evolution of Witchcraft and the Meaning of Healing in Colonial Andean Society." *Culture, Medicine and Psychiatry* 7 (1983): 413–27.

———. *Moon, Sun, and Witches: Gender Ideologies and Class in Inca and Colonial Peru*. Princeton, N.J.: Princeton University Press, 1987.

Simmons, Marc, ed., and trans. *Indians and Mission Affairs in New Mexico, 1773. Pedro Femín de Mendinueta*. Santa Fe: Stagecoach Press, 1965.

———. "The Mysterious A Tribe of the Southern Plains. In *The Changing Ways of Southwestern Indians: A Historic Perspective*. Edited by Albert H. Schroeder. Glorieta, N. Mex.: Rio Grande Press, 1973.

———. *Spanish Government in New Mexico*. Albuquerque: University of New Mexico Press, 1968; paperback ed., 1990.

———. "Tlascalans on the Spanish Borerlands." *New Mexico Historical Review* 39 (Apr. 1964): 101–10.

———. *Witchcraft in the Southwest: Spanish and Indian Supernaturalism on the Rio Grande*. Lincoln: University of Nebraska Press, 1974.

Scurlock, Dan. *From the Rio to the Sierra: An Environmental History of the Middle Rio Grande Basin*. Fort Collins, Colo.: U. S. Department of Agriculture, Forest Service, Rocky

Mountain Research Station, 1998.

Slifer, Dennis. *The Serpent and the Sacred Fire: Fertility Images in Southwest Rock Art*. Santa Fe: Museum of New Mexico, 2000.

———. *Signs of Life: Rock Art of the Upper Rio Grande*. Santa Fe: Ancient City Press, 1998.

Snow, David. "A Note on Encomienda Economics in Seventeenth Century New Mexico." In *Hispanic Arts and Ethnohistory in the Southwest*. Edited by Marta Weigle with Claudia Larcombe and Samuel Larcombe. Santa Fe: Ancient City Press, 1983.

Stanislawski, Michael B. "Hopi-Tewa." In *Southwest*. Edited by Alfonso Ortiz. Vol. 9 of *Handbook of North American Indians*. Washington, D.C.: Smithsonian Institution, 1979.

Steele, S. J, Thomas, and Rowena A. Rivera. *Penitente Self-Government: Brotherhoods and Councils 1797–1947*. Santa Fe: Ancient City Press, 1985.

Suggs, M. Jack, Katharine Sakenfeld, and James Mueller, eds. *Oxford Study Bible*. New York: Oxford University Press, 1992.

Summers, Montague, ed. *The Malleus Maleficarum of Heinrich Kramer and James Sprenger*. New York: Dover Publications, 1971.

Swadesh, Frances Leon. *Los Primeros Pobladores: Hispanic Americans of the Ute Frontier*. Notre Dame, Ind.: University of Notre Dame Press, 1974.

———. "They Settled by Little Bubbling Springs." *El Palacio* 84 (fall 1978): 19–20, 42–49.

Taussig, Michael T. *The Devil and Commodity Fetishism in South America*. Chapel Hill: University of North Carolina Press, 1980.

Taylor, Colin. *The Plains Indians: A Cultural and Historical View of the North American Plains Tribes of the Pre-Reservation Period*. London: Salamander Books, Ltd., 1994.

Thomas, Alfred Barnaby. *After Coronado: Spanish Exploration Northeast of New Mexico, 1696–1727*. Norman: University of Oklahoma Press, 1935.

———, trans. and ed. *Forgotten Frontiers: A Study of the Spanish Indian Policy of Don Juan Bautista de Anza Governor of New Mexico 1777–1787*. Norman: University of Oklahoma Press, 1932.

———. "Governor Mendinueta's Proposals for the Defense of New Mexico, 1772–1778." *New Mexico Historical Review* 6 (Jan. 1931): 21–39.

———. *The Plains Indians and New Mexico, 1751–1778*. Albuquerque: University of New Mexico Press, 1940.

Thomas, David Hurst, Lorann S. A. Pendleton, and Stephen C. Cappannari. "Western Shoshone." In *Great Basin*. Edited by Warren L. D'Azevedo. Vol. 11 of *Handbook of North American Indians*. Washington, D.C.: Smithsonian Institution, 2001.

Thomas, Keith. *Religion and the Decline of Magic: Studies in Popular Beliefs in Sixteenth- and Seventeenth-Century England*. London: Weidenfeld and Nicolson, 1971.

Thybony, Scott. *Rock Art of the American Southwest*. Portland, Ore.: Graphic Arts Center Publishing, 2002.

Twitchell, Ralph Emerson. *The Spanish Archives of New Mexico*. Glendale, Calif.: Arthur H. Clark Co., 1914.

Tykal, Jack B. "Taos to St. Louis: The Journey of María Rosa Villalpando." *New Mexico Historical Review* 65 (Apr. 1990): 61–74.

Valadez, Susana Eger. "Wolf Power and Interspecies Communication in Huichol Shamanism." In *People of the Peyote: Huichol Indian History, Religion, and Survival*. Edited by Stacy Schaeffer and Peter T. Furst. Albuquerque: University of New Mexico Press, 1996.

Van Ness, John R. *Hispanos in Northern New Mexico: The Development of Corporate Community and Multicommunity*. New York: AMS Press, 1991.

Walker, Deward E., Jr., ed. *Witchcraft and Sorcery of the American Native Peoples*. Moscow: University of Idaho Press, 1989.

Weber, David J. *Bárbaros: Spaniards and Their Savages in the Age of Enlightenment*. New Haven, Conn.: Yale University Press, 2005.

———. "Pueblos, Spaniards, and History." In *What Caused the Pueblo Revolt of 1680?* Edited by David J. Weber. Boston: St. Martin's Press, 1999.

————. *The Spanish Frontier in North America.* New Haven, Conn.: Yale University Press, 1992.

————. "The Spanish-Mexican Rim." In *The Oxford History of the American West.* Edited by Clyde A. Milner II, Carol A. O'Connor, and Martha A. Sandweiss. New York: Oxford University Press, 1994.

————. *The Taos Trappers: The Fur Trade in the Far Southwest, 1540–1846.* Norman: University of Oklahoma Press, 1971.

————, ed. *What Caused the Pueblo Revolt of 1680?* Boston: St. Martin's Press, 1999.

White, Lesley. "The Pueblo of Santa Ana, New Mexico." *American Anthropologist* 44 (Oct.–Dec. 1942). Reprint, New York: Kraus Reprint Co., 1969.

White, Richard. *The Middle Ground: Indians, Empires, and Republics in the Great Lakes Region, 1650–1815.* Cambridge: Cambridge University Press, 1991.

Wozniak, Frank J., Meade F. Kemrer, and Charles M. Carrillo. *History and Ethnohistory along the Rio Chama.* Albuquerque: U.S. Army Corps of Engineers, 1992.

INDEX